David Hume

edited by MARK G. SPENCER

David Hume

HISTORICAL THINKER, HISTORICAL WRITER

THE PENNSYLVANIA STATE UNIVERSITY PRESS
UNIVERSITY PARK, PENNSYLVANIA

Library of Congress Cataloging-in-Publication Data
David Hume : historical thinker, historical writer / edited
by Mark G. Spencer.
p.   cm
Summary: "A transdisciplinary collection of essays
focusing on David Hume as historian, and arguing that his
'historical' and 'philosophical' works are more intimately
connected than scholars have often assumed"—Provided
by publisher.
Includes bibliographical references and index.
ISBN 978-0-271-06154-2 (cloth : alk. paper)
ISBN 978-0-271-06155-9 (pbk. : alk. paper)
1. Hume, David, 1711–1776—Criticism and interpretation.
2. Great Britain—Historiography.
3. England—Historiography.
4. Hume, David, 1711–1776. History of England.
I. Spencer, Mark G., editor of compilation.

DA759.7.H86D38 2013
942.0072'02—dc23
2013023131

Copyright © 2013 The Pennsylvania State University
All rights reserved
Printed in the United States of America
Published by The Pennsylvania State University Press,
University Park, PA 16802-1003

The Pennsylvania State University Press is a member
of the Association of American University Presses.

It is the policy of The Pennsylvania State University
Press to use acid-free paper. Publications on
uncoated stock satisfy the minimum requirements
of American National Standard for Information
Sciences—Permanence of Paper for Printed
Library Material, ANSI Z39.48–1992.

For

FREDERICK A. DREYER (1932–2012)

historian, teacher, friend

ACKNOWLEDGMENTS / ix
METHOD OF CITATION / xi

Introduction: Hume as Historian / 1
Mark G. Spencer

1
Hume and Ecclesiastical History: Aims and Contexts / 13
Roger L. Emerson

2
Artificial Lives, Providential History, and the Apparent Limits
of Sympathetic Understanding / 37
Jennifer A. Herdt

3
"The Spirit of Liberty": Historical Causation and Political
Rhetoric in the Age of Hume / 61
Philip Hicks

4
"The Book Seemed to Sink into Oblivion": Reading Hume's
History in Eighteenth-Century Scotland / 81
Mark Towsey

5
Reading Hume's *History of England:* Audience and Authority
in Georgian England / 103
David Allan

6
Medieval Kingship and the Making of Modern Civility: Hume's
Assessment of Governance in *The History of England* / 121
Jeffrey M. Suderman

Contents

7
Hume and the End of History / 143
F. L. van Holthoon

8
David Hume as a Philosopher of History / 163
Claudia M. Schmidt

9
Fact and Fiction: Memory and Imagination in Hume's
Approach to History and Literature / 181
Timothy M. Costelloe

10
Hume's Historiographical Imagination / 201
Douglas Long

11
The "Most Curious & Important of All Questions of Erudition":
Hume's Assessment of the Populousness of Ancient Nations / 225
M. A. Box and Michael Silverthorne

SELECTED BIBLIOGRAPHY / 255
CONTRIBUTORS / 267
INDEX / 271

Acknowledgments

Many people have helped to make this book possible. For financial support, I am especially grateful to the Social Sciences and Humanities Research Council of Canada and the Humanities Research Institute at Brock University. At The Pennsylvania State University Press, Sandy Thatcher (now retired) gave the fledgling idea his backing early on. Kendra Boileau, with her assistant Robert Turchick, guided the project through to production, where Laura Reed-Morrisson, Kathleen Kageff, Steve Kress and Patricia Mitchell expertly saw things through to the end. My colleagues and students in the Department of History at Brock University listened with keen interest (not always feigned) and lent their encouragement along the way. Exacting research assistance from Mathieu Robitaille (BA, Brock University, 2009) and Janet Baines (MA, Brock University, 2010) is evident in the bibliography. As always, my greatest supporters are found at home, where Kelly and our two boys, Thomas and William, indulge with such good-natured ease the curious pursuits of their resident historian.

Mark G. Spencer
St. Catharines

Method of Citation

In this volume, citations to Hume's texts are provided parenthetically. Unless stated otherwise, citations give the titles (abbreviated as described in the list below) and page numbers of the edition cited. For example, *E* 563 refers to page 563 of Miller's edition of Hume's *Essays*. For citations to some of Hume's texts, however, it is useful to provide more information than the page number of a particular edition. References to Hume's *History* take the following form: title, volume, page. Thus, *H* 2:525 refers to volume 2, page 525, of Todd's edition of Hume's *History*. References to Hume's *Enquiries* provide the title, section, and paragraph number of the Beauchamp edition, followed by the page number of the Selby-Bigge/Nidditch edition, where applicable. For example, *EHU* 12.4/150 refers to section 12, paragraph 4, in Beauchamp's edition of the first *Enquiry*; page 150 in Selby/Nidditch. Similarly, references to Hume's *Treatise* provide the title, book, part, section, and paragraph number in the Nortons' edition, followed by the page number of the Selby-Bigge/Nidditch edition, so that *T* 1.3.4.2/82–83 refers to *Treatise* book 1, part 3, section 4, paragraph 2; pages 82 and 83 in Selby-Bigge/Nidditch.

List of Abbreviations

E	*Essays Moral, Political, and Literary,* edited by E. F. Miller, rev. ed. (Indianapolis: Liberty Classics, 1987).
EHU	*An Enquiry concerning Human Understanding,* edited by T. L. Beauchamp (Oxford: Clarendon Press, 2000).
	An Enquiry concerning Human Understanding, in *Enquiries concerning Human Understanding and concerning the Principles of Morals,* edited by L. A. Selby-Bigge and P. H. Nidditch, 3rd ed. (Oxford: Clarendon Press, 1975).
EPM	*An Enquiry concerning the Principles of Morals,* edited by Tom L. Beauchamp (Oxford: Clarendon Press, 1998).

	An Enquiry concerning the Principles of Morals, in *Enquiries concerning Human Understanding and concerning the Principles of Morals,* edited by L. A. Selby-Bigge and P. H. Nidditch, 3rd ed. (Oxford: Clarendon Press, 1975).
H	*The History of England, from the Invasion of Julius Caesar to the Revolution in 1688,* edited by William B. Todd, 6 vols. (Indianapolis: Liberty Classics, 1983).
L	*The Letters of David Hume,* edited by J. Y. T. Greig, 2 vols. (Oxford: Clarendon Press, 1932).
NHR	*The Natural History of Religion,* in *A Dissertation on the Passions* and *The Natural History of Religion,* edited by Tom L. Beauchamp (Oxford: Clarendon Press, 2007).
NL	*New Letters of David Hume,* edited by R. Klibansky and E. C. Mossner (Oxford: Clarendon Press, 1954).
T	*A Treatise of Human Nature,* edited by David Fate Norton and Mary J. Norton (Oxford: Clarendon Press, 2000).
	A Treatise of Human Nature, edited by L. A. Selby-Bigge, 2nd rev. ed. P. H. Nidditch (Oxford: Clarendon Press, 1978).

INTRODUCTION:

HUME AS HISTORIAN

Mark G. Spencer

David Hume (1711–1776) appreciated the centrality of historical thinking and writing to the enlightened world within which he lived. As the aging scholar put it reflectively in 1770 in a letter to his London publisher, William Strahan, "I believe this is the historical Age and this the historical Nation" (*L* 2:230). By then, of course, Hume had done much to contribute to that state of affairs in Britain and beyond. All six volumes of his *The History of England, from the Invasion of Julius Caesar to the Revolution in 1688* (1754–62) had been published and were circulating far and wide throughout the British Atlantic world. Hume's *History* would continue to attract large numbers of readers for the remainder of the author's lifetime and remained a best seller well into the nineteenth century. Little wonder that the card for Hume in the catalogue of the British Library differentiated him then (as it still does) as "David Hume, the historian." The records left by the earliest readers of Hume's *History*—even its noisiest critics—provide telling evidence of how influential Hume's account was and also of just how much history mattered to Hume and his contemporaries.

If we want to recapture the essence of Hume's place in the eighteenth-century history of ideas, then surely his historical thinking and writing ought to inform our understandings to a significant degree. But modern scholars have been far less interested in Hume as historical thinker and writer than were Hume's contemporaries. It is Hume the philosopher, and especially Hume the philosopher of book 1 of *A Treatise of Human Nature* (1739–40), whom scholars of Hume and general readers alike now know best. The *Treatise*—the work that Hume lamented "fell *dead-born from the press*"—rose to become standard reading in undergraduate philosophy courses around the world, while the *History* had died a slow death by the early twentieth century, so that now few besides specialists know its contents well. The number of book-length studies on Hume as historian published in the past hundred years are few, and there have been even fewer attempts to consider Hume as historical thinker and writer in a broader sense than as a historian of England. The chapters that follow cannot hope to right this historiographical imbalance, but each is an outstanding contribution toward that end, and together they provide a solid foundation on which future work may build.

The aim, of course, should not be to replace a misguided concentration on only Hume's philosophical writings with a misguided concentration on only the historical ones. Indeed, each of the chapters in this volume shows that the relationship between Hume's "historical" works and his "philosophical" works is more intimate than scholars have often assumed. Gone for good are the days when one can offhandedly assert, as R. G. Collingwood once did, that Hume "deserted philosophical studies in favour of historical" ones. Taken together, though, the following chapters offer much greater insight than that.

Casting their individual beams of light on various nooks and crannies of Hume's historical thought and writing, these chapters illuminate the whole in a way that would not be possible from the perspective of a single-authored study. Their transdisciplinary and international perspectives are complementary, while at the same time they complicate our understanding of Hume's intentions, texts, and impact. The approaches to Hume in this volume vary, sometimes considerably. A number of chapters offer close readings of themes in Hume's *History of England*. Others approach Hume the historical thinker and writer through his *Essays Moral, Political, and Literary* (in which many of the essays have historical leanings or are informed by historical dimensions), through his *Natural History of Religion*, or through the ecclesiastical history Hume contemplated but did not write. Clearly, none of those works was divorced from Hume's broader and long-developing philosophical concerns as the chapters below so aptly demonstrate. Other contributors to this volume fill in essential parts of the context in which Hume's historical thought developed or flesh out the reception his historical writings received. Others still tease out the historical features of Hume's more seemingly philosophical writings, his *Treatise of Human Nature*, and his later recasting of that work in *An Enquiry concerning Human Understanding* (1748) and *An Enquiry concerning the Principles of Morals* (1751). In short, it is not just that it is wrongheaded to pigeonhole Hume as "philosopher" at one point in his literary career and as "historian" at another; history and philosophy are commensurate in Hume's thought and works from the beginning to the end. Only by recognizing this can we begin to make sense of Hume's canon as a whole. Only then are we able to see clearly his many contributions to fields we now recognize as the distinct disciplines of history, philosophy, political science, economics, literature, religious studies, and much else besides.

In chapter 1, "Hume and Ecclesiastical History: Aims and Contexts," Roger L. Emerson asks why Hume "might have wanted to write an ecclesiastical history and what sort of a history he would have written had he done one."

Starting with the surviving textual evidence, Emerson establishes Hume's interest in the topic of ecclesiastical history and, drawing on a plethora of printed and manuscript sources, situates Hume's aims in the contexts of his own life, the Scottish Enlightenment, and larger trends in European history. Emerson notes that "to write ecclesiastical history as Hume had seen it in *The History of England* would be to destroy the field in the interests of more enlightened ways of thinking." Moreover, that was where "lasting fame and more money" were to be found and perhaps where "some contribution to what he called at the end of this life 'the downfall of some of the prevailing systems of superstition'" might be made. Hume would have been tempted by all of this. Emerson fleshes out Hume's Scottish context with extended accounts of Patrick Cuming, Charles Mackie, and William Rouet, among others whom Emerson knows well but who are not often referred to in the Hume literature, as vast as it is. By 1720, long before Hume turned his critical gaze in that direction, practitioners found it increasingly "difficult to see ecclesiastical history in the blinkered way that had previously prevailed." But Hume's ecclesiastical history, had he written one, may not have been the sort that enlightened contemporaries such as Voltaire and other *philosophes* wanted Hume to write. After all, Hume the historian always "sought to play a moderating and evenhanded role." So when Hume "said he did not want to write an ecclesiastical history because he prized his peace, he may not have been referring only to attacks by the orthodox." Emerson concludes that the "peace [Hume] was loath to forego" toward the close of his life "would have been disturbed by Catholics and Protestants but also by infidels and *philosophes* who wanted to *écraser l'infâme*" in a way that was not Hume's.

Chapter 2 is also concerned with the intersection between Hume's historical thought and his religious concerns. In "Artificial Lives, Providential History, and the Apparent Limits of Sympathetic Understanding," Jennifer A. Herdt considers Hume as "a proponent of a hermeneutic philosophy of history," maintaining that Hume considered religious lives a breed apart. Moreover, it "remains the case in contemporary historiography that religion is often subjected to reductionistic analysis in scholarship otherwise devoted to the task of understanding people on their own terms." Herdt provides a historiographical overview, giving attention to seminal works by David Fate Norton and Richard Popkin, and especially Donald W. Livingston, whose account of Hume's limits of moral explanation she challenges head on. With reference to the *Essays* but also the *Treatise* and "A Dialogue," which was appended to Hume's *Enquiry concerning the Principles of Morals*, Herdt pieces together Hume's historical perspective, seeing clearly what many twentieth-century commentators did not, that "Hume was optimistic about the possibility of achieving sympathetic understanding of foreign points of view, and insistent that this understanding did not imply moral relativism." The key for Hume in understanding any historical situation was what Herdt here and elsewhere helpfully names "thicker description." Hume saw "a limit to the scope of sympathetic understanding" because such a perspective was "possible only where people are governed by 'maxims of common life and ordinary conduct'; not where they live artificial lives, governed by speculative beliefs that contradict the maxims of ordinary life." Drawing on a key passage in the second *Enquiry*—one that figures in important ways in other chapters in this collection—where Hume derides monkish virtues, Herdt argues that Hume does not succeed "in drawing a sharp boundary between natural and artificial lives, maxims, and practices." Rather, he "illegitimately excuses himself from the task of sympathetic understanding by suggesting that lives dedicated to the pursuit of ends that do not conform to his own substantive understanding of what is truly 'useful' or 'agreeable' are in fact pursuing no goods at all and undermine the conditions of the possibility of human life and flourishing." She hints—with a nod to Hume's method of "thick description"—that a fuller appreciation of the providential histories available to eighteenth-century thinkers will show "that Hume's own grand story line of the improvement of the human mind will no longer appear sharply distinct from at least some forms of providential history." "If religious belief is utterly incoherent and religious lives utterly self-defeating, sympathetic understanding is inherently impossible," Herdt writes; "so why attempt it at all?" In her critical reading, Hume did not show "that in theistic convictions or monkish virtues sympathetic understanding comes up against its limits." This she finds unfortunate, for "the historian's first task"—whether in the eighteenth century or now—"remains that of seeking sympathetic understanding."

Emerson and Herdt both complicate our understanding of Hume's historical approach to religious topics; and so too does Philip Hicks, in his chapter, "'The Spirit of Liberty': Historical Causation and Political Rhetoric in the Age of Hume." Hicks writes that "one of Hume's goals was to write an utterly secular account of the English past," but using the phrase "the spirit of liberty" was ironic, as it "actually made it resemble providence to a startling degree." What is up here? Before turning to Hume's text for an answer, Hicks traces the history of the phrase as employed by Machiavelli and others, and especially as it was used by Henry St. John, Viscount Bolingbroke, and, following him, James Thomson. Hicks reminds us that "Hume first cut his teeth as a political thinker observing the titanic struggle between Bolingbroke and Walpole," and in his political essays and then in the *History of England*, Hume distilled the British civil wars down to a battle between Charles I and "the spirit of liberty." Reading Hume's *History* as a unified whole in the light cast by his *Essays*, Hicks shows Hume to be a master of historical summary. The *Essays* also give us a better context for understanding the close relationship between "liberty" and "enthusiasm" in Hume's historical narrative. Quoting an important passage from the *History* in which Hume had argued that the spirit of enthusiasm "strongly disposed [the Puritans'] minds to adopt republican tenets; and inclined them to arrogate, in their actions and conduct, the same liberty, which they assumed, in their rapturous flights and ecstasies," Hicks rightly sees that for Hume, "the spirit of enthusiasm and the spirit of liberty more or less worked in tandem, mutually reinforcing one another's influence." Thus, "the overall effect of using this bare phrase in the way Hume did was to minimize or ignore liberty's religious connotations and play up its positive, civic qualities." Hicks began with the historical use of the phrase "the spirit of liberty" before Hume, and he concludes by investigating the phrase in writings after Hume, including writings by British authors such as John Brown, William Robertson, and Catharine Macaulay. Tracing the phrase to American shores, Hicks teases out its meaning for American revolutionaries such as John and Abigail Adams, Josiah Quincy Jr., and Mercy Otis Warren, thereby masterfully illuminating Hume's place in connecting the "revolutionary politics" of the seventeenth century with that of the eighteenth century.

Several other chapters in this volume also contribute to our understanding of Hume by elucidating the different contexts in which Hume wrote and was read. In chapter 4, "'The Book Seemed to Sink into Oblivion': Reading Hume's *History* in Eighteenth-Century Scotland," Mark Towsey explores known readers of *The History of England* to see what they can tell us about Hume the historian. In particular, Towsey attempts "to explain the extraordinarily widespread consumption of Hume's *History of England* in spite of readers' serious (and very widely documented) reservations about its political and religious shortcomings." Towsey discusses the assessments of Hume in prominent reviews—such as Roger Flexman's in the *Monthly Review* and Tobias Smollett's in the *Critical Review*—but the real charm of this chapter is the attention given to lesser-known readers of Hume, who range from David Boyle of Sherralton to Hanna Hume, from the Jacobite Sir James Steuart of Coltness to the Duchess of Atholl, and even to the Church of Scotland minister the Reverend William Cameron. Towsey finds that "Hume's *History* was standard issue for polite libraries and genteel drawing rooms across the country, eagerly acquired by dukes, MPs, and lairds; transatlantic merchants and enterprising industrialists; lawyers, physicians, and clergymen; as well as more modest consumers such as William Munro, a Highland cattle dealer; Duncan Chisholm, a leather merchant in Inverness; and John Surtees, an iron founder in Markinch." Delving into the borrowing records of the charitable Gray Library in Haddington, we find that "Hume's borrowers included a tanner, a tailor, a haberdasher, and a shoemaker, alongside the more usual clergymen, lawyers, bankers, customs officials, and town magistrates." Towsey finds that "there are strong grounds for regarding Hume's *History* as one of the most influential pedagogical texts of the Georgian period. It was consistently recommended by professional reviewers, literary critics, conduct writers, and didactic novelists as the best guide to English history yet written, while amateur readers embraced its canonical status by including it in their autodidactic commonplace books, abridgements, and abstracts." We can see much more clearly than we could have without assembling this evidence that Hume's *History of England* "forced contemporary readers to negotiate for themselves Hume's various critics, the 'English, Scotch, and Irish, Whig and Tory, churchman and sectary, freethinker and religionist, patriot and courtier [who] united in their rage' against him." In coaching his readers in his light-handed way, Hume "helped fashion in them the sense of moderation, tolerance, and fair-mindedness that was crucial to polite readers in the Age of Enlightenment."

In chapter 5, we turn from Towsey's eighteenth-century Scottish readers of Hume to "Reading Hume's *History of England*: Audience and Authority in Georgian England." Here, David Allan aims to go a step beyond recent research into the printed reception accorded Hume, asking "how those who did not feel compelled—or who simply lacked the opportunity—to cast their experiences as readers in published form responded" to Hume. We find that there were many readers indeed of Hume's *History* in late eighteenth- and early nineteenth-century England: Anglican clergymen, middling-sort professionals, merchants, industrialists, and men (and women) of the landed elite are all known to have had Hume's *History* on their bookshelves. Those who did not own the *History* personally often had access to Hume's text through its place on the shelves of library societies, circulating libraries, and other collections of books that were accumulated during this period. What did these various readers make of Hume's text? Allan susses out surveying evidence in the form of annotations in surviving copies of Hume's *History* while also exploring more extended encounters with Hume found in the pages of various commonplace books. It is here that Allan makes his most substantial findings. Commonplace books offer us a window on "sophisticated reflections on people's experiences with texts." Allan brings to light several key commonplace reflections of Hume. William Constable, a Catholic gentleman from Yorkshire, kept a volume entitled "Notebook of Extracts from Works of David Hume," in which he appeared to be particularly interested in passages that "were capable of being read as comparatively well-disposed toward the traditional Catholic position." Others who commonplaced Hume include Charles Lee, who considered Hume a "Monarchical Writer;" the Reverend James Gambier in Kent, who recorded in one passage that the "Spirit of Philosophy which animates his Work gives it a manifest Superiority over most of the English Histories by which it is preceeded"; and James Smith, "a Unitarian wool merchant from Norwich." Hume's *History*, Allan justifiably concludes, "is a rare example of a text with which it is possible to make meaningful progress" in our efforts to document the responses recorded by "long-lost early readers."

Towsey and Allan show us a range of contemporary British responses to Hume's *History of England*, and in chapter 6, Jeffrey M. Suderman explains why it was that Hume's early readers were often baffled by his narrative. In "Medieval Kingship and the Making of Modern Civility: Hume's Assessment of Governance in *The History of England*," Suderman argues that the "modern reader, already inclined to ignore Hume's *History* in favor of his more overtly philosophical works, is tempted to pass lightly over the assessments of England's kings scattered throughout the medieval volumes." But Suderman rightly reminds us that these volumes "constituted the last major production of [Hume's] literary career" and that it is here that we have "Hume's most seasoned judgments on the nature of executive government." This approach also allows Suderman to see "civility" as an overarching concern of Hume's—one that encompassed "liberty," a topic that scholars have given much attention to, but not in this context. Surveying Hume's assessment of kings worthy (Alfred is the prime example) and reprehensible (John I, and to a lesser degree Richard III and Edward II, for instance), Suderman finds a story line centered on themes of liberty and tyranny. Hume seems to be saying, "If the want of liberty was the consequence of weak governance, then perhaps liberty itself, at least that which can be found in the medieval world, depended upon the efforts of bold and powerful monarchs." Moreover, the "term 'tyranny,' if applied equally to innocent but powerless kings and to vigorous and innovative monarchs, can have little meaning." Hume knew well that these terms had been "thrown about incautiously by party apologists"; as a philosophical historian, he would be more cautious and measured. Still, Hume's assessment of those, like Edward, who fall between these extremes contains other lessons. Suderman's reading makes good sense of several passages from the *History* that commentators have had difficulty interpreting; he finds that for Hume, "the most admirable monarchs in English history are to be found" in "barbarous ages," when there was an "absence of a continuous rule of law." In a "remarkable piece of philosophical detachment," Hume "chastises Edward only for the unnecessary severity of his administrative style and the counterproductive assaults upon Scottish customs." Suderman's nuanced reading shows that "Hume seldom made direct comparisons of good and bad monarchs, effective and ineffective reigns." Here, like in so much else that he wrote, Hume expected his readers to be active participants. Hume's heroes "were not kings who bent tamely before a timeless constitution, but instead powerful, innovative, and aggressive kings who created the rule of law out of chaos." What baffled his contemporary audience was that "Hume was retelling a Whig story with a Tory cast of characters." Moreover, "Hume hoped that, by showing his audience how their modern freedoms had really been won, he could help spare them from the absolutism that had made such freedoms possible."

Like Suderman, F. L. van Holthoon sees Hume as a historian who aimed "to judge persons and events" in an effort to "learn from the past so that we do not become its prisoner." In chapter 7, "Hume and the End of History," van Holthoon identifies three ways in which scholars have interpreted the historical lessons of Hume's *History of England*: "Hume as a *neoclassical historian*, the *History* as the product of a *scientific Whig*, and *reason in history* as the leading theme of Hume's *History*." Van Holthoon sketches the historiography related to each of those approaches, finding each has things to offer but suggesting an alternative approach in their stead. Drawing on his vast research into Hume's revisions to the *History*, van Holthoon points our attention to a key change that Hume made at the conclusion to the history of the Stuarts. In the edition of 1757, Hume had first "presented his story as an antidote against Whig propaganda," but by 1770, it had become "a cautionary tale against the risks of liberty to authority and the need to keep a balance between the two." Another noteworthy passage informing van Holthoon's assessment is Hume's conclusion to the second volume on the Middle Ages, one also quoted by Suderman. Like Suderman, van Holthoon cautions that Hume scholars have too often looked to Hume's *History* for its story of liberty. We are better served to think of it as "A Study of Authority," with a prominent part being played by Elizabeth I, "Hume's heroine." When we approach the *History* from this perspective and in its entirety rather than piecemeal, seemingly troublesome passages fall into place. For instance, the "four appendices are like slides in a magic lantern," each offering a stock-taking "of the functioning of authority in English history at certain moments in time." We also see that although Hume "earned his reputation as a Tory historian because of his defense of Charles I," like the other Stuarts, Charles did not have "the prudence and the skill to ensure stability," and that is what led to 1688, "the end of history" for the English. These themes van Holthoon traces through Hume's political and economic essays, showing that as a historical thinker and writer, "Hume had a remarkable unity of purpose," and this is partly why "his *History* has stood the test of time."

Both van Holthoon and Suderman emphasize the importance of historical context in Hume's scheme of historical judgment. In chapter 8, the late Claudia M. Schmidt has added to that developing image in her broad-ranging considerations in "David Hume as a Philosopher of History." Providing a survey of the origins and development of the "philosophy of history," Schmidt argues this historiography lends itself to a "twofold typology" aligned with "two divergent conceptions of philosophy in general: the 'speculative' or 'substantive' and the 'analytic' or 'critical.'" Schmidt recommends a third possibility, one that comes out of her reading of Emil Falkenheim and David Carr and which she describes as the "existential philosophy of history," an "approach to the philosophical study of history and human nature that examines the influence of historical existence on human consciousness." Viewing Hume's corpus in light of these three divisions, Schmidt finds that "a sequence of seemingly disparate passages" might advantageously be linked to reveal Hume's coherent philosophy of history. A speculative and analytic philosopher of history, Schmidt's Hume offers "a tentative theory . . . of progress" and recommends a causal understanding of human actions and historical testimony. But Schmidt also argues that Hume's existential philosophy of history "is an underlying principle in his philosophical system." Here she emphasizes Hume's attentiveness to historical context, a theme others touch on to good effect in this volume as well. Hume presents to his readers "an account of the influence of historical existence over human consciousness, which directs us to consider the historical context of human thought, emotion, and action." In a final section, Schmidt traces Hume's subsequent impact as a philosopher of history in the works of Auguste Comte, Hegel, John Herschel, J. S. Mill, Carl Hempel, Johann Gottfried Herder, and J. G. Hamann, among others.

Several of the contributors to this volume, including Schmidt, note that there are interesting links to be worked out between Hume's comments on aesthetics and his study of history. Timothy M. Costelloe takes up part of that challenge in chapter 9, "Fact and Fiction: Memory and Imagination in Hume's Approach to History and Literature." Noting that Hume both "*juxtaposes*" and "*compares*" what he artfully refers to as "the craft of the historian to the art of the poet," Costelloe investigates further to see what this reveals about Hume's understanding of the rules for literary and historical composition. Starting with the poet and drawing heavily on Hume's sections on memory and imagination in book 1 of the *Treatise of Human Nature*, Costelloe shows how for Hume there are "three general rules of criticism that are tantamount to techniques, which if followed can guide the creation of successful poetry, and if ignored would produce the opposite." Turning with that knowledge to Hume as historian, Costelloe argues that for Hume "history is a true copy, a veridical depiction, in contrast to the speculation of narratives that from error, fancy, or dogmatism, depart from matter of fact." Or, as he puts it later: "Historians, in short, distinguish fact from fiction, as ideas of memory can be separated from those of imagination; historians discern the real shape of events under the clutter which contemporary reports and time have effectively obscured them." But that is not to say there is no role for the imagination—far from it. Hume perceives that there is "a chain . . . that leads from the present into remote regions of the past, but the links are images of events and the connections between them dark corners to be illuminated." Important choices must be made about what facts are to be included in any narrative and how those facts are to be relayed. For Hume, "history still involves manipulating the reader" in an effort "to effect the easy transition of ideas in the imagination." Costelloe constructs from Hume's text a number of "rules of historical criticism": historical accounts must "*carry conviction,*" have a "*plan and design,*" and aim to "*imitate nature.*" Compositions that followed those rules, Hume thought, might live up to history's essential role as an instructor in morals.

Chapter 10, Douglas Long's "Hume's Historiographical Imagination," shares some ground with Costelloe and Schmidt but recommends an even more central place for the imagination in Hume's thought and writings. For Hume, says Long, it is "by means of our imagination that we construct the context in which we situate our direct experiences of the world." In the first part of his essay, Long pursues his theme by looking closely at two important qualities of the imagination: its "sympathetic character" and "constructive power." In part II, Long differentiates Hume's thought from that of Adam Smith, Thomas Hobbes, and Michel de Montaigne. Bringing Smith's understanding of sympathy into the mix, Long differentiates Hume's thought from that of his close friend. This allows us to see more clearly that the *History of England* "is philosophical history—it is a conventional historical narrative transformed and enlivened by the unprecedented application to historical narrative of Hume's sympathetic imagination." Long also maps the "universe of the imagination," by comparing Hume to Hobbes and Montaigne, two thinkers with whom Hume engaged. In a third section, Long turns to Hume's discussions of space and time in the *Treatise* for "insights into the nature and value of the historian's activities." He shows that "Hume's image of a 'universe of the imagination,' centered on and bounded by the self, yet paradoxically conveying a vivid sense of the isolation of the self in a vast sea of spatial and temporal phenomena, deserves to be carefully examined as one of the seminal metaphors of modern social, historical, and political thought." Approaching Hume's *History* from this vantage point, Long draws several conclusions, including that the *History* is "a Herculean attempt to overcome the resistance of historical data to narrative ordering—a sort of fling at cleaning out the Augean stables of historicity." It is, then, Hume's effort to map the imagination that so closely links the goals of the *Treatise* with the *History of England* and much else that Hume wrote in between. Long reminds us that Hume, in his intriguing essay "Of the Study of History," tellingly remarked, "we should be for ever children in understanding, were it not for this *invention*, which extends our experience to all past ages, and to the most distant nations; making them contribute as much to our improvement in wisdom, as if they had actually lain under our observation."

In chapter 11, "The 'Most Curious & Important of All Questions of Erudition': Hume's Assessment of the Populousness of Ancient Nations," M. A. Box and Michael Silverthorne turn our attention to Hume's essay on that topic. This essay—which has received relatively little scholarly attention—has penetrating light to cast on Hume's dimensions as historian. Box and Silverthorne note at the outset that Hume here seems to have had two goals in mind: "In its curious aspect, the essay is a virtuoso examination of a historical question about comparative populations; in its implications, it is a polemic about police, manners, and constitutions." Moreover, "the thesis of the curious examination is expressly skeptical, prescribing suspension of judgment. That of the polemic is an endorsement of modernism and a condemnation of the ancients' ways." Box and Silverthorne provide a schematic outline of "Hume's Skeptical Argument," whereby Hume offers a critique of Isaac Vossius, Montesquieu, and Robert Wallace. Hume's arguments related to physical and moral causes are outlined and seen in the context of other essays he wrote as well as the *Treatise*. But Hume's "skeptical argument is only as good as Hume's scholarship." A real strength of this chapter is its masterful account of Hume's sources, of which there are dozens, including many classical historians. Plutarch is cited most; Polybius is a "favored source"; Thucydides and Xenophon are "trusted," as is Xenophon, whose "reliability as a historian rests for Hume on his being a contemporary of the events he narrates." Less trusted are Herodotus and Livy. Hume's assessments of Tacitus, Strabo, and Pliny the Elder are more complicated, and extended attention goes to Hume's critique of Athenaeus's account of the population of Athens. Several other topics—slavery and infanticide included—are also dissected from the perspective of Hume's use of sources. Box and Silverthorne conclude that "Hume accumulated from his having 'read over of almost all the Classics both Greek and Latin' an astonishing amount of evidence, much of which scholars of population in antiquity still use today, and that he deployed it relentlessly to question, and in many cases, to invalidate definitively, the overconfident generalizations of those admirers of antiquity who had uncritically exaggerated its populousness." That survey is brought to bear on Hume's account of "ancient virtue" and "modern luxury." So what are we to make of Hume's account? More than anything else, Hume's "Of the Populousness of Antient Nations" was "a work of history," but it was also one with ample room for Hume's skepticism. Hume appears to lead his readers to a rather ambiguous conclusion: "Though we cannot prove that population was lower amongst the ancients, it would be enthusiasm to attempt to fashion society on the supposition that it was higher."

Far from presenting the final word on Hume as historical thinker and historical writer, the chapters in this book offer fresh and insightful points of departure for further research. Some readers may wish to dip in to particular chapters only, and of course each can be read as a stand-alone piece. But their real power—or so it seems to the volume's editor—comes in reading them as a connected whole. Historical thinking and historical writing were clearly at the core of Hume's being. Together, these chapters provide an exceptionally rich account of David Hume as historian.

HUME AND ECCLESIASTICAL HISTORY:
AIMS AND CONTEXTS

Roger L. Emerson

I

Ecclesiastical history, in so far as it deals with the Church Triumphant, concerns things not of this world, but things beyond experience about which we can know nothing. Its subjects lie in the realm of grace and amid the mysteries of faith. In so far as sacred history has a mundane side, it lies originally in the Hebrew scriptures, which were held to contain miraculous prophecies of the coming of Christ the Savior, and in the New Testament, which outlined the new dispensation of salvation culminating in the Last Judgment and the reception of the saved into Heaven to enjoy God forever. That history was held to have been validated by miracles.

The history of the otherworldly kingdom of God is not directly discussed by Hume.[1] However, by 1762, Hume had dealt with the Bible, miracles, saints, and much else in an ironic or duplicitous manner. Religious beliefs resting on miracles he had shown to be unreasonable, if not unbelievable; we should not believe miracles because the testimony supporting them is never such as to compel belief. Hume treated the events of sacred history no differently from those of secular affairs. He thought the revelations and miracles of Judeo-Christian history were things we could not know had really happened, and he saw them as reflections of the ignorance of barbarous or simple peoples, the results of madness and delusion, or rooted in superstition that was grounded in fears. All of that became entangled with "priestcraft" and the calculations of kings and rulers. *The Dialogues concerning Natural Religion* (mostly written by 1751 but not published until 1779) continued that polemic against Christian beliefs. When ecclesiastical history dealt with the things of this world, with the Church Militant and the people of God as they acted in time, he explained its history with causal principles no different from those he applied to other topics. Here he differed profoundly from William Robertson, who thought one could discern the providence of God in world history. God had prepared the way for Christ by the expansion of the Roman Empire, in which Christianity could flourish and spread. There was no sharp line between the history of the Church and churches; both revealed the providence of God. Robertson's restatement of old arguments must have seemed to Hume like speculative nonsense.[2]

Hume continued to pursue those themes in his *History of England* (1754–62), which contains a good deal of ecclesiastical history treated as but another set of events. The *History* was full of ironic and derisive comments about religion informed by his reading of Fra Paolo Sarpi, Pierre Bayle, and English deists like Conyers Middleton, whose own work against Christian miracles had upstaged Hume's own.[3] Hume's comments were sometimes directed toward superstitious Roman Catholics but also against Protestant fanatics and even Muslims. Hume's clerics remained generally as bigoted, political, power hungry, and self serving as they are in his essays. The religion they served seemed often absurd. Hume's comments on the portions of the "true cross" are like many others:

> But notwithstanding these disputes, as the length of the siege had reduced the Saracen garrison to the last extremity, they surrendered themselves prisoners; stipulated, in return for their lives, other advantages to the Christians, such as restoring of the Christian prisoners, and the delivery of the wood of the true cross; and this great enterprize, which had long engaged the attention of all Europe and Asia, was at last, after the loss of 300,000 men, brought to a happy period. (*H* 1:387–88)

The note to that passage reads: "This true cross was lost in the battle of Tiberiade, to which it had been carried by the crusaders for their protection. Rigord, an author of that age, says, that after this dismal event, all the children who were born throughout all Christendom, had only twenty or twenty-two teeth, instead of thirty or thirty-two, which was their former complement, p. 14" (*H* 1:388n). Here Hume is playing off Bernard de Fontenelle's famous story of the Golden Tooth. The *History* is replete with such cynical and derisive comments; many were aimed at Protestants, even Scottish ones: "The famous Scotch reformer, John Knox, calls James Melvil, p. 65, a man most gentle and most modest. It is very horrid, but at the same time somewhat amusing, to consider the joy and alacrity and pleasure, which that historian discovers in his narrative of this assassination [of Cardinal Beaton]: And it is remarkable that in the first edition of his work, these words were printed on the margin of the page, *The godly Fact and Words of James Melvil*" (H 3:347n). Few of the religious escape some form of criticism or derision.

Hume was not an obvious candidate to write ecclesiastical history, but he was attracted by the field and seems for about ten years to have thought of writing an ecclesiastical history of some sort. This chapter asks why he might have wanted to write an ecclesiastical history and what sort of a history he would have written had he done one. But first the evidence he was really interested in the topic.

II

In early 1762, having finished his six-volume *History of England*, Hume was wondering what to do next. He had "not laid aside thoughts of continuing my History to the Period after the Revolution," but he had clearly been talking to people about writing an ecclesiastical history. He tells us both those things in a letter to his publisher, Andrew Millar, written on 15 March 1762, as Millar was getting ready to publish the complete *History of England* in quarto. Hume told Millar "to contradict the Report, that I am writing or intend to write an ecclesiastical History."

> I have no such Intention; & I believe never shall. I am beginning to love Peace very much, and resolve to be more cautious than formerly in creating myself Enemies. But in contradicting this Report, you will be so good as not to impeach Mr [David] Mallet's Veracity: For tis certain I said to Lord Chesterfield [Phillip Stanhope, 4th Earl of Chesterfield] (from whom Mr Mallet first had it), that I had entertain'd such a Thought. But my saying so proceeded less from any serious Purpose, than from a View of trying how far such an Idea would be relished by his Lordship. (*L* 1:352)

Millar had heard the rumor and was eager to print what sounded like a scandalous best seller. If Hume was telling the truth, he had started this rumor himself. He loved to joke, and this might have also tickled the funny bone of an earl who was no better a Christian than Hume and who probably would have found the project laughably bizarre.

Chesterfield and Mallet both had interests in history that suggest things about Hume's intentions. The earl thought grace was about deportment

(*Letter* 140) and religion important only in its appearance, which seemed to guarantee good morals and character (*Letter* 100) if it was expressed without enthusiasm, bigotry, fanaticism, or sincerity.[4] He was as at home among freethinkers as was Mallet, whose wife thought Hume a deist like herself and her husband.[5] Their views were not uncommon in the London and Paris circles in which Hume moved. Chesterfield would not have found ecclesiastical history of much interest unless it related to secular subjects such as politics and statecraft (*Letter* 33). Useful history concerned the modern world (800 A.D. on) and could be written only when textual evidence was plentiful. Otherwise history was diversion that often allowed us to see through the motives and deceptions of others. Chesterfield, Mallet, and Hume lived in the same world as Voltaire, who had been writing useful ecclesiastical history of a sort since the 1740s. Chesterfield had remarked approvingly in 1753 of a work he thought to be by Voltaire, *Les Croisades*, that the Crusades were "the most immoral and wicked scheme that was ever contrived by knaves, and executed by madmen and fools, against humanity."[6] Popes had "generally been the ablest and the greatest knaves in Europe, wanted all power and money of the East; for they had all that was in Europe already."[7] Hume would see the effects of the crusades differently, but he too regarded them as "the most signal and most durable monument of human folly, that has yet appeared in any age or nation" (*H* 1:234). Hume's talk with Chesterfield would likely have followed such a pattern.

Hume continued to think about an ecclesiastical history and must have discussed it with others both in London and later in Paris. On 8 November 1762, he wrote to Mallet, "The Undertaking you mention was rather founded on an Idea I was fond of, than on any serious, at least any present Purpose of executing it" (*L* 1:369). That was not quite what he had told Millar and shows a bit more commitment to the project. Mallet, the deist who had edited Bolingbroke's *Works* (five volumes, 1754), was not to find an open ally in Hume, but the ecclesiastical history project figured in Hume's correspondence with d'Alembert and Helvetius.[8] The latter, in June 1763, when rumors were still circulating that Hume would write such a work, urged him to do so. In April 1766, Grimm, in the *Correspondance littéraire*, noted that the philosophic tribe in Paris had "frequently begged M. Hume, during his stay in France, to write an Ecclesiastical History." He added that "this would be, at the present time, one of the most beautiful undertakings in literature, and one of the most important services rendered to philosophy and humanity."[9] That piece appeared after the Jesuits had been expelled from Portugal (1759) and France (1765), and in the year before, they were forced out of Spain and its empire. Grimm would have seen Hume's contemplated work as another blow against *l'infâme* against which Voltaire and other *philosophes* had been crusading for years.¹⁰ D'Alembert echoed those hopes until 1773. He and his friends wanted Hume to "take the trouble to paint in her true colours our Holy Church."¹¹ Had he done so, the premier British man of letters would have joined their cause. Hume seems to have thought about this project for about ten years with enough seriousness to raise hopes that he too would write to crush *l'infâme*.

In 1762, Hume was well prepared to write on this subject. His philosophical works gave powerful arguments that undermined beliefs in miracles, revelations, providence, the soul, and notions of an afterlife. Hume's explanations of action and thought left no place for simple ideas of grace as had the philosophy of Jonathan Edwards. Some of those arguments were restated in *The Dialogues concerning Natural Religion* already almost complete in the draft of 1751. The *Essays, Moral and Political* (1741) included the essay "Of superstition and Enthusiasm," which made the first the basis of Catholicism and the second the ground of many kinds of Protestantism. He added "Of National Characters" to the collection in 1748; that included an attack on the character of clerics of all kinds.¹² The conjectural histories like "The Natural History of Religion" (1757) sketched the origins and cyclical progresses of religions that naturally root among primitive, ignorant, and fearful people. This contradicted the biblical account of the origins of religion both among the people of God and among the pagans.¹³ For Hume, there were no differences in the origins. In all those works, the deists and rational theologians, as well as those who thought Christianity had to be understood from a unique standpoint grounded in faith, were refuted by the skeptical philosopher. Hume had attacked bigots and superstitious fools while posing as a good Calvinist—and Calvinists, when, as a skeptic, he considered the enthusiasts.

By 1762, Hume had already written a good deal of ecclesiastical history since it figured in *The History of England*, where it was given a wholly secular treatment. There, greedy and power-hungry clerics, fanatics and the superstitious, and politicians manipulating and being manipulated by them are to be found in abundance. Hume had mastered the standard sources of British history from ancient times to 1688, including a lot of medieval chronicles and other works dealing with Europe, particularly with France.¹⁴ He had become learned about the Roman and other churches because he needed to be to understand English religious history. He now knew enough to write a history independent of his work on the Church of England. He could have prefaced his ecclesiastical history with a general conjectural account of religion and then showed how Christianity conformed to the patterns offered by other religions, or he could have written a factual history of the Church in Europe with examples to show that it followed the patterns he had set out in his earlier works. Steeped in what he regarded as the follies of the English past, he had only to generalize his views to satisfy Chesterfield, the Mallets, and his Parisian friends.

III

Writing an ecclesiastical history must have been a tempting project in the 1760s, when European Catholicism seemed on the defensive and when Britain was beset by enthusiasts represented by Methodists in England and the "High-flyers" in the Kirk. The latter had harassed him and his friends, and this would be revenge. To deal critically with the whole of world history since the Creation was an ambitious end, but Hume was not without ambition. In doing so, Hume would then have joined the ranks of the open radicals—not the deists but the skeptically irreligious among whom he privately belonged. That he did not write this work in part reflects his sense of the danger of doing so. It would have cut him off from some friends, perhaps have barred some employment, and could have endangered his pension.[15] In the end, he did not satisfy the urge to become a more open enemy of Christianity.

There is a second reason ecclesiastical history might have attracted Hume in 1762. The most prominent of the European historians of the time, Voltaire, had been writing just this sort of history and was becoming known for it. A man as emulous of other writers as Hume would not have ignored ecclesiastical history. Hume tells us that "a passion for literature" was "the ruling passion of [his] life" (*H* 1:xxvii). To write an ecclesiastical history might win him more laurels; that would have tempted him.

From 1753 to 1756, Voltaire published what became known as *Essai sur les moeurs*, translated into English in 1759 as *An Essay on the Manners and Spirit of Nations*, a work later prefaced by his *La philosophie de l'histoire* (1765). In 1754 Voltaire directly attacked Bishop Bossuet's *Abrégé de l'Histoire Universelle*. Voltaire had aimed to replace the Bishop's Christian vision of universal and ecclesiastical history set out in *Discours sur l'histoire universelle* (1681). That and others like it privileged the biblical chronology worked out to show that the Jews were the oldest people with the oldest and best history. The Hebrews were the first people of God, who had been succeeded by the Christians. Voltaire's universal history made the oldest people the Chinese, Indians, and Egyptians, not the Jews who were somewhat ignored in his article on "Histoire" in the *Encyclopédie*.[16] He explained the religious beliefs and practices of the gentile nations not as the corruptions of Hebrew originals but as the creations of primitive peoples much like those whom Hume had described. There had to be a new universal history constructed around climate, race, manners, laws, the arts, commerce, and the evolution of those as they were changed and were shaped by peoples and their great men.[17] Christian history should have no privileged status in the realm of learning. God's providence was not to be inferred from the disasters of the past. There was no special causality needed to understand history sacred in name only. Voltaire found occasions to say more about the real nature of religion and its relation to manners and politics, priestcraft, and irrationality. He carried on a running critique of *l'infâme* in his squibs, satires, and biblical criticism, which circulated in manuscripts with even a bit being printed, and in his political pieces and other historical works. All that had contributed to Voltaire's fame even though some of it was slapdash and not very good.[18] Hume could see and envy the fame it brought Voltaire at the same time knowing such work could be better done. To write ecclesiastical history as Hume had seen it in *The History of England* would be to destroy the field in the interests of more enlightened ways of thinking.

Hume had already shown that the English church from the beginning was a political creation founded on the ambition of Pope Gregory, the fears of a pagan ruler in Kent who was "promised eternal joys above, and a kingdom in heaven without end," and politic compromises about altars. Elsewhere, as in Wessex, it was introduced with violence and because of marriage agreements.[19] Its benefits to the Saxons were very mixed:

> Even Christianity, though it opened the way to connexions between them and the more polished states of Europe, had not hitherto been very effectual, in banishing their ignorance, or softening their barbarous manners. As they received that doctrine through the corrupted channels of Rome, it carried along with it a great mixture of credulity and superstition, equally destructive to the understanding and to morals. The reverence towards saints and reliques seems to have almost supplanted the adoration of the Supreme Being: Monastic observances were esteemed more meritorious than the active virtues: The knowledge of natural causes was neglected from the universal belief of miraculous interpositions and judgments: Bounty to the church atoned for every violence against society: And the remorses for cruelty, murder, treachery, assassination, and the more robust vices, were appeased, not by amendment of life, but by pennances, servility to the monks, and an abject and illiberal devotion. The reverence for the clergy had been carried to such a height, that, wherever a person appeared in a sacerdotal habit, though on the highway, the people flocked around him; and showing him all marks of profound respect, received every word he uttered as the most sacred oracle. Even the military virtues, so inherent in all the Saxon tribes, began to be neglected; and the nobility, preferring the security and sloth of the cloyster to the tumults and glory of war, valued themselves chiefly on endowing monasteries, of which they assumed the government. The several kings too, being extremely impoverished by continual benefactions

to the church, to which the states of their kingdoms had weakly assented, could bestow no rewards on valour or military services, and retained not even sufficient influence to support their government.

Another inconvenience, which attended this corrupt species of Christianity, was the superstitious attachment to Rome, and the gradual subjection of the kingdom to a foreign jurisdiction. (*H* 1:50–51)

Writing an ecclesiastical history might give him lasting fame and more money and make some contribution to what he called at the end of his life "the downfall of some of the prevailing systems of superstition."[20] There were reasons enough to think about writing an ecclesiastical history.

IV

To fully appreciate the effects of what he contemplated one needs to see how ecclesiastical history functioned in Hume's world—first in Scotland, then in Europe. It was important and had had a long career. Indeed, ancient historians such as Varro had separated sacred from secular history, the stories of the gods from those of heroes and the founders of states.[21] Early Christians had coordinated the chronologies and histories of the Hebrews with those of other ancient peoples but had preserved the distinction between God's chosen people and the gentile nations. For the Hebrews, there was both a religious and a secular history, particularly after the coronation of Saul. For the gentiles, there might be a providentially directed history, but they lacked inclusion in the Church, the community of the saved. By the second and third centuries A.D., Christians like Eusebius of Caesarea (c. 263–339) were working out a chronology of world history and of the events in it that constituted the story of God's provision for the salvation of some and then, with the death of Christ on the cross, the offer of salvation to all. That account had been made canonical by the work of Saint Augustine (354–430) and others. His scheme or variants of it were still in place by the 1750s; indeed, it formed the backdrop to the universal and ecclesiastical histories of men like Charles Rollin, Dom Calmet, Jacob Vernet (a Genevan pastor and Voltaire's onetime friend), and many others including, however insincerely, the *philosophe* Turgot in his *Sorbonniques* of 1750. Hume, if he attacked those views, would not be tilting at windmills but would create for himself enemies and he certainly would have no peace.

Ecclesiastical history was very much an apologetic tool of the churches and sects. For Catholics, it established the primacy of their church and of the Bishop of Rome. It showed the continuity of revealed and traditional beliefs and their validation by miracles. Historians delineated the heresies of those who opposed both. It relied unquestioningly on a history derived from the Bible and the stories of the people of God as they were related in the writings of the saints and martyrs, the Fathers of the Church, the records of Church councils and others made by ancient, medieval, and Reformation writers. For Protestants, it answered the old question "Where was your church before Luther?" Ecclesiastical history gave divinity students the learning to defend their faith while attacking the errors of others. This history was the history of a chosen people living in time but aware of a divine origin, a providential past, and a future containing judgments. Some would be damned, but others would be saved to spend a blissful eternity enjoying the presence of God. Ecclesiastical history showed the teleology imposed on all history by the Creator, who created and shaped our ends to His own unfathomable designs. It was providential and had causes and effects we can neither understand nor alter. Hume's classical models for his own histories, Tacitus,[22] Livy, Thucydides, and others, said nothing about those matters.

Hume's first exposure to such traditional histories would have come in Scotland, where ecclesiastical history had always been taught in the divinity halls. University chairs were established fairly late and were posts that were not very lucrative and did not attract scholars of distinction. Like the study of Hebrew and oriental languages, ecclesiastical history did not flourish during the Scottish Enlightenment. Patrons used the chairs to place deserving men of little distinction, but the chairs were also of little concern to the moderates, who often determined the policies of the Kirk after the 1740s. Some of them were Hume's friends and became in the 1750s members of the Moderate Party. They were among those who changed the nature of the courses.

The first lectureship in the field was held by "Blind [William] Jameson," who in 1692 became a lecturer in civil and ecclesiastical history at Glasgow University.[23] Jameson was a polemicist who excoriated the errors of the Roman Church but also of some Protestants. His sort of history required a knowledge of the ancient and modern churches since it was meant to prepare ministers to defend the Established Church of Scotland. An account of God's providential actions in history was carried on into the present by Jameson's friend Robert Wodrow, whose *History of the Church of Scotland from the Restoration to the Revolution* (1721–22) contained the story of God's grace shed over a tested remnant who proved firm in their faith. Ecclesiastical history was the story of what really mattered in this and the other world in which true Christians lived. Something similar was taught at Edinburgh, where a regius chair of ecclesiastical history was founded c. 1702. In the eighteenth century, this chair had only one distinguished incumbent, William Dunlop. He taught the subject from 1715 to 1720 as centered on the defense of the Scottish version of Calvinism. St. Andrews received its regius chair in 1707; it quickly became a sinecure. Glasgow received a professorship in 1716, but neither King's nor Marischal University had University chairs. Throughout the century, the subject was taught in those universities by professors of divinity as was some general history by others.

The ecclesiastical history taught in Scotland changed between c. 1720 and the 1750s. At Glasgow, the subject from 1721 to 1752 was taught by William Anderson, a polite man who had been a travelling tutor and had seen much of Europe. He seems to have broadened the course by making it more secular, but no notes of or from his lectures have been found. His inaugural lecture as professor was entitled "The Credibility of History" and shows that he was at least interested in matters of evidence and sources.[24]

During Hume's college years (1721–25), the Edinburgh professor of ecclesiastical history was Matthew Crawford. He was not popular with his colleagues or with students, who found his courses uninspired. Robert Wodrow (who did not much like the man because he had supported toleration and the restoration of patronage to heritors and had favored John Simson, the heretical professor of theology at Glasgow), described Crawford's teaching as attended by only "six or seven hearers."[25] Wodrow claimed that the professor gave only one course, not the usual two, because he expected fees for the second, but no one was willing to pay them.[26] Crawford was believed to be the author of a life of John Knox, which George Ridpath, a Berwickshire minister, thought "stupidly wrote by some dull well meaning Whig."[27] Knowing that Crawford was something of an antiquary and had preserved and copied the "History of Scotland" left by his father would not have changed the judgments of Wodrow and Ridpath very much. Hume would have known that the traditional ecclesiastical history was dull, biased, and not worth much money. That was the judgment of others who began to change what its professors taught in order to make it more polite and useful.

Crawford was succeeded in his Edinburgh chair early in 1737 by Patrick Cuming, the ecclesiastical manager for the Argathelian political faction led by the Earl of Ilay and his brother, the second Duke of Argyll, whom Ilay succeeded in 1743. This was not a post for which Cuming had any special training or obvious interest beyond a general curiosity about historical matters. He shared that with Lord Ilay, who appointed him. Cuming's Latin lectures ran in a six-year cycle with one given publicly each week for four months.[28] His text was J. A. Turretin's *Compendium Historiae Ecclesiasticae*, written in the seventeenth century but many times revised and brought up to date for later periods. It was widely used in Scotland and in Holland, where Cuming is thought to have studied.

Cuming's course assumed the veracity and authority of the Bible and the truth of revealed religion. It saw the works of Moses as the oldest and best histories. The professor spent a good deal of time on evidences of the authenticity of the Mosaic revelations and of those given to prophets and to the inspired Hebrew historians. He refuted those who believed the world was eternal or that the Chinese records were older than those contained in the scriptures. He was carrying on a debate with seventeenth-century libertines such as Isaac de La Peyrère and English deists like Charles Blount, who knew of the views of Spinoza.

Cuming sought to show that the Calvinist Presbyterian system was the one warranted by the Bible. Like his colleague who taught universal civil history and the Roman antiquities, Charles Mackie, Cuming began with the Creation and traced the uneven declines and progresses of mankind. History was the unfolding of God's plan. The course of history was irregular and cyclical. It spiraled down after the fall of Adam and later as the revelations of God were forgotten and the meaning of the death of Christ was perverted by a corrupt church. With the "10th age" (roughly 1000 and beyond) history became progressive; men tended now to be better even if not all are to be saved. Until c. 1300 history was primarily the story of human error, but thereafter the world seemed to be progressing toward truth and becoming more as God would have it. Progress seems to be the intention of God and the unintended results of human actions taken for various reasons usually unrelated to each other.

While he called his subject "ecclesiastical history," Cuming did not sharply differentiate secular from sacred history. He embedded ecclesiastical history in a universal history. He sketched the development of the arts and sciences that originated in Noah's time. Tubal Cain was the Vulcan of the Hebrews. The professor also found a place for the Trojan War, which he thought occurred in the time of King Saul. David was thus a near contemporary of Homer—but earlier. The first great poets were Hebrews. Cuming carefully pointed out parallel developments in the Hebrew and gentile worlds and gave some of the chronologies of the pagan nations. By "the 10th age," ecclesiastical and civil history mingled easily in his English summary of his lecture on it:

> We are now arrived at the 10th age which is generally acknowledged to be the most ignorant but it is from the history of those darker ages that some of the original of many superstitions which are defended in the Church of Rome And the Seeds of great revolutions which happened afterwards are to be traced.... The court of Rome was governed by Whores and some of their Sons were made Popes... the tenth centurie because of almost universal ignorance is called by the Church of Rome it Self

> Seculum obscurium Most of the Popes of Rome in this century were rather Monsters of wickedness than men; affairs of the Court of Rome were managed by the lewdest The most cruel and abandoned Women. Second marriages were declared to be unlawful without a dispensations by this means the Treasures of the Church of Rome were greatly increased. The Christian Religion was received by the Normans, Poland too became Christian as did Russia Denmark & Sweden But the Religion of those times was made to consist chiefly in Fasts and Festivals pilgrimages Worship of Images the Virgin Mary Angles and Saints in a Veneration relicts the bones and ashes of the Saints and Superstitious practices Bells were consecrated and baptized by Pope John 13 Nothing was more frequent in this age than determining differences whether civil or Ecclesiastical by the tryal Ordeal that is passing bars of Iron blindfold, if they passed with out wacking [blistering] them they were declared Innocent if wacked guilty and Such like Methods The Monastic Life was in High reputation And Several New orders were instituted.[29]

But, with the "10th age," events leading to the Reformation providentially appear, and history's irregular downward spiral took an upturn.[30] Whatever coherence Cuming's course has was supplied by the faith that there is a providence that will bring history to a close as the light that began to shine in the Reformation continues to spread and to dispel darkness.

All that was a somewhat amazing pastiche. Archaic elements jostle with ideas that came from more modern sources such as the works of Friedrich Spanheim, Jean Mabillon, John Clerk, Henry Dodwell Sr., Humphrey Prideaux, and other *érudits*. Cuming seemed as much concerned with the course of Western civilization as with strictly religious topics. His explanations were couched in terms of the actions of individuals motivated by their passions. In his classes, the story of the people of God has been somewhat displaced by the story of the errors of the men, not their sins. Pious people were noticed. National characteristics have a role to play, but particular providences, such as Wodrow or his friend Cotton Mather reveled in, were not much noticed. This was not a wholly modern course and was probably not revised after the lectures were first written in the late 1730s or early 1740s. They would have looked antique by the time Cuming retired in 1762. Nevertheless, the story was broader and more secular in tone than the lectures that survive from his brighter predecessor, William Dunlop.[31]

Cuming had competition in the teaching of history at Edinburgh from Charles Mackiethe, professor of universal civil history and Roman antiquities who held this chair from 1719 until his retirement in the 1750s. Mackie was a polite man who had been a traveling tutor. He became a member of the Rankenian Club (c. 1720) and of a Whig club that hoped to re-edit George Buchanan's *History of Scotland* (1582).³² Later, he was a member of the Philosophical Society of Edinburgh (c. 1737). An intellectual interested in what was current among scholars, including historians, he wrote a report on the first appearance of syphilis in Scotland (1496) and an account of a house struck by lightning. Both were noticed in the *Philosophical Transactions of the Royal Society of London*.³³ His book purchases show us a man who read widely and wanted to own works such as Bayle's *Dictionaire Philosophique et Critique* (1697). He drew on that and on Thomas Stanley's *History of Philosophy* (1655–72) for some of the intellectual history he included in his courses.

Mackie taught two courses.³⁴ His universal history course (which might be called "Western Civilization") ran over two years. The other was a yearly course on Rome designed to make the study of Roman law easier. The first began with Creation, but it turned into a mostly political history, which went up to the Reformation and included bits of Scottish history too. Mackie did not give undue attention to religion and often treated it as another aspect of society to be discussed in a secular fashion. He wanted his boys to know who the principal Fathers of the Church were and why they were famous, but he treated them much as he did their pagan rulers.

Politics dominated the affairs of nations and helped to explain nonpolitical events. Mackie was also interested in politics at the international level and wanted his students to read parts of Thomas Rymer's mostly posthumous *Foedera* (1704–35), a great collection of charters and treaties. Those tended to see churches as social factors among others. All churches in this world are, to some extent, merely political institutions reflecting the national character of the people who attend them.

Mackie's historical world was full of nations with distinctive national characters. After it appeared in the 1730s, he recommended Charles Rollin's *Ancient History* to his students, who found there sketches of the characters of ancient peoples, which were used to explain their histories. Rollin's work saw the character of peoples reflected in all their institutions. National character in Rollin's works, or in Mackie's lectures, did not change much over time, but their treatment of it was one that leads to Montesquieu and Hume. They would see manners and institutions interacting in social wholes of a dynamic sort. That message was implicit in much that he taught.

The Franks described by Gregory of Tours, on whose works Mackie relied, could not possibly be a genteel people. They acted on passions they had not learned to control. Mackie on the world of Chilperic might have seemed long-winded to his students, but they would have come from his lectures with an appreciation of how much manners and customs mattered and how religious values affected them and were affected by them. The acceptance of the Christian religion among the Franks as described by Gregory was one that required the alteration of barbarian manners and the acceptance of new values that would result in chivalric attitudes and the formation of a new ethos. Ecclesiastical history in his classroom had little to do with the Church Triumphant but a lot to do with the sordid affairs of men in the Church Militant. Mackie knew that manners change with the growth of politeness and knowledge and that they change in what seems a cyclical manner.

Professor Mackie, like Anderson, the Glasgow historian, was interested in questions of evidence and in rules by which we might eliminate the "many vulgar errors which have crept into history."[35] The first of those he listed was "a strong passion for illustrious origins" such as the Greek's propensity to trace their descent from gods and goddesses. The early modern historians' eagerness to find among the Trojans ancestors for modern kings, who would then be the equals of the Roman founder Aeneas, was not much different. Mackie was as sure as Varro and Hume that all history came in three kinds—"obscure or unknown, fabulous, and Historical"—or that for which "vouchers" were to be had. Mackie even found his vouchers among artifacts and archaeological remains. If they paid attention to the vouchers, learned men would not have believed in the legend of the Golden Tooth ridiculed by Fontenelle, or in Pope Joan and the Pied Piper of Hamelin, about whom Mackie also spoke in class. Historians had to free themselves from such prejudices but also get their dates right.

Like many of his time, Mackie had a fascination with chronology. This rested on the fact that chronologies had not been established for most countries and were much contested for the ancient world, where the problems of relating Judeo-Christian chronology to the dating of events in the histories of other peoples had not been solved.[36] Ancient traditions had some value, but they needed to be critically scrutinized and the tales of bards and poets set aside as worthless. Other old accounts were clearly forgeries.[37] Credulity, religious and political biases, individual peculiarities, and the illusions of whole peoples all add errors to our perceptions of the past. Ecclesiastical history, if it was to be respectable, had to conform to the same standards as civil history. It was no better than its sources, and those seemed less adequate than they had once been.

While Hume took neither of Mackie's courses, he had relatives and friends who did; he would have known what was being taught by the professor.[38] Hume also knew William Rouet, who became professor of ecclesiastical history at Glasgow in 1752. Rouet may never have taught a course specifically on ecclesiastical history, but he tried to teach a universal history course that was polite.[39] Rouet has had something of a bad press as a sinecurist, but he deserves better. He shared Mackie's virtues but went beyond him in interesting ways. Rouet wanted history to give the causes of the events it narrated: "History should not be Confin'd to the bare recital of facts such as gaining or losing a battle, the rise or fall of an Empire, but we ought carefully to endeavour to Investigate the reasons & secret Causes which contributed to bring this or that remarkable event."[40] When it came to setting out those causes, Rouet showed that he owed as much to reading Montesquieu, Hume, and Voltaire as to Rollin, whose *Ancient History* he also recommended to his students:

> [We ought] to be well acquainted wt ye Manners, customs, Genius & Character peculiar to each Nations generally & of all ye Extraordinary men, who through ye importance of ye Station they bore in ye Countery, or from ye uncommon abilities they possess'd might possibly have greatly contributed to bring about any remarkable alterations in ye Changes of States or fortune of ye publick. When our knowledge in history is founded upon this firm and proper basis it can't fail of producing both pleasure & profit to ye Mind.[41]

Such history would be "providential" and would teach us "the vanity of earthly things."[42] His history preserved a pious gloss, but its substance was different. Moreover, he told his classes that there was no pure church history:

> church History consider'd entirely by itself, without any politicall Connections or references to ye Civil history of these times must in itself be imperfect, and unsatisfactory, but when carefully connected, & illustrated by a more accurate scrutiny into ye manners, Customs & political Maxims of ye Different Countries, or Governours, where ye Religious revolutions happen'd, Church history, consider'd in this view becomes one of the most regular & instructive & most interesting connected parts of Universal history, & actively contradict[s] that Sarcasm of Grotius Dum Historiam Ecclesiasticam legis Quid legis nisi Episcoparum.[43]

Rouet's history is this-worldly and rather like Hume's in several respects. Charlemagne is like the Alfred of *The History of England*. Rouet's periodization resembles Hume's, and the bases for it are much the same, although Rouet gives less attention to economics. They were similar in their attitudes to medieval sources. Those can be used but with caution, for they are the products of benighted times and have information mostly about the lifetimes of the writers. For both, modernity comes not with Charlemagne but with the Renaissance and Reformation. Rouet gave more time to politics and diplomacy, but, like Hume, he was also interested in the arts. Fragments of "Lectures on Ancient Painting" survive in his papers. Rouet presented the history of art in a cyclical mold with the Renaissance recapitulating the discoveries of the Greek and Roman artists, albeit at a higher level of achievement.[44] Rouet had moved his universal and ecclesiastical history in a more polite and secular direction than had any other teacher in Scotland to that date. Hume would have seen that trend as needing extension.

Outside the Scottish universities, there was much to interest a would-be ecclesiastical historian. Both Colin Kidd and David Allan have drawn attention to the differing accounts of the Scottish Church given by Catholics, by English and Scottish Episcopalians, and by Presbyterians of various sorts.[45] Politics could not be avoided in their discussions, which were aimed at establishing the independence (or dependence) of the Scottish church and state from (or upon) England or Rome. Much of that publishing came at a time when deists were challenging old accounts of religious history by deriding miracles, a superintending providence, privileging the Bible as a source of historical information, and finding in priestcraft and kingcraft the key to the development of states and churches. History had had, and still had, practical consequences for the Scottish economy and culture and for the peace and security of Britain and countries in Europe. After 1720, it had become difficult to see ecclesiastical history in the blinkered way that had previously prevailed. Realism also came from an understanding of the political and religious compromises made in 1690, 1707, and the years that followed.

V

There is also a wider context in which Hume's ecclesiastical history project should be situated. Having considered the history of the English church for about thirteen hundred years and seen it from the perspectives of men of diverse opinions, Hume must have thought it was surely time to rethink the enterprise of ecclesiastical historians. In many cases, the critical acumen applied to the understanding of manuscripts and textual problems was at odds with the lack of critical judgment shown when it came to larger questions of religion and politics. For details, high churchmen like George Hickes or Thomas Hearne were necessary guides but not when it came to the grander themes. Hume was also aware of a surprising number of their continental counterparts whose works also show up in the notes to *The History of England*. Most of those scholars were still captive to the inerrant Bible and to the progeny of Eusebius and Augustine. When Hume was in France, he seems to have had little to do with men in the Académie des Inscriptions, but he did meet a number of less orthodox historians including Charles Duclos, the Abbé Raynal, Présidents de Henault and de Brosses, and minor figures such as the Abbé Le Blanc, who had translated into French Hume's *Political Discourses* (1752) and William Robertson's *History of Charles V* (1769). Perhaps the man whose works affected him most was one whom he never met—Voltaire.

There was more going on among historians of religion than he may have been aware. We lack evidence that he was, but that should not dissuade us from looking closer at the nature of that work. Radical biblical criticism had been coming out steadily since the mid-seventeenth century from Hobbes, Spinoza, their epigones, and from Bayle and the deists. Many of the ideas expressed in their works were common knowledge, and Hume had read those authors. It is unlikely that Hume knew that Dr. Jean Astruc, to whom he delivered a letter in 1764, was the anonymous author of the groundbreaking *Conjectures sur les mémoires originaux dont il paroit que Moyse s'est servi pour composer le livre de la genèse* (1753). That short work undercut orthodox beliefs in the divine inspiration of the mosaic authorship of the Pentateuch by showing that parts of it were composed of different accounts that had been conflated into the present text.[46] It is also unlikely that Hume knew anything of the works of the German thinkers who had begun to approach the Bible in novel ways. Hermann Samuel Reimarius, in isolation and secrecy, had begun to recast Christological questions, which he assumed had to be treated like any other questions about the facts of the past. G. E. Lessing was moving in the same direction. The more orthodox philologist, Johann David Michaelis, as he reconstructed the society of the ancient Hebrews, reduced them to the status of just another rather uncivilized Middle Eastern people. In Aberdeen, where George Campbell was already at work on a translation of the Gospels, that message would be understood, although its radical implications were rejected. Germans were doing the sort of thing that had been done to some extent by Bishops William Warburton and Robert Lowth. Lowth had made it possible to see the Old Testament as the product of a rude people hooked on metaphors, a people who were not closely related to the Christians of the New Testament. Indeed, the Hebrews were closer to the Greeks of the Homeric world, but this was not quite the compliment which it had been in the lectures of Patrick Cuming. Once the Hebrews had been put into a historical context, the Bible had to be treated like any other old text. It could then be seen to deal with local and particular matters, not those of world historical importance. Such critics, often clerics, had come perilously close to breaking the prophetic thread that was, up to that time, held to connect the two Testaments. Theirs were not altogether new messages, but they were now not being stated by a disreputable Irish priest's son, like John Toland, but by respectable men holding university and church positions even as they relegated church history to a section of universal history mostly concerned with politics. Their theories and those of their French counterparts were the subjects of enlightened conversations.

Finally, there were other continental influences that had some importance for eighteenth-century men thinking about ecclesiastical history. Those lie in the struggles of European rulers to control and regulate religious life in their domains. The greatest example of this was seen in the policies adopted and the actions taken by Louis XIV against Jansenists and Huguenots. Those were related to Louis's efforts to bolster Roman Catholicism and to create what some saw as a universal monarchy. His career supplied many writers with all they needed to understand both priestcraft and kingcraft. In relatively tolerant Britain, the government faced nonjurors in both Scotland and England. It imposed greater controls on the Scottish Kirk through the imposition of toleration and patronage (1710–12) and by the management of the General Assembly. In England, it finally prohibited the meetings of Convocation after 1719. Everywhere those struggles centered on politics, on appointments, on the control of lands alienated to the Church, on the control of Jesuits and other orders, and on the rights of the Church and Papacy in various countries. Everywhere governments feared the enthusiasm provoked by Jansenists or expressed in the revivals conducted in France and Italy by Saint Alphonsus Ligouri. Protestant countries had to deal with enthusiastic Calvinists, Methodists, and dissenters from national churches who sometimes preferred exile and emigration to obeying their rulers. Greater freedom of the press and of expression now made it possible for men of letters to argue that religious behavior had always been like that and would be manipulated and controlled by those who found it in their interest to do so.

VI

Had Hume written an ecclesiastical history, he would have used the many elements already to hand. The conjectural historians, with their blend of social science and realistic data derived from the study of primitive societies, offered new perspectives on the ancient world of both the pagans and the People of God. Some of this, when provided by men like Lowth or Thomas Blackwell, the Marischal College principal and professor of Greek, had become quite acceptable although not when used to demean the Judeo-Christian myths and stories. Hume may have believed for a while that he could do better and that there was glory to be had if one succeeded. It might have gotten him into no more trouble than had the essay on miracles and the "Natural History of Religion." Adopting an ironic and ambiguous stance was something he had long ago mastered. Irony more delicately veiled and explanations more finely wrought would allow him to *écraser l'infâme* as well as Voltaire. Less conjectural historical studies had included church history in universal and civil histories that were essentially political. The ways of understanding history Montesquieu, Voltaire, and Hume himself had supplied offered other ways to secularize accounts of the past. And the very *philosophes* who teased Hume to write such a work could have given him a model from the *Encyclopédie*, on which some of them were working. There we find three related articles that are pertinent.

In the first, *"Ecclesiastique (l'histoire ecclesiastique)"*, "Ecclesiastical History" is defined as "whatever has happened in the Church since its beginnings," an ambiguous definition that applies either to the Church Triumphant or the Church Militant. It invited reflections on many unsavory topics. The ambiguities deepen as the very short article concludes:

> M. Fleuri[47] nous l'a donnée dans un ouvrage excellent qui porte ce titre; il a joint à l'ouvrage des discours raisonnés, plus estimables & plus précieux encore que son histoire. Ce judicieux écrivain, en développant dans ces discours les moyens par lesquels Dieu a conservé son Eglise, expose en même tems les abus de toute espece qui s'y sont glissés. Il étoit avec raison dans le principe, "qu'il faut dire la vérité toute entiere; qui si la religion est vraie, l'histoire d'Eglise l'est aussi; que la vérité ne sauroit être opposée à la vérité, & que plus les maux de l'Eglise ont été grands, plus ils servent à confirmer les promesses de Dieu, qui doit la défendre jusqu'à la fin des siecles contre les puissances & les efforts de l'enfer."[48]

The editors thought more needed to be added.

The foregoing article was immediately followed by one entitled *"Nouvelles Ecclesiastiques,"* the clandestinely circulated Jansenist periodical that was commonly thought to be somewhat fanatical.[49] It figures here largely for its accounts of the miracles that took place at the Parisian tomb of the Abbé Pâris in the 1730s. The controversies over those had been a scandal to the Gallican Church and to the government. Royal prohibition of gatherings at the tomb ended the miracles—as Voltaire gleefully noted. They served Hume as examples of well-authenticated modern miracles, ones that bothered Protestants since, if real, they would have been works of God having a probative value for the Roman Catholic faith. Both entries implicitly questioned the Catholic faith and Church and the truth of the miracles. Finally, the entry was crossreferenced to "CONVULSIONNAIRES."

In a third entry, "*Histoire*," Voltaire, its author, applauded the histories of opinion that were not mere "collections of human errors" and then quickly went on to say that his article would not deal with "sacred history."[50] That is "a succession of divine and miraculous events by which it pleased god in former times to lead the Jewish people and sometimes today tries our faith. I will not touch upon this important matter." But we are soon back in Voltaire's world. We quickly learn that the early history of all peoples is fabulous, that the Chinese have the oldest culture, the culture of the Egyptians being of an indeterminate age. Not the history of Palestine but of Rome most merits study because it is from Rome that Europe derived its laws and culture. The uses of history are mainly political, moral, and cultural.

It is also a probabilistic discipline offering but moral certainties. In its early periods, such as those about which Moses wrote, there are few certainties because the early history of all people is mythic and fabulous. If we would know the earliest times, we must look at archeological remains and decipher the meaning of their ceremonies, their festivals and myths. Those are mostly grounded in the needs and desires of agricultural peoples and in the great moments of their collective lives. In short, we need to attend to customs and manners. The article recommends Livy as the best historian for style but suggests that modern histories cover far more fields with more precision and with better-warranted evidence. "One expects from modern historians more details, confirmed facts, precise dates, sources, attention to customs and laws, to manners, to commerce, to finance, agriculture and population." Religion is absent from that list, but the history of the Jews and of the Church are implicitly included. Christianity is thus, by implication, seen as barbarous in origin, and its early history mythical. The sort of details ecclesiastical history should include are shown in the Chevalier De Jaucourt's entry for "Henri Wharton," which gave many details and facts about the married clergy of the early church.[51] There were similar messages in many small and obscure articles by Diderot, d'Alembert, and others.

Had Hume pleased his Parisian friends, he would have written a history that treated the churches as but other institutions in a complex secular whole. There were likely to have been other things in the history he did not write that would not have pleased them. In *The History of England*, there is a sense that the Church preserved over many centuries much that was worth preserving. It was a patron of the arts and to some extent of learning. It was not the Church which lost and scattered manuscripts containing a richer classical heritage than we now preserve but rapacious rulers like Henry VIII and Protestant enthusiasts who cared less for learning than the Dark Age monks who quoted Latin poems no longer to be found. Hume had no brief for the scholastics, but not all medieval philosophy was foolish. Popes like Aeneas Sylvius and Leo X come off well in *The History of England*. The Papacy never looks as grim in Hume's work as it does in the works of many Protestants or in those of Voltaire. Hume sought to play a moderating and evenhanded role as a historian. We could expect to find in any ecclesiastical history by him things that would burnish and not blacken the image of some churches at some times. The *philosophes* might also have been surprised to find that Hume saw no immediate advantages coming from the sixteenth-century reformations but many losses. The freedoms fathered by enthusiasts had a long gestation period. When he said he did not want to write an ecclesiastical history because he prized his peace, he may not have been referring only to attacks by the orthodox. The peace he was loath to forego would have been disturbed by Catholics and Protestants but also by infidels and *philosophes* who wanted to *écraser l'infâme*.

NOTES

1. The searchable Past Masters disk containing Hume's writing has no references to "Church Universal" or "Church Triumphant," and its references to "the kingdom of saints" are ironic and refer mostly to the period of the English Civil War. History for Hume was only of events in this world. What Hume thought of the history contained in the Hebrew scriptures is shown by his 1751 broadside commonly called "The Bellmen's Petition." In that, the lineage of Christ is shown to be garbled, which makes His descent from the House of David uncertain. Hume thus undercut the link between King Zerubbabel, seen as a type of Christ the King, and Jesus of Nazareth. See Roger L. Emerson, "Hume and the Bellman, Zerobabel MacGilchrist," *Hume Studies* 23 (1997): 9–28.

2. Robertson's views of the relation of historical events to providence were set out in a 1755 sermon, "The Situation of the World at the Time of Christ's Appearance." He reiterated ancient views of the Roman world as civilized, unified, peaceful, and extensive—a proper place for the Gospel to be propagated. All these conditions had been brought about by providence acting though secondary sources. Robertson's ideas are discussed by several of the authors collected in *William Robertson and the Expansion of Empire*, ed. Stewart J. Brown (Cambridge: Cambridge University Press, 1997), including ones by Stewart J. Brown, Nicholas Phillipson, and Colin Kidd. The background to such views has been set out in an extended essay by C. A. Patrides, *The Phoenix and the Ladder: The Rise and Decline of the Christian View of History* (Berkeley: University of California Press, 1964) and more recently at length by J. G. A. Pocock, *Barbarism and Religion*, 5 vols. to date (Cambridge: Cambridge University Press, 1999–2010), 3:69–73.

3. Middleton was not unusual among the deists for secularizing history and undercutting traditional notions of ecclesiastical history. He was simply the best of the lot at doing so. The best account of Middleton's work is Hugh Trevor-Roper, "From Deism to History: Conyers Middleton," in Hugh Trevor-Roper, *History and the Enlightenment*, ed. John Robertson (New Haven: Yale University Press, 2010), 71–119.

4. The edition of the letters I have used appears in the Universal Classic Library as *Letters to His Son by the Earl of Chesterfield*, 2 vols., ed. Oliver H. G. Leigh (Washington: M. Walter Dunne, 1901).

5. Ernest Campbell Mossner, *The Life of David Hume* (Edinburgh: Thomas Nelson and Sons, 1954), 395; Sandro Jung, *David Mallet, Anglo-Scot: Poetry, Patronage, and Politics in the Age of Union* (Newark: University of Delaware Press, 2008), 145.

6. Voltaire's *Une histoire des Croisades et Un nouveau plan de l'histoire de l'esprit humain* (1752) was often printed with the *Micromégas* (1752) and was later incorporated into a grander work published in 1756, *Essai sur les mœurs et l'esprit des nations*. See also Chesterfield, *Letters*, letter 185; 2:147.

7. That was also the opinion of Chesterfield's friend Voltaire; see J. H. Brumfitt in *La philosophie de l'histoire*, 2nd rev. ed. (Geneva: Institut et Musée Voltaire; Toronto: University of Toronto Press, 1969); vol. 59 of *Les Oeuvres complètes de Voltaire / The Complete Works of Voltaire*, 16.

8. Helvetius to Hume, 2 June 1763, in *Letters of Eminent Persons Addressed to David Hume*, ed. J. E. Hill Burton (Bristol, 1995), 13–14; D'Alembert to Hume, 28 February 1767, in ibid., 183. D'Alembert wrote the short article on ecclesiastical history for the *Encyclopédie*, 5:223.

9. Friedrich Melchoir Grimm, *Correspondance littéraire, philosophique et critique par Grimm, Diderot, Raynal, Meister, etc.*, 16 vols., ed. Maurice Tourneux (Paris: Garnier Frères, 1879), 7:13. The original passage in French is: "Nous avons souvent sollicité M. Hume, pendant son séjour en France, d'écrire une Histoire ecclésiastique. Ce serait en ce moment une des plus belles entreprises de littérature, et un des plus importants services rendus à la philosophie et à l'humanité."

10. Voltaire's attacks on the Church and blasphemy laws intensified in the 1760s owing to the judicial murder of Jean Calas in 1762. D'Alembert himself had written in 1765 a notable work on the Jesuits, *Sur la destruction des Jesuites en France*, and the final volumes of the text of Diderot's *Encyclopédie* appeared in 1765 and 1766. They contained many attacks on religions and the churches despite the censorship of one of its publishers.

11. "Je ne me consolerai, pourtant, jamais d'être privé de cette Histoire Ecclésiastique, que je vous ai demandé tant de fois, que vous seul peut-être en Europe êtes en état de faire, et qui seroit bien aussi intéressante que l'histoire Grecque et Romaine, si vous vouliez prendre la peine de peindre au naturel notre mère Ste. Eglise." D'Alembert to Hume, 1 May 1773, in *Letters*, ed. Hill Burton, 218.

12. See "Of National Characters," *E* 199–201n3.

13. Hume's French friends missed his belief in the inevitability of the continuance of religion; see Roger L. Emerson, "Hume's Histories," in *Essays on David Hume, Medical Men, and the Scottish Enlightenment: "Industry, Knowledge, and Humanity"* (Farnham, UK: Ashgate, 2009), 137.

14. See the forthcoming bibliography compiled for *The History of England* by Roger L. Emerson and Mark G. Spencer. This shows, in particular, Hume's surprising familiarity with medieval sources.

15. Under a 1697 English act, it was illegal to blaspheme or to deny the doctrine of the Trinity or the articles of the creeds approved by the Anglican Church. In Scotland, Hume could have been prosecuted under the same laws that led to the hanging in 1697 of Thomas Aikenhead.

16. All quotations from the *Encyclopédie* are to the following edition: *Encyclopédie, ou Dictionnaire raisonné des sciences, des arts et des métiers* . . . (Paris: Brisson, David, Le Breton and Durand, 1751; reprinted in 5 vols., New York: Readex Microprint Corporation, 1969). Page numbers are to that set and not to the original volumes; 2:335–38.

17. A fine account of Voltaire's work in the books named above is given by Brumfitt in *La Philosophie de l'histoire*.

18. Hume's general verdict on Voltaire was, "I know that author cannot be depended upon with regard to Facts; but his general Views are sometimes sound, & always entertaining," *L* 1:423. Like Hume, he emphasized the uncertainty of all accounts of ancient peoples.

19. *H* 1:29–46 passim.

20. Adam Smith to William Strahan, 9 November 1776, in *L* 2:450.

21. On Varro, see *Enlightenment Discovering the World in the Eighteenth Century*, ed. Kim Sloan (London: British Museum Press, 2003), 169.

22. There is a short passage in Tacitus on Jews, *History*, bk. 5, 1–6, in *The Complete Works of Tacitus*, trans. A. J. Church and W. J. Brodribb (New York: Modern Library, 1942), 657–60. This depicts them as odd and despicable and Moses as a power-hungry fraud.

23. See Roger L. Emerson, *Academic Patronage in the Scottish Enlightenment* (Edinburgh: Edinburgh University Press, 2008), 31–32, 52, 71; James Coutts, *A History of the University of Glasgow* (Glasgow: Maclehose and Sons, 1909), 170, 192.

24. Anthony Browning, "History," in *Fortuna Domus*, ed. J. B. Neilson (Glasgow: University of Glasgow Press, 1952), 41–57; 44.

25. Robert Wodrow, *Analecta or Some Remarkable Providences* . . . , 4 vols., ed. Mathew Leishman (Glasgow: Maitland Club, 1842–43), 4:212.

26. Divinity students were not generally charged for the courses they took to prepare for the ministry.

27. James Balfour Paul, ed. *Diary of George Ridpath, Minister of Stitchel, 1755–1761* (Edinburgh: Scottish Record Society, 3rd ser., vol. 2, 1922), 200.

28. The manuscripts of those lectures can be found in the Library of New College, Edinburgh University, MS W12a 5\2. Each Latin lecture as an English language summary on loose sheets, which are still in the volumes. I have depended mainly on those summaries for what follows.

29. The summary uses spaces as punctuation and is not always written in full sentences.

30. This was rather like Jonathan Edwards's *History of the Work of Redemption* (written 1739; published Edinburgh, 1774), but Cuming did not see the cycles of life (degeneracy—revelation—moral improvement—backsliding—revelation, etc.) as always falling lower; his tended, after 1300 A.D., to be upward and the work more optimistic, as was characteristic of moderate men in the Kirk of his day.

31. His course somewhat resembled Antoine Goguet's *The Origin of laws, sciences and their progress among the most ancient nations* (Paris, 1758; Edinburgh, 1761). The translator was the Reverend Robert Henry.

32. George Chalmers, *The life of Thomas Ruddiman* (Edinburgh: John Stockdale; London: William Laing, 1794). The Rankenian Club is sometimes cited as the first Edinburgh club of adult intellectuals devoted to the discussion of religious and philosophical ideas.

33. The first letter was sent anonymously but is contained in the Leven and Melville Papers, National Archives of Scotland, GD 26\13\602. The second is in *Philosophical Transactions* 42 (1743), 420–21.

34. What follows rests largely on the notes for Mackie's lectures and on "A discourse read to the Philosophical Society, 4 March 1741" on "vulgar errors and how to detect 'em," both held at Edinburgh University Library [EUL]. Those are discussed by L. W. Sharp, "Charles Mackie, the First Professor of History at Edinburgh University," *Scottish Historical Review* 41 (1962): 23–45. See also Esther Mijers,*"News from the Republic of Letters": Scottish Students, Charles Mackie, and the United Provinces, 1650–1750* (Leiden: Brill, 2012); her discussion of Mackie as a historian runs pp. 157–84.

35. EUL, Laing Manuscript 2:37.10; there are also notes dealing with this topic that seem related to his course in MS Dc.5.24.2.

36. The Scottish chronology for the Middle Ages was first sorted out by Thomas Innes and David Dalrymple, Lord Hailes, in books published in 1729 and 1776.

37. This had been apparent to Sir Robert Sibbald and his friends in the 1680s when they rejected some of the fabulous genealogies offered to them by others. One for the Dukes of Argyle showed them as descendants of King Arthur and through him of Brut (Brute or Brutus), a descendant of Aeneas the Trojan. The mythical history of the Scots kings can still be seen, in part, in Holyrood Palace, Edinburgh, where the portraits of forty of them, painted by Jacob de Wet in the late seventeenth century, still hang.

38. Among the latter were Gilbert Elliot, Sir Harry Erskine, William Mure of Caldwell, James Oswald of Dunniker, Sir James Steuart of Goodtrees, and many more men whom Hume knew socially throughout his life.

39. The College reserved the right to make its professors also lecturers in civil history. Professors were paid mainly by students' fees. There were not enough to support two men. The threat

to render the chair virtually valueless gave them a voice in appointments. Rouet may have taught only a civil history course but that is unlikely.

40. William Rouet, Universal History Notes, National Library of Scotland [NLS], 4992\188.

41. Ibid., 34.

42. Ibid.

43. Ibid., 36.

44. Ibid., 1–31. The lectures are undated but probably come from c. 1752–55. The lectures may have been given to the Glasgow Literary Society, which met after 1752 and of which Hume was later a member. On the other hand, they may have been part of a special course for students or discourses given to the University. See also Carol Gibson-Wood, "George Turnbull and Art History at Scottish Universities in the Eighteenth Century," *RACAR* 28 (2001): 7–18, especially 10–12.

45. Kidd, *Subverting Scotland's Past: Scottish Whig Historians and the Creation of an Anglo-British Identity* (Cambridge: Cambridge University Press, 1993), and "Religious Realignment Between the Restoration and Union" in *A Union for Empire: Political Thought and the Union of 1707*, ed. John Robertson (Cambridge: Cambridge University Press, 1995), 145–68; Allen, *Virtue, Learning, and the Scottish Enlightenment* (Edinburgh: Edinburgh University Press, 1993).

46. *NL* 88–89.

47. The *Histoire ecclésiastique par M. Fleury, Prêtre, Prieur d'Argenteüil, & confesseur du Roy* (vols. I–XXX) was continued by others as *Histoire ecclésiastique pour servir de continuation à celle de Monsieur l'Abbé*. The book is not by Cardinal Fleury, who also wrote history, but by Claude Fleury (1640–1723).

48. "M. Fleuri has given us an excellent work which bears that title; he has added to that a *discours raisonné* more estimable and precious than his history. This judicious writer, in developing in his discourse the means by which God has conserved His Church, sets out at the same time the abuse on which this species of writing is apt to slip. It is right in principle to say 'that it is true that truth is one and entire; that if religion is true, the history of the Church is also; that truth ought not to be opposed to truth, & that the ills of the Church have been great, but they serve to confirm the promises of God who will defend it to the end of time against the powers and efforts of Hell.'" *Encyclopédie*, 1:1052n44.

49. Ibid., 1:1052.

50. Ibid., 2:335–37.

51. Ibid., 3:642–43. Wharton did write a treatise on clerical celibacy, but he was best known as an editor of historical sources, many of which Hume had used in writing his *History of England* and for attacks on the Jesuits.

ARTIFICIAL LIVES, PROVIDENTIAL HISTORY, AND THE APPARENT LIMITS OF SYMPATHETIC UNDERSTANDING

Jennifer A. Herdt

Once regarded as the hero of positivism, Hume is now widely appreciated as a proponent of a hermeneutic philosophy of history. In pursuing his project of developing a science of human culture, of "introducing the experimental method of reasoning into moral subjects," Hume recognized that human actions cannot be understood unless grasped as intentional, as performed for reasons, and not simply explained as falling under a covering law. This enterprise requires that the historian be capable of entering into the logic governing foreign beliefs and practices. Still, Hume draws limits to the scope of hermeneutic analysis. On Hume's account, theistic belief is self-contradictory, requires self-deception, and gives rise to unintelligible behavior. The "moral scientist" is thus licensed to suspend the hermeneutic enterprise and turn to other kinds of explanation. Are these limits justified? We cannot assess them by recourse to external standards, since no such standards are available to us. We can, though, assess them from within, developing an internal critique. The boundaries Hume sets for the range of sympathetic understanding are plausible only if "artificial lives" can be clearly distinguished from the wide range of variation exhibited by "natural lives." As we will see, on closer examination the distinction crumbles; theistic belief and practice offer no intrinsic barrier to understanding. Indeed, Hume's own historiographical practice offers evidence of this. Further, Hume's refusal of providential history can be made plausible only if something like his distinction between natural and artificial lives can be maintained; absent this, Hume's own philosophical history emerges as itself providential in character.

Hume's argument that religious lives constitute a special exception to the task of arriving at an internal grasp of foreign perspectives is sometimes replicated by Hume scholars, as we see in Donald Livingston's endorsement of Hume's critique of providential history. Moreover, the special treatment Hume gave to theism has helped to legitimate modern historiography as an enterprise that is not merely methodologically naturalistic but actually metaphysically naturalistic. It remains the case in contemporary historiography that religion is often subjected to reductionistic analysis in scholarship otherwise devoted to the task of understanding people on their own terms.[1] The cost, in terms of missed opportunities for understanding, is high.

Relinquishing the Search for External Standards

David Hume: Philosophical Historian, published in 1965 by David Fate Norton and Richard Popkin, played a key role in catalyzing a reassessment of the relationship between Hume as historian and Hume as philosopher. It did so by characterizing Hume's historical writings as an expression of his constructive skepticism. The selection of texts—from Hume's *Treatise, Enquiry concerning Human Understanding, History of England*, essays, and letters—along with the editors' introductory essays, issued a challenge to the established view that there was no intrinsic connection between Hume's philosophical and historical work. At times, Hume's philosophy had been viewed as antihistorical; indeed, even his overtly historical writings had been judged to be antihistorical.[2] Norton and Popkin insisted instead that even Hume's "most 'philosophical' work is historical."[3] While the essential nature of reality cannot be known, the regularities of experience can be, and it is with these that the historian is occupied. Nevertheless, Norton argued that Hume's new skeptical science was hounded by the same skeptical problems that its focus on appearances was designed to avoid. What is appearance and what is reality, in this case with respect to the past? "In the science of man as much as in purely speculative metaphysics, a criterion of truth appears to be lacking, so that custom and education, one's personal experiences, play an overriding, though logically indefensible, part in the formation of the judgments and claims making up that science—just as the skeptics had claimed they did in the formation of man's speculative theories."[4] Norton argued that Hume developed an implicit critical method in response to this problem, seeking to authenticate written documents and weigh the value of testimony. Nevertheless, Norton concluded that the assessment of evidence remains finally "a matter of personal opinion and prior decision"; there is "still no external or shared standard by which evidence can be evaluated."[5] He appealed to "Of Miracles" to bolster his claim that Hume consciously accepted the fact that individual experience is our final standard, seeing this as the only way to avoid a patent circularity in the argument (i.e., disputes over the past are settled by appealing to the past). We decide a priori whether we will take certain kinds of evidence seriously or not, and we do so on the basis of our own experience. Hume's method, then, is permeated with subjective elements. Norton concludes that "Hume's critical method, and with it, the science of man, failed, failed as he surely suggests all enterprises conceived after his model must fail"—even if we cannot refrain from forming opinions, and in this sense are licensed by nature to continue the enterprise.[6]

If Norton saw Hume as a constructive skeptic, later interpreters would tend to emphasize the "constructive" aspect of this characterization. So Donald Livingston, who declares himself indebted to *David Hume: Philosophical Historian* for helping him see the unity of Hume's philosophical and historical work, argues that Hume adhered to a philosophy of common life, according to which philosophy's task is to "methodize and correct" the customs and judgments of common life, repudiating philosophy's false pretension to stand above and outside all social convention.[7] Hume gave up on the misguided attempt to know the real apart from human custom and judgment and accepted instead the task of reflecting on the real through these human conventions. This might be regarded as a form of mitigated skepticism, but it is better understood as a form of pragmatism, although Livingston himself does not invoke the term. Total skepticism, in contrast, is understood to be the outcome of a falsely autonomous conception of the task of philosophy. It continues to lurk as a threat only insofar as the temptation to an autonomous philosophy also continues to exercise residual charm. Within the philosophy of common life, in contrast, the process of piecemeal internal criticism continues unscathed.

It is hardly surprising that such an interpretation of Hume's thought would prove compelling in a postfoundationalist context, nor that Hume so understood would become the focus of a surge of philosophical attention. What, then, becomes of Norton's diagnosis of the failure of Hume's critical method, on this interpretation? "Custom and education" do play a key role in the formation of judgments and claims, including the evaluation of historical evidence. But if there is no "external" standard, there are nevertheless "shared" standards; the alternative is not between subjectivism on the one hand and autonomous, external, philosophical judgments on the other. Repudiating as an illusion the aspiration to external standards, Hume regards objectivity as constituted by intersubjective standards. These may, to be sure, be corrupted or provincial, but they are also, by the same token, always open to correction.

History and the Task of Sympathetic Understanding

There remains a danger that the philosophy of common life, having given up on objective standards of judgment in the strongest (if illusory) sense, will strive to portray as shared, communal standards the judgments of a narrow minority. And indeed Hume has been seen as having done precisely this. R. G. Collingwood, for instance, indicted Hume for imposing eighteenth-century values on the past and found Hume incapable of understanding a past age on its own terms. Alasdair MacIntyre accused Hume, more precisely, of championing the values of the English landowning class.[8] But Hume was certainly well aware of the challenges posed to human society by differences in perspective: "'twere impossible we cou'd ever make use of language, or communicate our sentiments to one another, did we not correct the momentary appearances of things, and overlook our present situation." (*T* 3.3.1.16/582)[9] Moral judgment, he argued, requires that we give up our particular point of view, and consider character "in general, without reference to our particular interest" (*T* 3.1.2.4/472). It is not enough that we be disinterested, though; we must achieve a "sympathy with those, who have any commerce with the person we consider" (*T* 3.3.1.18/583). So a sympathetic understanding of the perspectives of others is vital to our capacity to evaluate others and hence bound up with the enterprise of history, which Hume unabashedly regards as normative.[10] Historians, unlike poets, philosophers, and politicians, are the "true friends of virtue, and have always represented it in its proper colours" (*E* 567). History "keeps in a just medium" between the extremes of a cold and abstract philosophical perspective on the one hand and the "warped" judgment of the man of business on the scenes of life on the other; history "places the objects in their true point of view" (*E* 568). History is capable of doing this because it gives us a sympathetic understanding of those whose perspectives are initially alien to us, allowing us both to perceive and to assess their reasons for acting.

This normative task is regarded by Hume as enhancing, rather than interfering with, the explanatory enterprise; "history is not only a valuable part of knowledge, but opens the door to many other parts, and affords materials to most of the sciences" (*E* 566). Hume's science of man did not amount to a reductive naturalism. Doubtless Hume held a naturalist ontology, regarding social and psychological phenomena as taking place at a secondary level of organization that is materially dependent on a more basic or primary level of material reality. And it is true that within the *Treatise* Hume employed association as a far-reaching explanatory principle, which might lead to the conclusion that he adhered to a kind of descriptivism, wishing to explain all phenomena at one privileged level of explanation.[11] But while he certainly does offer covering-law explanations to account both for regularities in human behavior and particular historical events, he finds it most satisfying to offer explanations that refer to the reasons an agent had for acting.[12] It is a mistake to oppose this kind of hermeneutical understanding to the enterprise of explanation, for understanding agents' reasons for action can allow us to more fully explain an event. The business of explanation is highly context dependent, and it is crucial to know what particular why-question is being asked. The simple question, "why did she die?" may be satisfactorily answered in a variety of ways that refer to different levels of explanation: "because of the poison in her system," "because she committed suicide," "because she was depressed," "because of an imbalance in brain chemicals," and "because of her estrangement from her son'" may all be appropriate answers in particular contexts, some of which have their home in the social exchange of reasons, others in the search for covering laws, whether at biological, psychological, or sociological levels of organization.

Hume was optimistic about the possibility of achieving sympathetic understanding of foreign points of view, and insistent that this understanding did not imply moral relativism.[13] We see this particularly clearly in "A Dialogue," appended to the *Enquiry concerning the Principles of Morals*. There the well-traveled Palamedes describes for Hume the strange inhabitants of the country of Fourli, where incest and homosexual liaisons are smiled on, marital fidelity disparaged, infanticide accepted, and honor disregarded. Hume's response is disbelief: "such barbarous and savage manners are not only incompatible with a civilized, intelligent people, such as you said these were; but are scarcely compatible with human nature" (*EPM* 112–13/328). To call manners "barbarous" and "savage" is to declare them beyond the reach of sympathetic understanding. But in this case the label turns out to be, in Hume's own judgment, falsely applied. Fourli turns out to be Athens, and only a thicker description is required in order to see these foreign practices in the light of community life as a whole, and thus as performed in the pursuit of intelligible goods. Whereas Palamedes, confronted with the cultural variation between ancient Greece and contemporary Paris, finds it impossible "to fix a standard for judgments of this nature," Hume advises him that the problem can be resolved "by tracing matters . . . a little higher, and examining the first principles, which each nation establishes, of blame or censure" (*EPM* 116/333). So, for instance, "Greek loves" arose from the frequency of gymnastic exercises and were regarded as a source of friendship and fidelity. Moreover, the Greeks recognized incest as contrary to reason and public utility but simply defined its limits differently than canon lawyers. And infanticide was practiced only in the face of extreme poverty and was regarded as saving the child from an evil greater than death. Even where Greek practices remain blameworthy, they are understandable, directed toward ends that we, too, can recognize as good.

The Problem of Artificial Lives

As optimistic as Hume was about the possibility of extending sympathetic understanding across cultural and historical boundaries, he believed that he had at the same time identified inherent limits to its scope. He sought to differentiate between natural variations in moral sentiment and practices, on the one hand, and artificial lives and manners, on the other. When it comes to the latter, the "maxims of common life and ordinary conduct" no longer apply; instead, speculative principles determine morality. Palamedes offers Hume two examples, one culled from ancient philosophy, the other from modern Christianity: the Cynic Diogenes and the Jansenist Blaise Pascal. To Palamedes's request that he reconcile these examples with his account of morality, Hume replies:

> An experiment . . . which succeeds in the air, will not always succeed in a vacuum. When men depart from the maxims of common reason, and affect these *artificial* lives, as you call them, no one can answer for what will please or displease them. They are in a different element from the rest of mankind; and the natural principles of their mind play not with the same regularity, as if left to themselves, free from the illusions of religious superstition or philosophical enthusiasm. (*EPM* 123/343)

Superstition and enthusiasm, then, are seen as interfering with the natural principles of the mind. More specifically, according to Hume, it is abstract speculations that interfere, when they intrude into the realm of morality. In the ancient world, religion had "very little influence on common life," but the philosophical schools sought "to regulate men's ordinary behaviour and deportment" and "produced great singularities of maxims and conduct." At present, argues Hume, it is religion, rather than philosophy, that has appropriated to itself this dubious honor; it "inspects our whole conduct, and prescribes an universal rule to our actions, to our words, to our very thoughts and inclinations" (*EPM* 122/342). Where natural lives are concerned, in contrast, however great the variations, it is always possible, argues Hume, to discern the operation of the same underlying principle, which lies at the heart of his account of morality: moral approval is given to those qualities that are either useful or agreeable, to the agent or to those affected by the agent (*EPM* 118/336).

Whereas the term "artificial" is rarely derogatory in Hume's thought—after all, the artificial virtues include justice and promise keeping—in this context, it clearly designates something very problematic. Both the maxims of common reason and artificial lives admit of a wide range of internal variation, but

Hume argues that there is an absolute division between the two: sympathetic understanding is possible only of the former. This is because sympathetic understanding requires grasping the goods for which agents act, their reasons for acting. But the actions of those who live artificial lives are unintelligible; they do not act for the sake of things that (Hume's rhetorically constructed) "we" can grasp as goods ("no man can answer for what will please or displease them"). They are, then, apparently like the insane, who may speak as though they have reasons for acting or pursuing particular goods, but whose actions do not follow from these purported reasons in any intelligible way. Their "actions" are thus merely pieces of behavior, to be explained, perhaps, but *not* understood.

Hume's twofold move is to identify artificial lives with actions performed for no good at all, that is, irrational actions, while identifying as natural those lives in which moral judgments admit of the particular account he gives in terms of usefulness and agreeableness: "It appears, that there never was any quality recommended by any one, as a virtue or moral excellence, but on account of its being *useful*, or *agreeable* to a man *himself*, or to *others*. For what other reason can ever be assigned for praise or approbation? Or where would be the sense of extolling a *good* character or action, which, at the same time, is allowed to be *good for nothing*?" (*EPM* 118/336). Hume's principle of sympathetic understanding requires that we be able to discern the reasons for which agents act, the goods they are pursuing. An action that is not directed toward anything under the denomination good is pointless, unintelligible. But it is not the case that an agent—or observer—must *think* of an action as useful or agreeable in order for it to have a point. In practice, the discernment of reasons for action is highly concrete and specific. If you pick up your umbrella as you head out the door on a rainy day, your action is immediately intelligible to me as having a point—to stay dry. If you pick up your umbrella and head out the door on a sunny day, having just heard a forecast of glorious weather, I will need some help in understanding the reason for your action—perhaps you wish to return the umbrella to your car, where you usually keep it; or perhaps there is a hidden camera in your umbrella, and you plan to use it to spy on your colleagues. The more foreign and distant your way of life, the more thick description I will need of surrounding beliefs and practices in order to make sense of a particular action. Perhaps you live in a culture that regards umbrellas primarily as parasols, protection from the sun. Perhaps you are a member of a gang that identifies itself by carrying a particular kind of umbrella. When we attempt to describe reasons for action in general, we abstract from all of this concreteness, saying things like, "actions, unlike pieces of behavior, are intentional," "actions are performed for reasons," "actions are directed towards ends perceived by the agent as good."

The monkish virtues were for Hume the epitome of character traits that are "good for nothing":

> celibacy, fasting, penance, mortification, self-denial, humility, silence, solitude, and the whole train of monkish virtues; for what reason are they everywhere rejected by men of sense, but because they serve to no manner of purpose; neither advance a man's fortune in the world, nor render him a more valuable member of society; neither qualify him for the entertainment of company, nor increase his power of self-enjoyment? We observe, on the contrary, that they cross all these desirable ends; stupify the understanding and harden the heart, obscure the fancy and sour the temper. (*EPM* 9.3/270)

We can see that the monkish virtues, at least as described by Hume, seem neither useful nor agreeable to anyone. However, is it really the case that Hume is unable to grasp virtuous monks as acting for reasons? Is he unable to discern the goods for which they act? Is he unable to see their actions as expressions of intentional agency, unable to see them as acting at all, rather than simply exhibiting pieces of behavior?

What lends Hume's statements regarding the impossibility of sympathetic understanding of artificial lives some initial plausibility is the analysis he offers of theistic beliefs—and the artificial lives based on these beliefs—as utterly self-contradictory and as requiring sustained self-deception. This analysis, which is most fully developed in the *Natural History of Religion*, essentially presents theists as insane—as perpetually driving themselves insane through their fears and insecurity, their simultaneous tendencies to exalt the deity and to regard the deity as a harsh and arbitrary tyrant, their efforts to laud the deity even as they secretly hate him. According to Hume's "natural history," polytheism, though arising out of fearful ignorance, is not irrational or self-contradictory; polytheists simply imagine the unknown causes of the unpredictable events that determine their fates as personal agents subject to potential human influence. Theism emerges out of polytheism as the attempt to influence one deity, seen as particularly relevant, gives rise to ever more exaggerated praise, until this deity is honored as sole, omnipotent, infinite divine power. Contradictions begin to enter in as the deity is praised as transcendent and infinite and yet believers continue to anthropomorphize the deity in order to have some hope of influencing that god; "it is well, if, in striving to get farther, and to represent a magnificent simplicity, they run not into inexplicable mystery, and destroy the intelligent nature of their deity, on which alone any rational worship or adoration can be founded" (*NHR* 53–54). Since it is fear and anxiety that drives the formation of religious belief, believers naturally tend, argues Hume, to conceive of the deity as a malicious entity who must be placated. On the other hand, in order to have some hope of flattering the deity into compliance with their wishes, believers tend to praise their god not only as omnipotent and omniscient, but also as perfectly good. And while praise of the gods might initially be purely affected, once the deity is regarded as omniscient, it is no longer sufficient to display devotion. Believers thus struggle to suppress their hatred and fear of the deity: "while their gloomy apprehensions make them ascribe to him measures of conduct, which, in human creatures, would be highly blamed, they must still affect to praise and admire that conduct in the object of their devotional addresses" (*NHR* 78). Theistic belief is thus on Hume's analysis pervaded by self-contradiction and self-deception. In fact, it hardly amounts to real belief at all, argues Hume: "the conviction of the religionists, in all ages, is more affected than real, and scarcely ever approaches, in any degree, to that solid belief and persuasion, which governs us in the common affairs of life" (*NHR* 71). If the lives of theists were indeed dictated by such a contradictory set of pseudo-beliefs, Hume's claim that sympathetic understanding here confronts an absolute limit would seem plausible.[14] After all, anything follows from a contradiction.

Even if Hume's account of theistic belief as riven with contradictions renders specious the notion that modes of life dictated by these beliefs would offer barriers to sympathetic understanding, Hume must still show that "artificial lives" are not intelligible in terms of the ordinary goods of human flourishing. He attempts to do so in "A Dialogue," in which Pascal is represented as leading the kind of artificial life that results from allowing speculative opinions—particularly of such a contradictory nature—to interfere with the "natural principles" of the mind:

> The aim of Pascal was to keep a perpetual sense of his dependence before his eyes, and never to forget his numberless wants and infirmities.... [He] made constant profession of humility and abasement, of the contempt and hatred of himself; and endeavoured to attain these supposed virtues, as far as they are attainable. The austerities... of the Frenchman were embraced merely for their own sake, and in order to suffer as much as possible.... The most ridiculous superstitions directed Pascal's faith and practice; and an extreme contempt of this life, in comparison of the future, was the chief foundation of his conduct. (*EPM* 122–23/342–43)

Pascal is represented as cultivating self-hatred, as pursuing suffering for its own sake, as condemning this life, as allowing "ridiculous" superstitions to determine his way of life. He is depicted as engaging in self-destructive behavior that is detrimental to human flourishing and potentially even counter to the basic need for survival. But note that Pascal's actions are not, after all, wholly unintelligible to Hume. Hume is able to identify the goods Pascal pursues, even if he regards those goods—of the life to come—as illusory. And in fact, the goods of eternal life can be made intelligible in terms of, or at least by analogy with, the goods Hume does recognize, those of ordinary human flourishing. Pascal seeks only true and secure goods, and concludes that these cannot be this worldly, given the finitude and unreliability of earthly goods. Given his belief that this world is a finite creation of an infinite and loving God, it makes sense for Pascal to seek communion with the source of that creation, the source of all the limited goods we encounter in this life. This is, of course, hardly a full specification of Pascal's beliefs and their relation to his way of life, but it is enough to call into question Hume's accusation that Pascal's way of life, as self-defeating and self-destructive, undermines the very conditions for the pursuit of any goods at all. Pascal does not seek suffering for its own sake; he seeks to recognize his true identity as a fallen creation of God. He does not cultivate contempt of this life but cultivates the awareness that all finite goods issue from God as goodness itself. While Hume argues that sympathetic understanding has arrived here at an absolute limit, there is no reason that thick description cannot accomplish here what it accomplished in the case of Greek infanticide and infidelity—render comprehensible, as ways of pursuing intelligible goods, practices that might still be judged by the observer to be worthy of blame. Hume has not succeeded in drawing a sharp boundary between natural and artificial lives, maxims, and practices. The task of sympathetic understanding remains in place even here.

Does this mean that the monkish virtues are, in fact, useful and/or agreeable? It would certainly be possible to redescribe them in this way—they are "useful" for transforming oneself into the person who will be acceptable in God's kingdom, say, or for earning God's favor, or for preparing oneself for the reception of grace. Likewise, they are "agreeable" for those who experience them as anticipations of the glorified life, free of bodily limitations, and as receptivity to divine indwelling. This is not to say, though, that monks cultivate these virtues for the sake of their usefulness or agreeableness. Rather, they cultivate them out of their desire for God. Hume's explanatory account is flexible enough to accommodate a very broad range of reasons for action—as is economists' category of "utility." Does it add to our understanding, though, to reduce the monks' reasons for action to this other, purportedly more basic, level of explanation? We might expect it to do so, insofar as it gives a unified account of apparently disparate phenomena. On the other hand, if this account lumps together reasons that are meaningfully experienced as distinct, it is not so clearly useful. Ernest Nagel's comments about the limited usefulness of reductive explanation is applicable here:

> [In problematic cases] the distinctive traits that are the subject matter of the secondary science fall into the province of a theory that may have been initially designed for handling qualitatively different materials and that does not even include some of the characteristic descriptive terms of the secondary science in its own set of theoretical distinctions. The primary science thus seems to wipe out familiar distinctions as spurious, and appears to maintain that what are prima facie indisputably different traits of things are really identical.[15]

Having seen that in fact the monkish virtues, too, can be described as "useful" and "agreeable," we are able to see that such an explanatory account works only insofar as "useful" and "agreeable" function as thin specifications of ends for action, which can be filled in radically divergent ways. Either Hume's account amounts to no more than the claim that "in order to be subject to moral assessment, an action must be performed for the sake of some perceived good," in which case the monkish virtues cannot be excluded as artificial, or "useful" and "agreeable" are substantive, not merely formal, categories. And if "useful" and "agreeable" are substantive, it cannot be claimed that these are the *only* goods that can be pursued through intentional action, or that any actions not performed for the sake of the "useful" or "agreeable" are pointless and unintelligible. They are "good for nothing" only from some particular perspective.

Sympathetic Understanding in the *History of England*

The preceding discussion has focused on Hume's articulating of the principle of sympathetic understanding and its limits and has held this up against contemporary hermeneutically oriented philosophy of history. How is this put to work in Hume's *History of England*? Hume famously prided himself on having offered a truly unbiased account, writing in "My Own Life" that "I thought I was the only historian, that had at once neglected present power, interest, and authority, and the cry of popular prejudices"(*E* xxxvii). Instead, he reports, he was assailed from all sides, "English, Scotch, and Irish, Whig and Tory, churchman and sectary, freethinker and religionist, patriot and courtier, united in their rage against the man, who had presumed to shed a generous tear for the fate of Charles I, and the earl of Strafford." As the reference to his "generous tear" indicates, Hume does not hesitate in his *History* to employ the rhetorical tools of sentimentality. He does so specifically in order to dislodge readers from their party prejudices and encourage them to enter sympathetically into foreign points of view. A major concern of Hume's *History* is with the destructive effects of various forms of party and faction; Hume's aim is to narrate the history of England in a way that heals factional divisions and makes way for a more harmonious (and prosperous) future.

It is no surprise that religious belief is presented as a major root of the kinds of social conflict that are most difficult to treat. Moreover, Hume regards this particularly resistant form of zeal as rooted in the self-deceptive or hypocritical character of theistic belief: "The religious hypocrisy, it may be remarked, is of a peculiar nature; and being generally unknown to the person himself, though more dangerous, it implies less falsehood than any other species of insincerity" (*H* 6:142). In its treatment of religion, Hume's sentimental history seeks to dislodge readers from their religious prejudices, in order to cultivate sympathy not with alien religious perspectives but rather with the "party of Mankind" as such. Yet Hume's treatment of individual cases varies considerably. Quite often in the *History*, he refers to instances of sincere conviction; in Thomas à Becket, for instance, Charles I, and Henry III of France (*H* 1:333–34; 5:213). For the most part, however, these acknowledgments come barbed: Becket was caught up in a mass delusion; Charles I trusted in a Being whose favor is expressed in incomprehensible ways; Henry III's belief was sincere enough but did not have the force to regulate his conduct. There are, though, rare instances in which Hume recognizes sincere conviction with actions following intelligibly from that conviction. So, for instance, he recognizes that Sir Thomas More relinquished his position "foreseeing that all the measures of the king and parliament led to a breach with the church of Rome, and to an alteration of religion, with which his principles would not permit him to concur" (*H* 3:197).[16] More acts on religious principle, but his actions are nevertheless intelligible even to the historian who does not share those principles. So Hume's historiographical practice belies at times his own general statement of limits.[17]

Providential History

As we have seen, then, while Hume did not reject the attempt to identify covering laws in history, he also sought to develop moral explanations, to achieve sympathetic understanding of historical actors. He understood this as an enterprise that would serve to refine and cultivate moral judgment. At the same time, Hume argued that there was a limit to the scope of sympathetic understanding. Sympathetic understanding is possible only where people are governed by "maxims of common life and ordinary conduct"; not where they live artificial lives, governed by speculative beliefs that contradict the maxims of ordinary life. Where moral explanation is possible, we can understand alien practices or individual actions, even if we judge them to be blameworthy. But when confronted by artificial lives, actions are unintelligible, pointless, possibly subject to causal explanation but not sympathetic understanding of agents' reasons for acting. I have argued, though, that Hume illegitimately excuses himself from the task of sympathetic understanding by suggesting that lives dedicated to the pursuit of ends that do not conform to his own substantive understanding of what is truly "useful" or "agreeable" are in fact pursuing no goods at all and undermine the conditions of the possibility of human life and flourishing. He does better in the practice of writing history than in articulating its theory.

Donald Livingston, too, explores the issue of the limits of moral explanation. The example he takes up in detail is Hume's treatment of the Saxon "barbarians" in volume 1 of his *History of England*. There Hume makes no effort to understand the point of view of those about whom he is writing, and his designation of the people as barbarians effectively captures why. Hume regards a barbarian as almost wholly unreflective, as lacking a conception of himself as a human being, and so as capable of very little self-conscious rational activity. "The Humean historian," notes Livingston, "must explain the actions of historical agents by rethinking in his own mind the rational activity that is the inside or moral cause of the action. But it is impossible to rethink rational activity where there is none or where knowledge of it is impossible."[18] The fact that barbarians lack a rational interior sets up a barrier to moral understanding. This example works well for Livingston since he is able to conclude his discussion by showing that Hume did, after reading Robert Henry's account of this historical period, come to recognize that the Saxons were not, after all, barbarians in this sense, and that it was therefore possible to achieve a moral understanding of their actions.[19] Precisely where Collingwood's judgment of Hume as incapable of *verstehen* thus seems most appropriate, Livingston has thus shown Hume to have recognized and corrected the deficiency. The more stubborn problem, however, is Hume's articulation of a general principle that excuses the historian from responsibility for seeking sympathetic understanding with those whom he regards as leading "artificial lives." Indeed, in endorsing Hume's critique of providential history, Livingston replicates the problem.

Livingston, echoing Popkin, sees as key to grasping Hume's enterprise as a historian the fact that Hume sought to undermine the dominant model of historical thinking in his day, which was providential. Instead of reading history as the arena of God's redemptive action and human response or failure of response, Hume, in Popkin's words, sought "to portray human history as meaningful and comprehensible in its own secular terms, according to a complex of human and natural factors."[20] This leaves open whether human history is to be comprehended in terms of covering-law explanations, in terms of historical agents' reasons for action, or as some combination of the two, but in any case, the Humean historian will have no need to appeal to divine action in order to explain a historical occurrence, nor will she regard historical agents as contributing unintentionally to the fulfillment of divine purposes. Livingston, for his part, makes clear that Hume appeals both to causal (covering-law) explanations and moral explanations, though he regards moral explanations as most significant in Hume's historical work. There are times when a moral explanation is available but no causal explanation, and vice versa, and there are times when we are able to offer both. Where we are unable to offer a moral explanation, we regard action as absurd or unintelligible, even if we have been able to formulate a covering-law explanation. This, argues Livingston, is the case where popular religion is concerned; Hume develops a causal explanation, but concludes nevertheless that "the whole is a riddle, an enigma, an inexplicable mystery" (NHR 87). "The suggestion is that a moral account of popular religious practices (of the sort Hume gave of the seemingly irrational behavior of Athenian politics) is needed but is not available. It is for this reason that Hume is forced to describe the practices of popular religion pathologically as 'the playthings of monkeys or sick men's dreams.'"[21]

Livingston offers a subtle account to show why Hume's rejection of providential history is justified. Hume, Livingston argues, regarded historical order as mind dependent. History is not a structure objectively present in the world but is "internal to a certain point of view of the world and would not exist at all if people did not adopt that point of view."[22] Still, like moral or aesthetic judgment, historical judgment is not arbitrary or merely relative to some partisan perspective; "the point of view in question is not considered by Hume to be relative to this or that historian; it is a point of view written into the very idea of history."[23] Historical order is, for Hume, perceived with reference to a grand story line, "the story of the 'improvements of the human mind.'"[24] This theme is not arbitrarily chosen or projected; rather, it is a "received historical theme," which serves to constitute the community to which Hume addresses himself, "all reasonable people," "the party of humankind" (EHU 10.27 /125; EPM 9.9/275). "The community would cease to be what it is if that story were no longer told."[25] Therefore, the project of narrating the story of the improvements of the human mind is a condition of the possibility of the existence of humankind.

Providential history, like Hume's history and his *History*, is governed by an overarching story line that brings order and unity to historical events. What is illicit about providential history is that it appeals to the *future* in order to judge the present, whereas Hume, argues Livingston, shows that it is only legitimate to appeal to the *past* in order to judge the present. In inferring a cause from an effect, Hume famously argues, we must carefully proportion the former to the latter; "the one can never refer to anything farther, or be the foundation of any new inference and conclusion" *(EHU* 11.14/137). It is only "vain reasoners" who "instead of regarding the present scene of things as the sole object of their contemplation, so far reverse the whole course of nature, as to render this life merely a passage to something farther; a porch, which leads to a greater, and vastly different building; a prologue, which serves only to introduce the piece, and give it more grace and propriety" *(EHU* 11.21/141). Providential historians assert that they have *knowledge* of future events. They attempt to narrate the future, to cast the future into the past tense.[26] It is not that they hope or anticipate something in the future, or even that they attempt to predict future events, but that they *foresee* or *foretell* the future. Thus, the present is viewed "in terms of future events thought of as, in some sense, already having happened."[27] Many of our concepts, Livingston argues, are past entailing; they hold only if some past-tense statement is true: "is a wife," "is a priest," "is a gold-medal winner." These are critical to the "narrative imagination" and "constitute the conceptual framework of the moral world."[28] We cannot make sense of the present, and certainly cannot coherently evaluate present states of affairs, except with reference to the past. From this Livingston concludes that "social and political legitimacy, in the broadest sense, is constituted by narrative relations holding between past and present existences where the past is viewed as a standard conferring legitimacy on the present and, as Hume paradoxically observes, where the present may also be taken as a standard for conferring legitimacy on the past."[29] Providential history, though, derives its standards not from past or present but from future events, "and these confer not legitimacy but, necessarily, illegitimacy on the present society."[30]

There are several difficulties with Livingston's analysis of Hume's attack on providential history. First, Hume's strictures against those who "reverse the whole course of nature" by making this life "merely a passage to something further" are aimed at those who act for the sake of life in the world to come, a supernatural mode of existence. Inferences to a historical future are something quite different from inferences to an eternal future, and Hume's attack does not clearly encompass the former, only the latter. Hume focuses on the difficulty of making new inferences from a cause whose existence has been inferred from a single work or production. "The Deity is known to us only by his productions, and is a single being in the universe, not comprehended under any species or genus, from whose experienced attributes or qualities, we can, by analogy, infer any attribute or quality in him" (*EHU* 11.26/144). We can thus infer from experienced effect to divine cause, but cannot infer from this anything that we have not actually experienced as caused by God. Given that human nature and agency are not, unlike God and the universe, a "single work or production," but rather something of which we have experienced very many instances, we can legitimately construct covering laws governing human agency and use these to infer to the future. The problem with providential history, in Hume's eyes, is thus not its reference to the future as such, but its claim that God is the cause of history, and more particularly with claims to know a future beyond history.

Second, even if Hume were successful in undermining the possibility of inferences from past or present to the future, this would not (as Livingston concedes) render illegitimate attempts to predict the future, hope for the future, or hypothesize about the future. Nor does it undercut criticism of the present order on the basis of an imagined and hoped-for future. This is important, since it is not at all clear that all forms of providential history, or even all forms of providential history present in eighteenth-century thought, involve a claim to know the future, to view the future as though it has already happened. Some forms of providential history look to the restoration of a past golden age, thus conforming to Livingston's stricture that the past be the source for present legitimacy.[31] Some combine keen *hope* for the future with an insistence on the impossibility of *knowing* the future, often rooted in Jesus's reminder that "about that day or hour no one knows, neither the angels in heaven, nor the Son, but only the Father" (Mark 13:32). Some see the *end* of history as inevitable but regard events within history as themselves open, an arena for free, undetermined human action. Some expect catastrophe to usher in a new transhistorical age, while others, focusing on the notion of a millennium, expect gradual improvement culminating in a new historical golden age; the latter, at least, are hardly alienated from the present or tempted to violent revolution.[32] And while there were many eighteenth-century theologians who thought it was possible and worthwhile to offer rational proofs of the existence of a future life beyond history, or, like Joseph Priestley, to attempt to discern in contemporary events the guiding hand of God, such efforts are not necessary concomitants of Christian or other sorts of religious faith and indeed have been subject to theological critique as misguided assertions of the power of human reason where a stance of faith is more appropriate. What is needed, then, is a more fine-grained description, which is capable of differentiating among a variety of Christian views of history, all of which might be termed providential in some sense, but not all of which are subject to Livingston's critique. One result will be that Hume's own grand story line of the improvement of the human mind will no longer appear sharply distinct from at least some forms of providential history. Hume rejected providential history but embraced his own teleology of progress, one that appealed not, as did nineteenth-century historiography, to an abstract scheme, but one that embodied hope for the future.[33] As Noel Jackson notes, "Hume offered a mode of historiography that catered to the needs of a credit economy that depended for its own prosperity upon the image of a stable and largely secular future."[34] Hume's ordering of the past certainly orients him to the future in a particular way; he hopes for the triumph of the "party of humankind" and for the demise of the monkish virtues, even as his inferences based on past experiences of human nature do not give him excessive confidence that his hopes will be realized. To be able to speak of improvements of the human mind implies not only a point of departure judged vicious or imperfect, but also an imagined perfection of the human mind, in light of which the present is discerned as improved but still imperfect.[35]

Finally, it is hardly clear that providential history is "in total alienation from the standards that constitute the present social and political order."[36] The present can be viewed as "passing" and "inadequate" without therefore being regarded as "illegitimate," but Livingston suggests that the former implies the latter.[37] In fact, Hume would surely agree that the present order is both "passing," that is, finite and subject to end or change, and "inadequate," that is, in less than perfect conformity to ethical standards. Given that the standards of Hume's social and political order were shaped in the context of Christian faith and eschatological hope, it is closer to the truth to say that Hume is the one who is in alienation from these standards. If, as Livingston argues, the present receives its legitimacy from the past, how is it legitimate, on Livingston's own grounds, for Hume to critique the legitimate Christian moral order? It can appear so only given a sharp distinction between artificial and natural lives, a distinction that has dissolved upon closer examination. Once the bright lines between artificial and natural lives—those between providential and Humean history—begin to fade, we—and Hume—are left with a more complex picture and a more differentiated critical task.

History as Rhetoric

Livingston rightly notes that "the providential view of history provides an a priori framework for interpreting historical events."[38] How does this differ from a Humean view of history? Hume often uses the term "true" when speaking of history. History, as we have seen, places objects in their "true point of view" *(E* 568), it perceives historical actors "in their true colours" (*E* 566), and historians are "true friends of virtue" (*E* 567). Nevertheless, while history is not written from some merely relative point of view, neither is it written into the objective structure of the world. Rather, the historical point of view is, in Livingston's words, the "point of view written into the very idea of history."[39] Once the distinction between natural and artificial lives is dismantled, along with the notion that providential history is a single discrete understanding of history that can be clearly opposed to Hume's own truly historical understanding, we are left with competing a priori frameworks for interpreting historical events, written into different ideas of history, and constitutive of different forms of community. These can be seen as in partial conformity with the standards that constitute the present social order, and in partial alienation from these standards. A wholly artificial form of life would be self-defeating and unable to sustain itself, just as an utterly alienated historical perspective would be unrecognizable as a historical perspective.[40] But anything short of this extreme is neither unintelligible nor illegitimate as a historical perspective.

This is not to deny that Hume is able to offer a critique of various forms of providential history, showing the historical accounts they offer to be wrong or blameworthy. But it is to insist that these must be engaged with substantively and piecemeal, rather than being dismissed a priori on formal grounds. Confronted with accounts of history shaped by Christian eschatology, it is obviously not sufficient to point out that these are alienated from the point of view Hume endorses, nor that Hume is alienated from the point of view endorsed therein. Rather, in critiquing the dominant conventions of his day, Hume must appeal to standards that are present or at least implicit within the society, and point out how they stand in tension with or contradict other commitments. And he must then persuade his readers to retain some of these while dropping incompatible commitments. Because common life is in fact pervaded by contradictions of various kinds, there will always be room for this kind of internal criticism, which preserves us from an immobile conservatism. But since logic by itself cannot determine which of two incompatible commitments should be dropped, criticism is always in part a rhetorical affair.[41]

Is this not what Hume has been up to all along? Surely he uses rhetoric to brand certain forms of life as "artificial" or "barbaric," certain forms of history as "true," certain communities as "the party of humankind"? Yes—but insofar as this rhetoric falsely claimed that certain forms of life are beyond the pale of sympathetic understanding, are incoherent or unintelligible in terms of the shared goods of "common life," it is a rhetoric that can and should be rejected. It is one thing to try to describe one's own conception of the useful and agreeable in ways that will be attractive and persuasive to others; it is quite another to argue that moral judgments and ways of life that do not align with these particular goods so described are incoherent and unintelligible. We can, in proper Humean fashion, both sympathetically understand Hume's temptation to do so and find it blameworthy. We are left, then, with something still meaningfully called a philosophy of common life, though no longer with the illusion that this common life neatly excludes popular theistic practices or providential history as artificial or unintelligible, nor that it is particularly unified or determinate.

There is a lesson to be learned here. Hume's highly influential *History of England*, along with his other writings, helped to foster the emergence of a secular historiography that interpreted human history as comprehensible by reference to a variety of psychological and social factors.[42] Hume's history was meaningful in terms of a story line that made no reference to God or to an otherworldly destiny. He helped to establish methodological naturalism as the modus operandi of the human sciences.[43] Moreover, in a context dominated by competing confessional histories, which privileged one religious group while tending to discount members of other confessions as self-deceived, self-interested, power-hungry, and/or insane, Hume prided himself on offering an impartial account. Hume's methodological naturalism and his impartiality are not unconnected; because Hume did not think that God was advancing the cause either of Puritans or of Anglo-Catholics, he traced the fortunes of these groups without reference to divine aid or retribution. And because he did not identify with any particular religious "party," he did not find it difficult to avoid privileging one over the others.

Naturalism as a methodological postulate, however, can easily give way to what one historian has called "the *dogma* of metaphysical naturalism."[44] Metaphysical naturalism, unlike methodological naturalism, does not hold simply that the tools of historians are capable only of discerning natural causes, but rather asserts that there is no transcendent reality beyond or grounding the natural. The metaphysical naturalist works "in a manner analogous to that of a traditional, religious confessional historian, insofar as one's analysis relies substantively on one's own beliefs."[45] Such a stance is hardly impartial between religious and nonreligious outlooks. Precisely because it is nonreligious, it fosters a reductionistic approach to religious belief and practice, in which religious phenomena are viewed as properly explained as a function of regularities at some more basic, primary, "real" level. So, for instance, Durkheim believed that the object of worship was in fact society, and he offered a functional analysis of religion as aiding social cohesion. Nor were functionalist and reductionist approaches a passing phenomenon; today, for example, early modern Christianity is widely viewed as "a means of political control and social discipline."[46] Yet as we saw earlier, even a naturalist can recognize that descriptivism, the drive to reduce all phenomena to one privileged level of description, can easily distort or wholly lose the very phenomena we wish to understand. Surely the task of historical understanding requires first that we seek to understand what beliefs and practices meant to those who held them and engaged in them. That is, it requires that we capture the level of description at which the agents themselves lived, and recognize that reducing this to some other, purportedly more primary, level of description may well elide precisely the distinctions we desire to have explained. Of course it is possible, even likely, that the historian will encounter instances of insanity, self-deception, and insincerity, and will need to probe beneath the level of description at which an agent purportedly proceeds. It is also possible that the historian will find explanations that proceed at some other level satisfying despite the fact that they lose some of the distinctions relevant to participants. This is because the historian is always mediating between the world as experienced by the subjects of his study and the world as she herself experiences it; the task of translation requires the conceptual apparatus of both.

What is particularly seductive about Hume's philosophy of history is that it marries a general commitment to sympathetic understanding—that is just the sort of thick description of the perspectives of historical agents that is in fact needed—with a critique of the artificiality of theistic lives that appears to legitimate making religious belief and practice an exception to the task of sympathetic understanding. If religious belief is utterly incoherent and religious lives utterly self-defeating, sympathetic understanding is inherently impossible; so why attempt it at all? But as we have seen, Hume has not in fact shown that in theistic convictions or monkish virtues sympathetic understanding comes up against its limits. No a priori dismissal is legitimate; the historian's first task, in each particular instance, remains that of seeking sympathetic understanding.

NOTES

1. For various explorations of this theme, see the special issue "Religion and History," ed. David Gary Shaw, *History and Theory* (December 2006), especially the essays by Shaw, C. T. MacIntyre, Catherine Bell, and Mark Cladis, as well as *Seeing Things Their Way: Intellectual History and the Return of Religion*, ed. Alister Chapman, John Coffey, and Brad S. Gregory (Notre Dame: University of Notre Dame Press, 2009).

2. Most influentially, R. G. Collingwood insisted that Hume had deserted philosophy for history: see *The Idea of History* (Oxford: Clarendon Press, 1946), 73. Similar judgments from the period include those of John Laird, *Hume's Philosophy of Human Nature* (New York: Dutton, 1932),

266; John B. Stewart, *The Moral and Political Philosophy of David Hume* (New York: Columbia University Press, 1963), 289; and Haskell Fain, *Between Philosophy and History* (Princeton: Princeton University Press, 1970), 9.

3. David Fate Norton, "History and Philosophy in Hume's Thought," in *David Hume: Philosophical Historian*, ed. David Fate Norton and Richard Popkin (Indianapolis: Bobbs-Merrill, 1965), xxxiii.

4. Ibid., xxxix.

5. Ibid., xliv.

6. Ibid., xlviii.

7. Donald W. Livingston, *Hume's Philosophy of Common Life* (Chicago: University of Chicago Press, 1984), 3. This argument is further extended in Livingston's *Philosophical Melancholy and Delirium: Hume's Pathology of Philosophy* (Chicago: University of Chicago Press, 1998).

8. Alasdair MacIntyre, *Whose Justice? Which Rationality?* (Notre Dame: University of Notre Dame Press, 1988), 295.

9. Livingston counters that Collingwood's accusation "is simply false." "Hume's doctrine of moral causes is, in fact," he states, "the earliest statement of the modern doctrine of *verstehen* or what Collingwood calls the reenactment of past thoughts," *Hume's Philosophy of Common Life*, 235. Livingston's analysis is indebted in part to James Farr's "Hume, Hermeneutics, and History: A 'Sympathetic' Account," *History and Theory* 17 (1978): 285–310; it was Farr who first invoked the term *verstehen* in connection with Hume's thought. A similar analysis is developed by S. K. Wertz in "Hume, History, and Human Nature," *Journal of the History of Ideas* 36 (1975): 481–96; republished in *Between Hume's Philosophy and History: Historical Theory and Practice* (Lanham: University Press of America, 2000).

10. I have given a fuller account of sympathetic understanding, its compatibility with moral judgment, and its purported limits, in Jennifer A. Herdt, *Religion and Faction in Hume's Moral Philosophy* (Cambridge: Cambridge University Press, 1997), chaps. 4–5.

11. For a critique of descriptivism, see Lee C. McIntyre, "Reduction, Supervenience, and the Autonomy of Social Scientific Laws," *Theory and Decision* 48, no. 2 (2000): 101–22. McIntyre's essay also helpfully elucidates the context-dependent character of explanation and defends the possibility of autonomous social scientific laws even given a naturalist ontology.

12. These are what Livingston terms "moral causal explanations," *Hume's Philosophy of Common Life*, 191.

13. I have elsewhere placed this aspiration within the context of other contemporary thinkers who shared Hume's concern with cultivating resources for coping with moral diversity and make no attempt to replicate that discussion here. See *Religion and Faction in Hume's Moral Philosophy*, chaps. 1–2. See also Daniel Carey's *Locke, Shaftesbury, and Hutcheson: Contesting Diversity in the Enlightenment and Beyond* (Cambridge: Cambridge University Press, 2006), chaps. 4–5, which depicts these thinkers as likewise "focused on the problem of diversity and the question of whether any moral consistency could be located in mankind," 1.

14. In fact, though, Hume's account of theism is perhaps most persuasive as an account of certain very particular forms of religious life, notably the one in which he grew up, a strict form of Scottish Calvinism. Even here, it can be argued that Hume's account is simply blind to the theological nuances that render the stance internally coherent—although he might counter that most uneducated Scots would not themselves have grasped the nuances.

15. Ernest Nagel, *The Structure of Science* (New York: Harcourt, Brace, and World, 1961), 340.

16. See also his account of Cardinal Pole (*H* 3:430).

17. For a fuller discussion of the place of the *History of England* in Hume's account of the limits of sympathetic understanding, see *Religion and Faction in Hume's Moral Philosophy*, chap. 5.

18. Livingston, *Hume's Philosophy of Common Life*, 240. Livingston is also concerned with the topic of barbarism in *Philosophical Melancholy and Delirium*, but here his focus is on how civilizations can fall back into a kind of "barbarism of refinement," 217–19.

19. Livingston, *Hume's Philosophy of Common Life*, 245–46.

20. Popkin, "Skepticism and the Study of History," in *David Hume: Philosophical Historian*, ed. David Fate Norton and Richard Popkin (Indianapolis: Bobbs-Merrill, 1965), xxx–xxxi.

21. Livingston, *Hume's Philosophy of Common Life*, 193. According to Livingston, Hume's critique leaves room for a form of philosophical theism, essentially amounting to a regulative belief about nature as an ordered whole that serves to guide inquiry, *Philosophical Melancholy and Delirium*, 63–66. This is a suggestive interpretation, but one that requires a strong reading of Hume's texts; I do not engage with it here.

22. Livingston, *Hume's Philosophy of Common Life*, 234.

23. Ibid., 234.

24. Ibid., 234–35.

25. Ibid., 235.

26. Ibid., 300.

27. Ibid., 143.

28. Ibid., 301.

29. Ibid., 301.

30. Ibid., 301.

31. On early modern European society (including, e.g., Calvinist ideals of the advancement of the kingdom of God) as dominated not by an idea of progress but by the notion of a return to a golden age in the past, see J. H. Elliott, *Spain and Its World, 1500–1700* (New Haven: Yale University Press, 1989), 98–101.

32. See George Marsden's account of Jonathan Edwards's "millennial optimism," in contrast with opposing contemporary views, in *Jonathan Edwards: A Life* (New Haven: Yale University Press, 2003), 333–40.

33. Ernst Breisach, *Historiography: Ancient, Medieval, Modern* (Chicago: University of Chicago Press, 2006), 215.

34. Noel Jackson, "Historiography: Britain," in *Encyclopedia of the Romantic Era, 1760–1850*, vol. 1, ed. Christopher John Murray (London: Fitzroy Dearborn, 2004), 504.

35. This is apparent in Livingston's characterization of Hume's true philosophical theism: "this metaphysical belief about the world *as a whole,* that it is ordered by 'some consistent plan' and reveals 'one single purpose or intention, however inexplicable and incomprehensible,' in turn guides scientific activity in its research *within* the world," *Philosophical Melancholy*, 66.

36. Livingston, *Hume's Philosophy of Common Life*, 285.

37. Ibid., 286, 291.

38. Ibid., 288.

39. Ibid., 234.

40. The reasons for this have been given classic formulation by Donald Davidson in "On the Very Idea of a Conceptual Scheme," *Proceedings of the American Philosophical Association* 47 (1973–74): 5–20.

41. Annette Baier argues that the test of reflexive self-survey is all Hume needs in order to justify the virtues he champions over against others; *A Progress of Sentiments* (Cambridge: Harvard University Press, 1991), 215–17. Lottenbach, though, points out that most rivals to Hume's position are not actually self-defeating, and are in fact capable of reflexive self-approval. He sees little to distinguish reflexive self-approval from "complacent self-congratulation," "Monkish Virtues, Artificial Lives," *Canadian Journal of Philosophy* 26, no. 3 (1996): 387. It is important to recognize both the power and the limits of this sort of internal criticism; it is inherently one part logic and one part rhetoric.

42. This is not to say, of course, that Enlightenment historiography won the day. Indeed, while Hume's *History of England* undeniably established his reputation as an author, it was not in its own day received as impartial. In the next generation, Romantic historiographers critiqued

Hume for a general failure of empathy with his subjects, not simply those dominated by religious convictions; Hume's approach was seen as too abstract, too detached. The Romantic ideal was itself to be displaced by nineteenth-century philosophical historians who likewise dismissed Hume, now for lacking insight into the structural forces driving historical change. See Mark Salber Phillips and Dale R. Smith, "Canonization and Critique: Hume's Reputation as a Historian," in *The Reception of David Hume in Europe*, ed. Peter Jones (London: Thoemmes Continuum, 2005), 312–13.

43. Jackson, "Historiography: Britain," 504; Catherine Bell, "Paradigms Behind (and Before) the Modern Concept of Religion," *History and Theory* 45 (2006): 33; Alister Chapman, "Intellectual History and Religion in Modern Britain," in *Seeing Things Their Way*, 232.

44. Brad S. Gregory, "The Other Confessional History: On Secular Bias in the Study of Religion," *History and Theory* 45 (December 2006): 138; emphasis in original.

45. Ibid., 138.

46. Ibid., 144.

"THE SPIRIT OF LIBERTY": HISTORICAL CAUSATION AND POLITICAL RHETORIC IN THE AGE OF HUME

Philip Hicks

In his *History of England* (1754–62), David Hume routinely used such phrases as "the spirit of independency" and "the spirit of opposition" (*H* 5:147, 6:387), commonplace language for eighteenth-century Britain. The notion that a person or collectivity might possess a "spirit" or distinguishing characteristic connected to a larger climate of opinion immediately calls to mind Montesquieu's *The Spirit of the Laws* (1748).[1] Yet such language actually predated Montesquieu and was comparatively new to British historical writing when Hume applied it to his account of the British civil wars. Hume adopted the phrase "the spirit of liberty" as a key explanatory device in his *History*, convenient shorthand for a combination of political and religious ideals that motivated Britons to oppose what they perceived to be excessive monarchical power. Hume plucked this term from the world of partisan politics and redefined it as part of a larger project promoting political moderation. Yet we shall see that choosing to deploy such a multivalent rhetoric had ironic consequences for his narrative. One of Hume's goals was to write an utterly secular account of the English past, but using "the spirit of liberty" according to the grammatical rules set forth by its progenitor, Henry St. John, Viscount Bolingbroke, actually made it resemble providence to a startling degree.[2] In a further irony, while Hume wanted to defuse this highly charged slogan, his own extensive use of the term only made it more popular, especially as a way of understanding political upheaval, past and present. On both sides of the Atlantic, Hume's *History* helped to shape the vocabulary used to explain the seventeenth-century British and eighteenth-century American and French revolutions.[3]

Given Hume's penchant for "the spirit of liberty," it is perhaps surprising to locate its intellectual origins in a Machiavellian tradition that ran counter to Hume's conviction that institutions and laws are more powerful determinants of a nation's political well-being than the manners and morals of its leaders.[4] During the Renaissance, Niccolò Machiavelli's study of the ancient republics convinced him that liberty in a republic could best be preserved not so much by adjusting the institutional machinery of government as by ensuring that the value of political liberty was nurtured in the people as a whole. Such a perspective emphasized structural and impersonal factors such as the spirit of the times and public opinion and imagined the polity as possessing its own characteristics and desires.[5] In Britain, Machiavelli's analysis influenced "Country" political groups that developed in the 1690s to defend parliamentary independence against encroaching executive power. These "True" or "Old" Whigs relied heavily on the political writings of such "Commonwealthmen" as James Harrington, Edmund Ludlow, Andrew Marvell, John Milton, Marchamont Nedham, Henry Neville, Algernon Sidney, and John Toland. In many cases, these thinkers were more concerned that the ethos of liberty be preserved than whether the actual form of government was a republic or a monarchy. It was in this ideological context that the expression "the spirit of liberty" was coined. Ludlow's *Memoirs* of the civil wars, written in the 1660s and redacted by Toland, twice referred to this "spirit" as an opponent of Oliver Cromwell's despotic actions.[6]

By the time the *Memoirs* were published in 1698, the phrase had begun to enter the lexicon of the British political class. In that year, a precocious nineteen-year-old, whose future as a Tory secretary at war and later a Jacobite secretary of state still lay ahead of him, wrote a letter to his mentor Sir William Trumbull. Henry St. John stated that whereas patriotism and "zeal for liberty" were once "imprinted on our hearts," the opposite values now held sway in Britain. St. John traced those traditional political virtues to the Romans. Even after ancient Britain threw off the Romans' legal system, he noted, "their divine spirit (if I might use the expression) shed its influence on us." After making this distinction between laws and their "spirit," and citing republican tags from Tacitus, Cicero, and Horace, St. John went on to observe that liberty-loving people had historically been enslaved not by force of arms but by the corruption of manners. He gave the Greek example of Cyrus, who failed to pacify the Lidians militarily because "the spirit of Liberty crost his designs, and stopt the course of his victories."[7] The spirit of liberty, as St. John viewed it, was thus more powerful than armies or laws; it was a god-like, "divine" influence; it was republican. These were the germs of a concept St. John would fully develop thirty years later and eventually bequeath to Hume.

During those years "the spirit of liberty" was occasionally mentioned in British political writings, essays, and histories.[8] Yet, as in the case of St. John's letter, it rarely appeared more than once in any given work; it was not deployed systematically in any purposeful way until St. John, now Lord Bolingbroke, mounted a decade-long political campaign, beginning in 1725, against the Whig regime of Sir Robert Walpole. To unite his coalition of fellow Tories and disaffected Whigs, Bolingbroke had to justify the very idea of political opposition and refute the charge that he was raising a treasonous "faction" of the sort that caused the civil wars. This was the goal of the *Remarks on the History of England*, twenty-four essays he published under the pseudonym Humphrey Oldcastle between September 1730 and May 1731 in his paper *The Craftsman*. Here Bolingbroke tried turning the tables on his opponents by pinning the label of "faction" on them. Drawing from Renaissance humanism's preoccupation with internal faction as the enemy of liberty and its technique of dividing history into good and evil periods based on republican criteria,[9] Bolingbroke went through English history showing how "the spirit of liberty" had always supported the national interest in the face of the self-interested "spirit of faction" that Walpole's Court Whigs now fomented.[10] England had the trappings of liberty, Bolingbroke argued, but Walpole's placemen, pensions, and bribes corrupted its political institutions, which were free in name only. The spirit of liberty alone could give life to the institutions of liberty, the English laws and system of government. Resuscitating the "Country" platform, Bolingbroke cited Machiavelli's *Discourses on Livy* as the source of this distinction between external constitutional forms and the true spirit of a government. To illustrate his point, he explained: "As losing the spirit of liberty lost the liberties of Rome, even while the laws and constitutions, made for the preservation of them, remained entire; so we see that our ancestors, by keeping this spirit alive and warm, regained all the advantages of a free government, tho a foreign invasion [by William the Conqueror] had destroyed them, in great measure, and had imposed a very tyrannical yoke on the nation."[11]

In this passage, "the spirit of liberty" described the preconditions for genuine liberty. Yet elsewhere in the *Remarks*, more interestingly, Bolingbroke endowed it with an agency all its own. He made it the subject of his sentences and paired it with active verbs. The spirit of liberty now "enacted" Roman laws; "prevailed" to secure Magna Carta; "exerted itself" in favor of Edward III; "diffused itself" through nobles, clergy, and commoners; "preserved" the constitution during the Wars of the Roses; "rose" to resist James I; and "baffled" his plans to wage war on the people.[12] In the process of anthropomorphizing this concept, Bolingbroke underscored its republican character. His adjectives describing the spirit of liberty as "generous" and "disinterested" indicated its public spiritedness; "vigorous" and "active" its aggressive political virtue (*virtù*); "watchful," "jealous," and "easily alarmed" its eternal vigilance.[13] More explicitly than its Machiavellian and Commonwealth sources, Bolingbroke's rhetoric depicted liberty not simply as the product of human creativity but as possessing its own creative powers. This idea of liberty received further elaboration from another member of Bolingbroke's circle, James Thomson. Inspired by the *Remarks* as well as classical mythology, Thomson traced the spirit of liberty to its ultimate source in the goddess of liberty. Thomson's poem *Liberty* (1735–36) credited this deity with "infusing" nations with "her spirit." This divine aid, "the Spirit of Liberty," was what enabled humans to love their country. Thomson thus brought to the surface what had always been a latent meaning of "spirit," a deity's power to create, animate, or inspire, a role not unlike that played by the Holy Spirit in Christian theology. Between them, Thomson and Bolingbroke had elevated liberty to a position above the human mortals on whom it might bestow or withdraw its favor.[14]

By incanting it hundreds of times as a centerpiece of his propaganda war, Bolingbroke gave "the spirit of liberty" currency in Anglophone political culture. More than ever before, it resonated in parliamentary speeches, political journalism, and private correspondence.[15] It now also began to appear in the writings of David Hume. Hume first cut his teeth as a political thinker observing the titanic struggle between Bolingbroke and Walpole. His earliest political essays criticized Bolingbroke's violent partisanship and basic premise that under Walpole, crown patronage had endangered the constitution. Nonetheless, Hume co-opted Bolingbroke's virulent language to help him conceptualize the English past. In his essay "Of the Parties of Great Britain" (1741), to compress into a few sentences the essential dynamic of the British civil wars, Hume imagined two entities that each "arose" and then collided: "an ambitious, or rather a misguided, prince" (King Charles I) and "the spirit of liberty" (*E* 68). Thirteen years later, Hume would adopt the same terminology to carry out his full-scale treatment of the same subject in *The History of England*. As early as 1741, then, writing in the waning days of Walpole's regime, Hume had already picked up this phrase and used it in the manner of Bolingbroke.[16] This usage, coming seven years before the publication of Montesquieu's *Spirit of the Laws* (1748), strongly suggests that Hume first encountered the concept in Opposition, not French, discourse. In other words, there was an English genealogy for this particular term from which Hume was drawing that ran back at least as far as Ludlow or Bolingbroke in 1698 and more immediately to the latter's essays in 1730–31. Montesquieu's magnum opus used a term translated as "spirit of liberty" (*un esprit de liberté*) in the two Bolingbrokean senses of an active force in history and a republican political culture. An earlier work, Montesquieu's *Considerations on the Causes of the Romans' Greatness and Decline* (1734), also employed this term.[17] These writings, together with Voltaire's *Essay on Manners* (1754–56), accustomed Europeans to speaking in terms of the *esprit* of nations and helped to invent the genre of philosophical history. Yet, interestingly, the historical thinking that informed Hume's *Essays* and *History* was largely independent of these models.[18]

Hume's source for "the spirit of liberty" was a polemical historical commentary in letter form, Bolingbroke's *Remarks*, not the French *philosophes* or the formal histories of England that preceded Hume's. Those histories by Thomas Carte, William Guthrie, James Ralph, Laurence Echard, Paul Rapin de Thoyras, White Kennett, and the first Earl of Clarendon portrayed events chiefly as the deeds of individual "great" men. Sometimes they discerned larger patterns of causation and highlighted the actions of "the people" or of divine providence. More occasionally, they used the formula "the spirit of" some idea, value, or feeling with which historical actors were imbued—faction, independence, jealousy, and so on.[19] In only a handful of instances, however, did they mention "the spirit of liberty."[20] In sum, this "spiritual" form of historical causation was not a common element in English historical writing before Hume made it so.

Hume's main purpose in adopting the concept of "the spirit of liberty"[21] was to explain the political catastrophe of the 1640s. The *History* expanded on the thesis of his 1741 essay to depict the British civil wars as a showdown between the spirit of liberty and early Stuart monarchy. By Hume's reckoning, Charles I was tragically overwhelmed and ill-equipped to deal with this formidable opponent:

> Unhappily, his fate threw him into a period, when the precedents of many former reigns favoured strongly of arbitrary power, and the genius of the people ran violently towards liberty. And if his political prudence was not sufficient to extricate him from so perilous a situation, he may be excused. . . . [T]he high idea of his own authority, which he had imbibed, made him incapable of giving way to the spirit of liberty, which *began* to prevail among his subjects. (*H* 5:543, 221)

Charles had inherited this political predicament from his father, James, who encountered the nascent spirit of liberty soon after his accession. James's first parliament "showed more spirit of liberty than appeared among his bishops and theologians" at the Hampton Court Conference, Hume observed (*H* 5:13). A few pages later, Hume noted that "this watchful spirit of liberty... appeared in the commons" to challenge royal judicial authority in the Goodwin electoral case (*H* 5:17). To account for this newfound spirit, Hume embarked upon one of the *History*'s famous digressions: "About this period, the minds of men, throughout Europe, especially in England, seem to have undergone a general, but insensible revolution," Hume wrote. The new learning, improved arts, and increased travel resulted in a "universal fermentation" in which "the ideas of men enlarged themselves on all sides" and "the love of freedom... acquired new force" (*H* 5:18). "This rising spirit" (*H* 5:19) could just be glimpsed in the previous reign, when one might "observe the faint dawn of the spirit of liberty among the English, the jealousy with which that spirit was repressed by the sovereign, the imperious conduct which was maintained in opposition to it, and the ease with which it was subdued by this arbitrary princess" (*H* 4:138). Analyzing Elizabethan political life, Hume again pared history down to its bare essentials, pitting the personal skills of a single monarch against the impersonal forces of the spirit of liberty. By contrast with Elizabeth's masterful response to the challenges presented by this new political reality, James "possessed neither sufficient capacity to perceive the alteration, nor sufficient art and vigour to check it in its early advances" (*H* 5:19). Although the spirit of liberty drew sustenance from deep-rooted intellectual, economic, and social changes in English society, its triumph over James and Charles was, therefore, by no means inevitable, provided these rulers possessed the political acumen and resolution to repress or accommodate it.

At James's accession, that spirit animated comparatively few Englishmen, Hume pointed out: "the principles of liberty... were, as yet, pretty much unknown to the generality of the people." Only in the work of "men of genius and of enlarged minds" such as Francis Bacon and Edwin Sandys did a "spirit of liberty" appear (*H* 5:550). By 1610, however, this growing force had spread, and Hume used it to explain the decisive shift in attitude articulated in the Commons' remonstrance against James's new impositions: "A spirit of liberty had now taken possession of the house: The leading members... less aspired at maintaining the ancient constitution, than at establishing a new one, and a freer, and a better" (*H* 5:42). In 1614, the new "house of commons showed rather a stronger spirit of liberty than the foregoing" (*H* 5:58). By 1626, Hume announced, "the spirit of liberty was universally diffused," and it accounted for the unprecedented challenge to the crown posed by the Five Knights' case (*H* 5:179). In the course of a generation, then, this spirit had spread from a few men to the entire House of Commons, thence to England at large, and finally to Scotland (*H* 5:257). It approached a saturation point in 1640, when Charles's attempts to impose forced loans were "repelled by the spirit of liberty, which was now become unconquerable" (*H* 5:278). So complete was this triumph that in 1642, even the king's own party "breathed the spirit of liberty," as its support was conditioned upon his submission to "a legal and limited government" (*H* 5:394). At this point in the *History*, the spirit of liberty virtually disappears.[22] It had served its two primary functions: registering the comparative extent of opposition to the crown at any given moment and illustrating how a change in intellectual climate precipitated the demise of Stuart monarchy. Because Hume saw the contest for liberty primarily in terms of political processes, not armed struggle, the spirit of liberty appeared in the run-up to the civil wars, but not the battles themselves.

At this stage in our analysis, we ought to consider the degree to which Hume was modifying this discourse as he had received it from Lord Bolingbroke. Linguistically, Hume and Bolingbroke used the term both in a passive form, as a descriptor, and in an active form as an agent. Both writers used the republican adjective "watchful" with it and spoke as if it were capable of human feelings, as when Hume wrote that after the Commons protested against arbitrary imprisonments and forced loans in 1628, "the spirit of liberty . . . obtained some contentment by this exertion" (*H* 5:191). Like Thomson, Hume even once made liberty itself, not its spirit, a historical character: James's latest scheme to raise funds foundered because "the jealousy of liberty was now rouzed" (*H* 5:84). For all these semantic similarities, however, Hume sharply repudiated Bolingbroke's and Thomson's doctrinaire, patriotic Whig paean to liberty. While Hume praised liberty as eloquently as they did, he also warned about its excesses and the need to balance it with authority.[23] Indeed, for Hume the civil wars and interregnum illustrated the dangerous consequences of the abuse of liberty. During those periods, he mentioned "the spirit of liberty" just once—to highlight the hypocrisy of Commonwealth officials "who possessed little of the true spirit of liberty, [but] knew how to maintain the appearance of it" (*H* 6:44). Whereas Bolingbroke had celebrated the spirit of liberty uncritically and traced it to the immemorial constitution of the ancient Britons and Saxons, Hume reined in the term, confining it to the early seventeenth century. Hume acknowledged that the idea of liberty was exemplified in the republics of classical antiquity, but he argued that true liberty, defined as the rule of law or justice, was a modern phenomenon dependent on an advanced level of civilization that began to emerge only in the fifteenth and sixteenth centuries. Before that epoch, England was in many ways a barbarous nation inhospitable to a regular plan of liberty, Hume believed.[24] In a further contrast with Bolingbroke, Hume challenged the commonplace view that the formation of a Protestant state had represented a high-water mark in the history of

British liberty. It was Bolingbroke's contention that by the time James came to the throne, "The spirit of liberty had blended our civil and religious rights together, and was become equally jealous of both."[25] Hume emphasized instead that the cause of liberty had been seriously compromised by its entanglement with religious fanaticism. The uneasy relationship between the spirit of liberty and the spirit of enthusiasm would in fact prove to be as important to Hume's narrative as the antagonism between liberty and faction was to Bolingbroke's.

To understand this aspect of the *History*, it is necessary to turn once again back to the *Essays*. In "Of Superstition and Enthusiasm" (1741), Hume had defined religious enthusiasm as the malady of presumptuous individuals whose overheated imaginations "inspire the deluded fanatic with the opinion of divine illuminations" (*E* 73–74, 77). He further observed that "enthusiasm, being the infirmity of bold and ambitious tempers, is naturally accompanied with a spirit of liberty" (*E* 78). In the *History of England*, Hume also stressed the close links between enthusiasm and liberty, describing how the spirit of enthusiasm "strongly disposed [the Puritans'] minds to adopt republican tenets; and inclined them to arrogate, in their actions and conduct, the same liberty, which they assumed, in their rapturous flights and ecstasies" (*H* 5:559). In the course of Hume's historical narration, the spirit of enthusiasm and the spirit of liberty more or less worked in tandem, mutually reinforcing one another's influence. Both first developed during Elizabeth's reign (*H* 4:123–24, 138), reached their apogee early in Charles I's (*H* 5:179, 221), and disappeared during Charles II's (*H* 6:274, 377). Hume once even went so far as to suggest that these two spirits were in fact one, referring to "that spirit, partly fanatical, partly republican, which predominated in England" (*H* 6:83).

If, by this account, the spirit of liberty was intimately bound up with the spirit of enthusiasm, it was an odd coupling, as the former had substantially less power than the latter but enjoyed all the prestige.[26] Explaining this unequal relationship, Hume wrote: "the spirit of civil liberty gradually revived from its lethargy, and by means of its religious associate, from which it reaped more advantage than honour, it secretly enlarged its dominion over the greater part of the kingdom" (*H* 5:559). Hume pressed this point further still: "the precious spark of liberty had been kindled, and was preserved, by the puritans alone; and it was to this sect, whose principles appear so frivolous and habits so ridiculous, that the English owe the whole freedom of their constitution" (*H* 4:145–46). In other words, "that great revolution of manners" (*H* 5:80) in the sixteenth and seventeenth centuries might have nurtured the spirit of liberty, but the republican idea of liberty was not sufficient to inspire successful opposition to the crown. On the contrary, that idea, paradigmatically derived from ancient history, was negatively associated with violent disorder. Only the Puritans, in their reckless zeal, dared to pick it up and wield it as a weapon of religious and political reform (*H* 4:123–24; 5:127, 563). This idea that the spirit of liberty was dependent on the spirit of enthusiasm, that it "naturally accompanied" (*E* 78) its "religious associate" (*H* 5:559), that it might even be identical to it, was, however, not apparent in the narrative portions of volume 5 where the spirit of liberty appeared most often and dramatically. Only in another volume of the *History*, in an endnote, and in an essay did these qualifications appear. Thus, the overall effect of using this bare phrase in the way Hume did was to minimize or ignore liberty's religious connotations and play up its positive, civic qualities.

Hume had good reason to make enthusiasm the secret engine driving the spirit of liberty, for this move diverted attention away from a subject he was at a loss to explain. "Of Superstition and Enthusiasm," of course, had given a psychological and philosophical account of religious enthusiasm, but inserting religious enthusiasm into the ebb and flow of historical events presented a greater challenge to Hume. "The religious spirit," Hume confided, "when it mingles with faction, contains in it something supernatural and unaccountable; . . . in its operations upon society, effects correspond less to their known causes than is found in any other circumstance of government" (*H* 5:67). Religious extremism thus tore asunder the skein of rational explanation by which Hume as a philosophical historian might show cause and effect according to natural, secular schema. To Hume's evident frustration, religious fanatics were not motivated by self-interest, rational calculation, or the common good. "The spirit of enthusiasm," he wrote, "disappointed all the views of human prudence, and disturbed the operation of every motive, which usually influences society. . . . The fanatical spirit, let loose, confounded all regard to ease, safety, interest; and dissolved every moral and civil obligation" (*H* 5:221, 380).

To the extent that such a fundamental aspect of "the spirit of liberty," namely, the religious enthusiasm that gave it life, defied logical explanation, it remained inscrutable. Hume's persistence in threading "the spirit of liberty" into key chapters of his story thus obscured the unknowable quality of this concept, giving the illusion of greater coherence and rationality than the *History* actually possessed. This practice, in turn, contributed to the surprisingly providential character of Hume's text. Like providence, Hume's spirit of liberty controlled human behavior in events so extraordinary that they could not be accounted for in human terms alone, but only by the interposition of this mysterious force. Like providence, it could "surmount every human opposition."[27]

Like providence, furthermore, it worked through unlikely instruments—the Puritans—all for the good of bringing forth "the whole freedom" of the English constitution.[28] As much as Hume reviled the Puritans, therefore, he adopted a distinctive element of their historiography. Hume refused to see the hand of God in unexpected happenings, but this notorious stance was, in the event, undermined by his own rhetoric. As he used it, "the spirit of liberty" echoed the traditional providential structure of Christian historical writing.

Whether or not these ironies were lost on Hume—a master ironist who may have intended his readers to savor them—he had numerous reasons for adopting "the spirit of liberty." Doing so allowed Hume to credit an idea with historical change, reinforcing his more general contention that changes in opinion are responsible for great historical movements.[29] At the same time, this discourse aided Hume in achieving a technical breakthrough that was a prerequisite for composing a philosophical history, a genre requiring that Hume somehow blend political narrative with structural, impersonal, and sociological explanation. Hume accomplished this feat by embedding the intellectual abstraction, "spirit of liberty," into his record of events, just as elsewhere he achieved similar integration through his judicious placement of philosophical analysis in appendices, endnotes, and digressions.[30] Finally, "the spirit of liberty" served as thematic spotlighting; it was an economical term that streamlined his fast-moving narrative. Hume's employment of such a poetic figure of speech marked a decisive reaction against the chronicle-like, document-laden histories of England that preceded his, and contributed a stylish liveliness to his narrative, one of its distinguishing features and claims to fame and a quality that contributed in no small way to its long shelf life.[31]

In order to round out this story of "the spirit of liberty" and Hume's engagement with it, our investigation needs to be extended to include the political and historical discourse of the 1760s and 1770s. Such an analysis reveals that despite his intervention in this discourse Hume never exactly swayed "Country" ideologues. While "the spirit of liberty" gained in popularity as a catchphrase in the second half of the eighteenth century, the term never in fact broke completely free from its moorings in republican tradition. Instead, it remained a favorite expression of eighteenth-century Commonwealthmen such as James Burgh, Thomas Pownall, Catharine Macaulay, and John Brown.[32] In 1757, the year Hume's second volume on the Stuarts appeared, Brown wrote a wildly popular jeremiad that threw the term back in Hume's face. Brown's *An Estimate of the Manners and Principles of the Times* called for a revival of the spirit of liberty. "This great Spirit hath produced more full and complete Effects" in Britain, he boasted, than anywhere in the world: "it shoots up here as from its natural Climate, Stock, and Soil." Yet despite these advantages, Brown warned, "The Spirit of Liberty is now struggling with the Manners and Principles, as formerly it struggled with the Tyrants of the Time." Brown's nationalistic use of this "spirit" and his republican critique of commercial society relied on Bolingbroke and Montesquieu, not Hume, whom he blamed for the luxury and irreligion that now imperiled the spirit of liberty.[33] For his part, Hume believed that the spirit of liberty was alive and well, in fact a selling point for the Hanoverian regime. In his essay "Of the Coalition of Parties" (1758), which addressed a different brand of malcontents, not Brown, Hume asked Jacobite sympathizers to consider how "the spirit of civil liberty, though at first connected with religious fanaticism, could purge itself from that pollution, and appear under a more genuine and engaging aspect" (*E* 501). Liberty and enthusiasm were not inextricably tied together, after all, Hume indicated. In his account, the spirit of enthusiasm had died with Oliver Cromwell a century ago, and ever since, the spirit of liberty had been free to pursue its noble work in its purest form.[34] By the middle of the eighteenth century, it was now "a friend to toleration, and an encourager of all the enlarged and generous sentiments that do honour to human nature." At last, a pleasing balance had been struck between liberty and authority: while the "high claims" of royal prerogative had been extinguished, Britons still retained "a due respect to monarchy, to nobility, and to all ancient institutions" (*E* 501).

If Hume could not get "Country" diehards like Brown to rethink the nature of modern liberty, he did succeed in altering the rhetoric of modern historiography. Among British historians writing in his wake, "the spirit of liberty" quickly became common parlance. Hume's friend, William Robertson, applied the term in *The History of the Reign of the Emperor Charles V* (1769) to explain the decay of continental feudalism and the challenges to royal and clerical authority in the sixteenth century. Histories of England also followed Hume's lead, regardless of political orientation. Oliver Goldsmith, Tory author of *An History of England* (1764) used the term, as did the radical Whig Catharine Macaulay. Macaulay's *History of England* (1763–83), a multivolume account of the seventeenth century, presented Hume with his primary eighteenth-century competition intellectually and commercially. Macaulay defended the regicide, paid homage to the republican regime of the early 1650s, and denounced the Revolution Settlement for failing to curb monarchical power. Unlike Hume, she saw liberty as a direct legacy from antiquity, threatened not by religious fanaticism but by luxury and effeminacy.[35] For all their differences, however, Macaulay borrowed "the spirit of liberty" from, or at least used it in much the same way as, Hume. Like Hume, she depicted it as the existing nemesis with which Charles I had to contend, and she focused this rhetorical ammunition on the origins of the civil wars. At his accession, the king "entertained the project of entirely subduing that spirit of liberty which had already formed a strong party in the nation." Again following Hume, Macaulay showed it animating orators in the House of Commons and then spreading more widely: "that noble spirit of Liberty . . . flamed in the lower house, and from thence diffused itself through the whole nation." Subsequently, it "repelled" Charles's arbitrary acts and "raised a successful opposition to his pretensions."[36] Since together Macaulay and Hume nearly monopolized the market for their subject, "the spirit of liberty" became imprinted on the historical consciousness of Britons and others who read British history in the 1760s and 1770s. Whether readers chose to get their history from a work Hume intended to be moderate but was widely seen as Tory, or from Macaulay's avowedly partisan "Old" Whig analysis, or from both, they came away with the same understanding that the spirit of liberty had been vital to the revolutionary politics of the seventeenth century.

During the political agitations of the 1760s, radicals like Macaulay were especially attracted to this language, and the goddess of liberty became a staple in the iconography of Opposition politics. Reprising verses from Thomson's poem, Macaulay put her *History*'s epigram in the form of a prayer to the goddess of liberty, then posed as that deity in the frontispiece.[37] Young women played Liberty in political parades, and John Wilkes was likened to the god of liberty.[38] Opposition political campaigns imagined that the same goddess or "spirit" that had once inspired the Greeks and Romans was now reborn. Nowhere was this perception more widespread than in the American colonies. Here, in the decade leading up to the American Revolution, many critics of the British government believed not only that they faced a conspiracy to enslave them or that their own actions were guided by divine providence, but also that they were empowered by the spirit of liberty.[39] As one pamphlet put it, the colonists had originally immigrated to America "animated with the spirit of liberty." At issue was whether enough of that spirit remained in Britain to prevent the unjust treatment of America or whether America had become the last bastion of liberty.[40] In 1765, one leading patriot, John Adams, wrote an essay holding out hope that "the spirit of liberty"—"the same great spirit (may heaven preserve it till the earth shall be no more)" that had destroyed Julius Caesar, secured Magna Carta, "severed the head of Charles the first from his body," and accomplished the Revolution of 1688—still survived in England. Nine years later, colonists were still debating the issue. Mercy Otis Warren, an American poet and playwright, anxiously asked Catharine Macaulay whether "the Genius of Liberty" had deserted Britain or "only concealed her lovely form untill some more happy period?" Macaulay, an ardent supporter of the American cause, affirmed that "the Goddess of Liberty" did endure. However, less sanguine observers argued that it had now become America's responsibility, in the words of the *Connecticut Courant* newspaper, to "rouse the dormant spirit of liberty in England."[41]

So far as Adams was concerned, the spirit of liberty was the surest constitutional safeguard Britain and its colonies possessed. Writing in the *Boston Gazette*, Adams reminded readers that the ancient constitution, "co operating with the invincible spirit of liberty, inspired by it into the people, has never yet failed to work the ruin of the authors of all settled attempts to destroy it." Spirited resistance to the Stamp Act appeared to bear out Adams's claim. In his diary, Adams marveled at the unprecedented unity achieved by the colonists in this endeavor, concluding, "So triumphant is the Spirit of Liberty, every where." In Massachusetts, he later observed, "the Spirit of Liberty circulates thro every minute Artery of the Province."[42] Thus, just as Hume used the device in his *History*, so American colonists used it to mark and explain a surge of powerful, unexpected opposition to the crown. They did so in more extravagant terms, however. Josiah Quincy Jr., bequeathing a collection of patriotic books, wrote of his son, almost as a blessing, "May the spirit of liberty rest upon him!" John Adams's wife, Abigail, universalized this spirit and made explicit its feminist and populist attributes. She reported to a correspondent in the wake of Lexington and Concord: "The Spirit that prevails among Men of all degrees, all ages and sex'es is the Spirit of Liberty." This shibboleth was now so well known that government apologists in Britain recognized its currency, even though they disputed its appositeness. Alarmed by reports of American fanaticism and barbarism, they blamed the revolution on "what they call the Spirit of Liberty, but what is in Fact the spirit of Licentiousness."[43] Although this term figured conspicuously in contemporary explanations of the origin and progress of the American Revolution, it is clear that competing conceptions of "the spirit of liberty" were in play at this time. Some observers still associated it with license and civil disorder, just as most sixteenth-century Britons—excepting some Puritans—conceived it, in Hume's account. Others, drawing from Commonwealth tradition, saw it as a transhistorical tool of political liberation, and John Adams underscored a violent strand in the republican legacy when he depicted it as the assassin of tyrants.

American colonists had learned about "the spirit of liberty" from reading Bolingbroke, Macaulay, Thomson, Brown, and Hume, whose works were all widely read in America. Although John Adams, like many Americans, was more exuberant and freewheeling in his use of the term than Hume had been, we know that Hume was in fact one of his sources. Adams wrote an essay that paraphrased volume 5 of the *History* at length. Describing the Goodwin episode, Adams copied out verbatim Hume's words "this watchful spirit of liberty" (*H* 5:17) and used similar phrasing in a nearby passage.[44] Compared with the other sources for this language, Hume was the odd man out, the only one not an outspoken publicist for Commonwealth values. Yet his outsider status had an advantage over the others, insofar as his work appealed to a broader political spectrum than theirs, encompassing moderates, Tories, and American loyalists alike. A second, related advantage the *History* had as a conduit for "the spirit of liberty" was its sheer popularity. To take just one measure of its appeal, in the period 1773–82 it was borrowed more frequently than any other work in the Harvard College Library. Simultaneously, it at last eclipsed Macaulay's *History* back in Britain. Exposing generations of readers to "the spirit of liberty,"[45] it dominated the market for histories of England well into the nineteenth century.

What, in an American context, was emerging as a watchword for revolution began its career in the late seventeenth century as a phrase scattered through the writings of quasi-republican figures inspired by the Machiavellian distinction between the values of the citizenry and the formal constitutional structures of the polity. It sprang to life in the brilliant polemical campaign against Robert Walpole, when Lord Bolingbroke reified liberty and James Thomson deified it, endowing it with a power greater than that of its human protagonists. David Hume gravitated to the term as a way to depict historical causation in capsule form and to construct a philosophical history of England. He defined it more narrowly than had the Commonwealth tradition from which it germinated, confining it chiefly to what was for him the perplexing marriage of republican ideals and religious fanaticism that brought about the British civil wars. While Hume emphasized its modernity and complexity, many of his contemporaries were so smitten with the idea of liberty that they could not resist viewing it as a timeless, unalloyed ideal. In fact, as we have seen, "the spirit of liberty" conjured up such an array of meanings—literal and figurative, secular and providential, Bolingbrokean and Thomsonian—that these could not be readily harmonized. Embracing such a protean and partisan expression was perhaps a rash move on Hume's part, considering he had such a politically moderate and highly nuanced understanding of liberty. Even Hume, it turns out, succumbed to this magical piece of rhetoric.

NOTES

1. See J. G. A. Pocock, *Politics, Language, and Time: Essays on Political Thought and History* (New York: Atheneum, 1971), 225.

2. For Hume's goals as historian, see Nicholas Phillipson, *Hume* (London: Weidenfeld and Nicolson, 1989), chaps 2–4.

3. The French Revolution is beyond the scope of this essay, but this rhetoric survived into this later period as well. See, for example, Edmund Burke, *Reflections on the Revolution in France* (1790), ed., intro. J. G. A. Pocock (Indianapolis: Hackett, 1987), 8, 25, 119; Mercy Otis Warren to

Catharine Macaulay, July 1789, in *Mercy Otis Warren: Selected Letters*, ed. Jeffrey H. Richards and Sharon M. Harris, 222 (Athens: University of Georgia Press, 2009).

4. See *E* 16, 24–25, 54–55; Duncan Forbes, *Hume's Philosophical Politics* (Cambridge: Cambridge University Press, 1975), chap. 7, esp. 229; Quentin Skinner, *The Foundations of Modern Political Thought*, 2 vols. (Cambridge: Cambridge University Press, 1978), vol. 1, *The Renaissance*, 44–45.

5. Peter Burke, *The Renaissance Sense of the Past* (London: Arnold, 1969), 77. Skinner, *Foundations of Modern Political Thought*, 1:175–76. For conversations regarding the sources and dating of this term in English political discourse, I am grateful to Peter Burke, Mark Goldie, J. G. A. Pocock, and Blair Worden.

6. Edmund Ludlow, *Memoirs of Edmund Ludlow...* [1698–99], 2nd ed., 3 vols. (London, 1720–22), 2:598; 3:20. Blair Worden, ed., intro., *Edmund Ludlow: A Voyce from the Watch Tower* (London: Royal Historical Society, 1978), 49, and "Part I," in *Republicanism, Liberty, and Commercial Society, 1649–1776*, ed. David Wootton, 57, 70–71, 100–101 (Stanford: Stanford University Press, 1994). Nigel Smith, "Popular Republicanism in the 1650s: John Streater's 'Heroick Mechanicks,'" in *Milton and Republicanism*, ed. David Armitage, Armand Himy, and Quentin Skinner (Cambridge: Cambridge University Press, 1995), 148–50. Mark Goldie, "The English System of Liberty," in *The Cambridge History of Eighteenth-Century Political Thought*, ed. Mark Goldie and Robert Wokler (Cambridge: Cambridge University Press, 2006), 64–68. Also see James Harrington, *The Political Works of James Harrington*, ed., intro., J. G. A. Pocock (Cambridge: Cambridge University Press, 1977), 750, 755–60.

7. Henry St. John to Sir William Trumbull, 31 July 1698, *Historical Manuscripts Commission: Report on the Manuscripts of the Marquess of Downshire*, vol. 1, part 2 (London: His Majesty's Stationery Office, 1924), 782–83. Compare the account in Herodotus, *The Histories*, 1.154–56, trans. Aubrey de Sélincourt, rev. A. R. Burn (Harmondsworth: Penguin, 1972), 103–4.

8. See, for example, Joseph Addison, *The Freeholder*, ed. James Leheny (Oxford: Clarendon Press, 1979), no. 41, 7 May 1716, 217; [John Oldmixon] *A Review of Dr. Zachary Grey's Defence of our Ancient and Modern Historians* (London, 1725), 81.

9. J. G. A. Pocock, *The Machiavellian Moment: Florentine Political Thought and the Atlantic Republican Tradition* (Princeton: Princeton University Press, 1975), 53–56. Skinner, *Foundations of Modern Political Thought*, 1:42. The *Remarks'* focus on these two opposing spirits has received little scholarly comment, but see Isaac Kramnick, "Introduction," in Lord Bolingbroke, *Historical Writings*, ed., intro. Isaac Kramnick (Chicago: University of Chicago Press, 1972), xl–xli; Forbes, *Hume's Philosophical Politics*, 198–201. For Bolingbroke's ideological strategies generally, see David Armitage, "Introduction," in Bolingbroke, *Political Writings*, ed., intro. David Armitage (Cambridge: Cambridge University Press, 1997), vii–xxiv; Bernard Cottret, *Bolingbroke's Political Writings: The Conservative Enlightenment* (New York: St. Martin's, 1997), 1–74; Quentin Skinner, "The Principles and Practice of Opposition: The Case of Bolingbroke versus Walpole," in *Historical Perspectives: Studies in English Thought and Society in Honor of J. H. Plumb*, ed. Neil McKendrick (London: Europa Publications, 1974), 93–128.

10. Bolingbroke, *The Works of the Late Right Honorable Henry St. John, Lord Viscount Bolingbroke*, 5 vols. (London, 1754), 1:277–82, 292, 303–4, 389, 460–64, 520–21.

11. Ibid., 1:319–21, 289–94.

12. Ibid., 1:472, 349, 319, 324, 317, 291. These active and passive uses of the word "spirit" correspond to definitions 7a and 7b, respectively, in the *Oxford English Dictionary*, 2nd ed. (Oxford: Oxford University Press, 1989).

13. Bolingbroke, *Works*, 1:476, 288, 302, 337, 472, 295. For these republican qualities, see Pocock, *Machiavellian Moment*, 177–78, 252; Worden, in *Republicanism, Liberty, and Commercial Society, 1649–1776*, ed. David Wootton, 71.

14. See the *OED* definitions of "spirit," 6a, 6b. James Thomson, *Liberty, The Castle of Indolence, and Other Poems*, ed., intro., James Sambrook (Oxford: Oxford University Press, 1986), iii, 103–10, 541, pp. 72, 372. Also see Christine Gerrard, *The Patriot Opposition to Walpole: Politics, Poetry, and National Myth, 1725–1742* (Oxford: Oxford University Press, 1994), chaps. 1–3, 5.

15. See, for example, Lord Orrery to Lady Orrery, 27 February 1739 in *The Orrery Papers*, ed. Emily C. Boyle, 2 vols. (London: Duckworth, 1903), 2:152; the speeches by Sir John St. Aubyn in 1734 and by William Pitt in 1736, *Cobbett's Parliamentary History of England from the Norman Conquest, in 1066, to the Year, 1803*, 36 vols. (London: R. Bagshaw, 1806–20), 9, cols. 404, 1221–25. Bolingbroke continued using the term in his most important ideological statement, *A Dissertation upon Parties* (1733–34). See Bolingbroke, *Political Writings*, 53–54, 56, 82, 91.

16. Bolingbroke had used a very similar construction, describing how the spirit of liberty "rose." See Bolingbroke, *Works*, 1:472. For Hume's view of Bolingbroke, see *E* 28–31, 44–46; Forbes, *Hume's Philosophical Politics*, 193–94.

17. Montesquieu, *Considerations on the Causes of the Romans' Greatness and Decline* (Dublin, 1734), 39, 67, 85. Though some monarchies did not aim at liberty, Montesquieu wrote, they nonetheless attained it because "a spirit of liberty . . . in those states is capable of achieving as great things, and of contributing as much, perhaps, to happiness, as liberty itself" (Montesquieu, *The Spirit of the Laws*, trans. Thomas Nugent, intro. Franz Neumann [New York: Hafner Press, 1949], 1:162; 2:31). Also see Melvin Richter, *The Political Theory of Montesquieu* (Cambridge: Cambridge University Press, 1977), 106.

18. For Hume's independence from these French sources, see Hume to the Abbé Le Blanc, 5 November 1755 (*L* 1:226); J. G. A. Pocock, *Barbarism and Religion*, 5 vols. (Cambridge: Cambridge University Press, 1999–), vol. 2, *Narratives of Civil Government*, 258–60. For Voltaire, see Karen O'Brien, *Narratives of Enlightenment: Cosmopolitan History from Voltaire to Gibbon* (Cambridge: Cambridge University Press, 1997), 50. Regarding the matter of influence, it should be noted that Bolingbroke personally knew both Voltaire and Montesquieu during his exile in France after 1715, though his letter of 1698 predated those encounters. As a rule, the language of liberty in the late seventeenth and early eighteenth centuries typified English, not French, political discourse (but see a French usage of the term by Pierre Joseph d'Orleans, *The History of the Revolutions in England under the Family of Stuarts* (1693–94) [London, 1711], 21). Bolingbroke's "Country" reading of English politics influenced Montesquieu and Voltaire on their visits to England in the late 1720s. For these relationships, see H. T. Dickinson, *Bolingbroke* (London: Constable, 1970), 156; Robert Shackleton, *Montesquieu: A Critical Biography* (Oxford: Oxford University Press, 1961), 65, 126–30, 165, 169, 297–301.

19. Examples of this "spirit" formula include: Edward Hyde, first Earl of Clarendon, *The History of the Rebellion and Civil Wars in England* (1702–4), ed. W. Dunn Macray, 6 vols. (Oxford, 1888), 1:55; 4:261; [White Kennett], *A Complete History of England; With the Lives of All the Kings and Queens . . .* , 3 vols. (London, 1706), 3:71, 84, 89; Paul Rapin de Thoyras, *The History of England . . .* , trans. Nicholas Tindal, 15 vols. (London, 1725–31), 8:265; Laurence Echard, *The History of England, From the First Entrance of Julius Caesar . . .* , 3 vols. (London, 1707–18), 1:388; 2:828. For providence, see Rapin de Thoyras, *History of England*, 1:138, 222; 2:216; Echard, *History of England*, 1:9, 44, 213, 577, 716–17; 2:714; Thomas Carte, *A General History of England*, 4 vols. (London, 1747–55), 4:3, 605. For "the people" as a political agent, see Carte, *General History of England*, 1:400–408; 3:355; Rapin de Thoyras, *History of England*, 1:410; 4:390; 6:78–82; 12:4.

20. See James Ralph, *The History of England during the Reigns of K. William, Q. Anne and K. George I . . .* , 2 vols. (London, 1744–46), 1:7–8; William Guthrie, *A General History of England from the Invasion of the Romans . . . to the late Revolution*, 4 vols. (London, 1744–51), 1:1–3, 40, 663; 4:990.

21. The most extensive discussion heretofore of the spirit of liberty in the *History* is Eugene F. Miller, "Hume on Liberty in the Successive English Constitutions," in *Liberty in Hume's History of England*, ed. Nicholas Capaldi and Donald W. Livingston, 85–86, 91–92 (Dordrecht, Netherlands: Kluwer Academic Publishers, 1990). Also see Daniele Francesconi, "The Languages of Historical Causation in David Hume's *History of England*," *Cromohs* 6 (2001): 10–11, also at http://www.cromohs.unifi.it/6_2001/francesconi.html .

22. The term appears only three times in the final volume of the *History*, 6:44, 76, 274.

23. For this balancing act, see Miller, "Hume on Liberty," 54, 88–90; Peter Jones, "On Reading Hume's *History of Liberty*," in Capaldi and Livingston, *Liberty in Hume's History of England*, 15, 19. For Hume's critique of "vulgar whiggism," see Forbes, *Hume's Philosophical Politics*, chap. 5; Pocock, *Barbarism and Religion*, 2:220–21; O'Brien, *Narratives of Enlightenment*, 69–72.

24. On liberty's modernity, see Philip Hicks, *Neoclassical History and English Culture: From Clarendon to Hume* (New York: St. Martin's, 1996), 182–88. Hume mentioned "the spirit of liberty" just four times prior to Elizabeth's reign. Of these citations, one noted the absence of this spirit (3:267), and another Hume subsequently deleted from his text (David Hume, *The History of Great Britain*, ed., intro. Duncan Forbes [Harmondsworth, 1970], 105); see also *H* 1:371–72; 2:286. For Hume's definition of liberty, see Donald W. Livingston, "Hume's Historical Conception of Liberty," and Nicholas Capaldi, "The Preservation of Liberty," in Capaldi and Livingston, *Liberty in Hume's History of England*, 112–17, 197; Forbes, *Hume's Philosophical Politics*, 153–55, 275. For liberty and ancient history, see *H* 5:127, Hume, *History of Great Britain*, 105.

25. Bolingbroke, *Works*, 1:450.

26. A point Hume restates, when he concludes that the 1640s were "ennobled by the spirit of liberty . . . [but] disgraced by the fanatical extravagances, which distinguished the British civil wars" (*H* 6:76).

27. Hume, *History of Great Britain*, 105.

28. For the attributes of providence as it was understood in the seventeenth and eighteenth centuries, see Blair Worden, "Providence and Politics in Cromwellian England," *Past and Present* 109 (November 1985): 55–99; J. C. D. Clark, "Providence, Predestination and Progress: Or, did the Enlightenment Fail?" *Albion* 35, no. 4 (2004): 559–89; Lester H. Cohen, *The Revolutionary Histories: Contemporary Narratives of the American Revolution* (Ithaca: Cornell University Press, 1980), 27–30, 39, 47–48.

29. For "opinion" in Hume's historical thought, see *E* 32–36, 51; Mark Salber Phillips, *Society and Sentiment: Genres of Historical Writing in Britain, 1740–1820* (Princeton: Princeton University Press, 2000), 49–52, 64; Pocock, *Barbarism and Religion*, 2:203–4.

30. For this technique, see Phillips, *Society and Sentiment*, 37–48, 52, 62–65; Hicks, *Neoclassical History and English Culture*, 188–90.

31. For contemporary complaints about those qualities of British historiography, see David Hume to John Clephane, 5 January 1753; Hume to James Oswald of Dunnikier, 28 June 1753; Hume to the Abbé Le Blanc, 12 September 1754 (*L* 1:170, 179, 193); Phillips, *Society and Sentiment*, 38–40, 64–65; Hicks, *Neoclassical History and English Culture*, chap. 1.

32. These writers are all featured in Caroline Robbins, *The Eighteenth-Century Commonwealthman: Studies in the Transmission, Development, and Circumstance of English Liberal Thought from the Restoration of Charles II until the War with the Thirteen Colonies* (New York: Atheneum, 1968). See [James Burgh], *Thoughts on Education: Tending Chiefly to Recommend to the Attention of the Public, Some Particulars Relating to that Subject; which are not Generally Considered with the Regard their Importance Deserves* (Boston, 1749), 15, and *Political Disquisitions; or An Enquiry into Public Errors, Defects, and Abuses*, 3 vols. (London, 1774–75), 1:185; Thomas Pownall, *Principles of Polity, being the Grounds and Reasons of Civic Empire* (London, 1752), 3, 15, 101–3, 108.

33. [John Brown], *An Estimate of the Manners and Principles of the Times*, 2 vols. (London, 1757–58), 1:17–22, 55–58, 152–61; 2:19–22, 31, 39, 57–58, 139, 149–51, 174.

34. For the way in which religious enthusiasm fizzled out, see *H* 6:377, 539, *E* 77; Pocock, *Barbarism and Religion*, 2:217.

35. For these themes, see Catharine Macaulay, *The History of England from the Accession of James I to that of the Brunswick Line*, 8 vols. (London, 1763–83), vol. 1, Introduction; Philip Hicks, "Catharine Macaulay's Civil War: Gender, History, and Republicanism in Georgian Britain,"

Journal of British Studies 41, no. 2 (2002): 170–98. For Macaulay as historian more generally, see Karen O'Brien, "Catharine Macaulay's Histories of England: A Female Perspective on the History of Liberty," in *Women, Gender, and Enlightenment*, ed. Sarah Knott and Barbara Taylor, 523–37 (Basingstoke, Hampshire: Palgrave Macmillan, 2005); J. G. A. Pocock, "Catharine Macaulay: Patriot Historian," in *Women Writers and the Early Modern British Political Tradition*, ed. Hilda L. Smith, 243–58 (Cambridge: Cambridge University Press, 1998). Oliver Goldsmith, *An History of England, in a Series of Letters from a Nobleman to his Son*, 2 vols. (London, 1764), 1:68, 108, 125, 139, 178, 223, 309; 2:68. William Robertson, "A View of the Progress of Society," *The History of the Reign of the Emperor Charles V*, 3 vols. (London, 1769), 1:41, 164, 265, 267.

36. Macaulay, *History*, 4:370; 2:353; 3:115; 2:82n, 449 (compare *H* 5:300); 1:283. For other uses of the term, see ibid., 2:307; 4:19; 5:376n; 8:191, 293.

37. Ibid., 1:xix. Thomson, *Liberty*, 1.339–58. For Macaulay as Liberty, see Philip Hicks, "The Roman Matron in Britain: Female Political Influence and Republican Response, ca. 1750–1800," *Journal of Modern History* 77 (March 2005): 35–69.

38. See John Brewer, *Party Ideology and Popular Politics at the Accession of George III* (Cambridge: Cambridge University Press, 1976), 163, 168–69, 185; Nicholas Rogers, *Crowds, Culture, and Politics in Georgian Britain* (Oxford: Oxford University Press, 1998), 243.

39. For these interpretive frameworks, see Gordon S. Wood, *The Creation of the American Republic 1776–1787* (Chapel Hill: University of North Carolina Press, 1969), 32–45, and "Conspiracy and the Paranoid Style: Causality and Deceit in the Eighteenth Century," *William and Mary Quarterly*, 3rd ser., 39 (1982): 401–41; J. C. D. Clark, *The Language of Liberty, 1660–1832: Political Discourse and Social Dynamics in the Anglo-American World* (Cambridge: Cambridge University Press, 1994), 39–40, 56, 119, 275, 336.

40. *Authentic Account of the Proceedings of the Congress Held at New York* . . . ([London], 1767), 11. Wood, *Creation of the American Republic*, 42–43.

41. *Connecticut Courant*, 15 February 1774, quoted in Trevor Colbourn, *The Lamp of Experience: Whig History and the Intellectual Origins of the American Revolution* (1965), 229. Catharine Macaulay to Mercy Otis Warren, 11 September 1774, *Warren-Adams Papers*, microfilm edition, 1 reel (Boston: Massachusetts Historical Society, 1954), reel 1. Mercy Otis Warren to Catharine Macaulay, 9 June 1773, in *Mercy Otis Warren*, ed. Richards and Harris, 15. For other examples of this language being used by members of Warren's circle, see *Warren-Adams Letters: Being Chiefly a Correspondence among John Adams, Samuel Adams, and James Warren*, 2 vols. (Boston: Massachusetts Historical Society, 1917–25), 1:16, 17, 35. John Adams, "A Dissertation on the Canon and Feudal Law," in *Papers of John Adams*, ed. Robert J. Taylor, 14 vols. (Cambridge: Harvard University Press, 1977–), 1:125. C. Bradley Thompson, *John Adams and the Spirit of Liberty* (Lawrence: University Press of Kansas, 1998), 52–55.

42. Entries for 1 July 1770, 2 January 1766, *Diary and Autobiography of John Adams*, ed. L. H. Butterfield, 4 vols. (Cambridge: Harvard University Press, 1961), 1:356, 285. For a similar perception that "the spirit of liberty is certainly contagious," see R. Alexander to the Committee of Correspondence, Baltimore town, 26 May 1774, in *Narrative of Events Which Occurred in Baltimore Town During the Revolutionary War*, ed. Robert Purviance (Baltimore: Jos. Robinson, 1849), 126. Adams borrowed familiar republican language to warn that "the spirit of liberty, is and ought to be a jealous, a watchful spirit," *Boston Gazette*, 9 February 1767, 27 January 1766, in Taylor, *Papers of John Adams*, 1:200, 169.

43. Quoted in Eliga H. Gould, *The Persistence of Empire: British Political Culture in the Age of the American Revolution* (Chapel Hill: University of North Carolina Press, 2000), 187–91. Abigail Adams to Edward Dilly, 22 May 1775, in *Adams Family Correspondence*, ed. L. H. Butterfield, et al., 1:202 (Cambridge: Harvard University Press, 1963). Quincy quoted in Bernard Bailyn, *The Ideological Origins of the American Revolution* (Cambridge: Harvard University Press, 1967), 45.

44. *Boston Gazette*, 16 February 1767, in Taylor, *Papers of John Adams*, 1:203–4. Also see Mark G. Spencer, *David Hume and Eighteenth-Century America* (Rochester: University of Rochester Press; Woodbridge, Suffolk: Boydell and Brewer, 2005), 93–95. For the popularity of these British authors in America, see ibid., 63–64; Carla H. Hay, "Catharine Macaulay and the American Revolution," *The Historian* 56 (1994): 301–16; Colbourn, *The Lamp of Experience*, 102–8, app. 2; Bailyn, *The Ideological Origins of the American Revolution*, 39, 41–42, 49n, 53, 87.

45. For the falloff in Macaulay's popularity in the 1770s and the upsurge in Hume's, see Bridget Hill, *The Republican Virago: The Life and Times of Catharine Macaulay, Historian* (Oxford: Oxford University Press, 1992), 121–24; Hicks, *Neoclassical History and English Culture*, 196–97. For Hume's appeal in America, see Spencer, *David Hume and Eighteenth-Century America*, esp. ix, 29–53, 80–81, 93–106, 118.

"THE BOOK SEEMED TO SINK INTO OBLIVION":
READING HUME'S *HISTORY* IN
EIGHTEENTH-CENTURY SCOTLAND

Mark Towsey

But miserable was my disappointment: I was assailed by one cry of reproach, disapprobation, and even detestation; English, Scotch, and Irish, Whig and Tory, churchman and sectary, freethinker and religionist, patriot and courtier, united in their rage against the man, who had presumed to shed a generous tear for the fate of Charles I, and the earl of Strafford; and after the first ebullitions of their fury were over, what was still more mortifying, the book seemed to sink into oblivion.

—Hume, "My Own Life"

Hume's assessment of the public response to the first volume of his *History of England* was typically witty, forthright, and astute, but it presents those of us who are interested in what Robert Darnton has called the "social history of ideas" with something of a conundrum.[1] The full range of criticisms outlined by Hume can be found in abundance in contemporary reading notes. Indeed, in several recent publications I have focused almost exclusively on Hume's negative reception in Scotland, arguing that his perceived irreligion and alleged atheism alienated contemporary readers to such an extent that it decisively shaped the social impact of the wider Scottish Enlightenment. Hume's skepticism—discerned by contemporaries as much in the pages of the *History of England* as in the *Essays and Treatises on Several Subjects*—drove contemporaries to read Common Sense philosophers such as Thomas Reid, George Campbell, and James Beattie, while their oppositional reading of Hume spilled over into correspondence, conversations, and heated debates in the public sphere. Intellectual culture in provincial Scotland thus became increasingly conservative, especially when the bloodshed of the French Revolution in the 1790s seemed to confirm the moral chasm into which modern skepticism had fallen.[2] Nevertheless, Hume's *History of England* was one of the best-selling works of the age, according to any measure we can now employ. In the second half of the chapter, therefore, I shall attempt to explain the extraordinarily widespread consumption of Hume's *History of England* in spite of readers' serious (and very widely documented) reservations about its political and religious shortcomings. In the process, I will outline some of the ways in which Hume's *History* was seen as a positive influence on the lives, behavior, and thought processes of contemporary Scottish readers.

I

There is little doubt that Hume's *History* was fiercely resisted by many readers within his native Scotland. The Glasgow University law student and future Lord President of the Court of Session, David Boyle of Sherralton (1772–1853), whose father had known Hume in the 1740s, was typical when he charged that Hume had failed in his self-imposed task of bringing impartiality to the history of England. Boyle lamented that Hume had been "unable altogether to conceal his partiality for the Royal cause, which . . . ought to be guarded against by every honest and candid historian."[3] James Forbes, an expatriate Scot in the service of the East India Company, came to a similar conclusion, inserting into his reading diary,

> A remark I have since met with in Stuart's View of Society in Europe; which struck me as very just, especially when we compare Hume's annals of the Stuarts with Mrs Macaulay's history of those monarchs. — "Mr Hume, struck with the talents of Dr [Robert] Brady, deceived by his ability, disposed to pay adulation to government; or willing to profit by a system, formed with art, and ready for adoption, has executed his history upon the tenets of this writer — yet, of Dr Brady, it ought to be remembered that he was the slave of a faction; and that he meanly prostituted an excellent understanding & admirable quickness to vindicate tyranny and to destroy the rights of this nation —
>
> With no less pertinacity, but with an air of greater candor and with the marks of a more liberal mind, Mr Hume has employed himself to the same purposes; and his history from its beginning to its conclusion,

is chiefly to be regarded as a plausible defence of prerogative — as an elegant & spirited composition it merits every commendation. But no friend to humanity, and to the freedom of this kingdom will consider his constitutional enquiries, with their effect on his narrative, and compare them with the ancient and venerable monument of our story, without feeling a lively surprise and a patriot indignation.[4]

Female readers were equally explicit in rejecting Hume's politics, although few did so with greater urgency than Hanna Hume (who was, as far as we know, no relation of David): "Mr Hume is charged with want of veracity in not telling the whole truth but only as much as serves his purpose by which an action may be represented quite contrary to what in reality it would appear if the whole truth was told." Writing desperately to dissuade her daughter from a youthful admiration of Hume's *History*, she outlined a range of conventional criticisms: "what is called his history is allowed to be an apology for the family of the Stuarts & written for that purpose only. The great deceit in his book is that he does not distinguish between the constitution & administration & so supposes that whatever is done by the most wicked kings or ministers is constitution." This time that other great polite historian of the Scottish Enlightenment, William Robertson, was enlisted in support: "It is certain that most of the kings before the Stuarts were as tyrannical as they but you who have read Robertson will easily account for their being so."[5] Although the individuals behind the scene of this exchange have not been firmly identified, the letter makes clear that Hanna Hume wrote to her daughter with the full support of her implacably Whig husband. Mother and father feared that their daughter's enthusiastic reading of Hume had been encouraged by her Tory-inclined husband. Hume meant very different things to readers deeply implicated in either side of the party political divide,[6] but his *History of England* had overwhelming political implications for one particular community in Scotland—the Jacobites.

The Jacobite philosopher and political economist Sir James Steuart of Coltness assembled a manuscript commentary on Hume's *History* that refuted, step-by-step, Hume's deconstruction of the then-totemic reputation of Mary, Queen of Scots.[7] His reading of the Marian myth was perpetuated after his death, with his widow making copies for fellow Jacobites in the northeast as a commemoration, she wrote, "of those valuable sentiments which formed the basis on which their Friendship was built, and mutually subsisted."[8] One copy, with the simple legend "Queen Mary" inscribed on its spine, still survives on the library shelves of the National Trust property Leith Hall—a monument not only to the Hay family's commitment to the Jacobite cause long after the '45, but also to the devotional industry of Steuart's widow in disseminating his views.

If preexisting political loyalties compromised the reception of Hume's *History*, his notoriously detached treatment of religion caused still greater offense.[9] The Duchess of Atholl, who as we shall see was otherwise an avowed admirer of the *History of England* despite her own family's Jacobite associations, complained of Hume's "inclination upon all occasions to have a fling at the clergy, be their profession what it will."[10] A younger aristocratic reader, Elizabeth Rose (daughter of the baronet of Kilravock, near Nairn), carefully removed all trace of Hume's skepticism from her youthful manuscript abridgment of the *History*. She ignored entirely Hume's account of the Reformation and subtly refined his narrative elsewhere. Where Hume criticized Edward VI's "narrow prepossession, bigotry and persecution," Elizabeth wrote instead that "he was staunch to the principles of the Reformation"; where Hume dispassionately computed how many Protestants had been "brought to the stake" by Mary Tudor, Elizabeth substituted the more reverential phrase "committed to the flames."[11] Elizabeth was the niece of Hume's close friend Dr. John Clephane (1701/2–1758), and her deliberate pruning of Hume's skeptical tendencies from her reading notes may have been framed by the availability of Hume's letters to Clephane at the family home. There is no solid evidence that she read them, but if she did, these candid letters would have put Elizabeth in an unusually privileged position as a reader of Hume in provincial Scotland. For a perceptive reader like Elizabeth, these letters would have thrown light on how Hume had developed his historical project and what he thought of its early reception, including his observation that "A few Christians only (and but a few) think I speak like a Libertine in religion: be it assured I am tolerably reserved on this head. . . . I composed it *ad populum*, as well as *ad clerum*, and thought that skepticism was not in its place in an historical production."[12]

In any event, Elizabeth clearly detected some residual signs of Hume's skepticism and set about quietly putting them right; for other readers, however, Hume's irreligion proved simply intolerable. The Reverend William Cameron, a Church of Scotland minister living just outside Edinburgh, was even provoked to compose a response in verse. In a slim volume of poetry he published in 1788, Cameron rhymed,

> As aim'd at Superstition's heart,
> The infidel directs his dart;
> And while his shafts at random fly,
> He wounds Religion standing nigh,
> Confounds them in his parallel,
> Tho' differing wide as heaven and hell.[13]

Cameron is one of the few contemporary Scots whose notes on reading Hume's *Essays and Treatises* survive;[14] he was particularly well placed to understand Hume's philosophy of religion—not least that Hume's real target was religious extremism caused by superstition and enthusiasm. Other readers were unwilling to make even this concession—or else incapable of doing so. Hanna Hume's more combative stance was entrenched yet further by the *History*'s association with Hume's "diabolical" skepticism (a view, pointedly, derived entirely from Beattie's *Essay on Truth*, as the letter makes clear). She assures her daughter that she will "detest him as a philosopher" for endeavoring "to overturn natural & revealed religion & all morality & to establish atheism."[15] Most dramatically, an anonymous member of the Stuart family of Castlemilk, clearly obsessed with the threat his irreligion posed the modern world, returned time and again to Hume's *History* in a commonplace book entitled "Amusements in Solitude." "That celebrated author appears to me the most detestable — & contemptible Historian I ever Read," she wrote after completing his account of the Norman conquest; "nothing can be more shocking than what he expresses with regard to the Reformation"; "[t]he war of the Cranes — or the Battle of the frogs is more instructive by far. The History of Tigers — Bares [sic] — wolfs & foxes; making wars upon herds of tamer Cattle & flocks of sheep; would make as good a figure & as improving an History in Mr Hume's Hand, as the History of England — indeed I imagine it would be a fitter subject for that author."[16]

The compiler of "Amusements in Solitude" cannot swiftly be discounted as an evangelical bigot, uninterested in polite letters more generally. Indeed, her favorite counterpoint to Hume's "contempt for human nature" was once again William Robertson, whose *History of America* "greatly entertained" her. Robertson, she wrote, "increases & strengthens my faith in Moses account of creation, & the history he gives of man, before & after the fall." She was thrilled by Robertson's account of the discovery of the Americas by Columbus; her mind instantly cast back to the "impiety" of Hume: "Ah! Thought I — How amazed would the fine genius of D: H—e be to find all the sublime truths of Christianity; which he doubted of — despised, & neglected, as below the regard of philosophy."[17]

II

Though I have argued elsewhere and at much greater length that "Amusements in Solitude" can be considered a somewhat exceptional account of one particularly pious reader's engagement with Hume,[18] there is no doubt that Hume's earliest professional reviewers encouraged this kind of private response. In particular, Roger Flexman's well-known criticisms of Hume in the *Monthly Review* for 1754 anticipated—and may well have influenced, however subconsciously—many of the complaints leveled against the *History of England* by contemporary readers in Scotland:

> The author's reflections, in many instances, are striking and manly, his manner masterly, and, when prejudice does not warp and bias his judgment, his characters are strongly and clearly marked. . . . If we take our notions of the two reigns this author assumes to write the history of, from what he says of them, we shall certainly form a very inadequate and unjust idea of those times. Many facts are concealed, or partially exhibited, that are necessary to be rightly viewed, in order to throw a true light upon them; and instead of a full and faithful representation of facts, the reader is often presented with half-views and side-glances of them. . . . We cannot but observe, how singular Mr. *Hume* is in his notions of religion. He seems to be of opinion, that there are but two species of it in all nature, *superstition* and *fanaticism*; and under one or other of these, he gives us to understand, the whole of the Christian profession is, and ever was, included. His treatment, indeed, of every denomination of Christians, to speak the most favourably, is far from being such as becomes a gentleman, and may, we apprehend, prejudice his reputation *even as an historian*, in the opinion of many intelligent and considerate readers.[19]

Flexman's striking conclusion that Hume's irreligion compromised his claim to be a historian is echoed in rants scattered throughout "Amusements in Solitude"—most intriguingly, when precipitated by a conversation with a young (and in the anonymous compiler's eyes, naïve) associate who had contradicted her by arguing that "Mr Hume was not writing Divinity. History was his province." Her response gets to the heart of the problem, both for Flexman and for the many pious readers who found Hume's carefully cultivated detachment so offensive:

> But the History of Rational, intelligent, immortal Creatures; the subjects of God — the great, the divine, moral governour of the universe can never be given with propriety, without a proper attention pay'd to religion. For religion is the distinguishing characteristic of Man; . . . Cut man of[f] from God, the Centre of Souls! What is he more than other Brutes that perish? — more wretched — more contemptible. This makes it Evident to me, that there is no being a Good Historian, without

being so far a divine, as to have a Regard for Religion. And the juster his apprehensions of Sacred Truths are, the better he is accomplished for this office.[20]

Similarly, the claim that Hume could not be trusted to tell the whole truth without distorting facts to suit his own agenda was replayed endlessly in contemporary reading notes. It was a leading theme of Hanna Hume's letters, as we have seen, and infiltrated the diary of the Reverend George Ridpath, one of the most well-informed Scottish readers of the 1750s and 1760s whose reading notes survive. Ridpath was disappointed to find "a great mixture both of trifling and blundering" in his friend's long-awaited *History*, complaining that "the detail is often wanting that is sufficient to enable a man to judge for himself."[21] In this instance, once again, there is evidence to suggest that Hume's controversial account of England's past became a hot topic of conversation among Scottish readers. Ridpath reported in his diary that Hume was subject to "much disputation" among his friends, drinking companions, and fellow members of the Kelso Subscription Library. On one occasion, indeed, their discussion devolved on a critical review of Hume's *History* in which the ensemble agreed "he is treated severely enough, yet not more than he deserves."[22]

The periodical reviews were clearly a decisive influence in shaping many readers' personal engagement with Hume's *History*, as so firmly reflected in the informal proceedings of the Kelso Library.[23] It is therefore vital to appreciate that, while the kind of criticisms made by Flexman would occasionally recur in the literary criticism of the later eighteenth century, for the most part professional commentators soon came to echo Tobias Smollett's conclusion in the rival *Critical Review* that it was "one of the best histories which modern times have produced."[24] Its transition from controversial pariah to literary classic was heralded as early as 1762 by a writer in the *Library; or Moral and Critical Magazine*, just one of the many short-term publications that sought to profit from the increasing cultural capital bound up in critical reviewing:

> A considerable number of historical performances have appeared of late years, which are eminent for the elegance of their composition. Among these the works of Mr. Hume will be reckoned, by all men of taste; and we have had the satisfaction of observing, that his merit, as an historian, has increased by every fresh publication. His first volume abounded with prejudices and misrepresentations, which no lover of religion and liberty could forgive, and no force of genius, or beauty of language, could atone for. His second volume was much less exceptionable. His account of the reigns of the Tudors is, on the whole, an excellent production, and wrote

in an admirable manner.... Though the peculiar principles of Mr. Hume may, perhaps, sometimes shew themselves, yet he has certainly given a very valuable present to the public; and his performance will be read with greater pleasure and improvement, than the full unaffecting narrations we have generally had.[25]

By 1776, then, David Hume could well afford to dwell on the poor reception of his *History of England* in such frank—and characteristically playful—terms. Far from sinking into oblivion, it had quickly risen to become the preeminent account of England's historical legacy, as the *Library*'s reviewer happily acknowledged. As a consequence, it was also one of the most commercially successful publishing enterprises of the Georgian age. Hume's *History* appeared in a dazzling number of editions and was translated into French and German. New editions were priced and formatted for different parts of the market: Richard Sher points out that contemporaries "could purchase Hume's philosophical and historical works in ten quarto volumes for as much as £9.3s., while those of more modest means could own the same texts in ten octavo volumes for as little as £3.2s., without recourse to pirated or used editions"—the last of which, of course, were very readily available in bookshops and specialist auctions in towns across the British Isles.[26] Hume's *History* was widely available in even cheaper formats, with John and Charles Cooke's pocket *Hume's History*, in nineteen tiny volumes, one of "the most popular and accessible genteel primers of . . . the 1793-4 season."[27] Such was its dominant position in the literary marketplace at the dawn of the nineteenth century that Hume's *History* had been stereotyped by 1810 as one of a small handful of works (and the only unabridged history of England, it should be emphasized) of which William St. Clair argues "a continuing large demand was expected."[28]

In Scotland, Hume's *History* was standard issue for polite libraries and genteel drawing rooms across the country, eagerly acquired by dukes, MPs, and lairds; transatlantic merchants and enterprising industrialists; lawyers, physicians, and clergymen; as well as more modest consumers such as William Munro, a Highland cattle dealer; Duncan Chisholm, a leather merchant in Inverness; and John Surtees, an iron founder in Markinch.[29] It was taken abroad by Scots implicated in the British imperial effort overseas, accompanying James Alexander Stewart-Mackenzie when he moved from the governor's residence in Ceylon to take up the position of Lord High Commissioner of the Ionian Islands in Corfu in 1840,[30] and taken to Halifax, Nova Scotia, on board HMS *Resolution* by Admiral George Murray in March 1794.[31] Hume's *History* could be borrowed from most circulating libraries and virtually all subscription libraries in Scotland[32] and was always among the most frequently borrowed books at any book-lending institution for which we have circulation records. In the earliest years of the Wigtown Subscription Library in the southwest, for instance, it was borrowed by Matthew Campbell, a banker and successful estate manager; the lawyer Robert McKeand; the physician Andrew Simson; and the widows McCulloch and Milroy.[33] At the far longer established library in Selkirk, where only the periodical *Edinburgh Review* and *Annual Register* were borrowed more frequently, subscribers who borrowed Hume's *History* in the opening decade of the nineteenth century included local gentry, tenant farmers, lawyers, physicians, schoolmasters, and merchants. Most notably, Hume's *History* was read at Selkirk by a dozen French Napoleonic prisoners of war paroled in the town between 1811 and 1814, and by a retired British army colonel, a landowning industrialist with manufacturing interests in the northeast of England, the two brothers of the explorer Mungo Park, and the Burgher minister George Lawson, who was Professor of Theology at the Associate Synod's Theological Hall.[34] At the charitable Gray Library in Haddington, Hume's borrowers included a tanner, a tailor, a haberdasher, and a shoemaker, along with the more usual clergymen, lawyers, bankers, customs officials, and town magistrates.[35]

III

We can be certain, then, that Hume's *History* was very widely encountered by readers in contemporary Scotland among a surprisingly diverse range of social groups, despite widespread discontent over his controversial politics and disturbing skepticism. Such sources do not help us understand why Hume's *History* was apparently so well received, however. Book catalogues are notoriously difficult to interpret, especially in an age that treated books as status symbols as much as functional texts to be read and digested, part of the cultural paraphernalia that marked their owners out as members of an increasingly broadly based genteel elite.[36] Library circulating records allow us to be much more certain that a book was actually taken down off the shelves, but tell us little about the precise nature of the reading encounter that occurred as a result.[37] As we have already seen, therefore, we need to turn to other types of source material to recover what readers actually thought of the books they read. On this score, historians of reading have so far enjoyed greater success in uncovering rebellious, disruptive, or deviant responses to books than in explaining their widespread popular acceptance.[38] This is a natural function of the kind of documentary material we rely on, since readers have always been more likely to interject when they disagree with something they have read rather than when it sits easily with them. For our present purposes, it is relatively simple to find evidence of individual readers' negative reactions to Hume's *History*—they abound in contemporary correspondence, marginalia, and reading notes, just as Hume attracted a succession of vociferous critics in print. This is not to say, however, that it is impossible to reconstruct something of the undoubted appeal of Hume's *History*, as attested so indisputably in the records of the eighteenth-century book trade. The remainder of this chapter therefore combines professional commentary (in the form of periodical reviews, literary criticism, and pedagogical advice on reading) with personal experiences (taken from correspondence, commonplace books, and personal reading notes of other kinds) to uncover some of the ways in which Hume's *History* was regarded positively by contemporary Scottish readers.

With his admirably drawn pen portraits of the virtues and vices of English history's leading characters, Hume's *History* provided a wealth of opportunities to study moral conduct in the traditional sense of history as "philosophy teaching by examples."[39] As the *Critical Review* acknowledged in 1762, "No writer hath more fortunately hit upon the method of rendering history instructive than our ingenious author, whose work may be regarded as a table of the human passions, stripped of all disguise, laid naked to the eye, and dissected by the masterly hand of a curious artist."[40] Many contemporary commonplace books reflect this perspective, scouring Hume's *History* (usually alongside other books) for moral maxims, instructive anecdotes, and improving *sententiae*.[41] A member of the Innes family of Stowe filled one such specialist reading notebook with notes under a wide range of subject headings, including standard topics of eighteenth-century moral philosophy such as *virtue, courage, liberty*, and *reason*.[42] Hume's *History* figured particularly prominently in Innes's reading, but the commonplace book does not offer much of a sense of how he or she regarded Hume. Indeed, in common with other such sources, the Innes reading notes were highly constrained by the generic requirements of commonplacing, being driven by a search for pithy phrases and memorable aphorisms that might later be used to enliven our reader's conversation and beautify his or her letter writing.[43] As a result, the personal meaning of such notes is often entirely irrecoverable; at times, indeed, it seems that the commonplacer's attention wandered from the search for edifying material toward more frivolous anecdotes, as in the note on "the English" apparently confirming their fondness for puddings: "David Hume relating the manner in which Henry the 8th gifted the revenues of the convents says, 'he was so profuse in these liberalities that he is said to have given a woman the whole revenue of a convent, as a reward for making a pudding which happened to gratify his palate.'"[44] Nevertheless, the reading methodology on display in the

Innes commonplace book implicitly valued Hume as an impeccable authority on manners and moral conduct; such commonplace books were usually compiled to record and organize a prescribed course of reading, usually with an avowedly pedagogical purpose. In this instance, as in many other late eighteenth-century examples, Hume was treated with as much decorum and respect as other canonical writers of the eighteenth century (including Addison, Chesterfield, Fielding, Sterne, and Young), with no mention of his questionable politics, provocative skepticism, or alleged atheism.

Commonplace books enshrined a philosophy of reading that remained significant throughout our period, but Hume's *History* was used for essentially pedagogical purposes in other ways. For instance, the celebrated Georgian actor and educational writer Thomas Sheridan particularly recommended Hume's *History* in his *Plan of Education* (1769):

> As our own history is that which chiefly imports us to know, Hume's *History of England* cannot be read too often, nor with too much attention. And this, not only because it is the clearest, and most impartial of any hitherto produced, but because of the goodness of the style, which will improve the taste of the boys in English composition. After having read it with care, each boy should be employed in making an abstract of it from the time of the conquest, taking notice only of the most material facts, without entering into the spirit of parties, policies or intrigues of the time. The abstract of each reign should be closed with an account of the principal laws made during that reign.[45]

It was precisely this kind of abstract that David Boyle produced in his abridgment of Hume's *History*, although Boyle focused only on the Stuart volumes and could not, as we have seen, entirely rise above the party politics of the era. Boyle only rarely chose to quote his source directly, preferring instead to note in sequential order summaries of Hume's text. The focus was not simply on party, policy, and diplomacy but also included, as Sheridan's advice and his own chosen career path dictated, the legal and constitutional developments of each reign as well as notes on cultural and literary history. This diversity is well illustrated in the following extract from his notes on the reign of James I, tellingly taken from one of Hume's characteristic "Appendices":

> The extent of the jurisdiction of the court of high commission was almost immeasurable and the star chamber may be stiled the engine of absolute monarchy. Monarchy undoubtedly was at its highest pitch in England upon the accession of the house of Stuart. Great ideas amongst

the writers of those times of the extent of Princes' Prerogative. By an order of Elizabeth, books were only allowed to be published at London, Cambridge, and Oxford. Stateliness and dignity alone distinguished the nobility from the common people. Civil subordinate to military honours. Greater prevalence of duelling than either before or since. The revenue of James as it stood in 1617, amounted to 450,000 pounds. However it would go farther then, than in our days. The militia of England consisted of 16,000 men. The English excelled in shipbuilding and the forging of iron cannon. The East India Company received a new charter during this reign, and had their stock increased to 1,500,000 pounds.[46]

Boyle's abstracts reveal how Hume provided a comprehensive guide to English history for an ambitious young man on the make, giving him a directory of basic information which he could later deploy in an eminent career in the Scottish law courts as well as in polite conversation. In precociously summing up his overall impression of the *History of England* at the end of his manuscript abridgment, Boyle focused on precisely the theme that modern commentators tend to highlight, acknowledging that Hume's narrative illuminated the "wonderful degree of party spirit displayed on both sides." Hume had revealed to him the "pretended sanctity under the veil of the deepest hypocrisy" that influenced men of all parties under the Stuarts and reflected further that it "is most astonishing how easily were the people in those days deluded by the most glaring absurdities."[47] Although, as we have seen, he dutifully noted Hume's perceived Tory bias, his conclusion was impeccably evenhanded—a touch of hero-worship perhaps betraying his father's former association with the great historian:

> Upon the whole, Mr Hume has maintained all the requisite dignity of an historian yet it must be confessed that he has been unable altogether to conceal his partiality for the Royal cause, which tho' founded on however just grounds, ought to be guarded against by every honest and candid historian.
>
> However the greatest of men have had their faults—*humanum est errare*.[48]

While Sheridan envisaged his to be an exclusively masculine method of reading history, Hume's *History* was treated in a similar manner by a number of Scotswomen whose reading notes survive—not least a youthful Elizabeth Rose, whose pious rewriting of Hume's account of the Reformation we mentioned earlier and who later inherited the title and lands of Kilravock *suo jure*.

There is no particular surprise in this: Hume acknowledged privately and in print the growing significance of female readers in the literary marketplace,[49] and his *History of England* was unashamedly commended as the most "useful and entertaining" guide to British history by bestselling conduct writers such as Lady Sarah Pennington and Hester Chapone.[50] Even Hannah More acknowledged Hume's contribution to national historiography, although she was more than a little suspicious of his motivations (she considered this "serpent under a bed of roses" unsuitable for all but the most well-prepared readers).[51] For the young Elizabeth Rose, Hume's *History* was a natural choice, given the family's close association with *Le Bon David* in the 1740s and 1750s. Yet her extended manuscript abridgment shows how the *History of England* could be used pedagogically by the women readers such conduct writers addressed, touching as it does not only on England's constitutional development, but also on female biography (she treats Henry VI's Queen Margaret as a model for her own duties as a single mother) and domestic economy (the price of livestock in 1199, for instance, and the introduction of "sallads, carrots and other vegetable roots" to English tables in the sixteenth century).[52] Rose used Hume's *History* to learn to read critically; she became a more skillful summarizer of Hume's original, able more effectively and more accurately to convey the significance of his narrative in her own words, and she developed a greater awareness of its implications in terms of both politics and sentiment. Indeed, Elizabeth Rose provides intriguing evidence to suggest that Hume did indeed pull at the heartstrings of his female readers. Her notes enhanced Hume's sympathetic yet condemnatory portrayal of Queen Mary, concluding that this "most lovely of women . . . died a Heroine to her Religion and Principles" (a eulogy never used by Hume).[53] More emphatically still, Elizabeth clearly joined Hume's celebrated friend Mrs. Mure in feeling "sorry for poor King Charles." Having already covered Charles I's reign in exceptional detail in her abridgment, Elizabeth Rose tellingly entered a digest of his most affecting moments into her prose commonplace book for 1775.[54] Here Elizabeth Rose really was shedding her own tear in sympathy with Charles I, literally engaging with the king's own "flood of tears" in a sequence of favorite transcriptions she could return to time and again.[55]

Though they censured Hume in their own distinctive ways, it was presumably a considerable benefit for both Boyle and Rose that his idiosyncrasies tested their nascent political and religious beliefs so thoroughly.[56] At the same time, the sheer effort their abridgments must surely have entailed demonstrates that his *History* remained unimpeachable on patriotic, sentimental, and stylistic grounds. Another measure of the moral conventionality of Hume's *History* is the fact that it was regarded as legitimate and, in the right circumstances, virtuous reading for the family circle. In common with many contemporary readers (especially, it seems, women), Elizabeth Rose had learned to read in the domestic sphere and remained throughout her life convinced of the moral benefits of sociable reading. Reading was at the heart of her closest female friendships, her diary reporting in December 1782 that she had had the "Miss Brodies to dinner . . . spent the evening in literary conversation"; an early summer's day in 1784 was spent "agreeably in reading, walking, music & conversation with the Brodies"; and at the end of April 1785 she "Read and walked with the Ladies of Lethen."[57] On these occasions, Elizabeth shared her reading strategies with younger female friends, perhaps lending them her extracts in an earnest attempt to further their education. Many years later, Elizabeth took an exceptionally active interest in her granddaughters' education, helping them develop appropriate reading habits and attempting to prevent them from choosing to read the wrong kinds of books.[58] We can only speculate whether Hume's *History* figured in Elizabeth Rose's virtuous reading communities (though a succession of furious extracts from Beattie's *Essay on Truth* compiled in 1806 almost certainly did,[59] serving to warn her dependents against Hume's skeptical philosophy), but elsewhere—in both contemporary fiction and in the historical record—the domestic sphere is precisely where it can be found.

The Ulster-Scot Elizabeth Hamilton was just one of a surprising number of contemporary female novelists to figure Hume's *History* as a virtuous text that would "reinforce or create family ties" when read sociably by the fireside.[60] Though she treated Hume's skeptical philosophy with utmost severity elsewhere in *Memoirs of Modern Philosophers*, Hamilton puts Hume's *History* in the hands of the "active and judicious" Harriet Orwell. Having "performed every domestic task, and . . . completely regulated family economy for the day," this conventional conduct model for impressionable young female readers can at one point be found "quietly seated with her aunt and sisters, listening to Hume's History of England as it was read to them by a little orphan girl she had herself instructed."[61] In the anonymous *History of Melinda Harley*, "good" Mr. Finchley includes Hume in a raft of reading designed to secure "the future good of his family": "Every morning one of the girls, by turns, reads aloud a paper of the Spectator; and, while the rest are at work in the parlour, another reads aloud, an hour before dinner, Hume's history of England. Before supper another paper of the Spectator or Guardian is read again, except on Sunday, when one of Fordyce's sermons to young women is then preferred."[62] In both novels the act of listening to the *History of England* being read aloud is therefore presented as the very model of virtuous domesticity, and this performance was repeated in real Scottish households throughout our period.

The mathematician Mary Somerville was raised in one such household in Burntisland, Fife, with her father insisting on some of the same prescribed reading as the fictional Mr. Finchley. In this instance, though, Somerville remembered her enforced exposure to Hume with little fondness: "he made me read a paper of the 'Spectator' aloud every morning, after breakfast, the consequence of which discipline is that I have never since opened that book. Hume's 'History of England' was also a real penance to me."[63]

The Murray family of Blair Castle seems to have relished reading books together rather more, despite their lofty social status and distinguished (though somewhat tainted) lineage. The teenaged Lady Charlotte Murray described in 1771 how her father "the Duke [John Murray, 3rd Duke of Atholl (1729–1774)] began reading a new book to us, Humphrey Clinker, it seems very entertaining so far as we have gone in it,"[64] while her mother (not the same duchess we encountered earlier) can be found in 1776 asking her son to "get me Campbell's Lives of the Admirals, as *we shall soon want a book to succeed* Hume's History, which I admire much. It is a very pretty style and fine language."[65] This was not the first time the Murrays had read Hume together. In fact, in the letter quoted earlier, Jean Drummond (d. 1795), the 2nd Duke's second wife, enjoins her absent nephew and son-in-law John Murray (who succeeded as 3rd Duke in 1764) to participate in the reading that the family at Blair Castle was currently enjoying—at once both an attempt to control from afar his ongoing political education and a recognition that the act of reading could bind the family together even when separated by hundreds of miles. Although, as we have seen, she admitted finding Hume's irreligion somewhat distasteful, she was rather more convinced about the benefits of the work overall: "I am just now reading Mr. Hume's History of England, and am more entertained and more instructed (that is to say, I can form more distinct notions, and retain them better in my memory of what were the transactions, laws and customs of the earliest times of this island) than I ever was by any history of England I have read formerly; were you to read it, I'm persuaded you would think your time very well bestowed."[66] Hume's *History* was clearly a regular item on the domestic reading list at Blair Castle, but the Murray family's protracted engagement with Hume also reveals one final element in his reception that was uniquely relevant to its Scottish audience. J. G. A. Pocock contends that "Hume does not feel much need to invoke Scottish history to explain the present that preoccupies him and his readers. . . . He thought Scots should study the English national context and not their own, but he thought them in some ways better qualified to do so."[67] This may be so, but at the same time Hume's *History* necessarily equipped Scottish readers for interaction with England, her institutions, and her people. The *History of England* may therefore have helped readers adjust to the consequences of Union in a very real and practical sense, fostering the new forms of "Anglo-British" identity to which Hume himself was so thoroughly committed.[68] In Jean Drummond's apparently nonchalant terms, Hume's *History* was regarded as such an indispensable part of contemporary print culture precisely because the history of "this island" was now unequivocally associated with the "history of England." That is why Hume's *History of England* was seemingly considered such an integral part of the education of the future judge David Boyle, the East India Company official James Forbes, the lady laird Elizabeth Rose, Lord High Commissioner Stewart-Mackenzie, Admiral George Murray, and, most intriguingly perhaps, his brother the future 3rd Duke of Atholl. John Murray's past was intimately bound up with Scotland's post-Union legacy: as the eldest son of the Jacobite commander Lord George Murray (1694–1760), the man who became the 3rd Duke fought relentlessly to redeem his tainted heritage, serving in the Hanoverian army in 1745, marrying into the loyalist branch of his family, and aligning himself with the Bute and Grenville administrations in Parliament.[69] Evidently his aunt considered a judicious reading of Hume's *History* instrumental in consolidating his carefully manicured Hanoverian identity and, ultimately, in securing the lands and title of Atholl. To get on in life in late eighteenth-century Britain, it seems, members of the professional and landholding elites in Scotland (as well, perhaps, as the cattle dealers, the merchants, the manufacturers, and the tailors for whom we have much less documentary evidence of reading experiences and responses) had to be intimately familiar with the English past—and this invariably entailed a close reading of David Hume's *History of England*.

IV

Although it is not normally considered as such, there are strong grounds for regarding Hume's *History* as one of the most influential pedagogical texts of the Georgian period. It was consistently recommended by professional reviewers, literary critics, conduct writers, and didactic novelists as the best guide to English history yet written, while amateur readers embraced its canonical status by including it in their autodidactic commonplace books, abridgments, and abstracts. Hume's *History* was praised for its correct literary style, for its entertaining narrative flow, and for its unrivaled scope and accuracy—and there is little doubt that its inclusion in so many contemporary commonplace books meant that it had a very real impact on readers' conversation and letter writing. Most importantly for readers in contemporary Scotland, perhaps, it helped disseminate the sense of "Anglo-British" identity that Hume and his friends were so keen to consolidate in post-Union Scotland, providing Scottish readers with the intellectual equipment to flourish not only south of the border but in the ever-increasing British presence overseas.

No wonder, then, that it was so widely owned, borrowed, and read in contemporary Scotland—as, indeed, it was elsewhere, in England, America, France, and Germany. But there is one final sense in which Hume's *History* played a part in improving and educating its readers. Almost without exception, the dozen or so contemporary readers discussed here criticized some element of Hume's approach, whether this be his controversial politics or his still more unsettling disregard for religion. These complaints tended to be terminal when readers had Hume's philosophical works in front of them,[70] but when confronted by the *History of England* they behaved very differently, as we have seen. Their eagerness to appreciate the *History* in spite of its well-known peculiarities, to paraphrase the *Library*'s critique, perhaps helps us understand why Hume was so keen to acknowledge the controversy caused by the publication of its first volumes. He intended his "My Own Life" to preface posthumous editions of his *History of England* from the outset, and it very probably prefigured many of the readers' responses discussed here. In recounting the "one cry of reproach, disapprobation, and even detestation" that met the release of the *History of England*, Hume may therefore be daring future readers to look beyond the conventional criticisms; to side with the voice of dispassionate Enlightenment; or, to recall another document that prefixed many posthumous readings of the *History of England*, to applaud "the most extensive learning, the greatest depth of thought and a capacity in every respect the most comprehensive." Of course, in the very same letter Adam Smith notoriously considered Hume "both in his lifetime and since his death, as approaching as nearly to the idea of a perfectly wise and virtuous man, as perhaps the nature of human frailty will permit."[71] Though Smith's eulogy was explicitly refuted by the compiler of "Amusements in Solitude" in the most vehement terms,[72] David Boyle's response was probably the more typical—his "*humanum est errare*" representing much more than simply a student's immature showmanship, but in itself a marker of the improving impact made by his encounter with Hume's *History*. For the *History of England* forced contemporary readers to negotiate for themselves Hume's various critics, the "English, Scotch, and Irish, Whig and Tory, churchman and sectary, freethinker and religionist, patriot and courtier [who] united in their rage" against him; in the process, it helped fashion in them the sense of moderation, tolerance, and fair-mindedness that was crucial to polite readers in the Age of Enlightenment.

NOTES

The author thanks David Allan, Siobhan Talbott, and delegates who attended the twenty-second annual conference of the Eighteenth-Century Scottish Studies Society in St. Andrews in July 2009 for their comments on earlier versions of this chapter. The research upon which it is based was supported by the Arts and Humanities Research Council of the United Kingdom and by the Leverhulme Trust.

The chapter's epigraph is derived from *H* 1:xxx.

1. Robert Darnton, "In Search of the Enlightenment: Recent Attempts to Create a Social History of Ideas," *Journal of Modern History* 43 (1971): 113–32; Darnton, "First Steps Toward a History of Reading," *Australian Journal of French Studies* 23 (Monash, 1986): 5–30.

2. Mark Towsey, *Reading the Scottish Enlightenment: Books and Their Readers in Provincial Scotland, 1750–1820* (Leiden: Brill, 2010); Towsey, "'Patron of Infidelity': Scottish Readers Respond to David Hume, c. 1750–c. 1820," *Book History* (2008): 89–123; Towsey, "'Philosophically Playing the Devil': Recovering Readers' Responses to David Hume and the Scottish Enlightenment," *Historical Research* 83, no. 220 (2010): 301–20. For the reception of Hume's *History* elsewhere, see Mark G. Spencer, *David Hume and Eighteenth-Century America* (Rochester: University of Rochester Press, 2005); David Allan, *Making British Culture: English Readers and the Scottish Enlightenment, 1740–1830* (Abingdon: Routledge, 2008).

3. Glasgow University Library MS Murray 170, Notebook of David Boyle of Sherralton, 77–78. For Boyle's career, see Arthur Grant, "Boyle, David, Lord Shewalton (1772–1853)," rev. Michael Fry, in *Oxford Dictionary of National Biography*, ed. H. C. G. Matthew and Brian Harrison (Oxford: Oxford University Press, 2004) [hereafter, *ODNB*].

4. Beinecke Rare Book and Manuscript Library, Yale University (hereafter Beinecke), Osborn Bound MS Fc132, Commonplace Book of James Forbes, 1766–c. 1800, [unpaginated]; taken from Gilbert Stuart, *A View of Society in Europe, in its Progress from Rudeness to Refinement* (Edinburgh, 1778), 327–28. Robert Brady (c. 1627–1700) was a Tory historian whose works included *An Introduction to the Old English History* (1684) and *A Complete History of England* (1685).

5. Beinecke Osborn MS 7733, Letter of Hanna (Frederick) Hume discussing David Hume, [unpaginated]. There is some debate about who Hanna Hume, her husband, and her daughter were, with the Beinecke catalogue identifying Hanna Frederick (wife of Sir Abraham Hume, d. 1772) as the most likely author. Identification is complicated by the author's use of initials, "AH snr," "AH jnr."

6. The classic view is Duncan Forbes, *Hume's Philosophical Politics* (Cambridge: Cambridge University Press, 1975); this has been revised in different ways by Nicholas Phillipson, *Hume* (London: Weidenfeld and Nicholson, 1989); J. G. A. Pocock, *Barbarism and Religion*, vol. 2, *Narratives of Civil Government* (Cambridge: Cambridge University Press, 1999); and Victor G. Wexler, *David Hume and the History of England* (Philadelphia: American Philosophical Society, 1979). The wider context of partisan historiography in which Hume's *History* appeared is best summarized in Philip S. Hicks, *Neoclassical History and English Culture: Clarendon to Hume* (Basingstoke: Macmillan, 1996).

7. National Library of Scotland [hereafter NLS], MS 9367, Notes on Hume's History of England, attributed to Sir James Steuart of Coltness. For an engaging study of eighteenth-century Mariolatry, see Karen O'Brien, *Narratives of Enlightenment: Cosmopolitan History from Voltaire to Gibbon* (Cambridge: Cambridge University Press, 1997), chapter 4.

8. National Trust for Scotland [hereafter NTS], Leith Hall Library, 77.8160 "Queen Mary" [MS copy of NLS MS 9367].

9. For Hume's "historical detachment," see Mark Salber Phillips, *Society and Sentiment: Genres of Historical Writing in Britain, 1740–1820* (Princeton: Princeton University Press, 2000), 58–78.

10. National Register of Archives for Scotland [hereafter NRAS] 234, Box 49/I/32; 5 February 1762, Duchess of Atholl to John Murray.

11. National Archives of Scotland [hereafter NAS] GD1/726/10, fol. 12v (compare *H* 3:196ff.); fol. 33r (compare *H* 5:213); fol. 17v (compare *H* 3:399); fol. 19r (compare *H* 3:441). For Elizabeth Rose, see my "'An Infant Son to Truth Engage': Virtue, Responsibility and Self-Improvement in the Reading of Elizabeth Rose of Kilravock, 1745–1815," *Journal of the Edinburgh Bibliographical Society* 2 (2007): 69–92.

12. David Hume to John Clephane, 1 September 1754; J. Y. T. Greig, ed., *The Letters of David Hume* (Oxford: Clarendon Press, 1932), 1:189–90; see also 1:204–5, 237.

13. William Cameron, *Poetical Dialogues on Religion, in the Scots Dialect, between Two Gentlemen and Two Ploughmen* (Edinburgh: Peter Hill, 1788), 38–39. Hume's nickname has often been revived, most recently by Roderick Graham, *The Great Infidel: The Life of David Hume* (Edinburgh: John Donald, 2005).

14. NAS CH1/15/3, commonplace book of William Cameron, minister of Kirkliston, fols. 72v–83r; for more analysis, see Towsey, "Patron of Infidelity," 96–99.

15. Beinecke Osborn MS 7733, [unpaginated].

16. NLS MSS 8238-40, Amusements in Solitude, quoting here from MS 8238, fols. 19r-v.

17. NLS MS 8239, Amusements in Solitude, fols. 16r–17r; compare William Robertson, *The History of America* (London, 1777), 1:264ff.

18. Towsey, "Patron of Infidelity," 99–104, 113–14.

19. [Roger Flexman], review in *The Monthly Review* 12 (March 1754), reprinted in James Fieser, ed., *Early Responses to Hume's "History of England"* (Bristol: Thoemmes, 2002), 1:21.

20. NLS MS 8239, Amusements in Solitude, fol. 17r.

21. *Diary of George Ridpath, Minister of Stitchel, 1755–61*, ed. Sir J. Balfour Paul (Edinburgh: Scottish History Society, 1922), 262, 264.

22. Ibid. 130, 6.

23. On the growth and influence of the periodical reviews, see Frank Donoghue, *The Fame Machine: Book Reviewing and Eighteenth-Century Literary Careers* (Stanford: Stanford University Press, 1996); Jon P. Klancher, *The Making of English Reading Audiences, 1790–1832* (Madison: University of Wisconsin Press, 1987).

24. Quoted in James Fieser, "The Eighteenth-Century British Reviews of Hume's Writings," *Journal of the History of Ideas* 57 (1996): 650; Hicks, *Neoclassical History*, 197–209.

25. *The Library; or Moral and Critical Magazine, for the year 1761, by a Society of Gentlemen* (London, 1762), 1:440.

26. Richard B. Sher, *The Enlightenment and the Book: Scottish Authors and Their Publishers in Eighteenth-Century Britain, Ireland, and America* (Chicago: University of Chicago Press), 58. Print runs and subsequent editions are also discussed in *H* 1:xviii–xx.

27. James Raven, *The Business of Books: Booksellers and the English Book Trade* (New Haven: Yale University Press, 2007), 249.

28. William St. Clair, *The Reading Nation in the Romantic Period* (Cambridge: Cambridge University Press, 2004), 515.

29. For the research on which this paragraph is based, see my *Reading the Scottish Enlightenment*, chapt 1; for Munro, Chisholm, and Surtees, see NAS CS96/1253, CS96/135 and CS96/203.

30. NAS GD46/15/140, Inventory of Books (1840) belonging to James Alexander Stewart-Mackenzie and Mary Elizabeth Frederica Stewart-Mackenzie. T. F. Henderson. "Mary Elizabeth Frederica Stewart-Mackenzie, Lady Hood (1783–1862)", rev. K. D. Reynolds, *ODNB*.

31. NRAS 234 [unlisted], Books taken on board HMS Resolution (1794). Malcolm Lester, "Murray, George (1741–1797)", *ODNB*.

32. Mark Towsey, "'All the Partners May Be Enlightened and Improved by Reading Them': The Distribution of Enlightenment Books in Scottish Subscription Library Catalogues, 1750–c. 1820," *Journal of Scottish Historical Studies* 28 (2008): 20–43.

33. National Trust for Scotland at the Hornel Library, Broughton House, Kirkcudbright: MS 5/27, Regulations of the Wigtown Subscription Library; MS 11/28-30, Borrowing Books of the Wigtown Subscription Library. For a detailed account of borrowings from the Wigtown Library in the 1790s, see my "First Steps in Associational Reading: Book Use and Sociability at the Wigtown Subscription Library, 1795-1799," *Papers of the Bibliographical Society of America* 103, no. 4 (2009): 455-95.

34. Towsey, *Reading the Scottish Enlightenment*, 69-76; Mark Towsey, "Imprisoned Reading: Napoleonic Prisoners of War at the Selkirk Subscription Library, 1809-1815," in *Civilians and War in Europe, 1640-1815*, ed. E. Charters, E. Rosenhaft, and H. Smith (Liverpool: Liverpool University Press, 2012), 241-61; Scottish Borders Archives and Local History Centre S/PL/7/1 and 2, Selkirk Subscription Library Registers, 1799-1808 and Daybook, 1808-1814; *Catalogue of the Selkirk Library, instituted 1777* (Selkirk, 1856).

35. NLS MS 16480, Book for the Receipts of Books lent out of Mr John Gray's Library [Haddington], 1732-1789; NLS MS16481, Account of Books borrowed from the public Library of the Town of Haddington, from 1st April 1792. For a general analysis, see Vivienne S. Dunstan, "Glimpses into a Town's Reading Habits in Enlightenment Scotland: Analysing the Borrowings of Gray Library, Haddington, 1732-1816," *Journal of Scottish Historical Studies* 26 (2006): 42-59.

36. Ian Gow, "'The Most Learned Drawing Room in Europe?': Newhailes and the Classical Scottish Library," in *Visions of Scotland's Past*, ed. Deborah C. Myers, Michael S. Moss, and Miles K. Oglethorpe (East Linton: Tuckwell Press, 2000); Claire Wainwright, "The Library as Living Room," in *Property of a Gentleman: The Formation, Organisation, and Dispersal of the Private Library, 1620-1920*, ed. Robin Myers and Michael Harris (Winchester: St. Paul's Bibliographies, 1991).

37. Paul Kaufman, *Borrowings from the Bristol Library, 1773-1784: A Unique Record of Reading Vogues* (Charlottesville: Bibliographical Society of the University of Virginia, 1960), 127-28; Kaufman, "Reading Vogues at English Cathedral Libraries of the Eighteenth Century," *Bulletin of the New York Public Library* 67/68 (1963-64): 654; Jan Fergus, "Provincial Servants' Reading in the Late Eighteenth Century," in *The Practice and Representation of Reading in England*, ed. James Raven, Helen Small, and Naomi Tadmor (Cambridge: Cambridge University Press, 1996).

38. Most famously, Carlo Ginzburg, *The Cheese and the Worms: The Cosmos of a Sixteenth-Century Miller*, trans. John and Anne Tedeschi (Baltimore: Johns Hopkins University Press, 1980). For more recent discussion, see Jonathan Rose, "Rereading the English Common Reader: A Preface to a History of Audiences," *Journal of the History of Ideas* 53 (1992): 47-70; James Raven, "New Reading Histories, Print Culture, and the Identification of Change: The Case of Eighteenth-Century England," *Social History* 23 (1998): 268-87; David Allan, "Some Methods and Problems in the History of Reading: Georgian England and the Scottish Enlightenment," *Journal of the Historical Society* 3 (2003): 91-124; Stephen Colclough, "Recovering the Reader: Commonplace Books and Diaries as Sources of Reading Experiences," *Publishing History* 44 (1998): 5-37; Anthony Grafton, "Is the History of Reading a Marginal Exercise?: Guillaume Bude and His Books," *Papers of the Bibliographical Society of America* 91 (1997): 139-57; Ian Jackson, "Approaches to the History of Readers and Reading in 18th-Century Britain," *Historical Journal* 47 (2004): 1041-54.

39. Phillips, *Society and Sentiment*, especially 65.

40. Quoted by Fieser, *Early Responses*, 1:xiv-xv.

41. On the historical development of the commonplacing tradition, see Robert Darnton, "Extraordinary Commonplaces," *New York Review of Books*, 21 December 2000; Ann Moss, *Printed Commonplace-Books and the Structuring of Renaissance Thought* (Oxford: Clarendon Press, 1996); Ann Blair, "Humanist Methods in Natural Philosophy: The Commonplace Book," *Journal of the History of Ideas* 53 (1992): 541-51; Lucia Dacome, "Noting the Mind: Commonplace Books and the Pursuit of the Self in Eighteenth-Century Britain," *Journal of the History of Ideas* 65 (2004): 603-26; Earle Havens, *Commonplace Books: A History of Manuscripts and*

Printed Books from Antiquity to the Twentieth Century (New Haven: Beinecke Rare Book and Manuscript Library, Yale University, 2001).

42. *Bell's Common Place Book, Form'd generally upon the Principles Recommended and Practiced by Mr. Locke* (London: John Bell, 1770), Innes copy held at NAS GD113/1/475. John Bell's was one of at least ten different editions of Lockean commonplace book templates that were published between 1770 and 1820 on both sides of the Atlantic. They came with printed introductions and heads, but were otherwise left blank to be filled out by readers.

43. Swift's quip, "What tho' his *Head* be empty . . . , provided his *Commonplace-Book* be full," reflects the conventional concern that too many commonplacers concentrated on such vacuous truisms; quoted by Robert DeMaria Jr., *Samuel Johnson and the Life of Reading* (Baltimore: Johns Hopkins University Press, 1997), 89.

44. *Bell's Commonplace Book*, 20; quoting *H* 3:255.

45. Thomas Sheridan, *A Plan of Education for the Young Nobility and Gentry of Great Britain* (London, 1769), 98.

46. Notebook of David Boyle, 14–15; compare *H* 5:124–55.

47. Notebook of David Boyle, 77.

48. Ibid., 78. David Boyle was the younger son of Hume's friend the Reverend Patrick Boyle (1717–1798), who had known Hume well while they both lived in London in the mid-1740s; E. C. Mossner, *The Life of Hume*, 2nd ed. (Edinburgh: Thomas Nelson, 1954), 173–74.

49. For Hume's recommendation of history to his female readers, see *E* 563. Hume's expectations for female readers are discussed by Phillips, *Society and Sentiment*, 60–61, 104–5; Phillips, "'If Mrs Mure Be Not Sorry for Poor King Charles': History, the Novel, and the Sentimental Reader," *History Workshop Journal* 43 (1997): 111–31. For Robertson's relationship with female readers, see Katharine Glover, "The Female Mind: Scottish Enlightenment Femininity and the World of Letters; A Case Study of the Women of the Fletcher of Saltoun Family in the Mid-Eighteenth Century," *Journal of Scottish Historical Studies* 25 (2005): 1–20.

50. Hester Chapone, *Improvement of the Mind* (London, 1773), 2:212; Lady Sarah Pennington, *Advice to Daughters*, 4th ed. (London, 1767), 62–63.

51. Hannah More, *Hints Towards forming the Character of a Young Princess* (London, 1805); quoted by St. Clair, *Reading Nation*, 621.

52. NAS GD1/726/10, fol. 3r (compare *H* 1:404); fol. 15v (compare *H* 3:327). Elizabeth may have cross-referenced such historical *minutiae* with her own domestic memorandum or account books, as was the habit of Mrs. Elizabeth Shackleton; see Amanda Vickery, *The Gentleman's Daughter: Women's Lives in Georgian England* (New Haven: Yale University Press, 1998), 127–60, especially 133.

53. NAS GD1/726/10, fols. 26v–27r (compare *H* 4:351–52). For the comparison with Elizabeth's notes on Queen Elizabeth I, see Towsey, "Infant Son," 79.

54. NAS GD1/726/6 Extracts made by Elizabeth Rose from her Reading (1775), 98–99; compare with NAS GD1/726/10, fols. 43v–44v and *H* 5:517, 529, and 537.

55. NAS GD1/726/6, 99; compare *H* 5:529.

56. Allan suggests that "responses to Hume also provided a reliable measure against which the political health and vitality of each individual reader could be accurately and reassuringly calibrated"; see *Making British Culture*, 213.

57. NAS GD1/726/1, Diary of Elizabeth Rose, [unpaginated].

58. Mark Towsey, "'Observe her Heedfully': Elizabeth Rose on Women Writers," in *Women's Writing* 18, no. 1 (2011): 15–33.

59. NAS GD1/726/9, Extracts made by Elizabeth Rose from her Reading (1806), 75ff; see Towsey, "Infant Son," 84–85.

60. Jacqueline Pearson, *Women's Reading in Britain, 1750–1835: A Dangerous Recreation* (Cambridge: Cambridge University Press, 1999), 171.

61. Elizabeth Hamilton, *Memoirs of Modern Philosophers* (Bath, 1800), 1:107–8.

62. *The History of Melinda Harley* (London, 1779), 36–37.

63. Martha Somerville, *Personal Recollections, from early life to old age of Mary Somerville* (London, 1873).

64. NRAS 234, Box 54/II/148, 17 September 1771, Charlotte Murray to John Murray.

65. NRAS 234, Box 25/II/8, 7 January 1776, Duchess of Atholl to her son (the emphasis is mine).

66. NRAS 234, Box 49/I/32; 5 February 1762, Duchess of Atholl to John Murray.

67. Pocock, *Barbarism and Religion*, 2:179, 261. Allan points out that some English readers considered Hume to constitute "a threat . . . to a sense of English nationhood itself," *Making British Culture*, 216. For Scottish readers' uses of their own national history, see my *Reading the Scottish Enlightenment*, chapt 7.

68. Colin Kidd, *Subverting Scotland's Past: Scottish Whig Historians and the Creation of an Anglo-British Identity, 1689–c. 1830* (Cambridge: Cambridge University Press, 1993), especially 209.

69. T. F. Henderson, "Murray, John, third duke of Atholl (1729–1774)," rev. Robert Clyde, *ODNB*.

70. Towsey, "Patron of Infidelity," especially 107–11.

71. *H* 1:xxxix–xl. For Hume's "My Own Life" and Smith's "small addition" to it, see Sher, *Enlightenment and the Book*, 55–56.

72. Towsey, "Patron of Infidelity," 113.

READING HUME'S *HISTORY OF ENGLAND*: AUDIENCE AND AUTHORITY IN GEORGIAN ENGLAND

David Allan

"The advantages found in history seem to be of three kinds, as it amuses the fancy, as it improves the understanding, and as it strengthens virtue": so reckoned David Hume in the whimsical essay "Of the Study of History," first published in 1741 (*E* 565). But how far did his own *History of England*, which began to appear more than a decade later, justify this carefully worded proposition about the intimate relationship between works of historiography and the individuals who read them? Much interest, of course, has lately surrounded the evaluation of this particular text by other contemporary writers whose formal responses to reading it were ultimately to be preserved in print.[1] It remains far less clear, however, how those who did not feel compelled—or who simply lacked the opportunity—to cast their experiences as readers in published form responded to this most popular and most problematic of historical works. Yet we can be almost certain that the *History*, given what was clearly a long and complicated publication history during Hume's lifetime and in the succeeding decades, at least *ought* to have been a reasonably familiar feature in the literary and intellectual landscape populated by a wide and growing community of literate men and women. It also seems a safe bet, given some of the evidence that has come down to us, that it must actually have been read by individuals in a great variety of settings—not all of them entirely propitious, or so one might have thought, for the concerted study of historical literature.

Travel overseas, for example, for all its immense practical inconveniences at this period, was clearly no bar to continued devotion to the modern British classics, among which the *History* was increasingly numbered by contemporaries—hence Lieutenant George Hopper of the Eighty-Ninth Regiment, when stationed at Halifax, Nova Scotia, in 1813, read this work, just like he read the poetry of Hume's compatriot Robert Burns, with great avidity, perhaps with the help of the local garrison library, while we know that George Whitmore of Lower Slaughter in Gloucestershire, who went to France in 1785 for his health (and, unfortunately, died there), took with him some of his favorite reading, which included the *History* as well as Tobias Smollett's *History of the World*.[2] Even prisoners, in a striking manifestation of the increasingly progressive values of an age of Enlightenment, seem to have retained access to Hume's peculiar perspective on England's historical development, though it is hard not to wonder how men as different as James Malton, the outspoken radical activist who was incarcerated in Coldbath Fields and devoured the *History* "with great interest and profit," and the considerably more urbane Marquis de Sade, who made sure to take his personal copy with him into the Bastille in 1784, might have reflected on Hume's subversive analysis of political liberty in the most painfully ironic of personal circumstances.[3] Most readers, however, needless to say, can only have encountered the *History* in somewhat less exotic surroundings than these. In this essay I want first to ask if we can say anything more systematically about who Hume's early English readers might have been and in what situations they might most often have come across the *History*; and then second to explore some of the evidence for the ways in which such people actually responded to the experience of reading this most multifaceted account of their own national history.

I

It is clear that personal owners of Hume's *History* must have been legion from the mid-1750s onward, representing literate English men and women from most social classes, most walks of life, and most outlooks and inclinations. In particular, the evidence confirms that aristocrats and landed gentlemen, many of them conspicuously well-read and so unlikely to spurn a text that was increasingly acknowledged as being canonical for the knowledgeable student of serious modern literature, were very often likely to keep a copy of Hume on their groaning bookshelves. Prominent individuals who did so, and whose substantial private book collections can easily be reconstructed from contemporary catalogues, ranged from the fifth Earl of Chesterfield at Eythorpe in Buckinghamshire and the Fourteenth Earl of Clanricarde at Warnford in Hampshire in 1809 to the eighth Earl of Bristol at his London house, the fifteenth Earl of Suffolk at Charleton in Wiltshire in 1797, the third Earl Cowper at Cole Green in Hertfordshire, and the thirteenth Baron

St. John at Melchburne in Bedfordshire.[4] Among the untitled gentry, whose collections were not necessarily much less impressive than those accumulated by the peers, the same was true of Samuel Tyssen of Narborough Hall in Norfolk, who in 1801 owned the 1763 eight-volume edition; John Holden of Warwickshire, who that same year had acquired the six-volume 1762 edition; Joseph Marks of Devon, whose personal library was auctioned in 1807, who had had the 1803 edition in sixteen volumes; and the Norfolk gentleman Joseph Windham, who, when his collection was dispersed in 1811, had owned an unnamed edition, duly claimed, according to an intriguing penciled note in a surviving sale catalogue, by a purchaser named "Bentham."[5] Sir William Wray, a Derbyshire baronet, was in one respect no different from these men whose unusually large collections were auctioned, reasonably enough, in the metropolis. When his rather smaller domestic library finally went under the hammer at Derby in October 1808, an 1802 octavo edition of the *History* was again among the items listed for sale.[6]

If the occupiers of substantial acreages—among whom during this period "bibliomania," as Thomas Frognall Dibdin amusingly described it, was an increasingly epidemic condition—can with predictable frequency be included among the identifiable early owners of Hume's work, so too were the occupants of that other prominent contemporary social group with an entirely justifiable reputation for incurable bookishness: the established clergy.[7] Anglican incumbents in particular were certainly not slow to appreciate Hume's importance as a historical writer, whatever their own intellectual affiliations led them subsequently to make of his troublesome motives. Sir William Wray, who was also rector of Derby, was once more typical. So too were ordinary provincial parsons like Wray's neighbour Richard Chapman, vicar of Bakewell, who still owned the *History* at his death in 1816; Thomas Newton of Calton, who lived across the Staffordshire border and whose books were eventually sold at nearby Ashbourne in 1829, among them a quarto edition of Hume; and Zachary Brooke, rector of Forncet in Norfolk in the 1780s, who actually owned what seems to have been a first-edition set.[8] But the higher clergy were just as likely, it seems, to own their own copies of Hume. Thomas Crofts, chancellor of the diocese of Peterborough in the 1770s, eventually amassed a substantial collection that included a first-edition set.[9] An even more striking case is Thomas Clarke, vicar of the Trinity Church in Hull. A leading figure in that town's burgeoning social and intellectual life as well as a bibliophile of considerable energy and ambition, Clarke must have been uncommonly attracted to Hume's historical masterpiece, to judge from the five different versions of it—a first edition plus further ones dated 1778, 1789, 1792, and 1796—he had acquired by his death in 1798.[10]

Neither the landed elite nor the clergy, however, although obviously making up collectively the most literate segment of contemporary society, enjoyed a monopoly on ownership of works like Hume's *History*. Indeed, middle-class professionals in particular, whose numbers were at this time rapidly increasing, often acquired the same text, as they did other titles of comparable stature and significance, which they increasingly found not only desirable but also affordable for people of their station. Nathaniel Edwards, for example, a Derby solicitor who died in 1826, and Edward Jerningham, another lawyer who lived on Mayfair until his death in 1822, both owned copies of the *History*, as did Dr John Monro, physician and pioneering psychiatrist at London's Bedlam, whose books were auctioned posthumously in 1792.[11] Businessmen and industrialists, groups with rising social profiles in this period and, as purchasers as well as library borrowers, an increasingly important part of contemporary book culture, also sought out the same kinds of books. Thus the Exeter merchant Thomas Binford was able to record a quarto version of the *History* when inventorying his own books in 1768, while Ebenezer Rhodes, a Sheffield master-cutler, whose household collection comprised just 217 items when it was auctioned off, also owned an unidentified edition of the same work in 1828.[12] Occasionally, we can even trace a surviving early copy of Hume to a particular early reader of this kind: the first-edition set belonging to Charles Hudson, for example, a South Sea merchant, survives at the W. S. Lewis Walpole Library in Farmington, Connecticut, while the one apparently owned by one Patrick Murdoch, probably a member of the local merchant class who inscribed his autograph signature on the title-page of the 1754 volume, is now in the possession of Chetham's Library in Manchester.[13]

Hume, of course, was perfectly well aware that "the fair sex" formed an ever more important part of the wider reading public, especially where historical literature was specifically concerned (*E* 564). And interestingly, despite the difficulties involved in documenting their independent ownership of property in this period, this observation seems to have been substantially vindicated by women's early proprietorship of his *History*. The Dowager Lady Selsey, for example, who lived at Newsells in Hertfordshire in 1817, certainly possessed a copy of Hume's work as well as of Robertson's *History of Scotland* and *History of Charles V* and Sir John Dalrymple's *Memoirs of Great Britain and Ireland*.[14] A decade or so later, Mrs. George Trevelyan, wife of the new incumbent of the Somerset parish of Halse, recorded her own possession of a few books, which included the *History*, along with Robertson's *History of America* and *History of Scotland*, Lord Kames's *Sketches of the History of Man* and Robert Watson's *History of Philip the Second of Spain*.[15] Mrs. Freeland, who lived at Westport House in Wareham in Dorset around the same time, had very similar literary tastes reflected in her household book collection: along with Hume's *History*, she owned, just to cite two of the works by other recent Scottish writers, Robert Henry's *History of Great Britain* and Alexander Tytler's *Elements of General History*.[16] It may well therefore be that the *History* was indeed recognized as a standard element in the emerging canon of historical texts to which female readers such as these—as "Of the Study of History" had playfully acknowledged—now looked in particular for instruction and amusement.

II

Georgian readers, notwithstanding their love, where feasible, of buying and owning books for themselves, also habitually flocked together, forming all manner of associations to facilitate the purchase and circulation of printed materials among themselves. In fact, so popular was this practice, which chimed perfectly with the contemporary preoccupation with the benefits of polite interaction and structured sociability, that even individuals who were undoubtedly in possession of very large personal book collections of their own—such as the nineteenth Earl of Exeter, with his sizeable library at Burghley House in Huntingdonshire, who also joined the subscription library at nearby Stamford, or the fourth Duke of Newcastle, who subscribed to a private lending collection at Nottingham—found participation in such organizations effectively irresistible.[17] By the early nineteenth century, every large town had at least one library established on this most agreeable of footings, as a place not only to borrow books but also to linger, to rub shoulders, and to converse. Moreover, as far as one can tell, Hume's *History* was a ubiquitous presence, even frequently appearing among the first items acquired by newly formed associations. At Kendal, for example, the committee decided on 27 January 1795 to order *en bloc* a batch of ten key works, evidently canonical in character and thus an obvious foundation on which to build, including Hume's *History*, Buffon's *Natural History* (1749–88), Gibbon's *Decline and Fall* (1776–88), and Adam Ferguson's *History of the Roman Republic* (1783).[18] Identical thoughts had crossed minds at Wolverhampton the previous year, where the *History*, which ever afterward bore the serial number "1" in the catalogue, was actually the very first work to be accessioned.[19] More generally, those involved in the subscription libraries—which is to say, merchants and urban professionals everywhere, local gentry in the country towns, entire chapters in cathedral cities, together with manufacturers in certain localities, clergymen in most cases, lay and ordained Dissenters in disproportionate numbers, and usually also a sizeable minority of women—tended to recognize Hume's *History* as an essential acquisition for any self-respecting collection, as it clearly was for libraries as widely scattered as those at Worcester, Shrewsbury, Norwich, Newark, Whitehaven, Ipswich, and Lichfield.[20]

The same was true not only of the prestigious intellectual societies that the same kinds of people also founded and frequented but even for the mechanics' institutes and artisans' libraries that they often established in parallel—essentially philanthropic bodies intended to provide instruction and illumination for working-class readers and employees. So the Ipswich Literary Institute and the Newcastle upon Tyne Literary and Philosophical Society, with their genteel and mannered memberships from among the local propertied elites, shared with humbler organizations such as the Liverpool Mechanics' Institute the desire to make available a lending copy of Hume's *History* (in this case, first borrowed on 1 March 1824 by an inquisitive local cabinetmaker named Hugh Campbell).[21] Less structured lending institutions, however, implicitly acknowledged the same work's undeniable canonicity by treating it as a compulsory acquisition. This was particularly so of the book clubs—conventionally distinguished from the subscription libraries by their eschewal of permanent holdings in favor of a continuous stream of new purchases funded partly by the regular sale of older texts.[22] At Hartington in the Derbyshire hills (where the *History* was bought on 14 February 1793), at Stafford (which owned a copy around 1807), and at Winchester (where the first two volumes were purchased as they were published in November 1754 and June 1756, though the first was sold off to a member in September 1755), those who created these small-scale organizations procured copies of Hume's work, perhaps understandably curious about its contents, probably keen to find out more, but also acutely conscious that to know the *History* and to have read it would make them appear more cultivated, more informed, and—above all, as so many of them fretted—more convincingly polite.[23]

Associationalism, though, was never the only or even the predominant context for institutionalized borrowing at this time. Indeed, for many commentators, some as appalled as they were amazed by the spectacular success of what they readily denounced as "book-renting," access to Hume's *History* was through commercially based lending by so-called circulating libraries, who charged fees for entry and for use. These venues soon emerged as one of the defining cultural phenomena of the age, endlessly remarked on by novelists and journalists and extraordinarily widely exploited by Englishmen and women of all social classes.[24] Readers as different as the future George IV, who subscribed to circulating libraries at Bath in the 1790s and Brighton in the 1820s; aristocratic married couples like the Richmonds, the Suffolks, the Haddingtons, and the Howes, who also patronized a profit-oriented library at

Bath; and working-class customers like the Hull painter Christopher Thomson and the Bath domestic servant John Jones, who both joined circulating libraries in their own neighborhoods— all shared in the incomparably liberating experience, hymned by Jane Austen's fictional Fanny Price in *Mansfield Park*, of paying cash to borrow—no questions asked—whatever books their hearts desired.[25] Significantly, many if not most of the entrepreneurs who ran these commercial collections and were necessarily constantly attuned to what the paying public currently wanted to read, made sure to offer Hume's *History* as part of their generally encompassing holdings that often stretched all the way from cheap romantic fiction and ephemeral journalism at one end of the spectrum right through to sober and durable works of divinity, moral philosophy, political science, and historiography at the other.

Certainly few of those contemporaries who visited or who lived at Bath, that iconic center of genteel recreation and socialization, would have been unduly surprised to find the *History* available in such significant local lending institutions as the libraries run at the close of the eighteenth century by shopkeepers like Thomas Gibbons on Bridge Street, Charles Godwin on Milsom Street, and Samuel Hazard on Cheap Street.[26] Nor, it should be said, would the experience in Bath have been unusual, in this respect at least, for in just about every urban community across England there was probably at least one commercial library of this description by the last years of the eighteenth century, willingly (and lucratively) providing local readers with an opportunity to read works like Hume's *History*. At Hereford, for example, those using John Allen's collection around 1780 would have found Hume on the shelves, as would those who frequented Anthony Soulby's at Penrith in Cumberland thirty years later, where an eight-volume octavo edition was kept, and subscribers to Jasper Sprange's library at Tunbridge Wells in Kent ten years earlier.[27] In the larger towns and cities, it would have been even easier for users of the commercial collections to get their hands on the *History*—as it was for patrons of the famous Marylebone Library on Duke Street in London in 1805 and for customers of William Ward's library in the incipient manufacturing center of Sheffield in 1762.[28] In short, whatever the complaints of contemporary critics that the circulating libraries, because of their supposed function in exposing vulnerable women and insubordinate servants to an unrelenting torrent of manipulative and corrosive fiction, were nothing more than "inlets of vice and debauchery," many did in truth offer large numbers of men and women the chance, for a relatively modest outlay in real terms, to read texts like Hume's famous *History of England*.[29]

No less against stereotype, God was sometimes almost as helpful as Mammon in bringing the Great Infidel, and other writers of comparable fame and notoriety, to contemporary readers' notice. Certainly it would be quite wrong to think—though it has been too often assumed—that the network of lending libraries maintained by the Anglican Church in this period existed solely to provide people with theological and classical literature of a rebarbatively old-fashioned kind. Indeed, recent research has confirmed that they often held literature that was both rather more relevant in character and far more recent in origin than many have suspected.[30] Hence minor local collections for which reliable records survive, like the traditional parish library maintained at Whitchurch in Shropshire, the Old Town Library at Ipswich (another parish library that had acquired, as its name suggests, an inclusively civic function), and the much more aggressively exclusive Church and King Library at Bolton in Lancashire (created by local communicants to flaunt their unswerving political loyalism after the French Revolution), as well as historic cathedral libraries such as those at Canterbury and Durham (extant borrowing registers at both places also happily confirm that it was frequently loaned out to readers), all in practice provided groups of Anglicans with free access to a copy of Hume's *History*.[31] In this respect at least, it does not seem unreasonable to conclude that even those of considerable outward orthodoxy may well have come to accept that contemporary English readers, whatever their specific doctrinal commitments, would positively *expect* to be able to consult a work like this, precisely because (rather than in spite of) the considerable interest and controversy that it had generated.

III

Some idea of what library users and book owners like these may have made of the *History*—providing, of course, that they actually removed it from the shelf and opened it—is offered in the first instance by the direct evidence left on the printed page by contemporary annotation in surviving copies. Often, it must be admitted, such intrusions by readers seem to have amounted to little more than an attempt to perform certain basic editorial duties in relation to a text. Just such an intervention in Hume's honeyed prose is what appears to be recorded in the alterations that were made to a copy of the first edition that is now in the Bodleian Library at Oxford. This particular individual plainly also knew the second edition intimately, since it was from a close-to-hand copy of the latter that he or she apparently set out to update the original first-edition text in light of the significant changes that the author himself had later made: where, for example, Hume had initially described the death of Queen Elizabeth in 1603, the passage is carefully given brackets by the reader and a suitable annotation is added, explaining simply "left out in ye 2^d edition"; on King James

I, too, where the first edition had given the simple formulation "Peace was his favorite passion," the addition of a handwritten amendment taken from subsequent editions effectively expands the text so that it now reads, "The love of peace was his ruling passion."[32]

A second early reader who approached an encounter with the *History* in essentially the same way, pen in hand and broadly determined to help enhance the experience of reading Hume by sympathetic amplification of the burden of the original text, was George Joseph Palmer, grandson of Charles Grave, whose copy of the first edition he had inherited and seems subsequently to have kept at his Leicestershire home. Palmer's manuscript note, probably written in the early nineteenth century, was eventually pasted inside the front cover of this valuable family heirloom, and it was presumably intended to provide assistance for anyone—Palmer himself, or perhaps another member of his household—studying Hume's complex account of English politics during the turbulent reign of James II, who happened to be familiar only with the much-altered circumstances of the last years of George III. As Palmer gently explains for the benefit of those whose understanding might be confounded by the unfamiliarity of the terminology:

> Whig is a Scottish, or Irish word for Whig or sour milk; When the duke of York took refuge in Scotland, his party being strongest, oppressed the opposite one, who were forced to retire into the Mountains & lived on Milk, for wch they were reviled by their opposers & called Whigs; they retaliated, & stiled <u>tories</u> or robbers.—Burnet says the word Whig arose from a march to Edinburgh wch Argyle headed called the Whiggamore's Inroad, from the word Whiggam used in driving their horses by the Leith corn carriers.[33]

Obviously striving to be as helpful as possible, Palmer manifestly assumed that such information formed a necessary background for an individual approaching the *History*, increasingly now conceived as the highly particular product of the first half of the eighteenth century, in a rather different political and linguistic context.

Not all the early readers who handled Hume's text with pen at the ready, however, were willing to treat his work quite so kindly. Given the many reservations that published critics and contemporary controversialists were registering about this work, there is little surprise in the fact that not everyone considered the experience of perusing their own well-thumbed copy might be improved merely by a little sensitive collation or, perhaps, some constructive supplementary commentary. Indeed, for some of those who wrote on its pages, the entire work was self-evidently toxic in a number of different ways—a highly dangerous book whose insidious challenge both to conventional religious faith and to public and private morality, or else, when viewed from a slightly different perspective, whose outrageous rejection of received political wisdom about the nature and destiny of eighteenth-century Britain, needed constantly to be countered, or at least contained, by a judicious process of contradictory annotation and intensely combative correction.

This seems very much to have been the considered opinion of Arthur Onslow, Speaker of the House of Commons through the middle years of the century, whose personal copy of Hume's *History*, replete with his own strategic attempts to limit the damage that this work seemed to be capable of causing, is now in the possession of the Houghton Library at Harvard University.[34] An unyielding Whig and self-conscious defender of what might reasonably be thought of as the orthodox interpretation of the history of English liberty, it is, perhaps, not surprising that Onslow should have been affronted by the *History*'s subversive treatment of the nation's political history, for, as a proud advocate of modern parliamentary prerogatives and of the constitutional settlement presided over by the House of Hanover, he naturally interpreted Hume's skeptical analysis as not merely unpleasantly Tory in party affiliation but actually as treasonably Jacobite in motive and consequence. This is why Onslow, faced with the evidence in front of him on the printed page, found it impossible to resist the temptation to confront Hume's continual insinuations, in which the *History*'s author famously cast doubt on the central significance of far-sighted English lawmakers and the ancient English legislature in the long-term evolution of England's freedoms: "I guess the author's meaning; but good Government is the best check," Onslow caviled at one point, where Hume's text had mischievously suggested that convention had usefully limited the power of Parliament; "See the Rolls of parl^t for the contrary," he also scribbled, here trying to deflect Hume's deliberately provocative comment that medieval parliaments had in any case met only infrequently.[35]

Similarly ripostes by another early reader, who was clearly unimpressed with the subversive games that Hume appeared to be playing in the *History*, mark the pages of a composite copy of the first edition that survives at Chetham's Library in Manchester, this time in the form of a series of pedantic challenges to the text's specific wording. In the 1762 volume, for example, beside a passage that discusses the Norman ancestors of John de Warenne, the thirteenth-century Earl of Surrey, this angry student wrote in the margin simply that "this has been stated before," evidently infuriated by what he took to be Hume's wearisome laboring of a point.[36] Equally, in the 1757 volume he objected to the description of William and Mary by 1689 as sovereigns of

England, France, and Ireland, impatiently underlining the second country to be mentioned and writing, presumably now in uncontrollable irritation with Hume's prose, "Should not this be—Scotland?"[37]

IV

Even more eloquent evidence of the reactions of contemporary readers survives in some of the extant commonplace books—essentially sophisticated reflections on people's experiences with texts—which were created during the period.[38] William Constable, for instance, a Yorkshire gentlemen from a long-established recusant family, even went so far as to compile, around 1758, what he called a "Notebook of Extracts from Works of David Hume" that clearly belongs securely to this *genre*. Certainly Constable utilised it to collect materials that, when taken together, amount to a series of excerpts from the *History* that, in an eventuality which may well have intrigued Hume himself, clearly appealed specifically to the committed reader who approached the work from a strongly Catholic standpoint. The printed text's remarks on some monarchs' support for the Reformation, for example, were laboriously copied out by Constable, perhaps because Hume had sought to emphasize their ulterior material motives while also stressing the continuing orthodoxy of most sixteenth-century rulers. As the resulting note now read: "Tho' the prospect of sharing the plunder of the Church had engag'd some princes to embrace the Reformation, it may be affirm'd, that the Romish System remain'd still the favourite religion of sovereigns . . . it reconciles the penitent to his offended Duty."[39]

In much the same way, Hume's assessment of a famous English primate, identified in the *History* (as by many of his own shocked contemporaries) as inclining perceptibly toward Catholicism, again earned Constable's close attention: "though Laud deserved not the appellation of papist, the genius of his religion was, though to a lesser degree, the same with that of the Romish: The same profound respect was exacted to the sacerdotal character, the same submission required to the creeds and decrees of synods and councils, the same pomp and ceremony was affected in worship, and the same superstitious regard to days, postures, meats, and vestments."[40]

As these examples make plain, Constable seems to have been attracted to precisely those parts of the *History* where its author had made observations that, particularly when extracted and viewed in the isolation that a commonplace book made uniquely possible, were capable of being read as comparatively well-disposed toward the traditional Catholic position.

A quite different English reader in many respects was Charles Lee, a distinguished army officer whose subsequent attachment to the colonists' side in the mid-1770s, and then trial for alleged complicity with the British, would eventually make him a hugely controversial figure in early American history. In the 1760s, however, Lee's thoughts, when engaged in diplomatic activities on the Continent, were very much on Hume's *History*, revealing themselves in a strongly worded series of letters to friends and family at home, in which his powerfully Whiggish instincts, and his innate hostility toward authoritarianism, seem to have been the driving intellectual force. In June 1765, for example, while in Poland, Lee chose to comment on the strange local hierarchies with which he was then trying to grapple, but he did so with a direct allusion to Hume's supposed preference for the reimposition of feudal ties in modern British society: "I would to God that our Tory writers, with David Hume at their head, and the favourers of our damnable administration, were to join this noble community, that they might reap the fruits which their blessed labors entitle them to, and that the effects might not fall on harmless posterity."[41]

By March 1766, Lee was at Constantinople, though evidently in no better mood with Hume, when he turned his mind once again to what he took to be the *History*'s seditious aim of advancing the cause of royal absolutism in England:

> On my journey I cou'd not help reflecting upon the vast obligations our Country has to Mr. David Hume and other Monarchical Writers who wou'd entail upon us their favourite absolute Government; at least we must imagine these to be their intentions when they wou'd weaken our jealousy which is the preservative of liberty, and lessen the horrors of despotism. Here they wou'd see their beloved scheme come to perfection; the finest provinces of Europe upon which Nature has pour'd a profusion of her gifts, one continued desert; the few Inhabitants who survive the oppression of Their Tyrants presenting famine and apprehensions of still greater misery on their countenances, to each trifling village burying places of so prodigious extent, as to denote the once existence of a considerable Town, in short every species of wretchedness I most sincerely wish that Mr. Hume and his fellow laborers were to join this happy community that they might enjoy the just fruits of their labours and not entail 'em on innocent posterity.[42]

Similar reservations about what the *History* seemed to imply were still revealing themselves three years later, this time in a letter sent by Lee to the Whiggish man of letters John Hall-Stevenson. On this occasion Lee reported that he had been sketching out his own work of history, "professedly in imitation of Mr David Hume's history of the house of Stewarts [*sic*], wherein I pretend to moderate the decent softening and coloring the ill humour and prejudice of mankind with regard to those injur'd characters—it is likewise dedicated to the same Mr Hume—but I will send you the dedication by which you will judge of the scheme."[43] Lee also added his own "An Epistle to David Hume, Esq." that makes the same point in a slightly different way: "No task can be equally laudable in a philosopher, an historian, and a gentleman, as to endeavour, to eradicate from the minds of our youth all prejudices and prepossessions against the memory of deceased, and the character of living princes; and by obviating the cavils and malice of republican writers, to inspire mankind with more candour in judging of the actions of governments and sovereigns."[44] As late as November 1772, Lee was still fretting about what he presumed to be the corrosive ideological effects of the *History*'s continuing popularity, an obsession clearly pathological enough in character for one kindly but long-suffering friend to feel it necessary to write to him (though we would rightly doubt the accuracy of the fact on which this correspondent decided to base his argument), "Come Lee, and leave Hume to cramb his history down the throats of his countrymen, for few others read it."[45]

The Revd. James Gambier, a Kentish parson around the turn of the nineteenth century, was yet another early reader who seems to have studied Hume intensively but with an understandable nervousness about the work's political ramifications. Like Constable, he ventured a series of notes on his reading in his commonplace book, this time entitled "On Hume's Hist^y of Engl^d." Here, however, showing an interest in critical commentary that seems to have colored his approach to other contemporary works, Gambier transcribed the observations of well-known literary judges on Hume's great work. Richard Hurd, for example, Bishop of Worcester, had been noticeably receptive to certain aspects of the *History*'s achievement, as Gambier's chosen extract made evident: "From Bp Hurd's Dial^s Vol2 p.326. Hurd says in the Text, that 'Eng. Liberty was inclosed in the ancient trunk of the Feudal Law, & was propagated from it': On this passage he gives the follow^g Notes viz. 'This appears even from Mr Hume's own acc^t of the feudal times; incomparably the best part of his H^y of Eng^d.'"[46] But Gambier was himself deeply worried by the wider implications of Hume's analysis of English history, countering Hurd's positive noises about parts of the text with the following transcription from the more antagonistic clergyman Francis Wrangham's *The British Plutarch* (1816). Hume, it was argued in a note copied out by Gambier, had mislead the reader in his treatment of Mary, Queen of Scots, "misrepresenting the conduct of the Reformers toward her" in an account that ultimately had been little better than "an overcharged satire."[47]

To this weighty riposte Gambier also appended the not-inconsiderable hostility of Thomas Jefferson, who for his part had applauded the critique of Hume offered in John Baxter's *A New and Impartial History of England* (1796): as Gambier wrote, "Thos Jefferson, speaking of Hume's *Hist^y*, says "Baxter has perform^d a good operation on it."[48]

Visceral antipathy of this kind, evidently spurred by a burning sense that the *History* posed a fundamental threat to political and religious principles that were widely accepted in English society in the second half of the eighteenth century, also marked the response of an anonymous Northern reader who lived somewhere in Westmorland in the closing decades of the eighteenth century. This man, whose private jottings on his reading subsequently found their way to Yale University, had clearly read and understood enough about Hume's work to feel able to offer his own lapidary judgments on the way in which its obvious merits—essentially confined to its status as high-class literary entertainment—had been more than outweighed by its glaring moral and political deficiencies. As he wrote,

> *Hume* as an historian has long enjoy'd an extraordinary Share of Popularity & his performance seems to be considered by the Majority of Readers, as the best Account of the Affairs of this Nation. His Abilities were competent to the production of an History, which might have surpass'd all the Efforts of his British Predecessors, and if his talents had been exerted with a just regard to Candour & Impartiality & with the sole View of exhibiting a fair & accurate Delineation of the transactions of former Days, his historic Fame would have rested on a more solid basis than that which now supports it. The Spirit of Philosophy which animates his Work gives it a manifest Superiority over most of the English Histories by which it is preceeded. His Style is elegant without affectation, & nervous without an appearance of labour. His Arguments in defence of a favourite Hypothesis possess all the acuteness of Sophistry, though their force is disarm'd by the Application of sound logic & the adduction of undistorted Facts. Under the Pretext of exposing the delusions of fanaticism, the Weakness of Bigotry, & the Arts of selfish & designing Ecclesiasticks, he indirectly endeavours to sap the Fabrick of religion itself & undermine the dearest Interests of Society. His political Principles are adverse to the Claims of Freedom and, under the cloak of impartial discussion, he vilifies the exertions of the patriot and depresses the generous flame of Liberty.[49]

It would be difficult to imagine a more concise, measured, and penetrating criticism of the *History*, as so many early readers seem to have seen it, than this bristlingly hostile assessment by someone who instinctively feared its profoundly ambiguous role in contemporary culture.

Yet another reader, James Smith, a Unitarian wool merchant from Norwich, was equally concerned about the ability of the *History*, precisely because it was superficially such a *good* read, to seduce the unwary into embracing its underlying doctrines. As Smith, who had apparently read it in 1766, wrote in his own commonplace book:

> Hume's abilities as a writer, made his history of England read with great expectation & it answers well to the ingenious character of the Author, his remarks & reflections are extremely judicious & Philosophical, almost always where they are upon the nature dispositions and circumstances of Mankind & Government in general, but when they relate to particular parties, opinions & sects, & even to Nations he is not devoid of prejudice & partiality, which often betrays him into self contradictions, & makes it much to be lamented that it is so difficult for Men of the finest Understandings and the most extensive geniuses, capacities to become true Philosophers & to make themselves masters of their principles & way of thinking.[50]

The same text and the same author long remained a preoccupation for Smith, since he subsequently took up the theme once more, lamenting, rather like Onslow and Lee, the serious ideological difficulties that the *History* continually raised for readers who clung tenaciously to conventional Whiggish principles: "Shew Mr Hume to be an uncandid partial Historian a great favourer of arbitrary principles and measures & an enemy to or detractor of every Genius that wrote in favour of Liberty. What every unprejudiced reader of his History must discover, is also that he always endeavoured to lessen the Character & exploits of the English."[51] Once again, the *History*'s potent challenge to the Whig account of the development of English freedom—seemingly as threatening to political liberty as it was to the very nationhood and self-confidence of so many of its early readers—had proved a major obstacle to complete enjoyment of what was all too obviously Hume's magnificent literary achievement.

V

The fates of the individual copies of Hume's *History* that were produced during the second half of the eighteenth and the first decades of the nineteenth centuries were many and varied, as these examples of how particular early readers actually responded to it have indicated. Indeed, some copies inevitably met an unhappy end, facing total destruction, as did the one that belonged to the Revd. Robert Hunter, vicar of Okeford Fitzpaine in Dorset, who lost the *History* in a disastrous fire on New Year's Eve 1846.⁵² Most copies of Hume's work, however, had somewhat less dramatic careers, inflaming only those who read them—some of them with a consuming passion for his purple prose and racy narrative, even if this natural reaction could also make them feel unmistakably guilty; others with unrestrained horror at his flagrant disregard for the niceties of religious and political piety, though these same people often were not completely immune, as they well knew, to the irresistible charms of his fluent writing and his mordant wit. It is relatively unusual, of course, for the historian to be able to document so precisely the responses that texts stimulate among their long-lost early readers, for by its nature the experience of reading generates far less evidence than the act of writing. But this remains in principle an inquiry eminently worth pursuing, above all because of the insights it promises into the context in which great works were written and the perceptions, beliefs, and arguments that encounters with them helped other people to forge. Fortunately Hume's *History of England*—precisely because it enjoyed, as we have seen, a prominent position in many English contemporaries' complex relationships with printed books—is a rare example of a text with which it is possible to make meaningful progress in this important direction.

NOTES

1. Most notably, James Fieser, ed., *Early Responses to Hume*, 10 vols. (1999; 2nd rev. ed., Bristol: Thoemmes Continuum, 2005).

2. Bristol: Bristol Record Office: 12453(6), Commonplace book of Lieut. Hopper, 89th Regt., fols. 8v–9v ; Gloucester: Gloucestershire Record Office: In D45/F39, "Catalogue of Mr Whitmore's Books, 1ˢᵗ of Janʸ 1786," fol. 6v.

3. David Vincent, ed., *Testaments of Radicalism: Memoirs of Working-Class Politicians, 1790–1885* (London: Europa, 1977), 111; Simon Schama, *Citizens: A Chronicle of the French Revolution* (London: Penguin, 1989), 391.

4. Farmington, CT: Walpole Library: *Catalogue of the Library of the Right Honble. Earl of Chesterfield . . . taken in June 1778*, 17; British Library: S.C. 820(S), *Catalogue of the Entire and Very Valuable Library of the Late John Thomas, Earl of Clanricarde. . . . January 1809*, 17; Bury St. Edmunds: Suffolk Record Office, 941/77/1, "Earl of Bristol's List of Book's [sic] London August 5ᵗʰ 1815," fol. 1r; Trowbridge: Wiltshire and Swindon Record Office: 88/10/97, "A Catalogue of Books in the Earl of Suffolk's Library at Charleton Taken December yᵉ 6. 1797," fol. 6r; Hertford: Hertfordshire Archives and Local Studies: D/EP/F336, "A Catalogue of the Earl Cowper's Books in the Library at Cole Green. . . . March 1777," 5; Bedford: Bedfordshire and Luton Archives Service: Z181/2, Inventory of property of the late Lord St. John at Melchburne, Beds, 24 October 1817.

5. British Library: S.C. 811(35), *Catalogue of the Entire and Valuable Library of the Late Samuel Tyssen . . .* , 35; S.C. 813(37), *Catalogue of the Magnificent Library of the Late John Holden . . .* , 7;

S.C. 813(7), *Catalogue of Books . . . Including the Library of Joseph Marks . . .* , 16; S.C. S.71(1), *Catalogue of the Entire and Very Valuable Library of the Late Joseph Windham . . .* , 37.

6. Derby: Derby Public Library: Vol. 5348, *Catalogue of the Valuable & Extensive Library of the Late Rev. Sir William Ulthorn Wray . . .* , 22.

7. Thomas Frognall Dibdin, *Bibliomania* (London, 1809).

8. Derby Public Library: Vol. 5348, *Catalogue of Part of the Library of the Late Rev. Richard Chapman . . .* ; Vol. 5348, *Catalogue of the . . . Library of Books . . . the Property of the Late Rev. Thomas Newton . . .* , 8; British Library: S.C. Sotheby.20(1), *Catalogue of the Elegant and Valuable Library of Z. Brooke . . .* , 7.

9. New Haven, CT: Beinecke Rare Book and Manuscript Library, Yale University: *A Catalogue of the Curious and Distinguished Library of the Late Reverend and Learned Thomas Crofts . . .* , 364.

10. British Library: 822.e.19, *Catalogue of a Valuable and Curious Collection of Books . . . Particularly Those of the Late Rev. Thomas Clarke . . .* , 47, 91.

11. Derby Public Library: Vol. 5348, *Catalogue of the . . . Library of Mr Edwards . . .* , p. 15; Stafford: Staffordshire and Stoke-on-Trent Archive Service: D641/3/I/5, "A Catalogue of Books belonging to the Late Edward Jerningham . . . ," fol. 7r; Beinecke Library: *Bibliotheca Elegantissima Monroiana. A Catalogue of the Elegant and Valuable Library of John Monro, M.D. . . .* , 33.

12. Exeter: Devon Record Office: 4508M/F49, "An Account Taken of My Books the 25th October 1768. Thos Binford," fol. 2r; Derby Public Library: Vol. 5348, *Catalogue of Mr E. Rhodes' Valuable Library . . .* , 7.

13. Walpole Library: 53 H882 754b.

14. Hertfordshire Archives and Local Studies: D/ERy/B527, "A Catalogue of Books at Newsells Library Herts, the Property of the Right Honble. Lady Selsey. May 27th 1817," fols. 10r, 12r, 16r.

15. Taunton: Somerset Record Office: DD/SF 4208, Catalogue of Books, n.d., 4, 10–11, 23.

16. Dorchester: Dorset Record Office: D/FIL F101, Inventory and Valuation of Books of Late Mrs Freeland, 13–14, 30.

17. David Allan, *A Nation of Readers: The Lending Library in Georgian England* (London: British Library, 2008), 70, 67.

18. Kendal: Cumbria Archive Service: WD/K/192, "Minutebook of the Kendal Library," 2.

19. Stafford: William Salt Library: bS2072, *Catalogue of Books belonging to the Wolverhampton Library . . .* (Wolverhampton, 1835), 60.

20. Worcester: Worcester Public Library: M368/W018.1, *Catalogue of the Worcester Library* (Worcester, 1818), 31; Shrewsbury: Shropshire Records and Research Centre: D87.6, *Catalogue of Books Belonging to the Subscription Library in Shrewsbury* (Shrewsbury, 1812), 43; Norwich: Millennium Library: N018.2, *A Catalogue of the Books belonging to the Society of the Norwich Public Library* (Norwich, 1792), 55; Newark: Newark Museum: L017, *A Catalogue of the Newark Library* (Newark, 1825), 36; Whitehaven: Cumbria Archive Service: D/LONSW20/2/1, *Catalogue of the Books Belonging to the Whitehaven Library* (Whitehaven, 1808), 13; Ipswich: Suffolk Record Office: 027.24264IPS(1), *Laws for the Regulation of the Ipswich Public Library* (Ipswich, 1791), 18; Lichfield: Lichfield Library: Library History Box, *Catalogue of the Books belonging to the Permanent Library, Lichfield* (Lichfield, 1815), 12.

21. *An Account of the Liverpool Mechanics and Apprentices' Library . . .* (Liverpool, 1824), 24.

22. Allan, *Nation of Readers*, chap. 2.

23. Matlock: Derbyshire RO: D307/All, "Hartington Union Book Society: Account Book 1787–1805," 14 February 1793; William Salt Library: S/5/17/1, *Laws for the Regulation of the Stafford Permanent Book Society* (Stafford, 1807), 21; Winchester: Hampshire Record Office: 44M69/H2/121, Memorandum book of a book society, fols. 42v, 58r 72v.

24. Allan, *Nation of Readers*, chap. 4.

25. Jane Austen, *Mansfield Park*, ed. Kathryn Sutherland (Harmondsworth: Penguin, 2003), 370.

26. Bath: Bath Central Library: B017.4 GIB, *Catalogue for Gibbons' Circulating Library . . .* (Bath, n.d.), 30; B017.4 GOD, *A New Catalogue of Godwin's Circulating Library . . .* (Bath, n.d.), 9; B017.4 HAZ, *A New Catalogue of Hazard's Circulating Library . . .* (Bath, [1796]), 70.

27. Hereford: Hereford Public Library, 027.3, *A Catalogue of Allen's Extensive and Increasing Circulating Library* . . . (Hereford, [1780?]), 33; Whitehaven: Cumbria Archive Service: D/HUD17/132/2, *Catalogue of the Circulating Library of Anthony Soulby, Printer & Bookseller* . . . (Penrith, 1808), 11; Tunbridge Wells: Museum and Art Gallery: 85/06(1), MS. Catalogue of Sprange's Circulating Library, 1773, fol. 9r.

28. Cambridge: Cambridge University Library: Munby.d.28, *A New Catalogue of the Books Contained in the Mary-Le-Bone Library* (London, [1805]), 29; Beinecke Library, Brit Tracts 1762 W21, *A Catalogue of Ward's Circulating Library* . . . (Sheffield, [1762]), 4.

29. [J. Cradock], *Village Memoirs* . . . (London, 1765), 54.

30. Allan, *Nation of Readers*, 164–83.

31. Paul Kaufman, *Borrowings from the Bristol Library, 1773–1784: A Unique Record of Reading Vogues* (Charlottesville: Bibliographical Society of the University of Virginia, 1960), 57.

32. Oxford: Bodleian Library: BOD DD35, 36 Jur., vol.1:2; 1:5.

33. Lewis Walpole Library: 53 H882 754b.

34. Cambridge, MA: Houghton Library: *fEC75 H8823H.

35. Ibid., vol.5:244.

36. Manchester: Chetham's Library: W.6.28, 64.

37. Ibid., W.6.32, 459.

38. The literature on commonplace books is exceptionally thin, but for introductions, see Earle Havens, *Commonplace Books: A History of Manuscripts and Printed Books from Antiquity to the Twentieth Century* (New Haven: Yale University Press, 2001); Ann Moss, *Printed Commonplace Books and the Structuring of Renaissance Thought* (Oxford: Clarendon, 1996); Richard Yeo, "Ephraim Chambers' *Cyclopaedia* (1728) and the Tradition of the Commonplaces," *Journal of the History of Ideas* 57 (1996): 157–75; P. Beal, "Notions in Garrison: The Seventeenth-Century Commonplace Book," in *New Ways of Looking at Old Texts*, ed. W. Speed Hill (Binghamton, NY: Medieval and Renaissance Texts and Studies, 1993), 131–47.

39. Beverley: East Riding of Yorkshire RO: DDCC/150/25, "Notebook of Extracts from Works of David Hume," fols. 2r–2v. This passage was later revised by Hume, but it exists in this form in *History of Great Britain*, 2 vols. (Dublin, 1755), 1:41.

40. "Notebook of Extracts," fol. 3v; cf. *H* 2:224.

41. *The Lee Papers 1754–1811*, 4 vols. (New York, 1871–74), 1:40–41.

42. Ibid., 1:43.

43. Ibid., 1:101.

44. Ibid., 1:103.

45. Ibid., 1:114–15.

46. Maidstone: Centre for Kentish Studies: U194 F9/2, Revd J. E. Gambier, Commonplace Book, 1789–, fol. 176r; Richard Hurd, *Works*, 8 vols. (London, 1811), 4:80.

47. Commonplace Book, 1789–, fol. 176r. For the source, see Wrangham, *The British Plutarch*, 6 vols. (London, 1816), 1:492n. Wrangham's critique of Hume was actually very extensive, although confined to intermittent footnotes: see ibid., 1:496n; 1:561; 2:332n; 2:370n; 3:12n; 3:67n.

48. Commonplace Book, 1789–, fol. 168v. The source is *Works of Thomas Jefferson*, ed. Paul L. Ford, 12 vols. (New York: G. P. Putnam's Sons, 1904–15), vol. 10, Jefferson to John Norvell, Washington, 14 June 1807. See also Mark G. Spencer, *David Hume and Eighteenth-Century America* (Rochester: University of Rochester Press; Woodbridge, Suffolk: Boydell and Brewer, 2005), esp. 253–59.

49. Beinecke Library: Osborn Shelves fc. 152, "Anon. Commonplace book," fols. 109r–109v.

50. Norwich: Norfolk Record Office: MS4379, T138C, "A Catalogue of Title Pages of Books Read . . . 1762–1786," 52–53.

51. Ibid., 171.

52. Beinecke Library: Osborn Shelves d.133, "Anon. commonplace book," 89.

MEDIEVAL KINGSHIP AND THE MAKING OF MODERN
CIVILITY: HUME'S ASSESSMENT OF GOVERNANCE IN
THE HISTORY OF ENGLAND

Jeffrey M. Suderman

David Hume paused in the middle of his second medieval volume, the last of *The History of England* to be published, to consider the reign of one of England's most glorious monarchs, declaring: "There is not a reign among those of the ancient English monarchs, which deserves more to be studied than that of Edward III" (*H* 2:283). Such an endorsement could have been made by any of a multitude of admiring chroniclers since the time of Froissart. But Hume was no antiquarian. He was a moral philosopher, a political essayist, and a philosophical historian who had by the end of the 1750s attracted a large and admiring popular audience. One suspects that he did not intend to offer up Edward's reign merely as an uncomplicated model of worthy kingship. And indeed Hume was quick to add: "Yet on the whole it appears, that the government, at best, was only a barbarous monarchy" (*H* 2:284). Hume seemed to suggest that although Edward III was a great king according to an antiquated standard of governance, he fell short of being a monarch worthy of the admiration of an enlightened audience. Nevertheless, there were a handful of rulers from these same barbarous ages who deserved to be called great kings, even by an enlightened historian. How did Hume distinguish between the deserving and the undeserving?

The modern reader, already inclined to ignore Hume's *History* in favor of his more overtly philosophical works, is tempted to pass lightly over the assessments of England's kings scattered throughout the medieval volumes. Hume himself had written, in an earlier volume on the Tudor period, "Whoever carries his anxious researches into preceding periods is moved by a curiosity, liberal indeed and commendable; not by any necessity for acquiring knowledge of public affairs, or the arts of civil government" (*H* 3:82). The medieval volumes were sequels of a kind, written to capitalize on the growing success of the Stuart and Tudor histories, and aimed less at a scholarly than at a popular audience.[1] One wonders if Hume's heart was really in these final volumes. Their organization is familiar, even old-fashioned, as if the iconoclastic philosopher could find no more innovative structure than an annalistic, reign-by-reign narrative. They were researched and written quickly relative to their bulk and to the breadth of the period covered. By the time he reached the fifteenth century, Hume could not help betraying obvious distaste, even revulsion, for the barbarity and lawlessness of European society and government before the modern age. Nevertheless, the modern reader should not forget that the two medieval volumes, appearing at the end of 1761, constituted the last major production of his literary career. His political and economic essays were almost all behind him, and there and in the earlier volumes of the *History* Hume had largely vented his spleen against the historical prejudices of Whigs and Tories. He had perfected his talent for character analysis by fashioning, in the style of his beloved Plutarch, moral and political assessments of nearly all of England's rulers. In a real sense, then, the medieval volumes represent Hume's most seasoned judgments on the nature of executive government. This matters because Hume had said remarkably little in his formal political essays about the qualities and character of a governor. But here in the medieval volumes we find ample reflections on the subject, covering the widest spectrum of ruling personalities from the very best to the very worst.

Moreover, Hume's assessment of medieval kingship throws light on a theme very much at the heart of Hume's entire body of work, that of civility. The origins and development of modern civility is perhaps a theme less obvious than that of liberty, on which a number of modern scholars have focused their attention.[2] But Hume's conception of liberty, unlike that of his supposed Whiggish nemeses, was merely one aspect of a wide-ranging account of the origins of civility, perhaps the greatest of Hume's goods. Hume consistently argued that there can be no true liberty without the rule of law, no law without the strict enforcement of equality before the law, and no such order without strong executive governance.[3] If such civility (which included liberty) existed in fact in Hume's enlightened age, it would seem to follow, even before examining the case a posteriori, that monarchs played some significant part in its origins. Which English monarchs then, according to Hume, most effectively employed their powers in the realization of the rule of law and of civility? And which monarchs, despite their fame, failed to advance England toward its civilized condition?[4] This essay will consider Hume's assessments of the characters and ruling abilities of the English monarchs found in the medieval volumes of his *History of England*, leaving the Tudors to another occasion and ignoring the better-studied and more controversial Stuarts.

Kings, whether they intended to or not, played a surprising and significant role in the creation of modern civility and of liberty.[5] The emergence of these goods was far from inevitable, but neither was it entirely accidental or inexplicable. Despite Hume's enlightened interest in conjectural history and sociological forms of explanation, he gave a great deal of credit to individuals in determining the course of England's constitutional development. And it was most often kings who had the capacity and interest to challenge the entropic tendencies of baronial power and the universalistic ambitions of the Church. In fact, it may have been the aggressive ambitions of a very few monarchs that did most to create the conditions permitting the development of the modern rule of law. If kings were critical agents in the emergence of civility, and consequently of liberty, then Hume was taking a broad swipe at the competing political prejudices of his age, employing a Tory cast of characters to tell a very Whig story.

―――

The worthiest English kings in Hume's story are easy to identify because they are few. They are found almost exclusively in the medieval volumes. The first (and really the only) monarch to merit Hume's unqualified praise is Alfred the Great (who reigned 871–901 by Hume's reckoning).[6] Hume depicts this celebrated monarch as the perfect mix of warrior and scholar, suggesting that it was the judicious balancing of these characteristics that accounts for his greatness (*H* 1:74–75, 80). Though inclined by nature to learning and literature, Alfred put aside his books to take up arms "in the defence of his people" (*H* 1:64), thereby turning back a seemingly overwhelming Danish invasion and creating lasting defenses against further incursions. Here Hume's narrative is reminiscent of Livy's account of Rome under the shadow of Hannibal; the invaders are made as ravenous as polite prose will permit and the Anglo-Saxons are brought to the depths of despair so as to make Alfred's remarkable adventures and military triumphs all the more memorable (*H* 1:66–69). Thus Alfred justly earned the title "Founder of the English monarchy" (*H* 1:74). But military accomplishments alone would not have merited Alfred glory beyond his barbarous age. Hume's more substantial admiration is reserved for Alfred's creation of a civil administration and judicial system; his encouragement of learning, commerce, and industry; and his unusual regard for liberty, which Hume equates not with wild Saxon freedom but with the acquisition of knowledge and morals (*H* 1:75–81). Without his martial and active qualities, Alfred could not have been a successful king to his own people. Without wisdom, learning, and love of law, he could not have been a worthy king in the eyes of enlightened posterity. The two very different sets of qualities together made Alfred—that rarest of beings—not merely a good but a great king, one who raised the very standards of worthy kingship. Alfred was not the only Saxon king to have been skilled in arms and leadership, but the rest of the Saxons are nearly an undifferentiated rabble in Hume's account, hardly rising above the treacherous standards of their age. In fact, Alfred is so unequaled as to be almost useless to a philosophical historian, too singular to have established a permanent standard of governance for a barbarous age, too virtuous to be faulted even by the most partisan of modern historians. Neither Whig nor Tory can find much to criticize in his reign, and so he remains universally praised for having shared so little in the prevailing spirit of his age. But Alfred does serve to highlight two characteristics that Hume will find in all of his most worthy kings: military ability—one might even say ambition—combined with a love of law and of learning.

The truly reprehensible English kings are nearly as rare in Hume's *History* as the worthy rulers. Hume gives particular attention to two. The first, John (r. 1199–1216), is as easy to despise as Alfred is to admire, a failure by the standards both of his age and of posterity. Hume characterizes him as "nothing but a complication of vices, equally mean and odious; ruinous to himself, and destructive to his people. Cowardice, inactivity, folly, levity, licentiousness, ingratitude, treachery, tyranny, and cruelty, all these qualities appear too evidently in the several incidents of his life, to give us room to suspect that the disagreeable picture has been anywise overcharged, by the prejudices of the ancient historians" (*H* 1:452). The unanimity of evidence and the absence of any obvious party interests mean that Hume can find no reason this time to disbelieve his sources. John was a poor leader of men, "always disgraceful" in the eyes of his nobility and "slothful and cowardly" in the defense of the realm, particularly in the case of Normandy (*H* 1:420, 416). Not only did John lack the chivalrous accomplishments of his brother Richard, but he was characterized by "stupidity and indolence," "imbecillity," viciousness, and lawlessness (*H* 1:416, 420, 378, 438). Moreover, he bore the criminal guilt of treason against his brother, and of the murder, by his own hand, of his innocent nephew, Arthur (*H* 1:395–96, 414). And if these incidents are not sufficient to horrify a polite audience, Hume finds in John a "natural propension to tyranny" (*H* 1:427), suggesting that the offensiveness of his rule derived from something inherent in his character rather than from any specific acts that might be excused as prudent necessities in other monarchs. John showed contempt for the system of laws so painstakingly created by his worthy father, reinforcing Hume's belief that laws once established, though innovations in their time, become part of the constitution and therefore binding on future generations. And for once, Hume finds that the self-serving barons were right to adhere tenaciously to "the defence of their liberties" (*H* 1:449). John was a thoroughly bad man, who, like the Stuart king James II, placed his private interests in defiance of the public good. His governance was consequently lazy and incompetent, creating no lasting order to balance his crimes. John's unforgivable failing was not in having exercised too *much* kingly power, but in having exercised too *little* vigor in pursuit of his public authority. Vigorous government, which is apt to be called tyranny in a more civilized time, was necessary to basic order in a lawless age.

Hume's condemnation of Richard III (r. 1483–85), like that of John, is based largely on moral considerations. Richard's unfitness for royal office was owing to a deficiency of humanity rather than of talent. Hume finds no objections to Richard's Yorkist lineage per se, which was better founded than Henry Tudor's. He certainly admires Richard's principled and competent father, Richard Duke of York, who might have made an excellent king. He recognizes King Richard's vigor and ruling abilities, his "courage and capacity" (*H* 2:518), and finds no evidence of the remarkable laziness or debauchery that had characterized the awful John. Yet Hume's hatred of Richard (we should say *Gloucester*, since Hume never quite accepts his right to rule) seems much more deeply felt than his disgust with John or any other ruler in the *History of England*. Hume regards Richard as a man whose passions were entirely self-serving, devoid of "all principles of honour and humanity" (*H* 2:499). He seems eager to attribute all of Richard's actions to the blackest of motives, perhaps unfairly considering that by the end of his project he well knows what moral niceties must be trampled by successful medieval kings. But as in the case of John, Hume seems most offended by Richard's inability to feel the natural ties of family, as in the murder of his helpless nephews, the famous princes in the tower. Indeed, Richard appears devoid of any humanity whatever, exemplified by the "utmost coolness and indifference" with which he murdered his political enemies (*H* 2:500). It seems Hume is here giving voice to the offended standards of common life. But why, in a century of unsurpassed betrayal, does Hume single out Richard's "most horrid crimes" and "detestable enormities" (*H* 2:518, 517)? Is he merely pouring onto Richard all the bile he feels toward a detestable age which Richard's reign so fittingly brought to an end? Or does Hume regard Richard's crimes as real enormities beyond even the pale of necessity, unjustified by any subsequent period of peace and law? The latter seems more likely—even Richard's contemporaries were shocked by his crimes (*H* 2:514–15). They served no greater good, offering to posterity only a "contagious example of vice and murder" (*H* 2:518). Unlike our modern historians, Hume retains little hope that Richard's ultimate character portrait might have been more balanced had he lived longer.[7] Good kings, like saints, may be forgiven their occasional sins, but bad men will never, by their own efforts, serve the greater good. In Hume's judgment, a bad man will always make a bad king. But it does not follow that a bad reign necessarily means the incumbent is deserving of moral condemnation.

The unworthy and even the disastrous kings in the *History of England* were not all bad men by Hume's moral reckoning. Most were the unfortunate victims of the cruelty of their times. "It is a shameful delusion in modern historians," says Hume, "to imagine, that all the ancient princes, who were unfortunate in their government, were also tyrannical in their conduct, and that the seditions of the people always proceeded from some invasion of their privileges by the monarch (*H* 2:173–74). Some, such as Edward II (r. 1307–27), met horrible and undeserved ends, earning Hume's humane pity. Although free of most royal vices (except the common weakness of favoritism), Edward was demonstrably unfit for executive office. He is even chastised by Hume for the surprising weakness of having failed to subdue Scotland (*H* 2:147–48). But Edward was no tyrant, and Hume suggests that his undoing was precisely his failure to become one. The English of that age, the "most intractable and most turbulent subjects in Europe," demanded a firm hand, and Edward, though "innocent and inoffensive" in his private character, ended a victim of the "turbulence of the great, and madness of the people" (*H* 2:199, 173–74). Edward's great-grandson, Richard II (r. 1377–99) met a similar end and for similar reasons. Despite early signs of promise, Richard proved to be "a weak prince, and unfit for government," though much less arbitrary than his beloved grandfather Edward III (*H* 2:323–24, 318, 324). Again, Hume suggests that it was the weakness of the crown, rather than any specific act of tyranny, that accounts for the troubles of this reign; "instead of being dangerous to the constitution, . . . [Richard] possessed not even the authority necessary for the execution of the laws" (*H* 2:318). The true tyrants of the age were "the princes and chief nobility" (*H* 2:303), responsible for countless acts of revenge and injustice. "The manners indeed of the age were the chief source of such violence: Laws, which were feebly executed in peaceable times, lost all their authority during public convulsions: Both parties were alike guilty: Or if any difference may be remarked between them, we shall find, that the authority of the crown, being more legal, was commonly carried, when it prevailed, to less desperate extremities, than was that of the aristocracy" (*H* 2:324). The infant parliaments of the age were the fickle creatures of noble factions rather than the guardians of law (*H* 2:319, 322, 483). Richard, though unworthy, was a lawful king.[8] He, like the unfortunate Edward II, met a horrible and inhuman end at the hands of his vassals, the great men whom he had offended with his weakness.

These unfortunate reigns are recounted in the final chapters of the medieval volumes, among the weariest in the entire *History of England*. Perhaps Hume can no longer hide his impatience with the seemingly endless catalogue of crimes, or his contempt for the behavior of powerful men, heaping blame on all parties and on the general manners of the age. But there is perhaps a subtler point here on the nature and meaning of tyranny. Tyranny, Hume seems to argue, is neither the antithesis of liberty nor a simple corruption of the legitimate office of a monarch. No English king has ever been great who has not imposed on his people profound changes in law and administration, and new habits of governance. The second Edward's want of tyranny endangered not only the peace and order of the kingdom but also the reforming legacy of his father. Edward I's more vigorous form of tyranny, as we shall see, had been indispensable to the humbling of the elite estates and the creation of both the rule of law and the House of Commons. In fact, the first Edward's innovations can hardly be called tyranny at all, for how could they have offended principles that Edward himself was in the very process of creating? The English free men of that age were no freedom-loving people. They were, by evidence of their manners during the reigns of several mild and inoffensive monarchs, ungovernable, knowing nothing of the rule of law, and having therefore no legitimate claim to the benefits of liberty. If the want of liberty was the consequence of weak governance, then perhaps liberty itself, at least that which can be found in the medieval world, depended on the efforts of bold and powerful monarchs. The term "tyranny," if applied equally to innocent but powerless kings and to vigorous and innovative monarchs, can have little meaning. Thrown about incautiously by party apologists, it is a term that should be used with greater care by philosophical historians. Hume's assessments of the remainder of England's monarchs will require finer historical judgments.

These have been the easy cases. Most English monarchs were neither as good nor as bad, nor as unfortunate, as these. The majority receive mixed assessments from Hume, tending to be either sadly ordinary in their abilities or hopelessly representative of their barbarous times. Such are the majority of the Anglo-Saxon kings, though Hume recognizes there is simply not enough evidence to construct well-rounded character portraits of most pre-Norman kings. Some monarchs are too significant and well known to be so easily dismissed; they combined remarkable talents with powerful personalities, but cannot be fitted easily into the ranks of good kings. The Tudors are notably of this category, inspiring Hume to his loftiest displays of ambivalence. One such king in the medieval volumes is William the Conqueror, without question a brilliant war leader, hardworking and able, who profoundly altered the course of English history, but who was unmistakably tyrannical and lacking in human feeling. Still, "the foundations which he laid were firm and solid, and . . . amidst all his violence, while he seemed only to gratify the present passion, he had still an eye towards futurity" (*H* 1:225). Despite his self-serving intentions, William contributed to the long-term stability of the kingdom and deserves grudging acknowledgment from the honest historian. But he also embodied the worst features of his violent age, and Hume can find sufficient cause neither to praise nor condemn him outright, since England had no knowledge of liberty and few established constitutional rights to offend.

Some medieval kings were admirable by the standards of their own times and even of posterity but have failed to withstand the scrutiny of a more enlightened notion of governance. Richard I (r. 1189–99), elder brother of the despicable John, was an exemplary king by the narrow and superstitious requirements of his age. He was everything that could be desired in a medieval man of arms, "candid, sincere, undesigning, impolitic, violent" (*H* 1:383), and an admirable model of chivalric leadership. "Equally martial and brave," he "passionately loved glory, chiefly military glory . . . [and] seems to have possessed every talent necessary for acquiring it" (*H* 1:393, 403). But here Hume the enlightened historian gets the better of Hume the sympathetic historian. Richard's military accomplishments produced only "a perpetual scene of blood and violence" (*H* 1:403), both at home and against a distant enemy, the Saracens under Saladin, whom Hume much preferred for their superior learning and humanity over the European invaders (*H* 1:393).[9] And Richard's good qualities, much admired by his subjects, were bundled with ones of little use to a wise governor: "He was open, frank, generous, sincere, and brave," observes Hume, but also "revengeful, domineering, ambitious, haughty, and cruel" (*H* 1:403). Hume is forced to conclude that Richard was, like his age, barbarous and inhumane, "so much guided by passion, and so little by policy" that, even in those rare months when he was at home or gave any thought to domestic policy, "his reign was very oppressive, and somewhat arbitrary," and his wars accomplished little but to ensure the economic ruin of his kingdom (*H* 1:377–78, 404). Richard altogether failed to rise above the unworthy standards of his age.

Edward III (r. 1327–77), whom we met at the beginning of this essay, was another such man of his age. He was, to be sure, gratifyingly free of the vices that had blotted the reigns of other monarchs, "a prince of great capacity, not governed by favourites, not led astray by any unruly passion, sensible that nothing could be more essential to his interests than to keep on good terms with his people" (*H* 2:283–84). Hume pays respect to his military accomplishments, describing in detail Edward's remarkable victory at Crecy (*H* 2:229–34), which made him a hero to his nation and to posterity. He shows that Edward's prudence, self-control, clear thinking, capacity for command, and even genius, were together instrumental in bringing his tiny forces to victory over seemingly insurmountable opposition. Hume also acknowledges the glorious court life that so impressed Edward's contemporaries. "This age was the reign of chivalry and gallantry: Edward's court excelled in these accomplishments as much as in policy and arms" (*H* 2:236). While Hume's audience is well acquainted with the glories of Edward's reign, the purpose of his narrative is to lead them, by easy steps, to an unfamiliar conclusion. "The English," Hume suggests innocently, "are apt to consider with peculiar fondness the history of Edward III. and to esteem his reign, as it was one of the longest, and most glorious also, that occurs in the annals of their nation" (*H* 2:271). But Hume quickly turns on his complacent readers, suggesting that "the glory of a conqueror is so dazzling to the vulgar, the animosity of nations is so violent, that the fruitless desolation of so fine a part of Europe as France, is totally disregarded by us, and is never considered as a blemish in the character or conduct of this prince" (*H* 2:272). Hume seems to invite his polite readers to look past Froissart's (one of his chief sources) fawning worship of Edward and to disassociate themselves from vulgar opinion, so as to reconsider the cost of Edward's policies and the price of his glory.

Edward was, even among his peers, "the most haughty and most aspiring of the age," his ill-founded claims to the French throne and "fatal pretensions" abroad (*H* 2:202, 203) beginning the destructive series of wars that had plagued western Europe to Hume's own day. This long Anglo-French rivalry implicitly included the Seven Years' War, in which the British were currently enjoying a string of seemingly miraculous victories even as Hume was composing his account of their fourteenth-century antecedents. But Edward's "foreign wars were . . . neither founded in justice, nor directed to any salutary purpose. . . . The success, which he met with in France . . . procured him no solid advantages" (*H* 2:272). Not only did they do great damage to France, for the sake of which he nominally fought, but also to his own kingdom, which amassed huge debts to assuage his chivalrous spirit (*H* 2:205). His economic policies were, at their most benign, founded in the sort of ignorance and jealousy common to most governments (*E* 309) but were more often pursued through violent and arbitrary means, impoverishing the kingdom for the sake of royal glory (*H* 2:275–76, 279–81). The best consequence of Edward's foreign policy was that it kept the great barons occupied, preventing civil war at home, to the clear benefit of domestic tranquillity (*H* 2:271). But the price was terrible, a fundamental disregard of the rule of law. The barons (as well as their king) kept company with murderers and robbers, shielding them from even the minimal legal restraints. "The gratifying of a powerful nobleman," Hume concludes sadly, "continued still to be of more importance than the protection of the people" (*H* 2:279). And by placing such value on the illusory virtues of chivalry, this glorious age turned its back on the more lasting accomplishments of learning, industry, and commerce (*H* 2:279).[10]

When Hume advises his readers that no age deserves more to be studied than Edward's, he is really inviting them to discontinue the long English tradition of thoughtlessly glorifying a chivalrous reign and to appreciate its miserable material existence and ignorant policies. To complete the passage that began this essay, Edward's government "was only a barbarous monarchy, not regulated by any fixed maxims, or bounded by any certain undisputed rights, which in practice were regularly observed." His kingdom lacked the rule of law, and none among his chivalrous merits could repair this fundamental want of consistency: "The king conducted himself by one set of principles; the barons by another; the commons by a third; the clergy by a fourth. All these systems of government were opposite and incompatible. Each of them prevailed in its turn, as incidents were favourable to it: A great prince rendered the monarchical power predominant: The weakness of a king gave reins to the aristocracy: A superstitious age saw the clergy triumphant: The people, for whom chiefly government was instituted, and who chiefly deserve consideration, were the weakest of the whole" (*H* 2:284). By this standard it would seem that no English era before the Glorious Revolution could produce an admirable reign. How could even an able monarch rule effectively without a firm constitutional foundation? And if such existed, what need of a great monarch? Yet despite the absence of a continuous rule of law, the most admirable monarchs in English history are to be found in these same barbarous ages. It is a curious paradox and requires some explanation.

Readers of Hume's medieval volumes who seek worthy monarchs are made to suffer through two centuries following the death of Alfred the Great to find a king remotely as accomplished in laws, learning, and arms. Then the Norman king Henry I (r. 1100–1135) provides a timely lesson to the polite reader, not in representing the manners of his age but in rising above them. In this era, "laws had . . . very little influence: Power and violence governed every thing" (*H* 1:253n.). Though a usurper of the throne, Henry nevertheless maintained a "profound tranquillity" in his many lands with a minimum of oppression (*H* 1:273). His government, though arbitrary, was "judicious and prudent" (*H* 1:273), much more so than the licentious and ignorant Normans had a right to expect. He administered justice as evenly and resolutely as was possible in light of the "manners and customs of the times" (*H* 1:278). And so, despite his sometimes criminal ambitions, Henry earns Hume's admiration. This suggests that such faults as he had—ambition and treachery—were faults more of the age than of the man. Hume recognizes that, in a violent and lawless age, a wise king cannot avoid all breaches of the law to maintain his throne; "when violence and usurpation are once begun, necessity obliges a prince to continue in the same criminal course" (*H* 1:277). But what most redeems Henry in Hume's eyes, and elevates him above his contemporaries, is his reputation as a man of letters. He was the *Beau-clerc*, "one of the most accomplished that has filled the English throne," who demonstrated "superior eloquence and judgment" (*H* 1:276), qualities indispensable to his lasting greatness, but always balanced by vigorous and forceful displays of authority.[11] Alfred had established the standard of medieval kingship, and Henry had come admirably close to meeting it (*H* 1:276): a truly great king had to be superior to his age in learning, in the administration of law, and in the use of arms.

Henry II (r. 1154–89), like his namesake, would be deemed a worthy king for no other reason than having maintained order and the semblance of law in an age that tended toward either aristocratic anarchy or clerical abuse. But Henry did more. Hume clearly admires his determination to reign in the incipient clerical despotism of Thomas à Becket. That such an ungrateful servant and usurper could have become a popular saint strikes Hume as clear evidence of the incurable superstition of that age. Although Hume finds many blamable moments in Henry's handling of the affair (*H* 1:318, 322), he cannot find Henry guilty of having betrayed England's fundamental laws in his rush to be rid of Becket, for there were no established limits to the exercise of royal authority (*H* 1:319, 361). Considering Henry's "largeness of thought as qualified him for being a legislator" (*H* 1:359), he was by far the more reasonable actor in the controversy, especially in the period following the churchman's banishment. Becket, by contrast, was an inflexible, violent, and aggressive antagonist (*H* 1:325, 330), though Hume is unusually willing to acknowledge the sincerity of his belief in light of the deeply rooted superstitions of the age (*H* 1:333). Henry brought about admirable and lasting improvements to the administration of English justice, protecting the property rights of commoners, curbing the powers of noblemen, limiting the ridiculous immunities of clergymen, and establishing regular circuit courts (*H* 1:359–62). He introduced several innovative taxes, including the first use of scutage (shield-money), a useful and enlightened innovation that helped break down the oppressive customs of feudalism without encroaching on property rights (*H* 1:373–74). Hume goes so far as to call Henry the "greatest prince of his time, for wisdom, virtue, and abilities, and the most powerful in extent of dominion of all those that had ever filled the throne of England" (*H* 1:370). In his retrospective at the end of the reign, Hume finds little to fault in Henry's character, and no criminal ambitions such as sullied the otherwise admirable rule of the first Henry. In all, Hume suggests that Henry II, like Alfred and Henry I, was a great king for having risen so far above the expectations of a barbarous age.

The Norman period, in Hume's view, was hardly better than the Saxon age; it "preserved such a mixture of liberty and oppression, order and anarchy, stability and revolution, as was never experienced in any other age or any other part of the world" (*H* 1:456). Heirs to the throne were liable to be ungrateful and rebellious, nobles feted more for barbaric military feats and superstitious piety than real virtue, and churchmen prone to violence in their pursuit of power and honor (*H* 1:375). The Normans, in sum, were "so licentious a people, that they may be pronounced incapable of any true or regular liberty; which requires such improvement in knowledge and morals, as can only be the result of reflection and experience, and must grow to perfection during several ages of settled and established government" (*H* 1:254). Here is one of the central lessons of Hume's medieval volumes, that liberty is the product of time and custom. But the rule of law was not to be found in the exertions of the common people, who had as yet no voice in government, and certainly not in the intentions of the barons (*H* 1:471, 474). Only, it seems, in the ambitions of a far-sighted king could such hopes of good government be placed. Henry II was, but for the testing of Becket, able to rise above the ills of his time and create a model of governance that anticipated the contours of a more enlightened and law-abiding age. In fact, Hume seems to argue that *only* a monarch of such exceptionally forceful character could have resisted the universalistic ambitions of the Church or the tendency of feudal kingdoms to disintegrate into impoverished baronial autocracies. At the end of the first medieval volume, Hume suggests that powerful kings were hardly the true impediments to English liberty. Instead, they were the only viable authors of the rule of law and the solitary hope of those seeking to escape the "perpetual iniquity and tyranny of the times" (*H* 1:479).

Perhaps Hume's most surprising choice, not just for "the model of a politic and warlike king" (*H* 2:141) but for a truly great and admirable monarch, is Edward I (r. 1272–1307). It is surprising because Edward has usually been known, both before and since Hume's time, as the "Hammer of the Scots," the personification of the English menace to Scottish liberty. Hume, however, admires Edward not in spite of his threat to Scotland's independence, but, as we shall see, in no small part because of it.[12] His account of Edward is one of the most substantial and rewarding chapters in the entire *History of England*.

Edward had shown promise from his youth and was known even during his father's reign as a liberal-minded prince of "scrupulous fidelity" (*H* 2:42–43), a moral quality respected by chivalrous and enlightened audiences alike. He had inherited the throne during a particularly difficult time, when the crown had been reduced to impotence, even contempt, and regular royal government had all but vanished during the long and ineffective reign of Henry III. Edward proved himself worthy of the chivalrous standards of his own age, shining in tournaments and making his reputation on crusade and in the military pacification of Wales. Yet he was also worthy by the standards of enlightened civility, rising above superstitious servility toward the Church, and determining to oversee "an exact distribution of justice, and a rigid execution of the laws, to give at once protection to the inferior orders of the state, and to diminish the arbitrary power of the great" (*H* 2:75). By virtue of his "active and ambitious spirit," he was effective in curbing the influence of the great barons, the "chief obstacle to the execution of justice," and in "restraining the usurpations of the church" (*H* 2:113, 143, 144). And so he justly earned his epithet "the English Justinian" (*H* 2:141). He it was who made Magna Carta an effective part of English law—by forcing the barons to follow it with regard to their own inferiors—rather than an empty symbol of the endless, destructive contest between a self-serving nobility and a despotic crown (*H* 2:75, 122). Not only were his laws numerous and durable, but the very practice of law by judges, lawyers, and the newly instituted justices of the peace became more regular, without the arbitrary meddling of the executive. The various exchequer courts were given distinct responsibilities, allowing mutual checks but also a healthy competition (*H* 2:142). And though he always held himself above his own laws, and was not unwilling to demand arbitrary exactions from his subjects, his taxes were moderate and his mercantile laws encouraged freer trade among his subjects, to the benefit of the kingdom (*H* 2:117, 142–43). In summary, says Hume, "the chief advantage, which the people of England reaped, and still continue to reap, from the reign of this great prince, was the correction, extension, amendment, and establishment of the laws, which Edward maintained in great vigour, and left much improved to posterity: For the acts of a wise legislator commonly remain; while the acquisitions of a conqueror often perish with him" (*H* 2:141).

But Edward was not negligent in conquest, at home or abroad. Hume finds in this English monarch "the ablest, the most warlike, and the most ambitious of all their princes," unmatched in energy and competence (*H* 2:122). While it is true that his foreign ambitions often invited the usual attendants of injustice and dishonesty—a "great source of the misery to which the human race is continually exposed" (*H* 2:133)—nevertheless Edward's undertakings "were more prudent, more regularly conducted, and more advantageous to the solid interests of his kingdom, than those which were undertaken in any reign either of his ancestors or his successors" (*H* 2:140). This is high praise indeed for a monarch whose undertakings included frequent and forceful pacifications of Scotland. Hume can find no legitimate basis for Edward's claim of feudal sovereignty over Scotland, not even in the biased English sources that he favors (*H* 2:88). He recognizes that Edward was far too interested a party to make an impartial arbiter, as he pretended to be, in resolving Scotland's succession issues (*H* 2:87). But Hume does not blame Edward for his unlawful determination to subjugate his northern neighbor, pragmatically concluding that such a conquest was "very advantageous to England, [and] perhaps in the end no less beneficial to Scotland" (*H* 2:88). Here, in the fraught question of the union of the crowns, we see the clear triumph of "reasons of state" (*H* 2:141) over honor, even over strict justice. Perhaps some North Britons among Hume's readers were taken by surprise. Hume does not deny that Edward employed "numerous acts of fraud and violence" (*H* 2:113) to achieve his end, even going so far as to steal the Stone of Scone, but neither does he seem offended by such policies, either as an enlightened historian or as a Scotsman. Hume even admits, "As few monarchs have lain under stronger temptations to violate the principles of equity, than Edward in his transactions with Scotland; so never were they violated with less scruple and reserve." (*H* 2:133). Still, "the advantage was so visible of uniting the whole island under one head" (*H* 2:141) that Hume finds it perfectly reasonable for Edward to seek the subjugation of Scotland. Here, in a remarkable piece of philosophical detachment, he chastises Edward only for the unnecessary severity of his administrative style and the counterproductive assaults on Scottish customs (*H* 2:125, 135), ill-calculated to reconcile the spirited Scots and their ungovernable nobility to vassalage. But on balance, as with Wales, Edward used mainly "wise and vigorous measures for reducing Scotland to a like condition" (*H* 2:141).[13] Edward's aggressive ambitions against his neighbors were no bar to, and almost certainly a necessary part of, his success as a ruler. And so he becomes the very model of a great (albeit barbarous) medieval king, the deserving head, if any there was, of a universal monarchy: "He possessed industry, penetration, courage, vigilance, and enterprize: He was frugal in all expences that were not necessary; he knew how to open the public treasures on a proper occasion; he punished criminals with severity; he was gracious and affable to his servants and courtiers: and being of a majestic figure, expert in all military exercises ... he was as well qualified to captivate the populace by his exterior appearance, as to gain the approbation of men of sense by his more solid virtues" (*H* 2:141).

The good kings of English history were strong and innovative, even aggressive, kings. Far from impeding the rule of law, bold monarchs were more likely than any other candidates to advance the rule of law and protect the kingdom from men "guided more by custom than by reason" (*H* 2:86). More timid monarchs would have been crushed by the domestic challenges faced by Edward, whose farsightedness helped begin the process of "protecting the lower and more industrious orders of the state" from the depredations of the privileged estates (*H* 2:105). It was the foresight of Edward (rather than the dim mists of time) that established the House of Commons as a counterweight against the tyranny of the great barons, who had up to that time been synonymous with parliament (*H* 2:104–5). This "faint dawn of popular government in England" (*H* 2:105) was a check not on the arbitrary rule of the monarch but on the arbitrary self-interests of the feudal barons, responsible for the greater part of the incivility of the age. Thus it was the innovation of a powerful king, who loved glory as much as any ruler in English history, that gave the commons its voice. It should be no surprise, then, that the first incarnation of the House of Commons (*H* 2:109) had no notion of impeding a king to whose machinations it owed its existence. Edward's peaceful innovation in law, which enshrined the financial power of the wealthy denizens of the boroughs—"the true commons"—originated quite suddenly but in time "became customary" (*H* 2:109, 107). And this custom, however recent, has become the foundation of the Commons' present legitimacy.[14]

Hume seldom made direct comparisons of good and bad monarchs, effective and ineffective reigns.[15] Such work his readers had to do for themselves, if they were so inclined. Hume's easy prose and engaging narrative suggest that he did not expect all of them to do so. Still, a few lessons and patterns must have become clear even to the less philosophical members of his audience. The best kings, for example, were always hardworking, while the least effective were usually lazy, a vice abhorrent to the solid middling virtues found in his essays.[16] The worst monarchs, exemplified by John and Richard III, were morally vicious, meaning that they placed their own narrow interests against the larger interests of the community, and above the fundamental demands of sympathy and humanity. But this did not mean that the best monarchs were always selfless, as Alfred came nearest to being. Indeed, most worthy monarchs were relentlessly ambitious. They were always active rulers, even aggressive in the pursuit of their royal prerogatives. This gave them the capacity on the one hand to threaten individual liberties (assuming there were any such to threaten), but on the other to impose order and the rule of law on lesser tyrants, the great barons and churchmen who proved to be the more consistent threats to securing individual liberties. Hume was an Erastian of a kind, hostile to the ruling ambitions of clergymen and determined to bring the Church (a social rather than a spiritual institution) under the rule of the state.[17] But in contrast to his Whig contemporaries, Hume was more scathing of the abuses of lesser princes than of nominal kings. The barons, above all, showed no interest in regular government or the consistent application of law (*H* 2:321, 323). Political slavery was more often the consequence of their petty tyrannies than of the ambitions of great monarchs (*E* 383–84). Kings, then, played a crucial role in the emergence of civility and of true liberty, providing a counterweight against the destabilizing ambitions of violent noblemen and manipulative churchmen. A proper constitutional balance of interests was the chief good that emerged from the chaos of the seventeenth century—this was a real Whig victory and the culminating good of the whole *History*. But only monarchs had ambitions large enough to rise above the localized perspectives of the medieval world and foresee the emergence of *general* laws, which were necessary to the triumph of *personal* freedoms, themselves the necessary antecedents of civil freedoms (*H* 2:524). Hume the historian remained ever cognizant that different circumstances required different kinds of rule; an effective medieval king must never be confused with a modern ruler. The medieval situation was always unsettled (*H* 2:311) and required a strong executive hand. Medieval kings were not in a position to act as constitutional Whigs would have them do; in fact, they had to create the rule of law before it could be applied to them.[18]

One of the chief historical lessons to emerge from Hume's medieval volumes was that weak kings were consistently more dangerous to English liberties than were strong ones. This was not because they were necessarily vicious characters or had any greater propensity to tyranny or arbitrary government, but because they were unable to prevent the more pervasive tyranny of great men (*H* 2:426). Weak monarchs did not inaugurate eras of improved liberty, as naïve Whigs might have imagined, but merely presided helplessly as liberty was eroded by the relentless pressure of humbler despots. The long reign of Henry III (r. 1216–72), for which Hume had a particular contempt despite the king's good intentions, was such an age of "licentious and powerful barons" who enlarged their own liberties at the cost of "outrages and disorders" borne by the lesser estates (*H* 2:11). The power of nobles, wrote Hume, is "always oppressive" and would, if unchecked, "subvert entirely the ancient constitution" (*H* 2:38). Even the celebrated Magna Carta was a threat to liberty, for it originated in a revolt of the feudal nobility against King John and "had set a dangerous precedent of resistance" (*H* 2:29), having been intended by the great barons to provide constitutional protections for none but themselves. Only the forceful innovation of Edward I later in the century extended its protections to all free men. Parliament too, as it took shape, was needed to protect the kingdom from "aristocratical as well as from regal tyranny" (*H* 2:57).[19] Henry III's weakness likewise left him vulnerable to the depredations of Rome (*H* 2:24, 70–72), and to the bigotries of London's citizens and charismatic mayors, who ought to have been defenders of personal liberties, but were, during this age, more liable to align themselves with the barons (*H* 2:46–47, 49–50, 64). Thus, even "the thoughtless and enraged populace" of the towns (*H* 2:201), those most advanced in arts and manufactures, could not be trusted to see the advantages of an enlarged conception of justice and a more consistently applied rule of law. Hume's study of Henry III's "incapacity for government" (*H* 2:64) showed that weak executive authority, vulnerable to the influence of favorites, was itself an arbitrary imposition and a greater threat to public happiness than the rule of able tyrants. The absolutism of the Tudors proved a more effective check on the self-serving ambitions of England's great men (quite the reverse of Montesquieu's argument).[20] Only with the dawn of civility in the time of Elizabeth, during whose long reign arbitrary royal power was effectively extended over the entire population, did the commons become free enough of petty tyranny and ecclesiastical dominion to acquire an inkling of true liberty (*H* 2:525).

The chronological construction of Hume's *History*, seen in this light, was neither unimaginative nor a sop to historiographical tradition. Hume's narrative had a very specific direction and purpose.[21] Unlike the Whigs, the reigning storytellers of his day, Hume did not suggest that history had an inbuilt structure or preferred outcome. But he did nevertheless employ reliable fictions to communicate his enlightened story to a popular audience, which included the casting of recognizable heroes and villains. As with the Whigs, his narrative purpose was to highlight the modern triumph of such admirable ends as civility and the rule of law. But his heroes, the active and purposeful agents of these ends, were not noblemen, superstitious clerics, selfless commoners, nor even religious enthusiasts (later the uncomprehending agents of progress). They were kings. And they were not kings who bent tamely before a timeless constitution, but instead powerful, innovative, and aggressive kings who created the rule of law out of chaos. In other words, Hume was retelling a Whig story with a Tory cast of characters. No wonder his audience was confused.[22]

Did Hume intend his studies of medieval kings to become models of exemplary governance, both good and bad, for his own enlightened age? Did he mean to justify the powers and prerogatives of kings, as a Tory historian might? Hume had no such pedagogical purpose. Despite his implicit list of good and bad kingly traits, Hume offered no definitive and universal model of executive governance. Custom may have been prescriptive, but history was not, as it usually was for Whigs and Tories. Instead, history was a tool for uncovering human nature, particularly the processes by which human habits and customs have been bent and molded to permit the triumph of the modern constitution. Most of the kingly virtues that Hume described would, he knew, have been intolerable in a modern monarch. Different times and circumstances demanded different rulers.[23] Such a conclusion would have been lost on sincere Tories, who had little interest in exploring the empirical foundations of ever-changing customs and political values. Yet the Whigs were no better, for they too were determined to find their party opinions enshrined in the English past. Hume was better positioned to wonder whether his contemporary system of laws would have wanted another English Justinian to overturn and improve it. Even the admirable Edward I had placed himself above the laws that he had wisely forced on his barbarous subjects, an abuse of the law in any modern king. Perhaps Russia would have benefited from a reborn Edward, but Hume had no wish to see such a figure appear in his own Britain. Here lies an instructive paradox: all of Hume's great kings were great precisely because they defied and surpassed the spirit of their (invariably barbarous) times, earning them the admiration of enlightened historians. Nevertheless, great rulers had to be suited to the needs (perhaps more than the spirit) of their times. The modern age, in spirit and in need, had become superior to any tyrant, however gifted.

The rule of law, brought into being primarily through the efforts of great kings, had made these same kings marvelously redundant in the modern world.[24] The lawlessness and inconstancy of the Middle Ages meant that the success of government depended too much on the character of individual kings. Hume was not unaware of political corruption and abuses in his own age; his essays dwelt almost obsessively on the abuse of public funds and the dangerous accumulation of debt that he saw as the chief hazards of his contemporary political world.[25] But he seemed genuinely to believe that his own age had stumbled upon "the most perfect and most accurate system of liberty that was ever found compatible with government" (*H* 2:525). His political essays said much about the rage of parties and about contemporary abuses of liberty, but little about the qualities of monarchs. He had sharp words for a governing Pitt, but where did he ever draw the character of a reigning George?[26] His civilized age had happily (though not inevitably) moved beyond the need of exemplary qualities, even good ones, in its kings, and so his essays offered little advice about the character of a governor. All the tears that Hume shed on behalf of a much-wronged Charles I did not alter the fact that he had no wish to see the return of any such monarch. Even Alfred, scholar and warrior, the wisest and most justly praised of all English monarchs, had no place in the modern constitution.

But Britain was not yet done with its kings. They had still an important role to play in the modern constitution. Hereditary monarchy provided, as it had in remote ages, continuity in government and especially in the court of public opinion.[27] It was a visible symbol of the "habits of order and obedience" (*H* 2:285), which were necessary to the maintenance of the Whig goods of civility and governmental legitimacy. The rule of law, like any habit of mind, had been acquired over a very long period of time (*E* 38–39). Progress and prosperity depended above all on the spirit of an age, that is, on the general state of manners and opinions, which were themselves the products of time and custom. Overly rapid changes could only threaten those beneficial associations of mind and "render the people giddy," causing them to "lose all notions of right and wrong in the measures of government" (*H* 2:323). Thus Hume concluded his great historical project with this reminder: "In each of these successive alterations, the only rule of government, which is intelligible or carries any authority with it, is the established practice of the age, and the maxims of administration, which are at that time prevalent, and universally assented to" (*H* 2:525). This was a conservative conclusion of a kind, but it was far removed from a Tory sentiment, and it did not construct ideological debts to the past in the way that a Whig would, nor pedagogical obligations in the manner of Bolingbroke. The enlightened study of the past was not the veneration of past practices. Perhaps this was the most significant innovation of enlightened historiography. Hume's praise of the vigorous and competent rulers of England's history constituted no model for the present, merely a reminder of a more barbarous and dangerous past. Enlightened audiences did not need to venerate great men in order to appreciate the actions of ancient kings who had, by establishing a more regular rule of law, rendered the arbitrary powers of their descendents obsolete. Good kings, then, were the unwitting parents of true liberty when the common people were in their nonage.

Hume hoped that by showing his audience how their modern freedoms had really been won, he could help spare them from the absolutism that had made such freedoms possible.

NOTES

1. Money was also a factor. Hume was promised £1,400 by Andrew Millar before he had even begun writing the medieval volumes, the first time Hume had ever made such an agreement for a literary work; see *L* 1:314.

2. The theme of liberty has been covered in a number of superb essays: Donald W. Livingston, "Hume's Historical Conception of Liberty," and Eugene F. Miller, "Hume on Liberty in the Successive English Constitutions," both in *Liberty in Hume's History of England*, ed. Nicholas Capaldi and Donald W. Livingston (Dordrecht: Kluwer, 1990). See also Miller's "Hume on the Development of English Liberty," *Political Science Reviewer* 16 (Fall 1986): 127–83. Civility, it seems to me, is a much more pervasive concept in Hume's body of writings and includes not just the consistent rule of law (i.e., liberty), but also literature, empirical philosophy, cosmopolitan manners, free commerce, and widespread material prosperity (even luxury).

3. Hume may have changed his mind on this point. In 1742, he declared that free states (i.e., republics) are by their nature inclined to support the rule of law, while absolute monarchies are by nature inimical to it (*E* 118); law, then, is the long-term consequence "of order and of liberty" rather than of wise lawmakers (*E* 124). But by the time of the *History*, he tended to argue that liberty was the *consequence* of law and order, which seems to give a larger role to the individual creators of law, wise or not.

4. I suspect Hume was more knowingly anachronistic than his frequent attacks on Whig historians, such as the French Huguenot Paul de Rapin-Thoyras, would suggest and despite his historically admirable idea that "it seems unreasonable to judge of the measures, embraced during one period, by the maxims, which prevail in another" (*H* 5:240). Hume did not believe progress was inevitable, but he very consciously preferred modern, even Whiggish, constitutional values.

5. Hume had been concerned with the abilities of monarchs as early as the 1742 essay "Of the Middle Station of Life" (withdrawn after the 1742 edition of the *Essays, Moral and Political*), where he compared the abilities of men of the middle ranks to those of the highest ranks. Among twenty-eight English monarchs since the time of the Conquest, he found only eight to have been of "great Capacity" (*E* 548), none reaching this rank by military accomplishment alone. Did this represent Hume's lasting opinion? It is hard to believe that, having studied in detail the challenges faced by English monarchs, Hume would have maintained that competence in kingship was easier to come by than competence at the bar. As he put it in the essay "Of the Coalition of Parties," composed in 1758 while he was working on the Tudors, "The power of the crown in that age depended less on the constitution than on the capacity and vigour of the prince who wore it" (*E* 644). But this line, though added to 1758–70 editions of the *Essays*, was removed thereafter.

6. Hume's marginal dates inexplicably have 901 for the year of Alfred's death, though modern sources agree on 899. Rapin-Thoyras said 900. Both historians, and most others of the age, took their material from Sir John Spelman's staunchly royalist *Life of Ælfred the Great* (first published posthumously in Latin in 1678 and translated into English in 1709 by Thomas Hearne). For an interesting account of Hume's personal interest in Alfred, see James Noggle, "Literary Taste as Counter-Enlightenment in Hume's *History of England*," *Studies in English Literature 1500–1900* 44, no. 3 (2004): 626.

7. Hume's account of Richard III depended heavily on Thomas More's famous biography, on which was also based Shakespeare's even more famous portrait of a king supposedly deformed in body and in mind; cf. *H* 2:518. See the historiographical introduction to Charles Ross, *Richard III* (Berkeley: University of California Press, 1981). Hume, says Ross, "though a great philosopher, deserves only a low rating as an historian" (xlix). Certainly his account of Richard III's

reign is not one of Hume's more balanced character portraits, even in comparison to other eighteenth-century accounts.

8. Hume's assessment of Richard II is controversial—Hume saw him as a victim of his times, whereas Whig historians saw him as a tyrant comparable to James II; see Constant Noble Stockton, "Hume—Historian of the English Constitution," *Eighteenth-Century Studies* 4, no. 3 (1971): 285–88 and 290–91. For an interesting debate between Horace Walpole and Hume on Thomas More's value as a historical source and on the best means of building a philosophical assessment of a historical ruler from limited evidence, see *Memoires litteraires de la Grande Bretagne*, vol. 2 (London: T. Becket and P. A. De Hondt, 1769), 13–35.

9. Perhaps more fundamentally, as Hume observed in his second *Enquiry*, martial bravery tended to overshadow other virtues; it had, in the Scythian people, "destroyed the sentiments of humanity; a virtue surely much more useful and engaging" (*EPM* 7.14/255).

10. Perhaps most revealing of Hume's real opinion is a tag attached to his discussion of the decline of shipping during Edward's reign as a consequence of military seizures: "So false is the common opinion, that this reign was favourable to commerce" (*H* 2:281). Hume had already attacked the disastrous effects of Anglo-French rivalry for both kingdoms in the essays "Of the Balance of Trade" (1752) and "Of the Jealousy of Trade" (1758). Despite this, William Robertson in 1769 continued to hold a much better opinion of Edward III's encouragements of trade and industry; see *The History of the Reign of the Emperor Charles V*, 4 vols. (London: A. Strahan and T. Cadell, 1792; rpt. Routledge/Thoemmes, 1996, [7th ed.]), 1:96. Hume's unflattering account of Edward III was perhaps meant to counter Bolingbroke's fawning treatment in letter 5 of the *Remarks on the History of England*, which first appeared in the *Craftsman* in 1730–31. Bolingbroke characterized Edward not only as a glorious warrior-king but as a sincere friend of liberty and a champion of English trade, in contrast to his grandson, the foolish tyrant Richard II, who, he suggested, richly deserved his unpleasant fate.

11. This recommendation is even odder considering that Hume himself noted Henry's general indifference to the strict execution of his own published laws (*H* 1:253–54). Hume must have had some inkling, as modern scholars do, that Henry's learning was not nearly as profound as his reputation suggests. Hume was likely making an implicit comparison to Henry's successor, Stephen, also a usurper, but unable to maintain order against the lawlessness of the barons.

12. William Robertson, like Hume, recognized Edward's abilities but drew much sharper attention to "the malicious policy of Edward I" toward Scotland; see *The History of Scotland*, 2 vols. (London: T. Cadell, 1794), 1:4.

13. Perhaps Hume's view was not that unusual among his enlightened peers; a few decades later, John Millar, a Scottish professor of law (who knew Hume's *History* intimately), said of Edward: "Had he lived somewhat longer, it is more than probable that he would also have completed the entire conquest of Scotland; in which case, there is good ground to believe, that the reduction of the northern and southern parts of the island into one monarchy, would have been productive of such advantages to both countries, as might in some measure have atoned for the perfidy and injustice by which it was accomplished"; *An Historical View of the English Government*, ed. Mark Salber Phillips and Dale R. Smith (Indianapolis: Liberty Fund, 2006), 275–76.

14. See Hume's *Treatise*, bk. 1, pt. 3, sections 8–10, and bk. 3, pt. 2, sec. 10, where he wrote, "Few governments will bear being examin'd so rigorously" [*T* 3.2.10.7/558]. The conventions of law and property are habits of the mind, but are not therefore of unaccountable provenance.

15. An exception is his comparison of Edward I to his son Edward II (*H* 2:174).

16. Hume of the *Essays* consistently valued hard work, industry, and the positive effects of international trade. Unlike many enlightened moralists, however, he believed that luxury was not an impediment, but more often a support, to hard work and other middling virtues; see particularly the essays that first appeared in *Political Discourses* in 1752, notably "Of Commerce" and "Of Refinement in the Arts." He consistently despised indolence (*E* 264, 266 and 355).

17. On Hume's attitude toward an established church, see Will R. Jordan, "Religion in the Public Square: A Reconsideration of David Hume and Religious Establishment," *Review of*

Politics 64, no. 4 (2002): 687–713; and Frederick G. Whelan, "Church Establishments, Liberty, and Competition in Religion," *Polity* 23, no. 2 (1990): 155–85.

18. Hume wrote, no doubt against Whig historians and their modern party adherents: "But always to throw, without distinction, the blame of all disorders upon the sovereign, would introduce a fatal error in politics, and serve as a perpetual apology for treason and rebellion: As if the turbulence of the great, and madness of the people, were not, equally with the tyranny of princes, evils incident to human society, and no less carefully to be guarded against in every well regulated constitution" (*H* 2:174). Successful medieval monarchs such as Edward I needed to be ruthless to survive their dangerous nobility (*H* 2:154). Even Richard of York, whom Hume clearly admired, and who might have been a great king but for his untimely death, was a victim of his own moderation (see *H* 2:442), since the ungovernable and factious nobility of the time tended to interpret moderation as weakness and as an invitation to rebellion.

19. Hume argued that the freedom and power of the commons was "totally incompatible" with the feudal system, particularly the power of the barons (*H* 2:57). During most of the later Middle Ages, the House of Commons was of little use in promoting or defending freedom, since it was unable to curb the nobility and since limiting the power of kings was not at all synonymous with promoting the freedom of the people (see *H* 2:525).

20. Montesquieu (1689–1755) was well known, especially in the 1750s (while Hume was composing his history), for his thesis that "intermediate" powers (by which he chiefly meant an independent nobility, animated by the principle of honor) constituted the principal check that prevented constitutional monarchies from degenerating into despotisms (wherein there could be no liberty whatever). See *The Spirit of the Laws*, II:4 (book 2, chap. 4), VIII:6, and XI:6 (the famous chapter on England). Hume, in contrast, seems to have regarded powerful monarchs as checks on the self-serving ambitions of petty-minded noblemen.

21. In the *Treatise*, Hume wrote, "Nothing but an absolute necessity can oblige an historian to break the order of time" (*T* 2.3.7.7/430). Donald W. Livingston argues that Hume believed we conceive of the world in terms of "narrative associations," in which case the structure of the *History* is almost certainly deliberate; *Hume's Philosophy of Common Life* (Chicago: University of Chicago Press, 1984), 130–37.

22. Likewise Hume argued that it was King William III, rather than Parliament, who deserved most credit for bringing into being the modern constitution; see Nicholas Phillipson, *Hume* (London: Weidenfeld and Nicolson, 1989), 106–7.

23. See *T* 3.2.10.16/563: "in the vast variety of circumstances, which occur in all governments, an exercise of power, in so great a magistrate, may at one time be beneficial to the public, which at another time wou'd be pernicious and tyrannical." Though undeniably disastrous in his own time, Charles I was a good man who had qualities that might have made him an admirable ruler in different circumstances (*H* 5:220–21).

24. Hume argued, in the 1741 essay "That Politics may be reduced to a Science," that a well-constructed constitution should make the personalities of rulers of little consequence (*E* 24–25, 29; see also 124). This same point is highlighted by Neil McArthur, "Laws Not Men: Hume's Distinction between Barbarous and Civilized Government," *Hume Studies* 31, no. 1 (2005): 123–44.

25. See, for example, *E* 60, 95, 349–65, 509.

26. See Hume's 1742 essay "A Character of Sir Robert Walpole," which in 1748 became a footnote to the essay "That Politics may be reduced to a Science," but was withdrawn after 1768. Hume's memorable reference to "that wicked Madman, Pitt," the chief author of Britain's hubristic victories over France during the Seven Years' War, can be found in *L* 2:301.

27. Hume had no particular love of republics. He argued that a hereditary monarchy is as likely to produce a worthy king as an elective one (*E* 18), is more stable over time, and is especially necessary in tumultuous ages (*H* 1:464). See also *T* 3.2.10. But Hume showed little interest in minute questions of legitimacy in matters of succession.

HUME AND THE END OF HISTORY

F. L. van Holthoon

Friedrich Meinecke regarded Hume's *History* to be a precursor of the proper and scientific approach to writing history.[1] David Hume, however, was a historian in his own right, and rather than as merely a precursor, he is, as a historian who wrote in a style distinct from nineteenth-century historiography, worth consideration. According to nineteenth-century historicism, the historian has to behave as an impartial spectator who describes but does not judge. Hume followed the classical dictum *historia magistra vitae* as a matter of course. We are free to judge persons and events using our own moral standard, and as to the lessons we draw from history, the most important is that we learn from the past so that we do not become its prisoner.

What particular lesson did Hume want to convey? Scholars have answered this question from different perspectives, which are not necessarily exclusive. Three perspectives will help my own analysis of Hume's *History of England*.[2] These are to see Hume as a *neoclassical historian*, the *History* as the product of a *scientific Whig*, and *reason in history* as the leading theme of Hume's *History*.

I

Philip Hicks regards Hume's *History* a successful attempt to write a neoclassical history. This label for Hume's *History* is a useful and an obvious one, but Hicks's description of Hume as a neoclassical historian needs further specification. He writes: "Hume helped to invent an 'enlightened' brand of history, a philosophical history that incorporated cultural history into an account of war and politics. Yet he managed to write this history of 'manners' with such attention to the integrity of his narrative and to several classical literary devices that his contemporaries, while acknowledging his innovations, nonetheless put him on a plane with the ancient historians."[3] Hume did not promote any enlightened message. He described violence and upheaval. He did not directly analyze nor applaud the evolution of polite manners. He described his British ancestors as rude, ambitious, and scheming. His purpose was often, as he explained in a note to the *History*, to illustrate "the manners and ways of living in that rude, not to say barbarous age" (*H* 3:469nC). The note describes the household book of the Earl of Northumberland in the early sixteenth century. To Thomas Percy, a descendant of the earl, who was offended by Hume's description, Hume wrote: "I hope it will give no Offence (and whether it do or not, I must say it) if I declare my Opinion, that the English, till near the beginning of the last Century, are very much to be regarded as an uncultivated Nation; and that even *When good Queen Elizabeth sat on the Throne* there was very little good Roast Beef in it, and no Liberty at all" (*NL* 198). Hume had the peculiar habit of debunking the past rather than promoting it.

Does Hume incorporate a "cultural history into an account of war and politics"? To some extent he does, but he does so in a curious way. As far as the social and cultural are concerned, he offers us only disjointed notes, and he even makes excuses that he sometimes takes the liberty "to expatiate a little on the present subject." That is the opening sentence to note W in volume five (*H* 5:568), and it indicates that Hume had difficulty in fitting his observations on cultural and social history into his general story.[4] In fact, the long note belonged to the text until the edition of 1778. And Hume attached an apology to the editions previous to 1778 that he thought it proper to "indulge" in this "digression" (on constitutional history), because "the philosophy of government, accompanying a narration of its revolutions, may render history more intelligible as well as instructive."[5] Four appendices and numerous notes (relegated to the back of the volumes since the 1770 edition) bear testimony to the fact that Hume was fascinated by the details of social history, but that he kept them separate, and that he had a constant struggle to keep the flow to his narrative. A large part of the revisions, particularly the excisions, deal with maintaining the narrative. So Hume did not write a historical narrative of manners, constitutional practices, and trade and industry: rather, he expatiated on them. In fact, you might say that Hume stuck closely to the principle of neoclassical history that history has to be a story, and Hume—like all historians since—had difficulty in combining political events and social and cultural developments.

It was the chief preoccupation of neoclassical historians to effect unity in their historical narrative. In a passage that appeared in his *Enquiry concerning Human Understanding* until the posthumous edition of 1777, Hume writes about the unity of history:

> The historian traces the series of actions according to their natural order, remounts to their secret springs and principles, and delineates their most remote consequences. He chooses for his subject a certain portion of that great chain of events, which compose the history of mankind: Each link in this chain he endeavours to touch in his narration: Sometimes unavoidable ignorance renders all his attempts fruitless: Sometimes, he supplies by conjecture, what is wanting in knowledge: And always, he is sensible, that the more unbroken the chain is, which he presents to his reader, the more perfect is his production. He sees, that the knowledge of causes is not only the most satisfactory; this relation or connexion being the strongest of all others; but also the most instructive; since it is by this knowledge alone, we are enabled to controul events, and govern futurity. (*EHU* 3.9)[6]

Here we have the reason Hume weeded his texts in subsequent editions; excised parts of the text or banished them to notes. The condemned passages obstructed the flow of events and concealed their interconnectedness. In 1753 (shortly before he published the first volume of his *History*), Hume wrote in a letter: "I make my work very concise, after the manner of the Ancients" (*L* 1:170). The interconnectedness of events means that politics dominates Hume's narrative, and indeed Hume primarily wrote a *political* history. He adopted the model of Tacitus's *Annales*, because he discussed history according to the reigns of the English kings, and, as did Tacitus, Hume ended each reign with a comment on the personality of the deceased king. Yet behind this chronicle there was a unifying theme. Hume's political history is a study of central authority: that is, of English kingship.

II

In *Hume's Philosophical Politics*, Duncan Forbes pays attention to an aspect of Hume's *History* that is missing in Hicks's analysis. Hume's *History* is part of a project, which Hume started in his *Treatise:* how to study the conditions under which a political community emerges and is contained. Forbes gives an attractive description of how a history of civilization and a political history work together for Hume. He writes "a history of civilization ... and a political history at the same time and the two aspects of the *History* fuse—the history of civilization bares its teeth in the arena of politics in the first volume Hume published."[7] Indeed, the historical facts on manners and practices are important, because they are the conditions under which authority can be exercised. The history of the reigns of the first two Stuart kings demonstrates what happens when those in authority disregard the emerging climate of opinion. Alas, Forbes spoils his dental metaphor with this verdict on Hume: "Hume presents a new-style history of liberty: the history of liberty is the history of civilization: the result of economic and social progress."[8] Political history as the development of legitimate authority is laced with the history of social and economic progress. It is, in other words, the story of the shifting balances of authority and liberty. So Hume's political views become similar to those of Edmund Burke, who appealed to "entailed inheritance" as a precept for contemporary politics. However, Hume was not a Whig. Nor was he a Tory. The point of his exercise in political science, of which his *History* was part, was to transcend that party division. Hume of course believed that eighteenth-century English society was a better place to live than in the time of Henry II and Thomas à Becket, but he did not use a single principle (or a set of principles) to explain how Englishmen got from Henry II to George II. On the contrary, it is crucial for Hume's understanding of history that Englishmen developed their state and their civil society by trial and error, and that major events—such as the Revolution of 1688—were to a large extent unintended consequences. You might say that Hume had an idea but not a theory of progress.

III

Forbes's statement that Hume wrote a history of civilization is closely linked to the supposition that Hume adhered to a theory of progress, and without this supposition there is no Humean history of civilization. The same is true of Claudia Schmidt's interpretation of Hume's *History*. She concedes that Hume did not present a theory of "continual progress" and tended to draw our special attention to the factors that "impede, threaten, or reverse the progress of civilization," yet she regards the victory of reason as the main theme of Hume's *History*.[9]

The remarkable aspect of the *History* is, however, that Hume hardly ever referred to the development of English society. Summing up his project at the end of the second volume on the Middle Ages, he abruptly closed the book of English history. Hume did not use a theory of progress, and Hume certainly did not want to suggest that reason is the engine of progress. Schmidt writes: "That Hume's philosophy, his study of history, and his contributions to the development of the other academic disciplines are part of a single integrated project: a constructive study of human cognition in its historical context; or, in other words, a study of reason in history."[10] Of course Hume used his reason to study history, but the twist is in the last words of this quotation, "in other words, a study of reason in history." I do not think that Hume is doing that, for what does he mean by *reason*? Is it the Hegelian *Vernunft*, that is, Hume's logical instinct? Or is it man's capacity for reasonableness? Presumably the latter, but then we should realize that Hume regarded that as a calm passion. He writes in his *Treatise* that we often confound reason with the calm passion of reasonableness, but reason is unable to influence the will, while the calm passion does: "Thus it appears, that the principle, which opposes our passion, cannot be the same with reason, and is only call'd so in an improper sense. We speak not strictly and philosophically when we talk of the combat of passion and of reason. Reason is, and ought only to be the slave of the passions, and can never pretend to any other office than to serve and to obey them" (*T* 2.3.3.4/415). And: "What we call strength of mind, implies the prevalence of calm passions above the violent; tho' we may easily observe, there is no man so constantly possess'd of this virtue, as never on any occasion to yield to the solicitations of passion and desire" (*T* 2.3.3.10/418). Reason cannot and should not be a guide to the human will, and the calm passion of reasonableness is a feeble one. If we want a single caption for Hume's *History*, it should be *Passion in History*. That caption explains why Hume was skeptical about human progress.

A History of Liberty?

There are two endings to Hume's *History*. At the end of his history of the Stuarts (volume 6; originally volume 2; Hume wrote his *History* backward), he originally took his stand against the "despicably" Whig propaganda about the events of 1688: "And because the ruling party had obtained an advantage over their antagonists in the philosophical disputes concerning some of their principles; they assumed a right to impose on the public their account of all particular transactions, and to represent the other party as governed entirely by the lowest and most vulgar prejudices."[11] In 1770, he replaced this sentence with the following: "And forgetting that a regard to liberty, though a laudable passion, ought commonly to be subordinate to a reverence for established government, the prevailing faction has celebrated only the partizans of the former, who pursued as their object the perfection of civil society, and has extolled them at the expence of their antagonists, who maintained those maxims, that are essential to its very existence."[12] In 1757, Hume presented his story as an antidote against Whig propaganda; in 1770, it became a cautionary tale against the risks of liberty to authority and the need to keep a balance between the two. Volume 6 is not a triumphant conclusion to a history of liberty.

At the end of the second volume on the Middle Ages (volume 2, the volume that completed Hume's *History*), Hume wrote and never revised:

> Above all, a civilized nation, like the English, who have happily established the most perfect and most accurate system of liberty that was ever found compatible with government, ought to be cautious in appealing to the practice of their ancestors, or regarding the maxims of uncultivated ages as certain rules for their present conduct. An acquaintance with the ancient periods of their government is chiefly *useful* by instructing them to cherish their present constitution, from a comparison or contrast with the condition of those distant times. And it is also *curious*, by shewing them the remote, and commonly faint and disfigured originals of the most finished and most noble institutions, and by instructing them in the great mixture of accident, which commonly concurs with a small ingredient of wisdom and foresight, in erecting the complicated fabric of the most perfect government. (*H* 2:525)

Hume's political recipe as derived from his *History* can be summed up:

1. The happy result is a matter of accident rather than foresight. Hume's skeptical bent is clearly visible. Human beings have very little capability to plan their future.
2. The glorification of the past is a dangerous thing. The usefulness of history is that it liberates us from the past and helps us to concentrate on our present achievements. Freeing ourselves from the past is the hallmark of Hume writing history. The "most accurate system of liberty" as "compatible with government": note the qualification. Here we have Hume's balance between authority and liberty again. And note also that it constitutes a "complicated fabric." We need wisdom and moderation to operate this system.
3. What helps is that it is an established system, meaning that it is based on a broad consensus in the population.

By the end of volume 2, Hume had reached not only the end of his *History*, but also the end of history. The English had stumbled on the recipe that could make a compound of authority and liberty work. Now they should stick to it.

A Study of Authority

Hume wrote to John Clephane in September 1757:

> I am now very busily engaged in writing another volume of History, and have crept backwards to the reign of Henry the VII. I wish, indeed, that I had begun there: For by that means, I should have been able, without making any digression, by the plain course of the narration, to have shown how absolute the authority was, which the English kings then possessed, and that the Stuarts did little or nothing more than continue matters in the former tract, which the people were determined no longer to admit. (*L* 1:264)

In a letter of the same year to William Strahan, he adds another important reason for beginning with the Tudors: "It is really the Commencement of modern History" (*L* 1:251). So the Tudor volumes (in the first edition, in one volume) became the lynchpin of the whole undertaking, and Hume's perspective of English history changed. Leo Braudy remarks that Hume's *History* betrays "a tension between the demands of sympathetic character analysis and those of detached narrative."[13] What this means is that Hume switched from character analysis to detached narrative in the Tudor volumes.[14] Character analysis was in the Stuart volumes a necessity for the description of those unsettled times. How did the first two Stuart kings react to the changing of a world contrary to their expectations? In the case of Charles I, Hume was seduced by the dramatic device of a most sincere and virtuous king earning the reputation of a tyrant. His description of Charles I is the weakest part of his history. As he could have learned from Dr. Birch, Charles deserved his reputation for duplicity, but Hume refused to accept this verdict, probably because it would have spoiled the dramatic effect of his character analysis.[15] However, it is true that from the time of the Tudor volumes, Hume more and more became the spectator of English history, who regarded history as an experiment—as we would say nowadays—in political science.

In 1762, Hume added a note to appendix three in volume 4.[16] Hume there distinguished constitutional phases "which prevailed before the settlement of our present plan of liberty," referring to 1688, and so Hume in an oblique way indicates that the period of the Stuart kings is a period of unsettlement. The phases Hume further distinguishes in this note are:

1. the phase of Tudor absolutism;
2. the period between the Magna Charta and Henry VII, when the barons "exercised great tyranny" over the people;

3. and the period before the Magna Charta, when the kings were the sole source of authority and when rule depended on the ability of the prince to wield his authority.

Hume ends the note with a characteristic sentence: "The English constitution ... has been in a state of continual fluctuation." Fluctuation, not development: the note is too imprecise to tell us what this means, but if we follow Hume's four appendices we get an adequate picture. Hume develops the theme of how central authority is being established and how it is being challenged by social and economic developments.

"The Commencement of modern History": At the end of appendix three, Hume wrote that Henry VII, by his situation and his character, "augmented the authority of the crown." "But the manners of the age were a general cause, which operated during this whole period, and which continually tended to diminish the riches, and still more the influence, of the aristocracy, anciently so formidable to the crown" (*H* 4:384). In their search for luxury, the barons squandered their immense fortunes, and their decline coincided with the rise of tradesmen in the cities and the gentry in the countryside.

> By all these means [rise of industry and the enclosures] the cities encreased; the middle rank of men began to be rich and powerful; the prince, who, in effect, was the same with the law, was implicitly obeyed; and though the farther progress of the same causes begat a new plan of liberty, founded on the privileges of the commons, yet in the interval between the fall of the nobles and the rise of this order, the sovereign took advantage of the present situation, and assumed an authority almost absolute. (*H* 4:384)

So Henry VII established a system "of *the most absolute* authority of the sovereign," which was "totally incompatible with the liberty of the subject." "But what ensured more effectually the slavery of the people, than even these branches of prerogative, was, the established principles of the times, which attributed to the prince such an unlimited and indefeizable power, as was supposed to be the origin of all law, and could be circumscribed by none" (*H* 4:367). So what in fact—Hume suggests—the rise of the new classes meant was that they accepted and perhaps wished for their own "slavery." There was one catch in this system of absolutism. The Tudor kings had no standing army and so had to obey "the established principles of the times."[17]

The monarch who used this system of absolutism to perfection was Queen Elizabeth. She was Hume's heroine. She was firm, even overbearing, and frugal and knew exactly what her subjects would accept. So she was immensely popular and even got an undeserved reputation for liberality. In his encomium, Hume refers to her terrible temper and misses "those amiable weaknesses by which her sex is distinguished" (*H* 4:352). "But the true method of estimating her merit, is to lay aside all these considerations, and consider her merely as a rational being,[18] placed in authority, and entrusted with the government of mankind. We may find it difficult to reconcile our fancy to her as a wife or a mistress; but her qualities as a sovereign, though with some considerable exceptions, are the object of undisputed applause and approbation" (*H* 4:352–53). See how Hume almost entirely focuses on the problem of authority. Liberty, though not entirely neglected, is a side issue. The gentry as the rising class in England did not consciously promote it. Liberty was the accidental product of religious and political conflict. Hume never fully endorsed the "noble principle of liberty" (*H* 4:368), which for him was always tinged with puritanical "enthusiasm," and as he described it in his volumes on the Stuarts, it was an unsettling principle. Only in the end did it have a fortunate outcome—in 1688.

From the appendix "The Anglo-Saxon Government and Manners" we can derive two remarkable subjects. The first is that many institutions, which later became important, were already there but did not yet add up to a viable political system. Kings were already in existence, but they had little power; the Wittenagot was a kind of parliamentary assembly. Who were entitled to be members of this council is, says Hume, not so easy to determine, but it is certain that the Wittenagot "in the period preceding the Norman conquest, was become extremely aristocratical" (*H* 1:165). There were three ranks of men in Saxon times: the noble, the free, and the slave. The great nobles who had large estates and many slaves also dominated the freeman, who could not protect himself, "except by courting the patronage of some great chieftain, and paying a large price for his safety" (*H* 1:169). Yet "there were still considerable remains of the ancient democracy," which gave at least some security to the inferior nobility. These were to be found in the functioning of the courts of the Decennary, the Hundred, and the County, which were "well calculated to defend general liberty, and to restrain the power of the nobles" (*H* 1:172).

The "remains of ancient democracy": Remarkably enough, the anti-Whig historian Hume accepted the Tacitean myth of the liberty of the German tribes. He went further: "The free constitutions then established . . . still preserve an air of independance and legal administration, which distinguish the European nations; and if that part of the globe maintain sentiments of liberty, honour, equity, and valour superior to the rest of mankind, it owes these advantages chiefly to the seeds implanted by those generous barbarians" (*H* 1:160–61). However, Hume could afford to make this concession to the notion of ancient rights, "ce beau système trouvé dans les bois," to quote Montesquieu,[19] because he made it clear that "the great body even of the free citizens, in those ages, really enjoyed much less true liberty, than where the execution of the laws is the most severe, and where the subjects are reduced to the strictest subordination and dependance on the civil magistrate" (*H* 1:168–69). The lesson delivered by this second point is that without a proper functioning system of government, preferably on the central level, there can be no "true liberty." There will be only license.

In retrospect, after four centuries of writings on English history, the conclusion that kingship gives its peculiar character to early English history since the Norman Conquest is rather commonplace. William the Conqueror introduced feudalism as a new institution, and, contrary to what happened in France, feudalism reinforced kingship as the seat of central authority. Not that the Norman barons and their successors were less rebellious than their French counterparts, but while these tried to build up a separatist power in the French kingdom, the Norman barons regarded control of royal power their big price.

The hot issue in the sixteenth and seventeenth centuries was whether the Conquest constituted a clean break with the Anglo-Saxon past, particularly in legal terms. Coke argued that the rights of the people went back to times immemorial and that the kings were subject to them as were their subjects. The royalist opponents of what became the Whig thesis were Spelman and Brady.[20] They argued that the Conquest constituted a new beginning in which feudal law, and in particular, the institution of kingship, had become supreme. Hume was closer to Spelman and Brady than to the Whigs, but he was not so much interested in the legal arguments of the controversy and whether the kings since the Conquest had a legal right to their prerogatives. The fact is that William as the conquering general introduced absolute power, and "England of a sudden became a feudal kingdom" (*H* 1:461). Feudalism—"that prodigious fabric, which, for several centuries, preserved such a mixture of liberty and oppression, order and anarchy, stability and revolution"—then caused a decline of this absolute regal power. This assessment shows Hume's constant preoccupation. Liberty and authority are not in balance, so liberty suffers.

However, the kings since the Conquest had not become powerless. The executive power was lodged in the king. He could summon the barons and their vassals to his court, and what the *curia Regis* meant was "to give sentence among the barons themselves." However, the plan of Anglo-Norman government "contributed to increase the royal prerogative; and as long as the state was not disturbed by arms, reduced every order of the community to some degree of dependance and subordination" (*H* 1:472). The supreme legislative power was lodged in the great council (or parliament), which assembled the barons and the bishops. This council forced King John to respect the rights of his citizens by accepting the Great Charter in 1215. However, those who benefited were the barons. The Commons was not represented in the council of 1215. It became a force only under Henry II in 1265, when, as a product of Simon de Mountfort's usurpation, it "gradually rescued the kingdom from aristocratical as well as from regal tyranny."[21] Hume concedes that the Great Charter restrained the "barbarous license of the kings, and perhaps of the nobles," and as "men acquired some more security for their properties and their liberties," the Great Charter "became a kind of epoch in the constitution" (*H* 1:488).

During the reign of the Stuart kings, the stability put together under the Tudors became unstuck. At the beginning of volume 5, describing the reign of James I, Hume writes that "the minds of Men, throughout Europe, especially in England, seem to have undergone a general, but insensible revolution" (*H* 5:18). And: "In consequence of this universal fermentation, the ideas of men enlarged themselves on all sides; and the several constituent parts of the gothic governments, which seem to have lain long inactive, began, everywhere to operate and encroach on each other."[22] The enlarged views stirred "the love of freedom," and the two Stuart kings did not know how to react to this change of public opinion. The voters who sent their members to Parliament took the initiative and by their attitudes created an unsettled constitution. As Hume wrote at *H* 5:569, note W: "It was the fate of the house of Stuart to govern England at a period, when the former source of authority [absolute royal power] was already much diminished, and before the latter [parliamentary power] began to show in any tolerable abundance. Without a regular and fixed foundation, the throne perpetually tottered; and the prince sat upon it anxiously and precariously." Hume earned his reputation as a Tory historian because of his defense of Charles I. In fact, however, he regarded him as an inept king who was blind to the winds of change and could not control events. "He deserves the epithet of a good, rather than of a great man; and was more fitted to rule in a regular established government, than either to give way to the encroachments of a popular assembly, or finally to subdue their pretensions" (*H* 5:542). The quality, which an English king needs, is the prudence and the skill to ensure stability, and none of the Stuart kings was capable of doing so. Hence 1688 was the outcome.

The four appendices are like slides in a magic lantern. They suggest not evolution, but rather a taking stock of the functioning of authority in English history at certain moments in time. In Saxon times, there was not liberty, but license, largely because there was no central authority to restrain the nobles; the period since the Norman conquest should be divided in two. William the Conqueror installed the central authority of the king. Since 1215, it was touch and go whether the barons or the reigning king wielded power. This unruly situation lasted until the system collapsed during the War of the Roses. The Tudors finally established a stable system of authority, which brought security to their subjects, and security had a tinge of liberty for many of Hume's contemporaries, and probably to Hume himself. Political liberty, Montesquieu wrote, consists of security.[23] Did 1688 introduce a new phase of stability, a new balance between authority and liberty? Hume was not so sure, because, as we shall see, he regarded *regimen mixtum*, which was the product of 1688, as an inherently unstable system of government.

The End of History

Hume had a genuine interest in social history. He was constantly adding observations on manners, and living conditions, but he did not write a social history. He used his observations on manners, customs, and institutions to test the viability of a system of government at a certain moment in English history, but he did not develop a narrative that allowed him to pinpoint the importance of social and economic factors in the unfolding of English history. That is why I said that he did not write a history of civilization.

The fact that Hume did not use a theory of progress or of development to explain events is remarkable. David Spadafora has made it clear that Britons in the eighteenth century, many of them clergymen, regarded themselves superior to their ancestors, because they were more civilized and wealthier.[24] Those who saw the dangers of corruption and decay nevertheless were proud about the achievements of their age. The idea that mankind *had to* progress was more a nineteenth-century notion.[25] Nineteenth-century observers became understandably nervous when the facts belied what the theory suggested. Eighteenth-century intellectuals, despite their skepticism, were buoyant about the present state of affairs. Hume believed that contemporary Britain was superior to the Britain of the past, but he expressed no thought on the subject and occasionally he used terms such as "progress" or "progression" in his *Essays* and *History* on an ad hoc basis.[26] Around 1750, the theory of the four stages in human history became popular.[27] Hume himself was aware of the theory and occasionally referred to it in his *Essays* (for example, his essay "Of Commerce"). However he did not speculate on what he considered to be the facts, and he did not use the theory explicitly.

Why did Hume not adopt the four stages theory for his analysis of English history? There are two answers to this question. The first is that Hume's focus on the study of authority left no room for this theory. The second answer is related. Hume certainly was convinced that his own age was superior to that of the ancient Greeks, but let us consider the *Dialogue* he published at the end of his *Enquiry concerning the Principles of Morals*. There his argument is that any moral system can function if the group to which it applies accepts and obeys its rules. The ancient Greeks, however despicable and wicked their morals, met this qualification. Hume was first a spectator and then a judge. He attached enormous importance to the established practices of a particular society during a certain period. *Custom* in his *Treatise of Human Nature* has epistemological, psychological, and sociological ramifications.[28] Without custom, human beings are the victim of unruly passions, and any change in established practices is serious, because until the members of society have managed to establish new rules, society is in a state of chaos. That is the reason Hume's observations on manners and customs, particularly in his appendices, have the character of an assessment rather than of a stage in a dynamic process.

Hume accepted the events of 1688, but in a reserved mood. Note that he wrote at the end of volume 2 about "the great mixture of accident, which commonly concurs with a small ingredient of wisdom and foresight, in erecting the complicated fabric of the most perfect government." The English had blundered into a new system "of the most accurate system of liberty." Note the reservation. Now they must make it work, and it is dangerous to appeal to "the maxims of uncultivated ages as certain rules for their present conduct." Why then did he accept what according to him was "if not the best system of government, at least the most entire system of liberty, that ever was known amongst mankind" (*H* 6:531)? The answer is that only this system enables the English to combine stable government and economic expansion.

Perhaps the most remarkable aspect of Hume's *History* is that it comes to a full stop in 1688.[29] There is no forecast of future events, no vista of further progress or progression. For the English, 1688 is the end of history. They know the recipe for stable government: a system of mixed government. They have learned the lesson that though this system is the best they can have, it is inherently unstable. So they also know that they must handle the system with caution.

Hazards of *Regimen Mixtum*

"The End of History" is of course a reference to Francis Fukuyama's book on the subject.[30] He used the concept to express that history ceases to exist in the sense that unpredictable changes and new developments taking place will be absent in the future. Events will be the result of the only possible recipe that man can apply or will certainly indicate that chaos exists if he does not. Of course Hume did not use the concept in any explicit and conscious way. The end of his *History* is the end of history because Hume was convinced that the only option the English, indeed the British, had, was to stick to the rules of *regimen mixtum* in order to maintain political stability. A short excursion into his political essays may be useful to prove how serious Hume took the lesson of 1688.

Hume's political essays can be divided into two batches. The *Political Discourses*, his first immediate success, deal with international affairs and economic matters. The second batch deals primarily with post-Walpole politics. Published before or during the writing of the *History* (except for one[31]), they represent the political analysis of the scientist, which analysis inspired the writing of his *History*, rather than the other way round.

In "That Politics may be reduced to a Science," Hume delivered the following "universal maxim": "It may therefore be pronounced as an universal axiom in politics, *That an hereditary prince, a nobility without vassals, and a people voting by their representatives, form the best* MONARCHY, ARISTOCRACY, *and* DEMOCRACY" (*E* 18). The obvious way to read this axiom is that Hume regarded absolute monarchies and (either aristocratic or democratic) republics as the most stable forms of governments, and as far as France was concerned he certainly thought so.[32] However, the point of Hume's dictum was not to celebrate the republic or absolute monarchy, but to suggest that *regimen mixtum* was not a stable system, even though—as in the case of Britain—it contained the best elements of all three systems. "But a limited monarchy admits not of any such stability; nor is it possible to assign to the crown such a determinate degree of power, as will, in every hand, form a proper counterbalance to the other parts of the constitution. This is an unavoidable disadvantage, among the many advantages, attending that species of government" (*E* 46). The instability of the system is the recurring theme of what I call the first cluster of essays. It is caused by the fact that the Commons as representative of civil society is infinitely richer than the king's demesne can ever be and "that there has been a sudden and sensible change in the opinions of men within these last fifty years" (*E* 51). The Commons, knowing of their potential power, want to get their way. The king on the other hand has one weapon to support his authority: the *civil list*. He can bribe members of Parliament by offering them lucrative appointments, effectively constituting a court party. And if in the short-term Parliament will prevail, in the long view, it will pave the road to an absolute monarchy or a dictatorship, because democracy will collapse in internecine fighting and chaos. And then follows Hume's famous sentence: "[Popular government] cannot long subsist, we shall, at last, after many convulsions, and civil wars, find repose in absolute monarchy, which it would be happier for us to have established peaceably from the beginning. Absolute monarchy, therefore is the easiest death, the true *Euthanasia* of the BRITISH constitution" (*E* 53). What then is the remedy to this threat of instability? For Hume it is moderation and promoting parties of interest. "Moderation is of advantage to every establishment: Nothing but zeal can overturn a settled power: And an over-active zeal in friends is apt to beget a like spirit in antagonists. The transition from a moderate opposition against the establishment, to an entire acquiescence in it, is easy and insensible" (*E* 500). Moderation should mean that parties leave zeal behind. What is remarkable in Hume's view of parties is that they are, first of all, the equivalent of factions and so potentially a dangerous and destructive influence. The best we can hope for is a sort of euthanasia of parties in Parliament. In the end, parties should "acquiescence" in government. Hume held to a particularly bloodless version of politics, at least as his ideal.

Hume made no distinction between parties and factions. Parties were a disturbing factor in politics. This applied in particular to the Tories and the Whigs. In "Of the Parties of Great Britain," Hume writes that affairs should have returned "to their natural state, that there are at present no other parties among us but *court* and *country*; that is, men, who, by interest or principle, are attached either to monarchy or liberty." However, the old differences between Whigs and Tories still exist. "This may convince us, that some biass still hangs upon our constitution, some extrinsic weight, which turns it from its natural course, and causes a confusion in our parties" (*E* 72). Note the terms "natural state" and "natural course." According to Hume, a clash of interests and will between those who support the Court and enjoy its benefits and those who are jealous of its powers on principle or because they do not enjoy these benefits, makes the distinction between Court and Country a "natural" one. The old party distinction is an ideological remnant of the past, which we should leave behind us. Hume had a jaundiced view of parties, but the Court and the Country, representing parties of interest, appealed at least to the rational behavior of individuals. It was a false hope of course that Hume thought he could convince his countrymen to leave their ideological differences behind them, and it is amusing to see that the philosopher who pointed out that sentiment is more important than reason in explaining human behavior was afraid of "irrational" passions in politics.

Well-known is Hume's reaction to the riots connected with John Wilkes, who was expelled from Parliament in 1769. He complained bitterly to William Strahan about the lack of firmness in central government to subdue the unrest. Giuseppe Giarizzo's conclusion is that Hume became more conservative in old age.³³ This may be, but that conclusion does not touch the nerve of his political expertise. The crisis around Wilkes occurred when George III took an active part in government. Politicians, such as Edmund Burke, disliked this "personal government" of the king and saw it as a breach with the emerging cabinet system by which the ministers and not the king are the center of decision making. However, Hume stuck to the lesson of 1688. The king and his advisers conducted the daily affairs of government *without the interference* of Parliament. Parliament had the right of petition and the authority to vote taxes but should not be meddlesome. Hume was oddly out of tune with public opinion in 1770.

The Conservatism of David Hume

I have presented Hume as a conservative, but not a conservative such as Edmund Burke, who believed that reforms for the future should be built on the past (and who so may rightly be regarded as the father of nineteenth-century Whigs). Instead, Hume was a conservative of a peculiarly eighteenth-century hue, who held to the view that the powers in the state should be strictly separate, each with its own function, and who for that reason cannot be seen as a pioneer for a representative democracy.

John B. Stewart thinks otherwise. He sees Hume's description of an ideal commonwealth as a proposal for parliamentary reform.³⁴ This view is, I think, mistaken. Hume's essay "Idea of a Perfect Commonwealth" explains the dispersion of political power by representation. The elaborate design, which Hume presented using Harrington's *Oceana* as his model, first of all acknowledged that it is not applicable to the United Kingdom. The danger is that the scheme will end with the dictatorship of the king or lord protector (*E* 527).³⁵ The mentioning of this risk is in line with Hume's conclusion, as we have seen, that a popular government will tend to end in an absolute monarchy, which is "the true *Euthanasia* of the BRITISH constitution."

At the end of his essay "Idea of a Perfect Commonwealth," Hume observes that the "common opinion" that a republic can survive only in a city-state is false. "The contrary seems probable. Though it is more difficult to form a republican government in an extensive country than in a city; there is more facility, when once it is formed, of preserving it steady and uniform, without tumult and faction" (*E* 527). This is not a call for parliamentary reform but an appeal to classical republicanism according to his own maxim that a republic is a stable form of government. My plan of government, Hume writes, is practicable because of "the resemblance it bears to the commonwealth of the United Provinces, a wise and renowned government" (*E* 526). Hume was aware of the problems of that government, but he probably underestimated them because, at the time, the Dutch republic was almost ungovernable, this because of its dispersion of power. Why did Hume want this dispersion of power? To answer this question I must turn to the second objection to the view that Hume was a conservative.

If Hume was backward looking in his views on authority, he was in the forefront of the new science of economics as a modernist. In his study *The Passions and the Interests*,[36] Alfred Hirschmann describes the message of those who believed that commerce would have a civilizing effect on human beings by softening their manners and preparing their minds for the benefits of economic cooperation on a national and international scale. Hume brought this message and turned it "into a neat and well-rounded theory," and Joseph Schumpeter, whom I am quoting, adds, "Adam Smith did not advance beyond Hume but rather stayed below him."[37] In terms of equilibrium analysis, Hume had a firm grip on the notion that if individuals cooperate, they create a situation in which all economic subjects can benefit from the joint effort, and Hume gave a short shrift to the zero-sum notion of mercantilism. To illustrate this point we do not have to go any further than quote from his essay "Of Commerce," which introduces the *Political Discourses*. "The greatness of a state, and the happiness of its subjects... are commonly allowed to be inseparable with regard to commerce; and as private men receive greater security, in the possession of their trade and riches, from the power of the public, so the public becomes powerful in proportion to the opulence and extensive commerce of private men" (*E* 255). And not only the state and private citizens will profit. Commerce will have the tendency to promote employment and a certain dispersion of wealth "among multitudes" (*E* 265) and because commerce promotes industry, England is a rich country compared with France, Italy and Spain. In another essay, "Of the Jealousy of Trade," published six years later, Hume brought forth another implication of the international division of labour. International commerce will promote peaceful relations between trading partners.

In his economic essays, Hume undoubtedly is on the side of the moderns against the ancients, and we may even call him a propagandist of early capitalism. However, he had his reservations. Hume (and Adam Smith) had an alarmist view of the threat of the public debt to the nation. If the public debt is allowed to grow, "it must, indeed, be one of these two events; either the nation must destroy public credit, or public debt will destroy the nation" (*E* 460–61). It was not only (and not in the first place) that Hume feared the economic consequences of the burden of debt, and those who think so—like Macaulay[38]—take a superficial view of his alarm. It is the injury to the body politic that comes first. The government can circumvent Parliament, which controls government expenses by borrowing money. The king becomes an absolute master and can indulge in irresponsible foreign adventures. And who will profit? The capitalists! Hume writes: "These are men, who have no connexions with the state, who can enjoy their revenue in any part of the globe in which they chuse to reside, who will naturally bury themselves in the capital or in great cities, and who will sink into the lethargy of a stupid and pampered luxury, without spirit, ambition, or enjoyment. Adieu to all ideas of nobility, gentry, and family" (*E* 357–58; see also 95). Suddenly an anticapitalist sentiment manifests itself, and it can only mean one thing. Hume wanted economic development, but not if it would destroy the status quo in which agriculture, trade, and industry would be in balance and the gentry would be the mainstay of civil society. It is at this point that the messages of the two clusters of political essays come together.

In fact, there were two ends to history in Hume's case. Mixed government was the most practicable system of government to preserve the status quo; a republic was in a sense Hume's utopia, because it spelled the end of the factitious spirit. In both cases, however, Hume's views implied a denial of the further development of capitalism, and of the osmosis of the state and civil society it effects, making parliamentary democracy the only possible option to meet the challenges of capitalism. The uncharacteristic vehemence of Hume's language in the final quotation suggest that he had a premonition that it was not the end, but only the end of the beginning to history he was witnessing in his lifetime.

David Hume, Historian

Hume remains a great historian, and his *History* has stood the test of time. William Robertson wrote very boring histories (with the exception of volume 1 of his *History of the Reign of Emperor Charles V*). Voltaire had such a mixture of sympathies that his historical account turned out to be uneven and chaotic. He set out to write a *eulogium* of the century of Louis XIV, but his stories of the court are the most damning part of his history. Hume had a remarkable unity of purpose, and in this respect only Edward Gibbon was his equal. Gibbon combined irony and learnedness, Hume irony and intelligence. Of course he was biased; who isn't? However, who but a man with a cool temper and a remarkable intellect could write about the Puritans: "Thus were the civil and ecclesiastical factions regularly formed; and the humour of the nation during that age [reign of James I], running strongly towards fanatical extravagancies, the spirit of civil liberty gradually revived from its lethargy, and by means of its religious associate [the Puritans], from which it reaped more advantage than honour, it secretly enlarged its dominion over the greater part of the kingdom" (*H* 5:559, note J). Chapeau bas!

Mark Salber Phillips discusses historical distance as an important theme in history writing in Britain between 1740 and 1820.[39] The term *distance* certainly applies to Hume. Nineteenth-century historians mixed a sense of loss with the sublime when looking at the past; Hume was a spectator, and that position allowed him to regard English history as the setting in which to study man as a political animal.

NOTES

1. F. Meinecke, *Die Entstehung des Historismus* (München: Oldenbourg, 1959).
2. Hume called the Stuart volumes *The History of Great Britain*. The Tudor and medieval volumes and the complete sets afterward carried the title *History of England*, while *The History of Great Britain* appeared as a subtitle in those Stuart volumes. The Liberty Classics (Indianapolis, 1983) reprint of the 1778 edition has omitted this subtitle.
3. Philip Hicks, *Neoclassical History and English Culture: From Clarendon to Hume* (London: Macmillan, 1996), 216.
4. Hume was not alone in having this difficulty. The conventional opinion was that history should be narrative or cease to be history, as one author expressed it; see Mark Salber Phillips, *Society and Sentiment: Genres of Historical Writing in Britain, 1740–1820* (Princeton: Princeton University Press, 2000), 88. Adam Smith told his students that dissertations "render them less interesting than those wrote by the Ancients" (Phillips, *Society and Sentiment*, 56). Yet Smith never wrote a proper history according to his own definition. Hume solved the problem of how to combine philosophical and plain narrative history by making the study of authority his main concern.
5. The references are to the Liberty Classics reprint. The variorum edition, CD-ROM (Charlottesville, VA: InteLex Corp., 2000), is based on this edition. The paragraphs of this edition are counted as records. In this case: Record 12597, note W; records 12592–97.
6. As in the case of his *History*, Hume excised such a passage because it was no longer relevant to his purpose, not because he had come to disagree with it. And, of course, he excised it long after he had completed his *History*.
7. Duncan Forbes, introduction to David Hume, *The History of Great Britain: The Reigns of James I and Charles I* (Harmondsworth: Penguin, 1970, reprint of the first edition of 1754), 39.
8. Duncan Forbes, *Hume's Philosophical Politics* (Cambridge: Cambridge University Press, 1975), 298.
9. Claudia M. Schmidt, *David Hume: Reason in History* (University Park: Pennsylvania State University Press, 2003), 406.
10. Schmidt, *David Hume*, 416.
11. Vol. 1a (1757), 445.30–34: The second volume on the Stuarts, first edition, 445.30–34, record 14626.
12. The passage was altered in 1770(8), 340.8–14; record 14669.
13. Leo Braudy, *Narrative Form in History and Fiction* (Princeton: Princeton University Press, 1970), 35.
14. Braudy, *Narrative Form*, 40.
15. See Hume's rewriting of note GG in volume 5 (page 576, record 12979). Notwithstanding Dr. Birch's proof of the contrary, he would not accept the fact that Charles tried to negotiate with the Catholic Irish. Gardiner, the great authority on the Civil War, mentions duplicity as Charles's major liability; see S. R. Gardiner, *History of the Great Civil War, 1647–1649* (London: Longmans, 1891), 603.
16. *H* 4:355, record 9499; the final version of this note was published in 1770.
17. Hume, who made many favorable comments on the French monarchy, nevertheless wrote at this page (*H* 4:370) that the French at present are "totally naked, defenceless, and disarmed" in relation to the monarchy.

18. Those who accuse Hume of misogyny, please note.

19. Montesquieu, *De l'Esprit des Lois* (Paris: Editions du Seuil, 1964), chap. 2, sec. 6, 590.

20. See J. G. A. Pocock, *The Ancient Constitution and the Feudal Law: A Study of English Historical Thought in the Seventeenth Century* (Cambridge: Cambridge University Press, 1957), particularly chap. 8, "The Brady Controversy."

21. As a Scot, Hume never had a good word for any of the barons who stood up against a king. Mountfort was no exception.

22. See records 9871–72 for some inconsequential revisions.

23. *De l'Esprit des Lois*, chap. 7, sec.1, 598.

24. D. Spadafora, *The Idea of Progress in Eighteenth-Century Britain* (New Haven: Yale University Press, 1990).

25. In giving his definition of progress (o.c.6), Spadafora could perhaps have made this distinction between eighteenth- and nineteenth-century notions.

26. D. Spadafora, *The Idea of Progress*, 277, 285, 289, 292, 299, 306, 308.

27. See R. Meek, *Social Science and the Ignoble Savage* (Cambridge: Cambridge University Press, 1976).

28. See F. L. van Holthoon, *Een Dialoog over David Hume* (Amsterdam: Boom, 2007), "Fifth Evening: Custom Belief and Fiction"; there is an online English version, which can be consulted at amazon.com.

29. Hume had vague plans to pursue his *History* beyond 1688, which never materialized. One might suggest that with the end to his study of authority in the past the inspiration had left him.

30. F. Fukuyama, *The End of History and the Last Man* (New York: Free Press, 1992).

31. "Of the Origin of Government" was published posthumously in 1777.

32. Bolingbroke and Burke were the first to regard parties to be necessary elements in the political system.

33. G. Giarizzo, *David Hume Politico e Storico* (Torino: Einaudi, 1962), 271: "Ne ritoccò la stile, ne attenuò ogni espressione troppo dura o troppo fervorosa, ne corresse—come abbiamo visto—dei giudizi, rafforzandone ulteriormente la tendenziosità *tory*." Another indication that Hume became less enthusiastic about liberty is his revision of his essay "Of Liberty of the Press." Originally he wrote that "liberty . . . is essential to the support of our mixed government." He scrapped that passage in 1770 and wrote instead: "It must however be allowed, that the unbounded liberty of the press, though it be difficult, perhaps impossible, to propose a suitable remedy for it, is one of the evils, attending those mixt forms of government" (*E*, 13, variant readings 604).

34. J. B. Stewart, *Opinion and Reform in Hume's Political Philosophy* (Princeton: Princeton University Press, 1992), 281, 316.

35. The inconvenience is that "the sword is in the hand of a single person, who will always neglect to discipline the militia [which was part of the scheme], in order to have a pretence for keeping a standing army."

36. A. O. Hirschmann, *The Passions and the Interests: Political Arguments for Capitalism Before Its Triumph* (Princeton: Princeton University Press, 1977).

37. J. A. Schumpeter, *History of Economic Analysis* (London: Allen and Unwin, 1963), 367.

38. Macaulay, *History of England* (London: Longman, 1864), 3:388: "David Hume, undoubtedly one of the most profound political economists of the time, declared that our madness had exceeded the madness of the Crusaders. . . . His prediction remains to posterity, a memorable instance of the weakness from which the strongest minds are not exempt."

39. M. S. Phillips, *Society and Sentiment*, 343.

DAVID HUME AS A PHILOSOPHER OF HISTORY

Claudia M. Schmidt

The discipline called the philosophy of history is often treated as a rather obscure branch of philosophy. At least in the United States, the philosophy of history is rarely included in the philosophy curriculum either at the undergraduate or at the graduate level and is perhaps never identified as an area of specialization for a prospective hire. Most philosophers have little or no occasion to think about the philosophy of history, and some philosophers, most notably Aristotle and Descartes, have even doubted the value of the study of history.[1]

On the other hand, a number of philosophers have taken a particular interest in history, with widely different perspectives and results. Among these we may include Augustine, Machiavelli, Hobbes, Vico, Smith, Kant, Herder, Hegel, Comte, Marx, Nietzsche, Dilthey, Heidegger, Collingwood, and Hempel. I will argue here that Hume should be included in this company. This claim might seem surprising, since Hume has traditionally been regarded as a skeptic in philosophy, who took up a second writing career as a historian, apparently without pursuing any connection between these two fields. However, I will argue, on the contrary, that Hume should be regarded as one of the leading figures in the philosophy of history, in light of both his philosophical and historical writings, and also in light of his influence on later philosophers of history.

Before I begin this discussion of Hume, however, I would like to offer a more general argument: that the traditional categorization of approaches to the philosophy of history is unsatisfactory, and should be replaced with a new division that would be more accurate and productive: both as a systematic framework for the philosophy of history, and for analyzing the works of individual philosophers of history. I will then apply this analysis to Hume and his influence on subsequent philosophers of history.

I. The Philosophy of History

The expression "philosophy of history" was apparently coined by Voltaire, in the title of his essay *La Philosophie de l'histoire* of 1764. Voltaire uses this phrase merely to designate a critical account of ancient history, as opposed to the uncritical acceptance of traditional or biblical history, and he does not propose any theory of history under this title.[2] The phrase "Philosophie der Geschichte" entered German with the translation of Voltaire's work in 1768 by J. J. Harder and was thereafter adopted by Herder, Schelling, Schlegel, and Hegel.[3]

In English, the phrase "philosophy of history" also appeared in the title of a translation of Voltaire's essay in 1766.[4] However, it soon came to signify a subdiscipline of philosophy. Its first significant use in this sense was by John Logan, who in his *Elements of the Philosophy of History* (1781) discusses the principles of historical explanation, in terms derived from other eighteenth-century Scottish authors, but with a degree of deliberation that makes this text the first example of a largely analytic treatment of the "philosophy of history" to be published under that designation.[5]

Since the 1950s, commentators writing in English have generally distinguished between two approaches to the philosophy of history, which are usually depicted as reflecting two divergent conceptions of philosophy in general: the "speculative" or "substantive" and the "analytic" or "critical." These two approaches to the philosophy of history are generally regarded as belonging respectively to the so-called continental and analytic traditions in contemporary philosophy, partly because of their styles and themes, and also because of their historical genealogies.[6] However, from the survey that I have presented above, I suggest that the expression "philosophy of history" has been developed and applied ad hoc to a diverse set of works by a variety of authors, rather than arising from a systematic analysis of what ought to be included in a discipline called the "philosophy of history."[7]

There are two problems arising from any simple distinction between the speculative and analytic approaches to the philosophy of history. First, this simple distinction is not always clear-cut once we apply it to individual authors and their works or to specific problems. Second, such a simple distinction does not accommodate many themes that are often included in philosophical reflections concerning history, including some that have been especially prominent in recent decades.[8]

Given these objections to the twofold typology for the philosophy of history, I would like to offer two proposals. First: the twofold distinction between the speculative and analytic philosophy of history should be replaced with a threefold distinction between the speculative, the analytic, and what I will call the "existential" philosophy of history. In offering this proposal, I do not intend to promote an arbitrary proliferation of types for its own sake. On the contrary, I am offering the phrase "existential philosophy of history" as a useful designation for a distinctive approach to the philosophy of history, and a distinctive set of questions, that already appear in the literature but do not clearly belong to either the speculative or to the analytic approaches. Second, we should be ready to trace elements of one, two, or all three approaches in the works of any given author, rather than characterizing specific authors as exclusively speculative, critical, or existential in their approaches to the philosophy of history. That is, my intent in proposing this typology is to guide our study of various themes in the works of individual authors, not to classify these authors as belonging to monolithic and mutually exclusive traditions in the philosophy of history.

By "existential philosophy of history," I mean any approach to the philosophical study of history and human nature that examines the influence of historical existence on human consciousness. I am using the word "existential" here not in a technical sense that is specific to any particular philosopher or movement, but as a term for the "situatedness" of the human individual within history, as the consciousness of this historical situatedness has developed in the modern era. In identifying the existential philosophy of history as a separate approach to the philosophy of history, I am developing an idea suggested by such authors as Emil Falkenheim and David Carr in their discussions of "historicity," a term derived from the tradition of Dilthey, Husserl, and Heidegger.[9] Others have already noted that the topic of historicity is not obviously included in either the speculative or analytic philosophies of history, and so, by proposing the expression "existential philosophy of history," I hope to incorporate historicity as a separate and coequal theme in the philosophy of history.[10]

How would these distinctions apply to particular philosophers? As indicated above, I suggest that we should treat these three approaches not primarily as separate traditions, but as approaches to different but often related questions that we may trace in the works of any given author. So I expect this threefold distinction to prove its value by the extent to which it can be used to illuminate the thought of various authors, and also to the extent to which it succeeds in clarifying and furthering contemporary discussions in the philosophy of history.

To test this hypothesis, I could consider any of the authors I have named above. For example, in the case of Hegel I might argue as follows. First, Hegel proposes a speculative theory of history in his account of the role of Reason or Spirit in guiding history as its own developing self-consciousness. Second, Hegel also pursues an analytic approach by proposing principles of explanation for the study of history: such as the principle that history is propelled by the actions of great individuals arising from their overriding passions or desires, though these actions often result in consequences that were not intended by the agent. Finally, Hegel presents an existential philosophy of history, by considering the influence of the historical situation of the individual, within a particular nation, culture, and period, over his or her thought and actions. Indeed, at the outset of his lectures on the philosophy of history, Hegel considers the existential situation of different types of historians: the original historian who writes from the perspective of the culture that he describes, the reflective historian who writes from outside that perspective, and the philosophical historian, who is aware of the principles that determine the whole of history.[11]

Marx, too, offers elements of all three approaches. As a speculative philosopher of history, he argues that the economic organization of each successive society in history determines its social structure and its culture, and that the internal contradictions in the economic, social, and political structure of each society determine a series of stages in history. Next, he presents an analytic philosophy of history, insofar as he proposes that individual human actions and states of consciousness may be explained as determined by material conditions, either as they generate a given social structure and its prevailing ideology, or insofar as these conditions prompt a recognition by individuals of the contradictions in the existing economic and social system. Marx also develops an existential philosophy of history insofar as he argues that the consciousness of each individual human being is determined by his or her place within a given economic system and may either be a false consciousness that uncritically accepts its place in this system, or a revolutionary self-consciousness that has become aware of its genuine interests by recognizing the conflicts in the given social structure and the ideological distortions produced by false consciousness.

Finally, it might seem that Carl Hempel, the author of the most influential article concerning the philosophy of history in the analytic tradition, could have little to say that is relevant to either of the other two approaches. Clearly, he contributes to the analytic philosophy of history by defending the application of the covering-law model to explanations in history. It might be difficult to identify a speculative philosophy of history in Hempel's writings, unless we attribute to him the view, shared with the first philosopher to identify himself as a "positivist," Auguste Comte, that human culture is progressing through the advance of science. I would argue, however, that Hempel develops an existential philosophy of history in one important respect: by arguing that the scientist relies on laws that are formulated through experience, since this experience is given through historical existence, in that the accumulated experiences of the past are presumed to justify the formulation of a general rule that can then be applied to predict events in the future, given sufficient knowledge of the initial conditions in any particular case.

In the remainder of this essay, I will show that the threefold division I have proposed here also provides an illuminating framework for examining Hume's contribution to the philosophy of history. I will show that this framework is useful both for examining his own approach to history, and for tracing his influence on subsequent authors.

II. Hume as a Philosopher of History

Hume did not write a specific work in what we would call the philosophy of history, except perhaps for "Of the Study of History," an essay on the benefits of this study, which he withdrew from the later editions of his essays after deciding that it was rather frivolous, at least in style (*E* 563–68). However, Hume develops a recurring discussion of historical knowledge in his main philosophical writings: *A Treatise of Human Nature*, *An Enquiry concerning Human Understanding*, and *An Enquiry concerning the Principles of Morals*. He also considers the use of history and various issues in the study of history in his *History of England* and in several of his essays besides "Of the Study of History." I will therefore refer to a sequence of seemingly disparate passages in his writings in order to reconstruct his distinctive views in the three thematic areas that I have identified above—speculative, analytic, and existential—as constituting his philosophy of history.

We may begin by considering whether Hume contributes to the speculative philosophy of history. The phrase "speculative philosophy of history" is generally used to designate a theory of history that aims to identify and explain the most significant events in the past, and to discover in them a principle that can be used to predict the future course of events.[12] While its origins include theological approaches to history within the Judeo-Christian tradition, the speculative philosophy of history received its classic expression as a secular philosophy of history in the nineteenth century, in the theories of Hegel, Marx, and Comte; and also in the works of some historians, such as Buckle in the nineteenth century, and Spengler and Toynbee in the twentieth century.[13]

Hume does not formulate a speculative theory of history in this sense. However, he does offer a tentative theory of the overall course of history, in his pragmatic and empirical version of the theory of progress. That is, he believes that the conditions of human life have generally improved from antiquity to the modern era: an improvement he traces in society, the economy, and government; in cultural and intellectual life; and even in manners and morals. On the other hand, he does not regard progress as either continuous or inevitable: some periods in European history represent a retrograde movement, such as was the early Middle Ages compared to the ancient civilizations of Greece and Rome, and the period of the English Civil War and Puritan Commonwealth compared to the Elizabethan period. Hume is also concerned about the regressive tendencies in his own day: in his essays and letters, he identifies, criticizes, and even seeks to counteract a number of trends in Great Britain that he regards as threats to this continued progress. Those threats included the growing national debt, protectionist trade policies, the military and colonial ventures of the British government, and the ideological partisanship of the Whigs and Tories.[14]

Hume argues that the forces propelling both progress and regress belong to human nature. On the one hand, human beings are motivated by a desire for activity, and for various material and social goods, to improve the conditions of their own lives and the lives of their friends and family members.[15] At the same time, our desire to improve our own circumstances and those of our companions gives us a motive to pursue our own interest and the interests of our associates through conflict with other individuals and groups. Indeed, Hume recognizes that while our capacity for sympathy provides a bond between members of the same family or group, and even generates moral sentiments and judgments, sympathy also reinforces the most destructive types of group loyalty: those that rest on and promote conflicts over religion, nationality, or political ideology.[16]

In Hume's view, the study of history is valuable at least in part because the historian can trace the stages of progress in history and is thus enabled to identify the motives and social circumstances that tend to promote progress. The historian may then offer these conclusions to public figures—such as moralists, politicians, and essayists—to guide their efforts to promote policies that might strengthen the progressive tendencies in their own time and place. On the other hand, Hume does not believe that progress is inevitable, or that a belief in such inevitable progress can be justified either by a consideration of human nature or by the study of history: on the contrary, both public figures and entire populations may be drawn to regressive measures by various types of ignorance, selfishness, ambition, or narrow group loyalty, as we have noted above.

Grand theories of historical development have become less popular since the mid-twentieth century.[17] However, other discussions have arisen from the speculative philosophy of history, especially when construed more pragmatically as a study of different ways of interpreting history. Here I am thinking of such topics as the use of narrative principles in writing history, the value of historical writing, and issues of style in historical writing. These topics seem related to the question of the "meaning" of history, which is often regarded as belonging to the question of the overall development of history.[18]

The study of narrative principles is often regarded as a recent development in the philosophy of history.[19] However, in the original version of section 3 of the first *Enquiry*, "Of the Association of Ideas," Hume develops a sustained comparison between fictional and historical narratives. He argues that these are similar insofar as they are constructs used by the author to depict a series of human actions, and to trace their causes and effects. But, for Hume, while the author of a fictional work is deliberately presenting an imaginary series of events for an aesthetic purpose, the historian is seeking to present an account of the causal relations in a selected series of past events, and to defend this account of these events as highly probable at least, on the basis of the evidence and the appropriate principles of reasoning, which we will consider below (*EHU* 2.1–2.25/132–43).

Hume also provides several discussions of the purpose and value of the study of history: above all in "Of the Study of History." In this essay, he argues that the study of history has a threefold value. First, it entertains the imagination by displaying a panorama of nations, cultures, personalities, and situations. Second, it contributes to our knowledge by enhancing our ability to judge the motives, characters, and circumstances of other human beings; and by making available to us the experiences of other nations and ages. Finally, it strengthens virtue, insofar as the historian depicts human motives and characters in a way that leads us to consider whether those motives and characters are to be praised or blamed (*E* 565–67).

It seems to me that one interesting topic for further work would be to consider the implications of Hume's writings in aesthetics for his remarks concerning the study of history: especially his reflections on the role of style in fiction and oratory for his practice in his historical writings. Such a study might draw on his discussions of fiction and history in the *Treatise* and the first *Enquiry*, and his essays on rhetoric, especially "Of Eloquence," "Of Simplicity and Refinement in Writing," and "Of Tragedy."[20] Through a consideration of these texts, one might for example be able to trace his views concerning the role of word choice in both the cognitive content and the emotional effects of a work of history, and even consider how this is reflected in his own use of language in the *History of England*.

Turning to our next approach—the analytic philosophy of history—we are in more familiar territory, since Hume contributed in a number of ways to discussions of such topics as the nature of historical explanation and the evaluation of human testimony.

First, Hume argues in the *Treatise* that historical knowledge consists in a "system" of judgments about a series of past events that is based on evidence available to us in the present: usually textual evidence, which is derived in some way from an original eyewitness, and is often transmitted by a series of copyists (*T* 1.3.9.2–4/107–8, *T* 1.3.13.3–6/144–46, *T* 2.3.1.15/404–5). These events are mainly human actions, and the basic task of the historian is to explain these actions as part of a series of causes and effects (*EHU* 2.12–20/136–41).

To find his account of the principles for explaining human actions, we may turn to Hume's more general account of causal reasoning, especially the philosophical form of probable reasoning, and its application to human actions. According to Hume, the main principle by which we explain events is the causal principle, which arises from our experience—in observing regularities, forming habits of expectation, and applying these expectations to similar cases. From his analysis of our judgments concerning causes, Hume derives a set of rules for judging causes and effects that enables us to distinguish the more probable from the less probable causes and effects of a given event (*T* 1.3.15/173–76).

In Hume's view, we explain human actions according to the same principle of causation, specifically by forming expectations based on the connections we observe between actions and motives, with motives constituted by the beliefs and desires of given agents as influenced by their characters and circumstances (*T* 2.3.1/399–407, *EHU* 8.1–25/80–96). However, Hume indicates in several of his texts, including the essay "Of Some Remarkable Customs" and "A Dialogue" at the end of the second *Enquiry*, that the attempt to discern and reconstruct the motives of an agent, especially in a different culture from one's own, is an ongoing challenge to the historian, requiring not only erudition, but also discernment and an extensive capacity for sympathy (*E* 366–70; *EPM* 112–23/324–43).

Since the transmission of historical information requires the contributions of eyewitnesses, subsequent compilers and interpreters, and even copyists, all of whom are themselves historical agents, Hume also applies this analysis more specifically to evaluation of testimony. In "Of Miracles," for instance, Hume argues that we should judge the reliability of testimony by forming probable judgments about the beliefs and desires of any reporters in the chain of transmission, which means that we must attempt to reconstruct the reporters' motives for writing their works or for claiming to be eyewitnesses. In an implicit application of his rules for probable reasoning, he famously argues that we should never accept testimony to an event that violates the laws of nature, since it is always more likely that the reporter is mistaken than that the event took place. He then describes a number of ways in which the beliefs, desires, and reasoning abilities of the witnesses, and of later reporters, might account for their testimony to a miracle, once we have ruled out the possibility of miracles both a priori and a posteriori (*EHU* 10.1–41/109–31). Hume applies this analysis to a specific example in his account of Joan of Arc in the *History of England*, by attempting to distinguish what was "miraculous" in her legend from those aspects of her story that, though "marvellous," are supported by "unquestionable testimony" and seem to be consistent with the "known facts and circumstances" (*H* 2:398).

Finally, and importantly, I would like to argue that Hume also develops an existential philosophy of history. This theme is largely implicit in his writings, but I hope to show that it is an underlying principle in his philosophical system.

In his consideration of the various operations of the human mind, Hume consistently regards the human agent as situated in a historical context: experiencing in the present, but remembering and making judgments about past events, and anticipating the future. This historical context is also a social and cultural context, in which individual agents are aware of each other and also able to communicate with each other, and in which they share elements of a culture that is both inherited and dynamic.

In Hume's view, human beings have a basic set of mental capacities for cognition, emotion, and volition. However, these all operate in a specific historical context, and the mental states and activities of the individual reflect the influence of that context in a number of important ways. First, we acquire experience within a historical context, through our own observation, or through the testimony of others as conveyed through education, documents, or conversation. In other words, experience is always historical since it consists in remembered events perceived within a cultural context. Hume also indicates that the terms and concepts that we use to classify objects and qualities are products of experience (*T* 1.1.7/17–25). In his various references to the history of modern science, he also indicates that the principles of experimental reasoning have been developed historically, especially through the work of modern astronomers and physicists.[21] In all these respects, Hume recognizes the historicity of human cognitive states and activities. Of course, Hume also examines the ways in which human cognition is influenced by the equally historical trajectories of credulity, superstition, and enthusiasm; but his writings reflect the hope that these can be counteracted by the development of a moderately skeptical and empirical philosophy, and by the development of modernity as a pragmatic, moral, and scientific culture.

Turning from cognition to the passions, Hume argues that human beings generally experience the same set of emotions, but that these may be directed toward different objects and qualities during different historical periods, according to whether these objects and qualities are valued or disvalued. Indeed, his first surviving work, a school essay entitled "On Chivalry and Modern Honour," examines the differing conceptions of honor in Europe during the Middle Ages and the modern eighteenth century.[22] Here he argues that moral sentiments and judgments are influenced by the specific cultural context: certain qualities of character may be morally approved in one culture and condemned in another because of differing assessments of whether they are useful and/or agreeable to the self or others. Indeed, our ability to sympathize with individuals in other cultures, or to expand the range of our moral sentiments, is partly a product of experience, and partly a product of education, which again operates in a historical context. Finally, the aesthetic tastes of individuals are influenced by their historical situations, within which certain works of art are regarded as classics, and are used as the basis for judging new works of art. In all these respects, I would argue that Hume presents an existential philosophy of history, or an account of the influence of historical existence over human consciousness, which directs us to consider the historical context of human thought, emotion, and action.

III. Hume's Influence in the Philosophy of History

I hope that I have made a convincing case for regarding Hume as a philosopher of history, even though his philosophy of history is based on separate passages in a number of his writings, philosophical and historical, rather than on any single work. I also hope that I have argued convincingly for the distinction between speculative, analytic, and existential themes in the philosophy of history. In the remainder of this chapter, I will show that Hume has also contributed to the development of these themes by subsequent philosophers of history, through lines of influence that are in some cases direct and in others more roundabout.

We may begin with the speculative philosophy of history. Here, we find that Hume is one of the first philosophers to have developed a secular version of the view that history has been largely progressive. This theme appears in his essays from the 1740s, which predate the writings concerning progress by Voltaire and Turgot in the 1750s and 1760s.[23] Like both Voltaire and Turgot, and subsequently Condorcet and Comte, Hume defended the view that history has generally been progressive in its advance toward the modern age.

However, Hume's theory is notable for the modesty and contingency of his claims: specifically in that he did not regard this progress as all pervasive or inevitable, and instead called attention to the possible sources of regress in his own era, especially ideological conflicts and misguided economic policies. In addition, Hume regards progress to be not directly the result of the advance of human reason, but the result of human passions, which (with the secondary help of reason) have increasingly found their satisfaction in activities that promote invention, commerce, stable representative government, courtesy, and sociability.

Among his successors, Auguste Comte identifies Hume as the first historian to have fixed his attention on "the march of civilization" and credits him with preparing the way for later efforts, beginning with Condorcet, to discover "the general law of the progress of the human spirit and of civilization."[24] This, of course, was the goal of Comte's own positivist approach to the speculative philosophy of history, although his conception of progress and its mechanisms is much more optimistic—and, one might say, more simplistic—than what we find in Hume's account of progress.

Hume's influence also extended to Hegel, who is generally considered to be the single most important speculative philosopher of history. In his lectures on the history of philosophy, Hegel is rather dismissive of Hume as a naïve empiricist and skeptic. However, H. S. Harris and Norbert Waszek have convincingly argued that Hegel developed his conception of the "cunning of reason" partly from his reading of Hume's *History of England*. In a notebook entry from sometime between 1795 and 1803, Hegel describes the central insight in Hume's account of English political history in the following terms: "Since the whole of an action, of which only a fragment belongs to each actor, is split up into so many parts, the whole work is a result of so many individual actions. *The work is not done as a deed, but as a result which is thought.* Consciousness of the deed as a whole is in none of the actors. The *historian* knows the work by the results, and is made attentive to that which brings them about, as already in what came before."[25] In this fragment, Hegel articulates the difference, already stated by Hume, between explaining the intentional actions of agents, and explaining the unintended outcome of these actions: an insight that Hegel evidently noticed in his reading of Hume's account of the political conflicts and civil war in seventeenth-century England.[26]

Next we may consider Hume's influence in the analytic philosophy of history. We may begin by considering his influence in the development of the philosophy of science, as background for the development of analytic philosophy in general, including the analytic philosophy of history. Here I believe we may trace a line between Hume's rules for judging causes and effects and the rules for scientific reasoning set out in the nineteenth century by John Herschel and J. S. Mill. In commenting on this lineage, Robert Butts has claimed that "Herschel provided the first rules of inductive procedure since Francis Bacon."[27] However, it seems to me that the structure and wording of Herschel's rules sufficiently resemble Hume's rules for judging causes and effects to suggest that Herschel was familiar with Hume's *Treatise*.[28] I have not been able to discover any external evidence for Herschel's acquaintance with the *Treatise*, but it is interesting to note that John's father, William Herschel, then a young musician, met "Mr. David Hume, the Metaphysician," while visiting Edinburgh in 1761, and was invited by Hume to dine with himself and a "considerable company."[29] During the next ten years, William Herschel's interests shifted from music to science, and he had become a famous astronomer by the time of his son's birth in 1792. It seems possible, even likely, that John, who shared his father's scientific interest, would have known of Hume from his father's memory of that meeting, and that they would perhaps have shared an interest in his writings, including the *Treatise*, either in its original edition or in the new edition of 1817.

We can trace Hume's influence more directly among the twentieth-century logical positivists, who considered him a predecessor to their program and their approach to the philosophy of science. For our purpose, Hume's influence is especially apparent in Carl Hempel's article "The Function of General Laws in History," which served as the catalyst for the development of the analytic philosophy of history in the mid-twentieth century. In that article, Hempel claims that historical explanations, like explanations in the natural sciences, are inferences from a set of initial conditions and a set of laws derived through induction: a claim he explicitly associates with Hume's analysis of causal explanation.[30]

Hempel's article provoked a lively discussion, but one that faded in the 1960s, as analytic philosophers began to restrain their ambitions in this area. However, Clayton Roberts has provided a valuable overview and reassessment of this debate in *The Logic of Historical Explanation*. Roberts provides a much more nuanced version of a covering-law approach to historical explanation. In Roberts's view, Hempel is correct in claiming that, in principle, historical explanations must show that human actions can be deduced from a set of initial conditions and lawlike generalizations. However, he argues that historical explanations cannot and should not be derived from macrogeneralizations, such as generalizations concerning the causes of war or of scientific revolutions. Instead, the laws that are used in historical explanations should be microgeneralizations concerning the actions of individual agents in relation to their characters and circumstances. This account, of course, strikingly resembles Hume's account of the explanation of human action, suggesting that the analytic discussion has come through a full circle back to Hume's analysis of historical explanation.[31]

Alongside the logical positivist tradition in the analytic philosophy of history, which holds that historical explanations can be assimilated to models of explanation in the natural sciences, many authors identify another tradition in the analytic philosophy of history, sometimes called the idealist approach, which regards historical explanations as fundamentally distinct from explanations in the natural sciences, because they rely on a distinctive type of insight called *Verstehen* or "understanding." This line of analysis extends back to Dilthey and Weber and received its classic twentieth-century expression in Collingwood's *Idea of History*.[32] Since Hume also suggests that sympathy is crucial to the ability to attribute motives to others and to discern these motives, it seems that an important theme in the *Verstehen* tradition is also anticipated by Hume.[33]

Finally, we may ask whether Hume influenced the development of the existential philosophy of history. If we were considering, not the term "existential" as defined in this essay, but "existentialism" as a movement in nineteenth and twentieth century philosophy, the answer might at first seem to be "not likely," since the general feeling of being at home in the world that Hume conveys in his writings seems far removed from the *angst* that is popularly regarded as an essential characteristic of the existentialist tradition. On the other hand, we can perhaps find one example of existential anxiety in Hume's account of the self-doubt and isolation of the skeptical philosopher, who feels like a "strange uncouth monster" cut off from normal human society (*T* 1.4.7.2 /263–64). I have argued above that Hume adopts an existential approach to the philosophy of history by considering the historical situatedness of human conceptualization, experiential cognition, emotion, and moral and aesthetic judgment. However, in spite of my argument for these implicit but pervasive themes, it might still seem an obvious truth that these themes were not recognized or acknowledged by Hume's earlier readers and could not have influenced later considerations of the historical dimension of human subjectivity.

Or is it obvious? On the contrary, at least two of the authors who contributed to the existential philosophy of history, as described above, were undeniably influenced by Hume. The first was Johann Gottfried Herder. As Kant's student in the 1760s, Herder shared in his mentor's enthusiasm for the study of history, literature, and culture: an enthusiasm that was tempered on Kant's part as he embarked on his reconsideration of metaphysics in the 1770s, but which guided Herder in his lifelong interests and endeavors.[34] Indeed, both Herder and Kant appeal to the example of Hume in their exchange of letters in 1768, which was evidently the occasion of the permanent breach between them: Kant recommends the example of Hume as a model of philosophical precision and clarity to Herder, whose work was becoming increasingly allusive in style, while Herder expresses his enthusiasm for Hume as "a philosopher of society in the most authentic sense."[35] In his own writings, Herder explores the diversity of human cultures and historical eras far beyond the scope envisioned by Hume. However, it is worthwhile to note that Herder's interest in these topics was first kindled by Kant and their shared interest in Hume's works on history, politics, and culture.[36]

The second direct line of influence from Hume to the existential philosophy of history begins with J. G. Hamann, who turned Hume's ironic treatment of faith upside down by claiming that Hume alone among contemporary intellectuals truly appreciated the true nature of faith in contrast to reason. Thus, for example, in his *Golgotha and Sheblimini!* of 1784, Hamann draws on Hume's *Dialogues concerning Natural Religion* in developing his own contrast between natural theology and a theology of historical revelation. Hamann illustrates this by quoting from the exchange between Cleanthes, who in the *Dialogues* argues that reason can prove the existence of God from the evidence of nature; and Philo, who ends the discussion by confessing his "fit of melancholy and astonishment over the greatness and obscurity" of questions concerning the nature and existence of God, and who hopes that Heaven will do something to overcome our ignorance by a particular revelation through an "adventitious instructor," a hope that Hamann regards as anachronistic, since it seems to seek "another gospel than that of the cross," which has already been revealed.[37] Hamann also translated the passage in the *Treatise* referred to above, in which Hume describes the feeling of the skeptical philosopher as an "uncouth monster" cut off from human society, and published this in the literary journal that he established in Königsberg, though he did not identify Hume as the author.[38] Hamann was in turn an important influence on Kierkegaard, who proposed a distinctive view of the human condition, as always historically situated and yet as confronting the eternal God through a textually mediated encounter with a historical figure who, as God, overcomes this mediation to encounter the believer within that believer's present moment.[39]

After this survey, the reader may be thinking that my account of Hume's philosophy of history amounts to nothing more than, so to speak, a bundle theory of Hume as a philosopher of history, reflecting my determination to trace as many trends back to Hume as I can. On the contrary, in concluding this paper, I would like to emphasize that Hume's philosophy of history is not merely a random combination of intellectual trends, but a coherent perspective in its own right. More specifically, in my view, Hume's distinctive achievement in the philosophy of history lies in his outlook, which, distinctively modern and yet distinctively serene, recognizes the historical situatedness of human consciousness, and considers the implications of this modern self-understanding for developing an optimistic and humanistic set of principles to guide personal and civic life in the modern world. As part of this project, he also provides an account of the nature and purposes of historical explanation and composition; and of the role of the study of history both in understanding human life and in guiding our present and future actions. Indeed, it is perhaps the very moderation and serenity in his depiction of modern historical self-consciousness, combined with his measured and cautious optimism in addressing the moral, political, economic, and cultural issues of his day, in contrast to both the narrower and grander ambitions of his successors, and the extremes of later optimism and pessimism, that show us the value of Hume and his approach to history—not only as a source of insights and perspectives, but as the model of a confident historical self-consciousness.

NOTES

1. Aristotle, *Poetics* (1451a36–1451b11), in *The Basic Works of Aristotle*, ed. Richard McKeon (New York: Random House, 1941), 1463–64; René Descartes, *Discourse on Method*, in *The Philosophical Writings of Descartes*, trans. John Cottingham, Robert Stoothoff and Dugald Murdoch (Cambridge: Cambridge University Press, 1985), 113–14.

2. Voltaire, *La philosophie de l'histoire. Par feu l'abbé Bazin* (Geneva: aux dépens de l'auteur, 1765). Voltaire originally published this essay as a free-standing text, attributed to "the late Abbé Bazin," but then recast it in 1769 as the introduction to later editions of his *Essay on the Customs and Spirit of Nations*, which he originally published in 1756.

3. *Die Philosophie der Geschichte des verstorbenden Herrn Abtes Bazin*, translated by Johann Jakob Harder (Leibzig: Hartknoch, 1768); Johann Gottfried Herder, *Another Philosophy of History and Selected Political Writings*, trans. Ioannis D. Evrigenis and Daniel Pellerin (Indianapolis: Hackett, 2004); F. W. J. Schelling, *System of Transcendental Idealism* (1800), trans. Peter Heath (Charlottesville: University of Virginia Press, 2001), 199–212; Friedrich von Schlegel, *The Philosophy of History in a Course of Lectures Delivered at Vienna*, trans. James Burton Robertson, 7th ed. (London: George Bell and Sons, 1883; St. Clair Shores, MI: Scholarly Press, 1971); and Georg Wilhelm Friedrich Hegel, *Lectures on the Philosophy of World History. Introduction: Reason in History*, trans. H. B. Nisbet (Cambridge: Cambridge University Press, 1975).

4. Two editions of an English translation of Voltaire's essay were published in 1766, both entitled *The Philosophy of History by M. de Voltaire*: one in London, "printed for I. Allcock"; and the other in Glasgow, "printed for Robert Urie." These two editions differ in their typesetting but apparently use the text of the same unnamed translator.

5. John Logan, *Elements of the Philosophy of History* (Edinburgh: printed by John Robertson, for W. Creech and C. Elliot, 1781). This text has been reprinted as John Logan, *Elements of the Philosophy of History*, with a new introduction by Richard B. Sher (Bristol: Thoemmes Press, 1995).

6. This distinction was perhaps first stated by W. H. Walsh in *An Introduction to Philosophy of History* (London: Hutchinson's University Library, 1951). It was reinforced by William H. Dray in his *Philosophy of History* (Englewood Cliffs, NJ: Prentice-Hall, 1964), and in Dray's article "Philosophy of History" in the *Encyclopedia of Philosophy*, ed. Paul Edwards (New York: Macmillan,

1967), vol. 6, 247–54. This is also the organizing principle used by Ronald H. Nash in editing his two-part anthology *Ideas of History*, 2 vols. (New York: E. P. Dutton, 1969).

7. In providing this survey I am especially indebted to two sources: Robert Flint, *The Philosophy of History in France and Germany* (Edinburgh: Blackwood, 1874; reprinted, Geneva: Slatkine Reprints, 1971); and Daniel Little, "Bibliography of the Philosophy of History" at http://www-personal.umd.umich.edu/~delittle/philosophy%20of%20history%20bibliography.pdf (posted in 2005, and retrieved on 29 August 2008).

8. Several other commentators have criticized this distinction, either explicitly or implicitly. These include Arthur Danto, *Narration and Knowledge* (New York: Columbia University Press, 1985), ix–xiv; Gordon Graham, "History, Philosophy of," in the online *Routledge Encyclopedia of Philosophy*, ed. E. Craig (1998) and David Carr, "Philosophy of History," in the *Encyclopedia of Philosophy*, 2nd ed., ed. Donald M. Borchert (Detroit: Macmillan, 2006), 386–99.

9. See Emil L. Fackenheim, *Metaphysics and Historicity* (Milwaukee: Marquette University Press, 1961); and also David Carr, *Time, Narrative, and History* (Bloomington: Indiana University Press, 1986), 1–7; and his "Philosophy of History," 397–99. See also Martin Heidegger, *Being and Time*, trans. Joan Stambaugh (Albany: State University of New York Press, 1996), 341–69.

10. See, for example, Dray, *Philosophy of History*, 1n1; and Carr, *Time, Narrative, and History*, 1–7; and "Philosophy of History," 397–99.

11. Hegel, *Lectures on the Philosophy of World History*, 11–24.

12. This characterization is provided by Arthur Danto in his *Narration and Knowledge*, 1–16. Danto uses the expression "substantive philosophy of history" for what I am calling the "speculative philosophy of history."

13. Karl Löwith provides a notable account of approaches to history within the Judeo-Christian lineage, tracing modern teleological theories of history back to biblical teleology, in *Meaning in History: The Theological Implications of the Philosophy of History* (Chicago: University of Chicago Press, 1949).

14. Claudia M. Schmidt, *David Hume: Reason in History* (University Park: Pennsylvania State University Press, 2003), 402–8.

15. Ibid., 300–305.

16. Ibid., 177–82, 278–79.

17. This especially reflects the influence of Jean-François Lyotard's *The Postmodern Condition: A Report on Knowledge*, trans. Geoff Bennington and Brian Massumi (Manchester: Manchester University Press, 1984), published originally in French in 1979.

18. See Löwith, *Meaning in History*.

19. Carr traces the discussion of narrative as it has emerged in the philosophy of history both in the analytic tradition, in the works of Arthur Danto, W. B. Gallie, and Louis O. Mink in the 1960s and 1970s; and in the continental tradition, as influenced by developments in literary theory and historiography, reflected for example in the works of Hayden V. White. See Carr, "Philosophy of History," 394–99; and his *Time, Narrative, and History*.

20. Schmidt, *David Hume: Reason in History*, 321–26.

21. Schmidt, *David Hume: Reason in History*, 100–103.

22. "David Hume's 'An Historical Essay on Chivalry and Modern Honour,'" ed. Ernest Campbell Mossner, *Modern Philology* 45 (1947): 54–60.

23. See Hume's essay "Of the Rise and Progress of the Arts and Sciences" (*E* 111–37), originally published in 1741, and his essays on economics (*E* 253–365), many of which were originally published in the *Political Discourses* of 1752.

24. See Mary Pickering, *Auguste Comte: An Intellectual Biography* (Cambridge: Cambridge University Press, 1993), 1:165. As Pickering notes, Comte provides an important early statement of this view in his initially unpublished review, "Compte rendu de *L'Abrégé des Révolutions de l'Ancien Gouvernement Français ouvrage élémentaire extrait de l'abbé Dubos et de l'abbé Mably*, par Thouret," reprinted in Auguste Comte, *Écrits de Jeunesse 1816–1828*, ed. Paulo E. de Berrêdo Carniero and Pierre Arnaud (Paris: Archives Positivistes, 1970), 453–54.

25. Johannes Hoffmeister, *Dokumente zu Hegels Entwicklung*, 273–74. This is a modified version of the translation by Clark Butler included in H. S. Harris, ed., "G. W. F. Hegel: Fragments of Historical Studies," *Clio* 7 (1977): 127–28.

26. See Harris, ed., "G. W. F. Hegel: Fragments of Historical Studies," and Norbert Waszek, "Hume, Hegel, and History," *Clio* 14 (1985): 379–92.

27. Robert E. Butts, "Science, 19th Century Philosophy of," in *Routledge Encyclopedia of Philosophy* (London: Routledge, 1998). See also Ralph M. Blake, Curt J. Ducasse, and Edward Madden, *Theories of Scientific Method: The Renaissance Through the Nineteenth Century* (Seattle: University of Washington Press, 1960), 144–52; and Gerd Buchdahl, *Metaphysics and the Philosophy of Science: The Classical Origins: Descartes to Kant* (Cambridge: MIT Press, 1969), 325–87.

28. John Frederick William Herschel, *A Preliminary Discourse on the Study of Natural Philosophy*, reprint of the 1830 edition (New York: Johnson Reprint, 1966), 151–52.

29. Constance A. Lubbock, *The Herschel Chronicle: The Life Story of William Herschel and His Sister, Caroline Herschel* (Cambridge: Cambridge University Press, 1933), 18. The quotations are from William Herschel's own chronicle of his life.

30. Carl Hempel, "The Function of General Laws in History," *Journal of Philosophy* 39 (1942): 35–48. The reference to Hume is on page 46n7.

31. Clayton Roberts, *The Logic of Historical Explanation* (University Park: Pennsylvania State University Press, 1996).

32. R. G. Collingwood, *The Idea of History* (Oxford: Clarendon Press, 1946). This distinction is stated by Walsh in *An Introduction to the Philosophy of History*, 42–47, and is also used by Nash to organize his *Ideas of History*, vol. 2, *Critical Philosophy of History*.

33. On sympathy, see for example Hume, *Treatise*, 206–8 and 234–35.

34. John H. Zammito, *Kant, Herder, and the Birth of Anthropology* (Chicago: University of Chicago Press, 2002), 98, 150–53, 183–88, 278–84, 312–13.

35. Ibid., 312–13. The letters are reproduced in *Immanuel Kant: Correspondence*, ed. Arnulf Zweig (Cambridge: Cambridge University Press, 1999), 94–100.

36. Hume and Voltaire were among the first to consider cultural history in their historical writings, and indeed Hume was somewhat nettled by those who suggested that he had imitated Voltaire in this respect: see *L* 1:226. On the other hand (and curiously), by the nineteenth century it was common among romantically inclined historians, at least in Britain, to regard Hume's treatment of historical periods and figures as intellectualist and unable to evoke an emotional appreciation of past persons and cultures: see Mark Salber Phillips and Dale R. Smith, "Canonization and Critique: Hume's Reputation as a Historian," in *The Reception of David Hume in Europe*, ed. Peter Jones (London: Thoemmes Continuum, 2005), 299–313.

37. See Johann Georg Hamann, *Writings on Philosophy and Language*, ed. Kenneth Haynes (Cambridge: Cambridge University Press, 2007), 200–201. Hamann's treatment of Hume is complex. He evidently recognizes here and elsewhere that Hume intended his apparent affirmations of faith to be ironic. Here Hamann takes it that Philo speaks for Hume, and that he is expressing hope for a new revelation in the future, though Philo's words could also be read as referring to the Christian faith.

38. See Philip Merlan, "From Hume to Hamann," *Personalist* 32 (1951): 11–18. For other discussions of Hamann and his relation to Hume, see Frederick C. Beiser, *The Fate of Reason: German Philosophy from Kant to Fichte* (Cambridge: Harvard University Press, 1987), 24; Günter Gawlick and Lothar Kreimendahl, *Hume in der Deutschen Aufklärung: Umrisse einer Rezeptionsgeschichte* (Stuttgart-Bad Cannstatt: Frommann-Holzboog, 1987), 174–98; and Manfred Kuehn, *Kant: A Biography* (Cambridge: Cambridge University Press, 2001), 118–26, 194–201.

39. The most sustained version of this argument appears in Søren Kierkegaard, *Philosophical Fragments; or, A Fragment of Philosophy*, trans. David F. Swenson, rev. by Howard V. Hong (Princeton: Princeton University Press, 1962).

FACT AND FICTION: MEMORY AND IMAGINATION IN HUME'S APPROACH TO HISTORY AND LITERATURE

Timothy M. Costelloe

I. Introduction

This chapter explores the central role Hume assigns to imagination in historical writing by comparing and contrasting it to the function the same faculty plays in poetry, the literary forms of lyric, dramatic, pastoral, and epic, to which the majority of Hume's remarks are directed.[1] It begins with the distinction he draws between memory and imagination. Both faculties are responsible for copying impressions to produce ideas, but, since each bears a distinct relation to experience, they give rise to different classes of ideas. Ideas arising from memory repeat original impressions, retaining much of the force and vivacity of originals, resulting in facts that inspire true belief; imagination, by contrast, robs ideas of an equivalent force and vivacity, giving rise to fictions that involve only belief-like states. For this reason, Hume routinely *juxtaposes* the craft of the historian to the art of the poet: whereas the former relies on memory to reiterate the sequence of past events in a narrative that conforms to real existence and matter of fact, the latter employs the imagination to create a fictional world that deliberately leaves experience behind. When historians depart from matter of fact, their narrative becomes fictional and false; when poets depart from fictions, their productions become real and un-poetic.

At the same time, however, Hume also *compares* the historian with the poet, recognizing that historical writing itself depends on the imagination. This comparison is explored by showing how the same principles that govern literary creativity are applicable to history: both poets and historians draw on the magical power of imagination to transform ordinary experience into something extraordinary, create ideas that are agreeable to an audience, and bring about their effects deliberately. Finally, in both poetry and history, identifying these principles makes it possible to specify rules of literary and historical criticism, which, extracted from the respective practices, determine whether a work is successful or not. Hume thus shows what makes both good literature and good history, and he specifies normative rules that, if followed in a certain manner, should result in the production of good or even great literary and historical works.

II. Literature and Imagination

Memory and Imagination

Hume's approach to understanding the form and function of both literature and history is based on his epistemological principle that all perceptions of the mind are divisible into impressions—either external (from the senses) or internal (from passions and sentiments)—and ideas, which are subsequent to and "faint images of these [impressions] in thinking and reasoning" (*T* 1.1.1.1/1–2). Original percepts differ from copies quantitatively, not qualitatively, in terms, that is, of the force and vivacity they contain. While the mind is a "faithful mirror" of past sentiments and affections and "copies its objects truly," it does so in colors that are "faint and dull, in comparison of those in which our original perceptions were clothed" (*EHU* 2.2/17–18); violent ideas can approach impressions, however, as faint impressions can come close to ideas (*T* 1.1.1.1/1–2).[2] Hume locates the power of the mind to make these copies in the faculties of imagination and memory, and, again, there is no qualitative distinction between the ideas each produces; they differ only in so far as ideas belonging to memory contain more force and vivacity than their counterparts arising from imagination.

There are, however, specific features of these two faculties that mark the nature of the respective ideas they produce. Since memory recollects, the ideas to which it gives rise are repetitions of impressions or "equivalent" to them (*T* 1.3.4.1/82–83); as such, "memory preserves the original form, in which its objects were presented" (*T* 1.1.3.3/9). The ideas of the imagination, by contrast, are pure, faint, or "perfect" because they lack the vivacity of original impressions. As Hume writes, "When we remember any past event, the idea of it flows in upon the mind in a forcible manner; whereas in the imagination the perception is faint and languid, and cannot without difficulty be preserv'd by the mind steady and uniform for any considerable time" (*T* 1.1.3.1/9). Ideas of the imagination are not simply feigned, illusory, or merely supposed since they form "a poetical system of things" (*T* 1.3.10.6/121), but they do have a different relationship to *experience* than those of memory: memory, we might say, connects *directly* to experience by recalling the past, whereas imagination does so *indirectly* via its distance from matter of fact; as a result, memory *preserves* experience, while imagination *subverts* it.[3]

This relation to experience and the kind of copying involved determines the respective strengths and weaknesses of each faculty. While the direct relation memory bears to experience makes its ideas accurate copies of originals, it "is in a manner ty'd down ... without any power of variation" (*T* 1.1.3.2/9); the indirect relation of imagination to experience, by contrast, means that it "is not restrain'd to the same order and form with the original impressions" (*T* 1.1.3.2/9). The imagination cannot reproduce the world in the bright colors of memory, but on the canvas of the mind it has wide scope to create new and marvelous things. This, in Hume's view, is the origin of creativity and genius.

As one might expect, poets draw on the imagination; they take ideas copied by the mind and proceed to mix, compound, separate, and divide them to create new and original ideas of objects without real existence. The creative mind does not mimic or straightforwardly copy experience—which would reproduce and preserve matter of fact—but represents and subverts what is given originally. As such, the poet creates *fictions*—"poetical fictions" as Hume calls them—which are always one remove from reality. Correspondingly, these fictions will not produce states that constitute belief. The "difference between a *fiction* and *belief*," as Hume writes, "lies in some sentiment or feeling, which is annexed to the latter, not to the former, and which depends not on the will, nor can be commanded at pleasure" (*EHU* 5.11/48). A fiction of the imagination fails to qualify as that "*strong and lively idea deriv'd from a present impression related to it*" (*T* 1.3.8.15/105), where "strong and lively" means that the idea produces the "same effect with those impressions, which are immediately present to the senses and perception" (*T* 1.3.10.3/119). Instead, a fiction terminates only in a *belief-like state*. In poetry, nature is "confounded" (*T* 1.1.3.4/10), not an object to be understood, but a subject of aesthetic representation limited in the first instance by the poetic genius of the author in question. This can be seen as a weakness of the imagination in so far as its poetic ideas lack the force and vivacity of original impressions; it is also its strength, however, since, unless liberated from repeating matters of fact, the poetic arts would be impossible.

The Art of the Poet

That ideas are fictions that attain the status of belief-like states, however, is not sufficient for them to be *poetic* fictions. Poets confer a particular status on their ideas by placing them in a "poetical system of things," which, while not giving them real existence, serves as a "sufficient foundation for any fiction"

(*T* 1.3.10.6/121). First, poets are like magicians or conjurors who effectively *transform* ordinary experience into something extraordinary. Their pens represent the world with "strong and remarkable" strokes that "convey a lively image to the mind," as Hume puts it in his essay "Of Simplicity and Refinement in Writing" (*E* 191–92).[4] "All poetry," in Hume's view, "being a species of painting, brings us nearer to the objects than any other species of narration, throws a stronger light upon them, and delineates more distinctly those minute circumstances, which . . . serve mightily to enliven the imagery, and gratify the fancy" (*EHU* 3.11). In addition, Hume emphasizes, the transformative power of poetic language at once *embellishes* the world; poetry highlights certain details while casting others into shadow, and through its lens what is in reality ugly, repellent, or mundane appears beautiful, appealing, or fascinating. "Sentiments, which are merely natural," Hume writes, "affect not the mind with any pleasure, and seem not worthy of our attention. The pleasantries of a waterman, the observations of a peasant, the ribaldry of a porter or hackney coachman, all of these are natural, and disagreeable. What an insipid comedy should we make of the chit-chat of the tea-table, copied faithfully and at full length? Nothing can please persons of taste, but nature drawn with her graces and ornaments, *la belle nature*" (*E* 191–92).[5] Simply to *present* the world in its "merely natural" aspect is to replicate the empirical content of experience in all its mundane detail; the poet, on the other hand, creates an alternative world, adorned and rendered beautiful by the power of language.

Second, in transforming and embellishing experience, the poet creates ideas that are *agreeable* to an audience. Poets achieve their effects by transforming merely natural objects and scenes into things of beauty, deliberately arousing a corresponding pleasure in the audience. Poetic genius lies not only in the ability to manipulate ideas, but, by appeal to the receptive capacity of the reader through the mechanism of sympathy, in the skill to rouse sentiments in an audience (see *EPM* 5.37/224). "Every movement of the theatre, by a skilful poet, is communicated, as it were by magic, to the spectators," Hume writes, "who weep, tremble, resent, rejoice, and are enflamed with all the variety of passions, which actuate the several personages of the drama" (*EPM* 5.26/221–22); "no passion, when well represented," he adds later, "can be entirely indifferent to us; because there is none, of which every man has not, within him, at least the seeds and first principles" (*EPM* 5.30/222).

Third, authors do not produce such agreeable sentiments by accident but employ techniques to bring them about *deliberately* as a particular response in the audience. Poets recognize that the imagination should not be strained, but engaged so that it can move easily among its ideas according to the principles of association. This deliberate use of poetic skill is a double-edged sword, however, since one cannot embellish the world in a fictional way without exaggeration and artifice. For poetry to be effective in transforming the world, practitioners must possess a certain genius, taste, or spirit—"a kind of magical faculty in the soul" (*T* 1.1.7.15/24)—without which they would create ideas that are dull and unable to convince, move, or otherwise affect an intended audience. Depending on one's emphasis, then, one might laud the genius of poetry for achieving its effects or condemn its power of manipulation through which reality is turned into fiction. When Hume acknowledges the former side of the imagination he praises poets, but when he recognizes the latter, he denounces them as a source of artifice and deceit: "liars by profession, [who] always endeavour to give an air of truth to their fictions" (*T* 1.3.10.5/121).

Rules of Literary Criticism

Once these principles of poetic art are recognized, it is possible to frame them as rules of criticism. These are appropriately thought of as abridgments since they express formally the regularities that give order to poetic practice. In matters of beauty and deformity, it is possible to isolate "what has been universally found to please in all countries and in all ages," as Hume observes in "Of the Standard of Taste," and thus "fix" "rules of composition"; reflection reveals common features of works that have consistently elicited pleasure rather than pain (*E* 231).[6] As *philosophical* principles, these have *descriptive* or *explanatory* value for the moral scientist, since they show how poets create ideas that elicit agreeable sentiments in an audience. As *critical* principles, on the other hand, they have *prescriptive* or *normative* force for the creative artist by offering guidelines for writing great poetry.

Accordingly, we can specify three general rules of criticism that are tantamount to techniques, which if followed can guide the creation of successful poetry, and if ignored would produce the opposite. First, in order to create a world that engages the audience, poetic depictions must be *plausible* fictions. The poet has the express task of persuading an audience of the poetic reality of events and thus enflaming them with the same passions that actuate the figures in the work. To check the "progress of the passions" and produce indifference is a recipe for poetic failure (*EPM* 5.28/222). The imagination is satisfied by an easy transition among its ideas, facilitated by the poet who inspires belief-like states with ideas that approximate truth—to "look like truth and reality," in Hume's words (*EPM* 5.30/223)—while remaining distinct from real existence and matter of fact. "In short," as Hume puts it, "we may observe, that even when ideas have no manner of influence on the will and passions, truth and reality are still requisite, in order to make them entertaining to the imagination" (*T* 1.3.10.5/121).

Second, a work of literature must exhibit order and coherence by having a *plan and design* created by the poet in conformity with the principles of association. For Hume, what is true of experience generally is true of poetry in particular: even in the wildest poetic reverie, thoughts cannot "be allowed to run at adventures, if we would produce a work, which will give any lasting entertainment to mankind" (*EHU* 3.10). Without the active imagination of the author employed to discover and express the connections in this chain, the passive imagination of the audience is left without direction, and it is impossible to take pleasure in the work: "A production without a design would resemble more the ravings of a madman, than the sober efforts of genius and learning" (*EHU* 3.5).

Finally, literature must exhibit *simplicity* in thought, expression, and composition, and since the noblest works of art are "beholden for their chief beauty to the force and happy influence of nature" (*E* 139), this can be realized only by imitating nature herself. "Art is only the under-workman, and is employed to give a few strokes of embellishment to those pieces," Hume declares, "which come from the hand of the master. Some of the drapery may be of his drawing; but he is not allowed to touch the principal figure. Art may make a suit of clothes: But nature must produce a man" (*E* 138). Objects are beautiful, in part, because they are structured in such a way that fits our capacity to be affected: we take pleasure from harmonious compositions (*EPM* 5.37/182) and figures that are balanced, like the parts of an animal moving together in a perfect whole (*EPM* 2.10 /179) or a pillar slender at its top and wider at its base (*EPM* 6.28/245). The same is true of poetic objects, which must exploit the natural fit between the beauty contained in their unity and the capacity of the imagination to be affected by it. Since nature already exhibits poise and balance, and her forms are fitted to produce pleasure in those with sufficient taste to detect them, poets must avoid excessive ornamentation and artifice. At the same time, they must still represent rather than reiterate her real features, offering readers *la belle nature* rather than mundane and unnecessary detail. Literature should balance the imitation of nature's inherent simplicity and refinement with representing her in a way that engages the imagination (*E* 191–93). This is difficult to attain—it is the work of genius—but a "faithful picture of nature" will produce a "durable work . . . transmitted to the latest posterity" (*H* 6:153).

III. Hume and History

Having outlined Hume's view of memory and imagination and shown how it informs his approach to literature, we are now in a position to elucidate the role of those faculties in his philosophy of history. In many remarks, Hume juxtaposes the craft of the historian to the art of the poet in order to emphasize its connection to memory. Unlike the poet who represents the world by subverting experience, historians depict it by reiterating the sequence of past events as accurately as possible; when it departs from matter of fact, historical narrative becomes false. While memory has a direct correspondence to real existence that it copies, however, the subject matter of history is available only indirectly, through the testimony of written record, itself based largely on the testimony of others. For this reason, historians find themselves confronting the twofold nature of the imagination. On the one hand, they must embrace the principles of memory to copy the world with accuracy and truth; on the other, they depend on the imagination to bring past events into a vivid present and portray them in such a way that inspires belief and carries conviction for the reader. Any historical depiction is thus a re-creation, a tensed representation of experience, to which direct access is, by definition, impossible. In the final analysis, Hume acknowledges, historical facts are qualitatively indistinguishable from poetic fictions but can be differentiated from them in the same way as impressions from ideas, or ideas of memory from those of imagination, that is, by the amount of force and vivacity they contain, the feeling of conviction they carry, and the degree of belief they subsequently inspire.

History and Memory

Hume begins volume 1 of the *History of England* by expressing "regret that the history of remote ages should always be so much involved in obscurity, uncertainty, and contradiction" (*H* 1:3), and promises to supplant the "fables, which are commonly employed to supply the place of true history" with a consideration of the language, manners, and customs that place history on a firm empirical foundation (*H* 1:4). The historian is beholden to evidence based on written record, for which reason, in Hume's view, the invention of modern printing is an important milestone in the progress of historiography. It is the beginning of the "useful, as well as the more agreeable part of modern annals," he observes, since events "preserved by printing" (*H* 3:82) are truths frozen in time from which the historian selects, confident that the events occurred as reported and that the narration they compose is certain. This allows history to realize its task of "distinguish[ing] between the *miraculous* and the *marvelous;* to reject the first in all narrations merely profane and human; to doubt the second; and when obliged by unquestionable testimony . . . to receive as little of it as is consistent with the known facts and circumstances" (*H* 2:398).

Hume captures this idea that history should be beholden to fact in his conviction that it should be "true" or "philosophical." This strikes the modern reader as a commonplace, though as Richard Popkin emphasizes, Hume's attitude was revolutionary since it marked the inception of "purely secular history" and made a decisive break with the "providential and prophetic" tradition that had regarded the Bible as a historical document.[7] This was recognized by no less a historian than Edward Gibbon, who described Hume as "our philosophical historian,"[8] and, as Laurence Bongie shows in his study of the *History*'s reception in late eighteenth-century France, the close connection between Hume's philosophical views and his historical work was immediately apparent to a readership whose taste demanded that history should follow the model of "*l'histoire raisonnée*, as opposed to *l'histoire simple*," the writing of which only "profound thinkers" like Hume with a sufficiently "reflective turn of mind" were qualified to undertake.[9]

This rejection of prophetic or "theological" history is clear in Hume's derision of "monkish" historians, whose writings reflect ignorance, superstition, and the narrow horizons of their "manner of life." The works of medieval chroniclers and annalists reveal individuals who "lived remote from public affairs, considered the civil transactions as entirely subordinate to the ecclesiastic, and ... were strongly infected with credulity, with the love of wonder, and with a propensity to imposture" (*H* 1:25). On occasion, Hume sees these chroniclers as giving voice only to their own beliefs, reporting miracles as fact and celebrating various "monkish virtues" (*H* 1:38, 133); at other moments, he accuses them of bombast, inaccuracy, exaggeration, and "spurious erudition" (*H* 2:88, 328, 477) or outright "invention and artifice" designed to blacken the name of those who challenged ecclesiastic privilege (*H* 1:85, 132, 241).

Religious dogmatism, however, is only the most common instance of hypothetical argument or "reasoning upon a supposition" that supplants the disinterested search for truth (*T* 1.3.4.2/83). Corruption of a similar sort also occurs when historians deliberately relate the "*secret* history" of events in order to excite curiosity (*E* 564), and when "national prepossessions and animosities have place," as Hume reports of English historians writing of Athelstan (*H* 1:86), or when accounts are "delivered by writers of the hostile nations, who take pleasure in exalting the advantages of their own countrymen, and depressing those of the enemy" (*H* 6:277). Similarly, "controversies of faction" affect the honest weighing of evidence, exemplified in assessing the consequences of the Norman invasion of 1066 (*H* 1:227), as do the tendencies of "passionate historians" to draw inferences based on sentiments divorced from sound reasoning (*H* 4:40). In general, Hume considers the early histories of nations and those who chronicled them to be soaked so thoroughly in the stain of superstition and ignorance that the philosophical historian should condemn them to obscurity rather than risk inserting hypothesis where matter of fact should have place.

Hume does not rule out *honest* historical error, however, nor does he think that a superstitious tarnish automatically impugns the integrity of an otherwise true narrative. Tacitus, after all, reports miracles in his history—that Vespasian cured a blind man through his spittle and a lame man by the touch of his foot (*EHU* 10.25/122)—as Quintus Curtius recounts without irony the supernatural courage of Alexander the Great (*EHU* 8.8/84). While Hume never considers these details to be legitimate elements of a true narrative, he himself is not beyond admitting extraordinary events to the historical record. He reports without comment, for example, on Herodotus's account that the Scythians used the scalps of enemies as towels (*EPM* 7.14/255). Some mistakes, moreover, are unwitting and arise from honest ignorance and inexperience (*H* 5:469), or are oversights due to benign prejudice. Such is the case with Livy's portrayal of Hannibal (*EPM* app. 4.17/320) and Timæus's partiality in describing Agathocles, whom he reproaches for tyranny but fails to praise for his "talents and capacity for business" (*EPM* app. 4.19/321). Historians can also be forgiven mistakes that are "natural and almost unavoidable while the events are recent" (*H* 2:173), and for errors arising from the sheer complexity of the narrative or where obscure evidence is a barrier to interpretive accuracy. Unraveling the course of naval battles suffers unavoidably from the former disadvantage (*H* 6:277), as does deciphering the conflict between the Houses of York and Lancaster from the latter (*H* 2:469).

It is the great *benefit* of historical investigation, however, that many errors are amenable to reflection and correction, either by narrators themselves or by subsequent generations of historians who peruse extant histories with the wisdom of hindsight and an improved knowledge of human motives and conduct (*EHU* 8.9/84–85); the accounts of predecessors might thus be confirmed or rejected and true history rescued from the corruptions of tradition. Hume makes this point in correcting previous evaluations of the effects of the Norman Conquest of Britain, for instance, and in confirming that the "disagreeable picture" of King John is not overblown (*H* 1:453). Even a dearth of available evidence can be corrected by a general knowledge of historical circumstances to support a judgment—that wellborn thanes resisted the rise of merchants or ceorls through the ranks of medieval society (*H* 1:170), for example—and the benefit of doubt can usually be conferred on contemporary reports, since writers with a stake in events are generally better informed and more accurately relay details than those with only academic interest; Hume makes this point with respect to Scottish historians reporting Robert the Bruce's first declaration of independence from English rule (*H* 2:137). Indeed, the true historian has an obligation to correct the errors of the past. While contemporary writers can be forgiven imputing all errors of a reign "to the person who had the misfortune to be entrusted with the reins of empire" (*H* 2:173)—as Hume writes of the unfortunate Edward III—the benefit of hindsight and enlarged perspective is an aid to historical erudition and accuracy. In contrast to honest, sometimes unavoidable, and at least partly correctable errors, genuine corruptions of the historical record are the result of systematic and principled distortion. Ideally, history is a true copy, a veridical depiction, in contrast to the speculation of narratives that from error, fancy, or dogmatism, depart from matter of fact. For this reason, Hume considers the "first page of THUCYDIDES [to be] . . . the commencement of real history. All preceding narrations are so intermixed with fable, that philosophers ought to abandon them, in great measure, to the embellishment of poets and orators" (*E* 422).

If the poet, as we have seen, personifies the power of imagination to represent and subvert experience, the historian thus reflects the force of memory to present and preserve it in its original form, due position, and temporal sequence. Past events are equivalent to impressions, and the products of the historian to exact, though fainter, copies taken from them and arranged in their proper order. Historians effectively *memorialize* the past and "confine themselves to strict truth and reality" (*EHU* 3.10) and matter of fact (*E* 564), their explanations grounded in causes rather than floating on spurious motives speculatively attributed to individual actors. The historical writer regards the past with a disinterested eye and bears witness to what actually happened by stripping away falsehood and allowing one "to see all human race, from the beginning of time, pass, as it were, in review before us; appearing in their true colours, without any of those disguises, which, during their life-time, so much perplexed the judgments of the beholders" (*E* 566). Historians, in short, distinguish fact from fiction, as ideas of memory can be separated from those of imagination; historians discern the real shape of events under the clutter by which contemporary reports and time have effectively obscured them.

The Craft of the Historian

On the face of it, then, the empirical character of philosophical history leaves little room for truck with the imagination, the faculty that trades precisely in the fictions and loose reveries that distort the true narrative of past events. Yet, while Hume emphasizes the ideally philosophical character of historical writing and its relationship to memory and matter of fact, he also acknowledges how historians rely on resources that only the imagination provides. First, the historian's originals are events long gone, temporally and spatially remote and available only in and through a historical narrative. The historian "extends our experience to all past ages, and to the most distant nations; making them contribute as much to our improvement in wisdom, as if they had actually lain under our observation" (*E* 566–67). This task is facilitated by the historian's capacity effectively to annihilate the distance of time and space and bring events into a vivid present in which they can be experienced by the reader. This can be achieved only by drawing on the power of the imagination, which allows the writer to project himself into the past, reviving events that compose it and giving reality to what would otherwise be inaccessible. "A man acquainted with history," as Hume writes, "may, in some respect, be said to have lived from the beginning of the world, and to have been making continual additions to his stock of knowledge in every century" (*E* 567). This is a function of the imagination, however, not of memory alone.

Second, even when historians recall the past by making it present, the originals with which they deal differ significantly from the impressions of sense and reflection that are copied by memory. When the memory recollects past impressions, it refers directly back to the *immediacy of lived experience*. The originals of the historian, by contrast, are beyond living memory; they are tensed representations in the form of reports, written records that are *already images* or indeed *images of images*, because copied by others and available as the testimony of events never experienced. This feature gives history its peculiar mode of reasoning, namely, to trace a "chain of argument or connexion of causes and effects" based on authority of "memory or senses." Without this, Hume observes, history sinks to the level of "*hypothetical* arguments, or reasonings upon a supposition; there being in them, neither any present impression, nor belief of a real existence." "Every link of the chain wou'd in that case hang upon another; but there wou'd not be any thing fix'd to one end of it, capable of sustaining the whole; and consequently there wou'd be no belief or evidence" (*T* 1.3.4.2/83). At bottom, there is some present impression or real existence—albeit obscure—that anchors a chain of historical narrative in the bed of lived experience, guiding the historian in writing a true narrative; history can in principle at least reach this original scene of action "beyond which there is no room for doubt or enquiry" (*T* 1.3.4.1/83). Without the temporal reach of the imagination, historical time would be irretrievable and knowledge of events that compose it impossible. At the same time, the original cannot be displayed by cutting the past at its joints; the past is not an open book to be read, but a scene of interpretation to be reconstructed. There is a chain, to follow Hume's metaphor, that leads from the present into remote regions of the past, but the links are images of events and the connections between them dark corners to be illuminated.

These two features of historical evidence—the remoteness of past events and the interpreted nature of testimony—mean that history cannot be a straightforwardly empirical discipline distinguished by its emphasis on veridicality and connection to memory. History is constrained by recollecting matter of fact, but is also a species of "invention" (*E* 567): it preserves the past and anticipates the future only by representing them, and that is a task that requires the aid of imagination. True historians might abjure the creative fictions of literature, but they at once *craft* scenes to create a historical system of things that confers a certain status on the ideas involved. Sharing this feature with the creative power of the poet, the craft of the historian is marked by the three qualities that characterize literary creativity: the magical power to transform ordinary experience into something extraordinary, the capacity to create ideas that are agreeable to an audience, and the rare gift of historical genius to bring this effect about.

First, as poets work on ordinary experience to create something marvelous, so historians *transform* the past by highlighting certain aspects of it and casting others into shadow. As in poetry, the creation of agreeable ideas involves embellishing the world, or "adorning" the facts in the process of selecting what is relevant for the narrative (*H* 3:82). In a historical account, as in a poetical creation, what was in reality ugly, repellent, or mundane appears beautiful, appealing, or fascinating. There is a difference between straightforward presentation of the world and its representation in a true historical imitation. Historians achieve this transformation in two related ways. On one hand, they approach the past as the sedimentation of action and events, from which the heavier elements are dredged and placed before the reader as *relevant* facts. History memorializes the past, but copying it "faithfully and at full length"—to recall Hume's remark on poetry—makes history as insipid as a comedy that repeats the "chit-chat of the tea-table," an antiquarian collection of artifacts merely laid out on a narrative table. "History," Hume writes, in a preamble to considering the reign of Henry III,

> being a collection of facts which are multiplying without end, is obliged to adopt such arts of abridgment, to retain the more material events, and to drop all the minute circumstances, which are only interesting during the time, or to the persons engaged in the transactions.... What mortal could have the patience to write or read a long detail of such frivolous events as those with which it [the reign of Henry III] is filled, or attend to a tedious narrative which would follow, through a serious of fifty-six years, the caprices and weaknesses of so mean a prince as Henry? (*H* 2:3–4).

From a mass of mundane details, the drama of history is revealed through events pertinent to the matter at hand. The historical lens brings events closer, but propinquity selects some and ignores others. Consequently, there might be more than one true history or correct representation of the past, but while different true histories are available, the content of any narrative and the philosophical defense of the methods that produce it depend on satisfying criteria governing what counts as relevant. On the other hand, historians are obliged to transform the sequence of events by representing *time* in a more or less foreshortened way. A history is not a transcription but a temporal representation to suit the purposes of historical narration. To some degree, this reflects the amount, quality. and availability of evidence, which tends to become more adequate as the historian moves through increasingly contiguous events and more extensive written testimony: in the *History*, Hume's account of Anglo-Saxon England from the Roman Empire circa A.D. 55 to the Norman Conquest in 1066 occupies only some 160 pages of narrative, and he does not date events systematically until the reign of Egbert in 827–38 (*H* 1:55ff.). More significantly, narrative time reflects the importance attached by the author to the events under discussion. As Hume examines scenes of increasing importance, detail, and drama—those leading up to the dissolution of the Long Parliament and the Restoration of Charles II, for example (*H* 6:111ff.)—his narrative grows protracted and the temporal sequence slows, sometimes abruptly, from years to months, to days, and even, as in events preceding the murder of Thomas à Becket, to a matter of hours (*H* 2:328ff.).

Second, the historian also produces ideas that are *agreeable* to an audience. Hume explicitly characterizes the aim of history in terms of instruction (*H* 3:82; 6:140), but he emphasizes at once that, by opening up the past and bringing the past into the present, it provides "agreeable entertainment to the mind" and "amuses the fancy" (*E* 565; see also *T* 3.3.4.14/613). History entertains by revealing the world in a unique way so that those "who consider the periods and revolutions of human kind, as represented in history, are entertained with a spectacle full of pleasure and variety, and see, with surprize, the manners, customs, and opinions of the same species susceptible of such prodigious changes in different periods of time" (*E* 97). Like poets, historians thus rely on the receptivity of an audience and the mechanism of sympathy. "The perusal of a history seems a calm entertainment," Hume writes, "but would be no entertainment at all, did not our hearts beat with correspondent movements to those which are described by the historian" (*EPM* 5.32/223). The historical drama, however, must not be painted in colors that are *too* vivid. Like scenes of self-mutilation in a theatrical work, some historical events resist narrative transformation because they are too recent or horrific. Such is the massacre of the English in Ireland during O'Neal's rebellion of 1641 (*H* 5:342) and the "horrid ... scene" at the execution of Charles I (*E* 223).

Third, and finally, historians produce such agreeable sentiments by *deliberately* bringing about a response in the reader. History does not suffer so acutely from the problem faced by the poet—creating fictions that must also convince an audience of their reality—since, instead of transforming reality into fiction, it represents matter of fact as accurately as possible. For this reason, Hume does not denounce historians as *essentially* corrupt—they are truth-tellers rather than liars by profession—since their efforts become false contingently, when the empirical record is distorted through hypothetical reasoning. History still involves manipulating the reader, however, in order to effect the easy transition of ideas in the imagination. In satisfying this demand, historians tread an equally fine line between representing events to produce agreeable ideas *and* achieving "true and establish'd judgement" (*T* 1.3.9.14/115). In Hume's view, this task can be accomplished because history refers to matter of fact and aims at bringing about the conviction of true belief rather than the persuasion of belief-like states. In the historical recollection of events, "every particular fact is there the object of belief. Its idea is modify'd differently from the loose reveries of a castle-builder" (*T* app. 4/625). Two people reading the same book, one as a romance and one as a true history, Hume observes, receive the same ideas, but while the "latter has a more lively conception of all the incidents ... the former, who gives no credit to the testimony of the author, has a more faint and languid conception of all these particulars; and except on account of the style and ingenuity of the composition, can receive little entertainment from it" (*T* 1.3.7.8/98). A historical narrative differs from a poetic romance, that is, by the true belief it inspires, which depends in turn on the *way* the ideas strike the imagination. Ideas in a historical reality still enliven the imagination and enflame the passions, though with less intensity than its poetic counterpart (*EPM* 5.41); the reader feels a sensible difference between the facts of the former and the fictions of the latter. History, we might say, can be false but never enthusiastic.

Rules of Historical Criticism

Despite Hume's emphasis on the philosophical character of history writing, then, like poets, historians are obliged to transform experience and produce agreeable ideas by deliberately manipulating an audience. As Hume points out, historical ideas differ not in kind from their poetical counterparts, but in degree, and via the response they elicit. The nature of the evidence and the causal reasoning involved opens historical narrative to the truth, constituted by the feeling accompanying the sentiments it arouses. As such, there exists what we might term *rules of historical criticism* comparable to those governing poetry, the satisfaction of which determines the success of a historical narrative. These rules of historical criticism are abridgments of historical practice—as those of poetry are abridgments of poetic practice—and amount to techniques that govern the success or failure of historical writing.

First, historians must produce ideas that *carry conviction* by painting a historical picture with colors bright enough to warm the passions of an audience, allowing them to enter into characters and events related in the narrative. For this reason, some themes are more suitable than others for treatment by the historian, since the imagination is naturally affected by events that are more dramatic and of greater consequence. The "histories of great empires" are more interesting "than those of small cities and principalities," Hume remarks, "and the histories of wars and revolutions more than those of peace and order. We sympathize with the persons that suffer, in all the various sentiments which belong to their fortunes. The mind is occupy'd by the multitude of the objects, and by the strong passions, that display themselves" (*T* 3.3.4.14/613). For the same reason, Thucydides and Guicciardin support the reader's attention with difficulty when they describe "trivial rencounters of the small cities of GREECE, and . . . the harmless wars of PISA." As compared to the terror and anxiety that arise from images of the Athenians at Syracuse or the dangers threatening Venice, the "small interest fill not the imagination, and engage not the affections" (*EPM* 5.33/223). Even narrating events that have this natural appeal to the audience, still history must include sufficient detail to engage the reader without falling into antiquarianism or dwelling—as in James V's unwise relationship with his favorite, Robert Carre, Viscount Rochester—on demeaning trivialities. "History charges herself willingly with a relation of the great crimes, and still more with that of the great virtues of mankind," Hume remarks, "but she appears to fall from her dignity, when necessitated to dwell on . . . frivolous events and ignoble personages" (*H* 5:53).

Second, a historical narrative should not run to adventures but must exhibit order and coherence by having a *plan and design* framed by the historian in conformity with the principles of association. As "a certain unity is requisite in all productions," Hume writes, "it cannot be wanting in history more than in any other" (*EHU* 3.14). Moreover, the "unity of action . . . to be found in biography or history, differs from that of epic poetry, not in kind, but in degree" (*EHU* 3.10), so the historian does not aim to enliven the imagination and enflame the passions with the same intensity as the epic poet, but he is not thereby freed from achieving narrative order. Like poets, historians enjoy some latitude in choosing the connections that give unity to the diversity of events. Contiguity in space and time might suffice, in which case, "all events, which happen in that portion of space and period of time, are comprehended in his design, though in other respects different and unconnected" (*EHU* 3.8). Unity can also be achieved by focusing on particular themes that distinguish a period, civil transactions, for example, which Hume sees as "the great ornament of history" under the Stuarts (*H* 5:469), or the "catalogue of reversals . . . fluctuation and movement" that unifies the history of ancient Britain (*H* 2:311). Given that history memorializes the past and secures conviction by tracing a chain of events to an original scene of action, however, the historian more usually produces unity through cause and effect. The historian "traces the series of actions according to the natural order," as Hume describes it, "remounts to their secret springs and principles, and delineates their most remote consequences. He chooses for his subject a certain portion of that great chain of events, which compose the history of mankind: Each link in this chain he endeavours to touch in his narration. . . . And always, he is sensible, that the more unbroken the chain is, which he presents to his reader, the more perfect is his production" (*EHU* 3.9). Hume follows this method in his own historical writing, where, as he remarks before embarking on his account of Anglo-Saxon Britain, he aims at "a succinct account of the successions of kings, and of the more remarkable revolutions in each particular kingdom" (*H* 1:25). Only out of respect for the rule of reporting relevant detail does he depart from this model, as in the case of Henry III, for instance, where he warns the reader that "till the end of the reign, when the events become more memorable, we shall not always observe an exact chronological order in our narration" (*H* 2:4–5).

In this respect, the technique of history is of a piece with the technique of epic poetry, where the writer is also obliged to construct a narrative through a chain of cause and effect, and the distinction between history and epic might even blur. Since the difference between the two forms of narrative lies "only in the degrees of connexion, which bind together those several events, of which their subject is composed," Hume observes, "it will be difficult, if not impossible, by words, to determine exactly the bounds, which separate them from each other. That is a matter of taste more than of reasoning; and perhaps, this unity may often be discovered in a subject, where, at first view, and from an abstract consideration, we should least expect to find it" (*EHU* 3.15). Epic poetry does differ from history, however, in terms of the nature of the writing and the effect it aims to bring about. The former carries the narrative over a greater extent of time and makes connections that are less "close and sensible" (*EHU* 3.10). The links forged in the chain of the latter, by contrast, are "closer and more sensible," Hume emphasizes, "on account of the lively imagination and strong passions, which must be touched by the poet in his narration" (*EHU* 3.14).

Finally, history must attempt to *imitate nature*. History, to recall Hume's remark on poetry (*E* 138), never equals the actuality of events but is the "under-workman" who gives a "few strokes of embellishment" to the past on which he works. Poets satisfy this requirement by simultaneously copying the simplicity and refinement of nature while representing her in all her beauty, *la belle nature*. Historical scenes also are successful when they copy the natural virtues exhibited by characters at the scene. Such is the "the picture, which TACITUS draws of VITELLIUS, fallen from empire, prolonging his ignominy from a wretched love of life, delivered over to the merciless rabble; tossed, buffeted, and kicked about; constrained, by their holding a poinard under his chin, to raise his head, and expose himself to every contumely. . . . Yet even here, says the historian, he discovered some symptoms of a mind not wholly degenerate. To a tribune, who insulted him, he replied, 'I am still your emperor'" (*EPM* 7.9/253). Moreover, since historians depict matter of fact, they also imitate nature in copying as far as possible the "natural order" of events. In general, "we always follow the succession of time in placing our ideas, and from the consideration of an object pass more easily to that, which follows immediately after it, than to that which went before it. We may learn this, among other instances, from that order, which is always observ'd in historical narrations." For this reason, Hume adds, "nothing but an absolute necessity can oblige an historian to break the order of time, and in his *narration* give the precedence to an event, which was in *reality* posterior to another" (*T* 2.3.7.7/430). "An historian may, perhaps, for the more convenient carrying on of his narration, relate an event before another, to which it was in fact posterior; but then he takes notice of this disorder, if he be exact; and by that means replaces the idea in its due position" (*T* 1.1.3.3/9).

Hume's references to and praise for historical writers who, following these rules, have produced successful work, are relatively few compared to his more numerous comments on literary figures. Where he does offer critical observations, ancient historians are heralded as best instantiating rules of historical criticism most perfectly, and they stand as the best and most trustworthy models for historical writers to emulate. Tacitus, in particular, stands out for his "candour and veracity," making him "the greatest and most penetrating genius, perhaps, of all antiquity" (*EHU* 10.25/123). Hume also esteems ancient historians for their illustrations of virtue and vice—an honor he does not confer on poets, one might observe—and when they enumerate details of religious practice.[10] Modern historians receive praise only when they approach their ancient forebears. "Raleigh," Hume observes for instance, "is the best model of that ancient style, which some writers would affect to revive at present" (*H* 5:154), and, he continues, "Camden's history of queen Elizabeth may be esteemed good composition, both for style and matter." "It is written with simplicity of expression, very rare in that age, and with a regard to truth. It would not perhaps be too much to affirm, that it is among the best historical productions which have yet been composed by any Englishman" (*H* 5:154). Like literary works, historical writing is still of value even when it fails to satisfy *all* the rules of historical criticism. Such is the case with Clarendon, who, in Hume's view, "will always be esteemed an entertaining writer, even independant of our curiosity to know the facts, which he relates. His style is prolix and redundant, and suffocates us by the length of its periods: But it discovers imagination and sentiment, and pleases us at the same time that we disapprove of it" (*H* 6:154).

Conclusion

This chapter has approached Hume's view of history by elucidating its connection with the repetitive power of memory, but also by showing its intimate relation to the creative power of the imagination. History is philosophical not only though memorializing the past, but in its necessary creativity, required by the historian if he is both to reclaim the past and simultaneously to transform and adorn it in order to entertain and convince the reader. The principles that make this possible, moreover, are manifest as historical techniques or, otherwise conceived, as rules of historical criticism, which, comparable to those of literary criticism, abridge historiographical practice and offer guidelines for producing great works of history. In these respects, historians share common features with poets, though where the latter trades in fictions, ideas that never move beyond belief-like states, those inspired by the historian feel different and rise to the status of true belief. History coincides with poetry in that it depends on the imagination to achieve its effects but departs from it in anchoring its investigations in matter of fact. The features of true history, moreover—that it at once memorializes *and* embellishes—fits it for a singular task: to paint the past factually and give instruction in moral virtue. It presents models that can show us our duty and recommend courses of action which, if followed, would constitute an excellent character and promote a good life.

NOTES

1. Hume also discusses eloquence, comedy and, famously, tragedy (*E* 216–25) under the rubric of literature. He sometimes includes history under the same heading, but, as this chapter shows, there are important differences between the writing of history and more strictly literary works. I shall use the terms poetry and literature interchangeably.

2. See Colin McGinn, *Mindsight: Image, Dream, Meaning* (Cambridge: Harvard University Press, 2004), 8–11.

3. See Don Garrett, *Cognition and Commitment in Hume's Philosophy* (Oxford: Oxford University Press, 1997), 26. Some commentators interpret Hume as arguing that the imagination turns the empirical world into an illusion. See John Bender, *Imagining the Fiction: Fiction and the Architecture of Mind in Eighteenth-Century England* (Chicago: University of Chicago Press, 1987), 35–38; and Leo Damrosch, *Fictions of Reality in the Age of Hume and Johnson* (Madison: University of Wisconsin Press, 1989), 3–4 and 65.

4. See Ralph Cohen, "The Rationale of Hume's Literary Inquiries," in *David Hume: Many-Sided Genius*, ed. Kenneth R. Merrill and Robert W. Shahan (Norman: University of Oklahoma Press, 1976), esp. 104–6.

5. See also *EPM* 3:15/189, where Hume describes the "*poetical* fiction of the *golden age*" in similar terms.

6. See Don Garrett, "The Literary Arts in Hume's Science of the Fancy," *Kriterion* 44, no. 108(2003): 173–74; and Timothy M. Costelloe, *Aesthetics and Morals in the Philosophy of David Hume* (London: Routledge, 2007), chap. 1.

7. Richard H. Popkin, "David Hume: Philosophical versus Prophetic Historian," in *David Hume: Many-Sided Genius*, ed. Kenneth R. Merrill and Robert W. Shahan (Norman: University of Oklahoma Press, 1976), 83, 89–90, and 92.

8. See Edward Gibbon, *Decline and Fall of the Roman Empire*, ed. J. B. Bury (London: Methuen, 1909–14), 7:215, quoted in Donald T. Siebert, *The Moral Animus of David Hume* (Newark: University of Delaware Press, 1990), 119.

9. Laurence L. Bongie, *David Hume: Prophet of the Counter-Revolution*, 2nd ed. (Indianapolis: Liberty Fund, 2000), 5.

10. See, for example, *EPM* 6:16, 26/240, 245; 7:9, 13, 14–15/253, 254–55; and *NHR* 146–48, 153, 162, 174.

HUME'S HISTORIOGRAPHICAL IMAGINATION

Douglas Long

This essay attempts to link the distinctiveness of David Hume's historiographical "voice" to the distinctiveness of his philosophical understanding of the imagination. Section I shows how two distinctive features of Hume's idea of the imagination—its "sympathetic" character and its "constructive" power—shape his account of history and historiography by influencing his understanding of historical identification and historiographical narration. Section II distinguishes Hume's understanding of the role of imagination in historiography from the views of Adam Smith, Thomas Hobbes, and Michel de Montaigne. Section III sketches briefly Hume's account of the definitive activity of the historian: the "ascent" into the past.

It is well known that in Hume's writings "imagination" plays an exceptionally important role in the development of our ideas of "self" and "soul" and "substance" (*T* 1.4.6.6/254). What has been far less noticed, and what I want to suggest here, is that this role has direct and significant implications for Hume's approach to the writing of history. Indeed, one could say that history and the imagination are associated through a relationship, in a Humean sense, of reciprocal causality: the imagination *generates* historical narratives, while history in turn amuses and instructs by its impact on our imaginings.

It is, for Hume, by means of our imagination that we construct the context in which we situate our direct experiences of the world, and that context is by turns social (spatial), political (causal), or historical (temporal)—indeed it may be all of these at once. When the application of the experimental method in morals takes us beyond the small circle of our sensations and simple impressions into the realm of complex impressions and ideas grouped in chains and clusters, we immediately invoke the imagination to impose some degree of coherence on the Heraclitean flow of events that seems to surround us in our lives.[1] We construct our identity, our "Commonwealth" and/or *our* history in our imagination. The flow of events, "cross-sectioned" so to speak temporally rather than spatially, is that to which we turn our attention in the writing of history. Historical identities, be they characters or commonwealths, are doubly imagined: they are imagined as spatially deployed relations of resemblance, contiguity, and causality; and imagined again as unfolding temporally in a historical narrative that exhibits a constructed, artificial continuity and clarity of focus. In writing and reading history, as in all areas of "morals," we behave in a way Hume characterizes as paradoxical: we "chace our imagination to the heavens, or to the utmost limits of the universe," yet in doing so "we never really advance a step beyond ourselves" (*T* 1.2.6.8/67).

In one sense, history is the stuff of direct experience and recollection, Hume's and his reader's, in the eighteenth century or in the twenty-first. But in another sense, history is neither experienced nor remembered. It is imaginatively constructed. Hume makes an important distinction between the operations of memory and imagination. "The memory," he says, is "in a manner ty'd down . . . without any power of variation" in relation to "the same order and form" of our "original impressions" (*T* 1.1.3.2/9). Our imagination, however, is not so "restrain'd." He argues that the imagination is at liberty "*to transpose and change its ideas*," as it does in "fables" where "nature . . . is totally confounded" (*T* 1.1.3.4/10). History is not simply the record of Hobbes's "decaying sense."[2] Historiography is an art form: the coherences, continuities, and causal connections that make history meaningful to the reader are imaginative constructs—fruits of the evocative tropes that enrich the historian's text. The world or scene that comes into imaginative existence as a background or context to the narrative flow of actions and events is vivid and plausible just insofar as the historian successfully places the techniques of the *ars rhetorica* in the service of the imagination. A good historical narrative is a comedy of manners, a drama "which paints the manners of the age, and exposes a faithful picture of nature," and as such it is of more lasting value than more pretentiously systematic works of rational analysis (*H* 6:153 discussed below). Hume's famous critiques of fanaticism and superstition, and of the styles of historical writing derived from them, should not blind us to the fact that his own *History* is as much a dramatization of characters and events as it is an explanation. His hostility toward the fanatical and the superstitious is aroused not so much by the imaginative basis of their arguments as by their refusal to acknowledge it. Fanatical ("Whiggish" or "Tory") and Superstitious ("Monkish") accounts of history pretend that their dramatizations are factual, objective—"true."[3] Hume's only claim is to be instructive, amusing, faithful to nature, and moderate—a moderation induced by a skeptical sense of the elusiveness of truth. This is in keeping with Hume's sense, famously expressed in "My Own Life," of his intellectual inclinations and of his literary path.[4] What makes Hume's work both accessible and iconoclastic is that the passion that drives the drama is not a partisan passion but a passion for an imaginative intimacy with the past which only a mind steeped in sympathetic imagining can generate.

For Hume, the writing of history is divested of its traditional aspect of ceremonial, public declamation. His historical narration assumes a conversational, almost intimate, tone. One is taken, imaginatively, into the confidence of the author. To be sure, Hume examines the historical record—he faithfully footnotes the authors his contemporaries would have expected him to cite—but he subjects even this record to an imaginative critique. At Hume's side, so to speak, the reader imaginatively constructs the temporal and historical context of the famous events and characters that occupy almost all of Hume's text, while Hume himself guides and channels this imaginative/constructive process with the deft hand of the historian/historiographer.

I. Imagination and Historical Inquiry

The imagination in Hume may be said to have two distinctive and intrinsically important characteristics: it is "constructive" and it is "sympathetic." In the *Treatise*, in the course of deploying his ideas on the nature, scope, and methodology of the social sciences—morals, politics, and history—Hume wrote that "the minds of men are mirrors to one another" (*T* 2.2.5.21/365). Moreover, in each of these three "scenes of thought," that is, the moral, the political, and the historical, we extend the reach of our imagination, although "we never really advance a step beyond ourselves" (*T* 1.2.6.8/67). We see ourselves reflected in the minds and figures of agents near us or distant from us in either space or time: "Every human creature resembles ourselves, and by that means has an advantage above any other object, in operating on the imagination" (*T* 2.2.5.4/359).

History is a hall of mirrors—it reflects us as we reflect its leading characters and events. But we also create, and are created by, those characters and events. The richness and complexity of historical narration—and its value—arise from reflection compounded by imaginative construction. Whether the object of study be ancient Rome, Joan of Arc, or some exotic locale, the process is the same. The historiographic imagination constructs historical narratives, weaving them dramatically and compellingly into a web of connections which, if not seamless, is coherent and reasonably continuous. This suffices to create a sense in the reader of "realism," for the historical imagination—the imagination of the reader of history—comes equipped, as our imagination always is, to sustain a sense of coherence and continuity in spite of the selectivity or even the contrived nature of the narrative. The imagination is the capacity whereby "we infer the continu'd existence of the objects of sense from their coherence, and the frequency of their union . . . in order to bestow on the objects a greater regularity than what is observ'd in our mere perceptions" (*T* 1.4.2.21/197). If this is true of the objects of direct sense experience, it is true a fortiori of the objects communicated to the historical imagination by the historian's narrative. But in the case of these latter, the power of the sympathetic imagination goes beyond endowing evanescent objects with an imagined "continu'd existence." Historical agents and events, qua historical, are not directly experienced—we have, a least initially, only ideas of them. In sympathy, however, "the force of the imagination" *converts these ideas into impressions* (*T* 2.3.6.8/427). The vividness of historical writing, and much of its capacity to instruct and amuse, must surely originate in this specific and remarkable capacity of the imagination.

The same feature of the operation of the imagination that enables us to understand objects (and ourselves) as having a continuous existence is enlisted by Hume for the task of endowing historical figures with a life of their own, so to speak. That feature is what I have elsewhere called "cognitive momentum": "the imagination, when set into any train of thinking, is apt to continue, even when its object fails it, and like a galley put in motion by the oars, carries on its course without any new impulse . . . as the mind is once in the train of observing an uniformity among objects, it naturally continues, till it renders the uniformity as compleat as possible" (*T* 1.4.2.22/198).[5] To be sure, objects directly present to our senses ought not to be conflated with the objects constructed by and for the historical imagination. Hume is aware that the "constancy of their appearance" makes it possible for us to believe in the continued existence of "all external bodies" as components of one great "edifice": in short, to believe in what we call the external world. The world opened up to the reader by Hume's *History* does not have this constancy—we can close the book. But Hume's narrative skills are such that, as long as the book is open, we remain deeply engrossed in it as though it were a "scene" or "world" with its own continuous existence.

Methodologically, however, there is no difference between the way we arrive at the notion of our "selves" and the way we arrive at our historical understanding of historical actors in the near or distant past. There is no difference between the way we arrive at an image of the "commonwealth" within which we live (our own spatial context) and the way we arrive at our historical understanding of commonwealths more or less distant from us in time. In short, it is the sympathetic and constructive imagination that generates our sense of psychological, sociological, political, or historical orientation in the world.

James Farr has argued persuasively that in Hume's account of sympathy, "the emphasis is on communication, not empathy or individual psychology."[6] Hume's concise summary comment at *T* 2.3.6.8/427 clearly describes sympathy in cognitive, not emotive, terms: "sympathy, as I have already observ'd, is nothing but the conversion of an idea into an impression by the force of imagination." As Farr observes, Hume gives two different explanations of sympathy. The *Treatise* places sympathetic communication within a framework of psychological "general" rules, the rules of association, which are represented as structuring, at least by implication, the very process of sympathetic communication, while in the *Enquiry concerning the Principles of Morals* sympathy is a sort of primum mobile of moral science: a "principle of human nature" so general and fundamental that its existence and operations are to be assumed, not subsumed under any other general causal category or principle: "sympathy no longer represents an instantiation of association. Rather, it represents a precondition for and a limit to our investigations of moral phenomena. . . . It is an essential part of human experience, and on the basis of it we 'enter . . . deeply into' others when we receive by communication their feelings, ideas and the like. . . . sympathy is a form of sharing or re-experiencing as a consequence of successful communication."[7] The idea of mirroring captures nicely this capacity for communication via an "entering into" the other's mind and perspective.[8] So, one might be tempted to say that the experimental moral / social sciences hold the mirror up to human nature in this restricted sense. The significant inaccuracy, however, of the language of holding up a mirror to nature—that is, reflecting it without distortion or omission—may be seen if we examine the process by which we arrive at an imaginative notion of ourselves. This is, after all, the imaginative construct in relation to which commonwealth (spatiality) and history (temporality) are understood. To the imagination, Hume explains, one "uninterrupted and invariable object" appears so similar to a rapid "succession of related objects" that by "mistake" we "confuse" them. "So great" is "our propensity to this mistake . . . that we fall into it before we are aware." This is our imaginative default setting, so to speak, a "biass" we are unable to "take off." Although our insistence on the continued existence of something called the "self" flies in the face of careful philosophical reflection, "in order to justify to ourselves this absurdity, we often feign some new and unintelligible principle, that connects the objects together, and prevents their interruption or variation. Thus we feign the continu'd existence of the perceptions of our senses, to remove the interruption; and run into the notion of a *soul*, and *self*, and *substance,* to disguise the variation" (*T* 1.4.6.6/254). The "true idea of the human mind," and the most apt parallel to the idea of the soul, Hume goes on to say, may be found in the idea of a "republic or commonwealth":

> I cannot compare the soul more properly to any thing than to a republic or commonwealth, in which the several members are united by the reciprocal ties of government and subordination, and give rise to other persons, who propagate the same republic in the incessant changes of its parts. And as the same individual republic may not only change its members, but also its laws and constitutions; in like manner the same person may vary his character and dispositions, as well as his impressions and ideas, without losing his identity. (*T* 1.4.6.19/261)[9]

The same commonwealth or republic sustains its identity in our imagination despite, indeed, "*in*" (emphasis added), "the incessant changes of its parts, just as individuals sustain by an act of willful imagining the idea that their identity remains unaltered through the incessant changes of a life lived. Thus the process of historical identification is a precondition of historical narration. Moreover, the power of the imagination to connect ideas not only assists us in forming durable and coherent notions of mind, self, soul, and commonwealth: it also is at the root of our representations of the power relationships that surround us in society. Two objects are causally linked in the imagination, Hume wrote, when "one produces a motion or any action in the other" or even "when it has a power of producing it": "And this we may observe to be the source of all the relations of interest and duty, by which men influence each other in society, and are plac'd in the ties of government and subordination" (*T* 1.1.5.5/12).

The same imaginative capacities that are indispensible to our belief in self and commonwealth are put to work in the construction (and consumption) of historical narratives. The "flow" of Hume's narrative is extraordinarily smooth. Even today the reader can easily be swept up in the drama of his depiction of the great deeds of Alfred the Great,[10] the contest between Henry II and Becket,[11] or the vicissitudes of Charles II.[12] The eloquence of Hume's evocation of Alfred's eminence, Henry's rage, or Charles's meanness of spirit was surely meant to generate precisely the sort of sympathetic communication that would transform imaginative ideas into vivid impressions on and in the reader. The distantness of the experiences communicated to us via sympathy, however, does add to the difficulty of forming strong impressions of them.[13] Hume clearly believed, as we shall see, that the writing of history was a challenging form of communication for this very reason. Nevertheless, the capacity of the imagination to sustain our ideas of the coherence and continuity even of "feigned" entities makes intertemporal sympathetic communication possible: "'Tis certain, that sympathy is not always limited to the present moment, but that we often feel by communication the pains and pleasures of others, which are not in being, and which we only anticipate by the force of the imagination" (*T* 2.2.9.13/385). Hume had in mind here the power of imaginative "anticipation" projected into the future. We shall see as our argument unfolds that imaginative retrospection, though more difficult, was feasible, and indeed the more to be prized because it was in Hume's view so difficult. History, as James Farr observes, is in fact for Hume "the paradigmatic sympathetic social science."[14] This is correct, insofar as history is for Hume the most direct (and dependent) beneficiary of the distinctive features of the operations of the sympathetic imagination.

The sympathetic imagination is ipso facto what David Raphael called it in an important essay on the "true old Humean philosophy": the "constructive" imagination.[15] The sympathetic imagination constructs historical "reality" by providing a grounding for our sense of the integrity and coherence of a narrative that is in fact highly discontinuous—an "interrupted" and "variable" account of a flow of experience too rapid and complex ever to be "re-collected." The sympathetic imagination can never incline us to write history that is utterly irrelevant or uninteresting to ourselves and our fellow citizens, for sympathy can communicatively capture only images in which we find ourselves somehow, to some extent. In its selectivity, the sympathetic imagination is ethnocentric. Humean history is never the history of an unmitigated "otherness." Hume's historical narrative tells a story that is gripping for his readers because, and insofar as, they are Britons, or insofar as they share a British idea of what it is to be human. The mirror of history, insofar as it is the mirror of sympathy, is "our" mirror.

II. Imagination, Philosophy, History: Hume, Smith, Hobbes, Montaigne

Hume's sympathetic imagination exhibits what I have called "cognitive momentum": in the narratives it shapes, the imagination "papers over the cracks" in our incoherent and discontinuous perceptions. Hume's friend, literary executor, and intellectual competitor Adam Smith placed an emphasis on this quality of the imagination that was as great as Hume's.[16]

> When objects succeed each other in the same train in which the ideas of the imagination have ... been accustomed to move, and in which, though not conducted by that chain of events presented to the senses, they have

acquired a tendency to go on of their own accord . . . the thought glides easily along them, without effort and without interruption. They fall in with the natural career of the imagination; . . . There is no break, no stop, no gap, no interval. The ideas excited by so coherent a chain of things seem, as it were, to float through the mind of their own accord, without obliging it to exert itself, or to make any effort in order to pass from one of them to another.[17]

Where Hume had divorced the idea of imaginative/sympathetic communication or understanding from any idea of a feeling, however, Smith emphasized the positive feeling—a feeling, one might say, of sympathetic sociability—that accompanied this smooth progress of the imagination along the line of flow of one's experiences of the world. Thus he asserted that "if this customary connection be interrupted," the agent will respond emotionally. "Surprise" is followed by "wonder," and the imagination struggles to fill in the "gap" it perceives, to build a "bridge" to restore continuity to the flow of events or objects—and to restore the feeling of comfort that accompanies the sense of continuity.[18] Philosophy, which Smith describes as "the science of the connecting principles of nature," "endeavours to introduce order into this chaos of jarring and discordant appearances, to allay this tumult of the imagination, and to restore it, when it surveys the great revolutions of the universe, to that tone of tranquility and composure, which is both most agreeable in itself, and most suitable to its nature."[19] Smith then undertakes to write, in the remainder of his essay, a history of the great "systems of nature" that have successively (and one might say paradigmatically) shaped Western thought. This history will be maximally "entertaining" and "instructive" if it examines not "their absurdity or probability, their agreement or inconsistency with truth and reality," but rather "how far each of them was fitted to sooth the imagination, and to render the theatre of nature a more coherent and therefore a more magnificent spectacle." "According as they have failed or succeeded in this, they have constantly failed or succeeded in gaining reputation and renown to their authors: and this will be found to be the clew that is most capable of conducting us through all the labyrinths of philosophical history."[20]

Although Hume and Smith both placed enormous emphasis on the constructive role of the imagination in philosophical inquiries, they did not share the same conception of sympathy. For Hume, sympathy was, as we have seen, a capacity for cognition and communication. For Smith, the experience of sympathetic communication was inseparable from a positive feeling or sentiment of connectedness, of sociability. Smith said as much in a letter to Gilbert Elliott. There he argued, explicitly against Hume, that sympathetic response to the "passions" of others is always connected with some emotional response. Depending on whether sympathy is connected to "approbation" or "disapprobation," the feeling actually mirrored in actor and spectator may be either "agreeable or disagreeable." However, Smith insists that "the emotion which arises from his observing the perfect coincidence between this sympathetic passion in himself and the original passion in the person principally concerned ... is always agreeable and delightful." Sympathy for Smith is always accompanied by what we might term a sentiment of sociability that is positive. This sentiment is the quintessence of the "sense of justice," which is in turn a condition of civilized society.[21] Thus it happened that sympathy became the cornerstone (via the related idea of propriety) of Adam Smith's theory of moral sentiments,[22] while it played a very different role in Hume's application of the experimental method to moral subjects, a role that could be said to be communicative, not sentimental, culminating in a sense of history, not a sense of justice.

Smith's application of (his version of) the idea of the sympathetic imagination to the study of "philosophical history," however, may serve to remind us that Hume and Smith did share a very distinctive conception of historiographical methodology: they both developed a form of "philosophical history" that was unapologetically imaginative.[23] The retrospective conceptual analysis of Smith's "History of Astronomy" in his essay "The Principles which Lead and Direct Philosophical Enquiries"[24] and the "four stages" theory that provided the structural framework for Smith's account of the history of law and government in his lectures on jurisprudence[25] share, at least generically, the imaginative framework used by Hume in *The Natural History of Religion*.[26] The "four stages" theory of the development of society and government, which sees history to date as culminating with the emergence of commercial society, is presupposed by, though not explicated in, both Hume's essay "Of Commerce" (*E* 253–67)and Smith's *Wealth of Nations*.[27] There are tantalizing occasional indications of the influence of this construct in Hume's *History*, but the fact remains that while Smith wrote only one kind of history—the more strictly abstract, conceptual, "philosophical" kind—Hume wrote two.[28] The argument of this essay, however, is that *all* of Hume's historical writing was philosophical in an important sense. The *History of England* is prima facie a "conventional" history of characters and events—but is it not in its own way a history of ideas as well? And is it not "philosophical" in its methodology, if not in its narrative topics? The *History of England* is philosophical history—it is a conventional historical narrative transformed and enlivened by the unprecedented application to historical narrative of Hume's sympathetic imagination.

In a famous passage from *Leviathan*, Thomas Hobbes argued that there can be "no Knowledge of the face of the Earth," "no account of Time," "no arts, no letters" and "no society" in "a time of Warre."²⁹ Hobbes's distinction between time of war and time of peace hinged not on the human disposition but on subjection to the will of a political sovereign. Thus for Hobbes, the validity and value of accounts of geographical and social space and of historical time are derived solely from their point of origin: sovereign political authority. Control over accounts of social space and historical time would naturally be an integral part, for Hobbes, of "the wel governing of Opinions" by the office of political sovereign.³⁰ In specifying the necessity of such control, Hobbes was explicitly responding to one of the basic needs of modern social and political theory: the need to situate the individual subject securely in a context of social space and historical time. Hobbes, like Hugo Grotius, provided his readers with an account of the laws putatively governing human motion and behavior in a societal and historical context, laws that would hold were it the case—though neither author wished to be thought to believe that it was the case—that there was no God. God was not, in the sense to be made famous by Nietzsche, dead, but the horizons of social space and historical time could be fixed sufficiently authoritatively that they would hold, and thus protect social peace, even if He were. This authoritative "fixing of horizons" was at least arguably one of the defining features of a distinctively modern mode of historiography deployed in support of modern ideas of social space and historical time. Hume made an extraordinary contribution to the development of such a mode of historical writing, but he did it in a way antithetical to Hobbes's.

Hume found Hobbes's authoritative "fixing" of the content of approved public accounts of the horizons of social space and historical time to be "dogmatic." The skeptical Hume could hardly endorse a Hobbesian sovereign's control over the will, understanding, and imagination of mankind. The contrast in their positions on these matters is clearly implied by Hume's general critique of the matter and style of Hobbes's works, a critical assessment of Hobbes's literary and philosophical achievements that is surprisingly seldom examined. In volume 6 of the *History*, in the course of an account of the "Manners and arts" of the Restoration period, just after some comments on the poet Sir John Denham (*H* 6:153) and before a short paragraph on Harrington's *Oceana*,³¹ Hume acknowledged that Hobbes was the most "celebrated" English author of his day. "In our time," he continued, "he is much neglected." Hume's explanation for such neglect is instructive. The root problem in his view is the dogmatically rationalist character of Hobbes's ethics and politics: "Hobbes's politics are fitted only to promote tyranny, and his ethics to encourage licentiousness. Though an enemy to religion, he partakes nothing of the spirit of scepticism; but is as positive and dogmatical as if human reason, and his reason in particular, could attain a thorough conviction in these subjects" (*H* 6:153). The "matter" of Hobbes's oeuvre showed him to be a secular dogmatist—an intellectual authoritarian lacking the proper "spirit of scepticism." His style, Hume conceded, was excellent—who could deny Hobbes's capacity for vivid imagery and adroit verbal constructs? But his skills were in Hume's eyes deployed in the service of a system of "reasoning and philosophy," and Hume as a historian and as a skeptical philosopher took a dim view of the value and durability of such systems. As he explained in the same paragraph, "a system, whether physical or metaphysical, commonly owes its influence to its novelty; and is no sooner canvassed with impartiality than its weakness is discovered." Hume's skepticism concerning the intrinsic merits of systems of nonskeptical philosophical reasoning does not seem to have been confined to Hobbes's work, for his negative portrayal of the evanescence of reputations and works built on reason and system is also set over against a flattering picture of comic drama—to be precise, comedies of manners: "A pleasant comedy, which paints the manners of the age, and exposes a faithful picture of nature, is a durable work, and is transmitted to the latest posterity." The key assertion here is that dramas "paint . . . a faithful picture of nature."

This is strikingly reminiscent of the naturalism of that great humanist skeptic so admired by Hume, Michel de Montaigne:

> Philosophical inquiries and meditations serve only as food for our curiosity. The philosophers . . . refer us to the rules of Nature: but these have no concern with such sublime knowledge. The philosophers falsify them and show us the face of Nature painted in too high a color, and too sophisticated, whence spring so many varied portraits of so uniform a subject. . . . The more simply we trust to Nature, the more wisely we trust to her. Oh, what a sweet and soft and healthy pillow is ignorance and incuriosity, to rest a well-made head![32]

It is hard to imagine Hume endorsing Montaigne's praise of "ignorance and incuriosity," but easy to see him carrying forward into the eighteenth century Montaigne's call to trust in nature. In his essay "Of the Study of History" (*E* 563–68), Hume echoed Montaigne in an attack on philosophers and poets for failing to paint human nature "in its proper colours":

> Poets can paint virtue in the most charming colours; but, as they address themselves entirely to the passions, they often become advocates for vice. Even philosophers are apt to bewilder themselves in the subtilty of their speculations; and we have seen some go so far as to deny the reality of all moral distinctions. But . . . the historians have been, almost without exception, the true friends of virtue, and have always represented it in its proper colours. (*E* 567)[33]

In his essay "Experience," Montaigne offered further suggestive insight into the relationship between the mind's "reasons" and the imagination: "Now I treat my imagination as gently as I can, and would relieve it, if I could, of all trouble and conflict. We must help it and flatter it, and fool it if we can. My mind is suited to this service; it has no lack of plausible reasons for all things."[34] Thus in place of Hobbes's "Leviathan" Montaigne simply postulated a "bag": in contrast to rational philosophical systems outlining the art of sociopolitical construction, Montaigne postulated that humans simply "pile up and arrange themselves" without system but to good effect "by moving and crowding together, just as ill matched objects, put in a bag without order, find of themselves a way to unite and fall into place together, often better than they could have been arranged by art."[35] Hume chose to emulate Montaigne rather than Hobbes when he entered the field of moral, social, and political thought. He chose a path of skeptical naturalism and structural minimalism, so to speak, both in his philosophical works and in the narrative trajectory of his *History*.

III. Space, Time, and History: The Ascent into the Past

It is to Hume's philosophical accounts of space and time that we next turn for his insights into the nature and value of the historian's activities. His investigation of these matters in *T* 1.2.1/26–68 begins and ends with paradox. More specifically, Hume begins and ends his analysis with allusions to Xeno. At the outset, he observes that doctrines such as that asserting the infinite divisibility of time and space can be believed only because the relationship between "philosophers and their disciples" is characterized by a "mutual complaisance" resting on the intrinsic pleasure that minds find in surprising and remarkable propositions. Truth has nothing to do with it: "any thing propos'd to us, which causes surprize and admiration, gives such a satisfaction to the mind, that it ... will never be perswaded that its pleasure is entirely without foundation" (*T* 1.2.1.1/26).[36] What is at work here is the spirit of the classical skeptic: certain knowledge of truth is not necessary for a happy life, nor perhaps is it available to the skeptical questioner. One attends to Xeno's paradoxes, as to Carneades's famous orations on justice, one wonders at the impenetrability of it all, and one gets on with life. Naturalism and the Practical Criterion are deeply implicated in this, the very beginning of Hume's account of space and time.[37] The implication for Hume as historian is that the writing of histories should be seen as an expression of sociability, of complaisance—not as an exercise in metaphysics.

The paradox with which Hume chooses to conclude his study of extension (and succession) is designed to show that the attempt to ground moral, political, or historical narratives on ideas that have no foundation whatever in original sense impressions necessarily leads to self-contradiction.[38] If we are to avoid self-contradiction, then, we must restrict ourselves in our theorizing to the postulation of discrete and finite points or locations extended in space or successively arranged over time. For such notions as eternity and omnipresence, infinite time or infinite space, there can be no basis in human imagining. This is the philosophical basis for Hume's hostility toward "Monkish" or "Whiggish" history. If one asks "why the allusions to Xeno?" then surely the answer is that from Xeno a proper sense of the irreducibly paradoxical and contingent nature of the intellectual categories of space and time can be gained. It is within the boundaries of paradox and contingency that the skeptic seeks to learn how to live and be happy—and, we may add, how to write history.

Hume emphasizes that he is illustrating, in his analysis of space and time, a complete and distinctive approach to philosophizing based on sense impressions, experience, and fallible human judgment and imagination. He anticipates an objection to his method: "'Twill probably be said . . . that I explain only the manner in which objects affect the senses, without endeavouring to account for their real nature and operations" (*T* 1.2.5.25/63). "I answer this objection, by pleading guilty, and by confessing that my intention never was to penetrate into the nature of bodies, or explain the secret causes of their operations. . . . I am afraid, that such an enterprize is beyond the reach of human understanding" (*T* 1.2.5.26/64). We cannot know "body"—or extension, or duration—"otherwise than by those external properties, which discover themselves to the senses": "I content myself with knowing perfectly the manner in which objects affect my senses, and their connections with each other, as far as experience informs me of them.*This suffices for the conduct of life; and this also suffices for my philosophy*" (*T* 1.2.5.26/64; emphasis added). There is a discernible echo of the Practical Criterion of the Skeptics here. And there is more than a hint of a strategy for the *secularization* of the philosophical analysis of space and time: "*Here is the whole of my system;* and in no part of it have I endeavour'd to explain the cause, which separates bodies . . . and gives them a capacity of receiving others betwixt them" (*T* 1.2.5.25/ 63/4; emphasis added). Hume had earlier pursued this secularizing strategy quite explicitly in the context of his consideration of geometrical figures:

> Our appeal is still to the weak and fallible judgment, which we make from the appearance of the objects, and correct by a compass or common measure; and if we join the supposition of any farther correction, 'tis of such-a-one as is either useless or imaginary. *In vain shou'd we . . . employ the supposition of a deity, whose omnipotence may enable him to*

> *form a perfect geometrical figure. . . . As the ultimate standard of these figures is deriv'd from nothing but the senses and imagination, 'tis absurd to talk of any perfection beyond what these faculties can judge of . . .* (T 1.2.4.29/51; emphasis added)

Could he not have said exactly the same thing about abstract ideas of time and space? In fact, as we have seen in a passage quoted above, Hume did return to this theme at the very end of part 2, book 1 of the *Treatise*, asserting that philosophizing must always be circumscribed by "the universe of the imagination": "Let us chace our imagination to the heavens, or to the utmost limits of the universe; we never really advance a step beyond ourselves. . . . This is the universe of the imagination, nor have we any idea but what is there produc'd" (*T* 1.2.6.8/67–68). Hume's image of a "universe of the imagination," centered on and bounded by the self, yet paradoxically conveying a vivid sense of the isolation of the self in a vast sea of spatial and temporal phenomena, deserves to be carefully examined as one of the seminal metaphors of modern social, historical, and political thought. The skeptical Hume made an astute diagnosis of the plight of the imaginative self adrift in this new secularized spatiotemporal context. He was appropriately hesitant about imposing on that context (or that self) the authoritative strictures of a "system," be it rational, fanatical, or superstitious.

Professor Donald Livingston has pointed out that there are two different and complementary accounts of time and space, especially of time, in Hume's *Treatise*.[39] Because of its focus on the ordering of points in time in a manner analogous to the spatial idea of arrangement, Livingston refers to the discussion of time in book 1 (which I have been discussing so far) as "tenseless." He emphasizes, rightly, that by contrast, Hume's second discussion, in book 2, part 3 at sections 7 and 8 (427–38), is all about tense. Yet, in it, the characteristic transposition of spatial language still takes place: Hume's discussion is of "contiguity and distance" in past, present, and future time. Looking at the same phenomenon with different eyes, I think of these two discussions as, in book 1, atomistic and, in book 2, Heraclitean, for in the second discussion we are presented with an analogy between the "flow of time" and the momentum Hume had attributed to the movement of the imagination in book 1 (*T* 1.4.2.22/198).

The account begins with a reference back to book 1, and to the anchoring of the imagination in the self and in the present as a "point in time": "'Tis obvious, that the imagination can never totally forget the points of space and time, in which we are existent" (T 2.3.7.2/427). Moreover, "it is necessitated every moment to reflect on the present" (*T* 2.3.7.2/428). Yet the imagination constantly "moves" (though presumably never advancing a step beyond its "self") toward points nearby or distant in time and/or space. The more distant the point, the more difficult the transition to it via intermediate points, and the less vivacious or vivid our impression or idea of it. Hume draws several interesting conclusions from this principle of "movement" of the imagination. First: it explains why "men" are so preoccupied "in common life" with what is immediately present to them in space or time (428); Hume's famous social formulation of "selfishness and confin'd generosity" as the bases of justice (T 3.2.2.17–18/495) is rooted in this way of imagining the spatial situation and behavior of the self. Second: insofar as the points or parts of space are all simultaneously present to the beholder at one time, whereas by definition the points of time are not, "the parts of extension being susceptible of an union to the senses, acquire an union in the fancy," while "the incompatibility of the parts of time in their real existence separates them in the imagination, and makes it more *difficult* for that faculty to trace any long succession or series of events" (T 2.3.7.5/429). Viewed from this perspective, the *History of England* is a Herculean attempt to overcome the resistance of historical data to narrative ordering—a sort of fling at cleaning out the Augean stables of historicity. The complementary implication is that systems for the imaginative ordering of space will take root in the mind more readily than those aimed at constructing histories. Third: a compensating factor perhaps, in relation to the preceding point—"We always follow *the succession of time* [emphasis added] in placing our ideas"; thus there is a natural basis after all, in a very general way, for the standard pattern of "historical narrations." Unfortunately, when we try to think back, so to speak, to a "past object," Hume feels that we swim against the current of the "stream of time"; when we imagine a future point, we "flow along" with it. So the imagination flows more easily toward the future than into the past (see T 2.3.7.6–9/430–32)—a highly impressionistic and dubious proposition on the face of it. Fourth: we are, Hume asserts, more impressed (presumably for the reasons given above) by objects distant in time than by those distant in space: "Ancient busts and inscriptions are valu'd more than *Japan* tables" (T 2.3.8.3/433).

All these observations and claims reinforce the root idea that the temporal imagination—the imagination "moving" through time—has a momentum derived from its own nature and either augmented or obstructed by the idea of a flowing "stream of time." Whereas in book 1 we were exposed to close analogies between points in space and points in time, in book 2 we are shown asymmetries between space and time, as well as asymmetries in time itself, and especially between time past and time future: asymmetries generated by the fact that there is a natural "flow" and momentum in the imagination and in time itself. Thus Hume summarizes: "In our common way of thinking we are plac'd in a kind of middle station betwixt the past and future; and as our imagination finds a kind of difficulty in running along the former, and a facility in following the course of the latter, the difficulty conveys the notion of ascent, and the facility of the contrary" (*T* 2.3.8.12/437). The ascent into the past is challenging; the glide into the future is natural.[40] Then why did Hume write history and not some prototype of futurology or science fiction? He provides an answer that speaks to "complaisance" rather than to truth. The imagination and "the soul," he argues, are stimulated and nourished by opposition to their normal, natural way of encountering the world:

> every thing, which invigorates and inlivens the soul, whether by touching the passions or imagination, naturally conveys to the fancy this *inclination for ascent*, and determines it to run against the natural stream of its thoughts and conceptions. This *aspiring progress of the imagination* suits the present disposition of the mind; and the difficulty, instead of extinguishing its vigour and alacrity, has the contrary effect, of sustaining and encreasing it. (*T* 2.3.8.9/435; emphasis added)

Surely we have in this passage an indication of the mentality of Hume the historian: the historical—and historiographic—imagination is here portrayed as the embodiment of a heroic human response to intellectual challenge. The writing of history expresses the "inclination for ascent" of a lively and "invigorated" soul, determined to "run against the natural stream" of easy, conventional thinking, bent on "progress" and sustained in its vigour and alacrity by the very difficulty of the task.

Having depicted the combination of passion and reason that animates the historian in the most dramatic terms, Hume nonetheless ends his examination of "space and time" with a cautionary note for those who would reconstruct the psychology of individuals distant from themselves in time and/or space (or even write autobiographies after long lives): "Upon the whole, this struggle of passion and of reason, as it is call'd, diversifies human life, and makes men so different not only from each other, but also from themselves in different times. Philosophy can only account for a few of the greater and more sensible events of this war; but must leave all the smaller and more delicate revolutions, as dependent on principles too fine and minute for her comprehension" (*T* 2.3.8.13/438). The voice of the skeptic thus returns to a discussion that had begun to sound rather enthusiastic. The historical imagination is dynamic, but this should not induce the historian to think that historical narrative can re-create past events or (pace R. G. Collingwood) rethink past thoughts.[41] A picture in broad strokes (risking caricature) of the "great war of passion and reason" that gives human life its diversity can be achieved. But many a "small and delicate revolution" must remain lost in the mists of time—or rather unattainably "upstream," given the natural flow of time and the leanings of the imagination. Such are the excitements and the limitations of historical narration for Hume.

Conclusion

Hume's philosophical and historiographical activities were shaped, at least in part, by the simple if ambitious objective of exploring the "universe of the imagination," the intellectual realm within which all of our ideas, in his view, have their origins (*T* 1.2.6.9/68, quoted above). It was a bold and innovative intellectual course to pursue, and at times Hume could hardly hold to it.[42] It was seminally modern, though not of course intentionally so. Hume was mining classical philosophical sources in order to find a way of coping with the very problem that had plagued skeptics from ancient times: how to live happily and well in conditions of epistemological uncertainty, eschewing metaphysical and moral dogmatism. Hume's attempt to construct a skeptical basis for a happy life by trying "to introduce the experimental method of reasoning into moral subjects" took on added urgency because of the accelerating pace of social transformation and the rising level of turbulence characteristic of the emerging commercial society in which he and his friend Adam Smith both lived.[43] My contention is that Hume offered his analyses of space and time as an essential step in a lifelong philosophical project of mapping the "universe of the imagination," and that the governing intention of his historical work, both in the *History of England* and in the *Essays*, was to advance that project. This "mapping" process aimed at a plausible though inherently conditional and imperfect articulation of the nature and the ordering of social space and historical time—an idea that could itself have no direct basis in sense experience, but which could be arrived at only by the patient and candid examination of the arrangement of objects and agents "in" space and time, together with an understanding of the imaginative processes by which the self came to be equipped with impressions as well as ideas of them. As a complement to his analysis of space, Hume's particular account of time was meant primarily to provide a view of the successive changes in social arrangements encountered by humans in their historical experience, which is to say in the process of maintaining their identity "in the incessant changes of [their] parts." Thus Hume's account of time directs our attention not to the contrast between temporal human experience and eternity, but to patterns of historical change.

In his 1969 Massey Lectures, published in a revised version in 1995 as *Time as History*, the Canadian moralist and theologian George Grant mounted a critique of modernity based on its distinctive conception of "Time as Historical Process."[44] He wrote that "through the ages men have tried to understand the temporality of their lives. In our age, astonishment about that temporality has been calmed by apprehending it above all as history."[45] Grant contrasts this conception of temporality with an earlier conception, which he derives from Platonism and from the Thomistic (not Roman) Christian natural law tradition. This ancient conception found the "nature" of humanity and its world to be revealed not in its temporal context but in the contemplation of the eternal. Plato, he asserts, understood time "as an image, the moving image of eternity."[46] David Hume's exploration of the ideas of space and time in his *Treatise of Human Nature* and his second *Enquiry* seems to be an intellectual moment at which the very transformation to which Grant alludes is, if not actually effected, at least recognized in an explicit and comprehensive way. Space is understood as "extension," its boundaries established by the capacity of the human imagination to work constructively with the sensations and impressions generated in human experience, its constituent units as numerous and diverse as the imagination can create, but still neither infinitely divisible nor infinite in number: "this idea, as conceiv'd by the imagination . . . is not infinitely divisible, nor consists of an infinite number of parts: For that exceeds the comprehension of our limited capacities" (*T* 1.2.2.9/32). For Hume, what extension is to space, succession is to time. Just as there can be no infinite diversity or divisibility of the units of extension that make up space, there can be no infinite divisibility, diversity, or number of the successive instants that make up time. Time conceived in this way may be many things, but it cannot be the "moving image of eternity." It can be only the imaginative record of experiential change: "nor can any thing unchangeable be ever said to have duration" (*T* 1.2.3.11/37). Time and eternity are antitheses. The idea of the eternal, or of an eternal unchanging Divinity, can have a "place in" human history only in a profoundly paradoxical sense—as an idea that lies entirely outside the boundaries of human imagining, an image of the unimaginable.

It would be seriously misleading to say, or think, that Hume somehow "qualifies" as a historian solely because he wrote the *History of England*. It would be more plausible and helpful to suggest that he might have turned to writing the *History* because his philosophical and literary work had such an important historical dimension. It is worth underlining the fact that his approach to the writing of history is both literary and philosophical, and indeed that the latter can properly be subsumed under the former. His reflections in the *Treatise*, as we have seen, included significant—and highly imaginative—ruminations on the idea of time and on the possibilities for imaginative communication across time on the basis of the sympathetic mirroring of minds. It should not be forgotten, moreover, that his *Essays* were in an important sense not only "moral, political and literary," but also historical.

Space does not permit at this point the full treatment the *Essays* richly deserve as repositories of historical insight and as applications/illustrations of Hume's playfully imaginative approach to the "verities" of fanatical and superstitious historiography. On one hand, they may be seen as illustrating, from the annals of history, the principles of human nature whose genesis via the sympathetic imagination is explored in the *Treatise*. On the other, they capture, as W. B. Todd observes, "all the aberrations of human behavior as there exhibited in 'wars, intrigues, factions and revolutions'" (*H* 1: foreword, xi). Thus in "Of the Origin of Government" (*E* 38), we are shown how the record of history exposes a "great weakness" that is "incurable in human nature": the very shortsighted self-interestedness that was the focal point of analysis in Hume's study of the origin of justice and property in the *Treatise* (*T* 3.2.2/484–501). One of the most famous moments in "Of the Independency of Parliament" comes when Hume puts forward an ostensible paradox: the assertion "*that every man must be supposed a knave*" is "true in *politics*," though "false in *fact*" (*E* 42–43, emphasis in original). This is "in fact" no paradox at all, as long as we understand that in politics, as in history, we construct our most fundamental generalizations imaginatively. Moreover, it is a clear allusion to the picture of human nature given in Machiavelli's *The Prince*, where princes are advised to assume *politically* that every man is a knave, though we can be quite sure that Machiavelli did not hold this to be true in fact when applied to the people of Florence or even of Rome.[47] But it is worth recalling in this context that Hume distinguished sharply between Machiavelli's moral merits as a "politician" and as a historian: "When he talks as a *Politician*, . . . he considers poisoning, assassination and perjury, as lawful arts of power; but when he speaks as an *Historian* . . . he shows . . . indignation against vice, and . . . approbation of virtue, in many passages" (*E* 567).

"Of the Rise and Progress of the Arts and Sciences" begins (*E* 111–14) with Hume's reflections on causality and contingency in history: "*What depends upon a few persons*," Hume writes, "*is . . . to be ascribed to chance, or secret and unknown causes. . . . What arises from a great number, may often be accounted for by determinate and known causes*" (*E* 112, Hume's emphasis). Thus the deeds of "HARRY IV. Cardinal RICHLIEU, and LOUIS XIV," though of enormous importance, must remain ultimately mysterious to us, since it is easier to explain "the rise and progress of commerce in any kingdom," than it is to explain either such deeds or other elite activities such as the rise of "learning"

(E 113).⁴⁸ The sloppy historian—or philosopher of history—is likely, then, to "assign causes which never existed, and reduce what is merely contingent to stable and universal principles" (E 113). In much the same vein, "Of Some Remarkable Customs" (E 366–76) attacks the use of "general maxims" in politics (aside from maxims that describe human nature itself—366) and attacks specifically the theoretical sacred cow of the indivisibility of sovereign power by pointing to historical evidence. The passage sounds almost mischievous: "A wheel within a wheel . . . is considered by Lord SHAFTESBURY as an absurdity in politics: But what must we say to two equal wheels, which govern the same political machine, without any mutual check, controul, or subordination; and yet preserve the greatest harmony and concord?" (E 370). "For this was actually the case with the ROMAN republic," in which "legislative power was . . . lodged in the *comitia centuriata* and *comitia tributa*" (E 371). Hume is a devastating and playful "debunker"—is this not precisely what one would expect from an adventurer in imaginative inquiry?⁴⁹

In fact, a unique historical sensibility runs throughout Hume's oeuvre. His approach to history and to historiography is skeptical, which is to say experimental, in a very particular sense; and it forms an integral part of his approach to "moral subjects" as a whole. This approach derives its distinctive character from the foundational idea that "the minds of men are mirrors to one another" (T 2.2.5.21/365, quoted above) and from Hume's strategic decision to use the idea of the sympathetic and constructive imagination to dramatize and explore communication between and among minds, including minds separated in space and/or time. Hume's skepticism is mitigated by, because it is grounded in, the capacity of the imagination to generate coherent ideas, beginning with "self" and "soul" and "substance" but including also our ideas of the human spatial context (commonwealth) and the human temporal context (history). In contextualizing ourselves, as it were, spatially and temporally, we "chace our imagination to the heavens, or to the utmost limits of the universe"; and yet "we never really advance a step beyond ourselves." This is the paradox of imaginative skepticism, and the paradox of historical writing. Historical narrative imitates the flow of time but can never duplicate it: interruptions and discontinuities are inevitable and ubiquitous. It is the cognitive momentum of the constructive imagination that allows us to override those interruptions and discontinuities, to "enter deeply into" the minds of historical figures and to entertain vivid impressions of dramatic historical events. The reader glides through Hume's history on the wings of imagination.

Recalling his rejection of Hobbes's rational "system" of thought, and his conviction that the influence of such systems must always be short-lived, it is tempting to see in Hume's *History*, and in the historical dimension of his philosophical work, the actualization of his idea of the "Pleasant comedy," which "paints the manners of the age, *and exposes a faithful picture of nature.*" Such a work, Hume no doubt hoped, would be "a durable work . . . transmitted to the latest posterity." In "Of the Study of History" (*E* 563–69), Hume said of the reading of history that "it amuses the fancy, . . . improves the understanding, and . . . strengthens virtue" (565): "we should be for ever children in understanding, were it not for this *invention*, which extends our experience to all past ages, and to the most distant nations; making them contribute as much to our improvement in wisdom, as if they had actually lain under our observation" (566–67; emphasis added).

NOTES

1. As John B. Stewart rightly points out, in *The Moral and Political Philosophy of David Hume* (New York: Columbia University Press, 1963), by "morals" Hume meant "the entire realm of words, deeds, institutions, and works of art, insofar as this realm is shaped by the minds of men" (82).

2. C. B. Macpherson, ed., *Hobbes: Leviathan* (Harmondsworth: Penguin, 1968), bk. 1, chap. 2, "Of Imagination," 88.

3. Fanatical ("Whiggish" or "Tory"): see Hume's (historical) objections to the use of "philosophical or speculative system[s] of principles" in political argument in "Of the Original Contact," *E* 465–87, at 465–66; Superstitious ("Monkish"): Hume blames the "barrenness . . . of the accounts transmitted to us" of the early "ages" of English history on the "Monks, who were the only annalists during those ages"(*H* 1:24–25).

4. "I . . . was seized very early with a passion for literature, which has been the ruling passion of my life, and the great source of my enjoyments" ("My Own Life," *E* xxxii–xxxiii).

5. For more on cognitive momentum, see my essay "Hume's 'Imagination' Revisited," in *Lumen: Selected Proceedings from the Canadian Society for Eighteenth-Century Studies* 17 (1998), ed. C. Gibson-Wood and G. D. Fulton, 134.

6. James Farr, "Hume, Hermeneutics, and History: A 'Sympathetic' Account," *History and Theory* 17 (1978): 289. Farr also writes that "sympathy is emphatically not a feeling or passion, but a species of communication" (292). This is supported by Hume's reference at *T* 2.3.6.8/427 to "the principle of sympathy or communication."

7. Farr, "Hume, Hermeneutics, and History," 295.

8. Adam Smith, who was clearly well aware of the nature of Hume's ideas on sympathy and imagination, argued that the process whereby we enter into the interests and perspectives of others should be understood by reference to a "philosophy of vision" in which "the weak eye of human reason" would be contrasted with the more powerful "natural eye of the mind." See E. C. Mossner and I. S. Ross, eds., *Correspondence of Adam Smith*, in the Glasgow Edition of the Works and Correspondence of Adam Smith (Indianapolis: Liberty Classics, 1987), Letter no. 40 to Gilbert Elliott, 10 October 1759, 56, 53, 55, respectively.

9. Hume's essay "Of the Populousness of Ancient Nations" (*E* 377–464) begins with an evocation of "the continual and rapid motion of matter," and of "the violent revolutions with which every part [of the world] is agitated," which seems to me to echo this passage in *T*.

10. Hume's peroration on Alfred (*H* 1:81) is a model of rhetorical elegance: "Both living and dead, Alfred was regarded, by foreigners, no less than by his own subjects, as the greatest prince

after Charlemagne that had appeared in Europe during several ages, and as one of the wisest and best that had ever adorned the annals of any nation."

11. "The king had raised Becket from a low station to the highest offices, had honoured him with his countenance and friendship, had trusted to his assistance in forwarding his favourite project against the clergy; and when he found him become of a sudden his most rigid opponent... rage at the disappointment, and indignation against such signal ingratitude, transported him beyond all bounds of moderation; and there seems to have entered more of passion than of justice, or even of policy, in this violent prosecution" (*H* 1:317–18).

12. Of Charles II, Hume said: "His good understanding lost much of its influence by his want of application; his bounty was more the result of a facility of disposition than any generosity of character; his social humour led him frequently to neglect his dignity; his love of pleasure was not attended with proper sentiment, and decency; and while he seemed to bear a good will to everyone that approached him, he had a heart not very capable of friendship, and he had secretly entertained a very bad opinion and distrust of mankind" (*H* 6:189).

13. Note that "sympathized with" is not an acceptable substitute for the phraseology "communicated to us via sympathy."

14. Farr, "Hume, Hermeneutics, and History," 299.

15. See the conclusion of D. D. Raphael, "'The True Old Humean Philosophy' and Its Influence on Adam Smith," in *David Hume: Bicentenary Papers*, ed. G. P. Morice (Austin: University of Texas Press, 1977), 23–48.

16. Smith noted, in his essay "The Principles which Lead and Direct Philosophical Enquiries; illustrated by the History of Astronomy," "how easily the learned give up the evidence of their senses to preserve the coherence of the ideas of their imagination." See W. P. D. Wightman, ed., *Essays on Philosophical Subjects*, in the Glasgow Edition of the Works and Correspondence of Adam Smith, 77.

17. Smith, "Principles ... History of Astronomy," 41.

18. Ibid., 41–42.

19. Ibid., 45–46.

20. Ibid., 46.

21. See A. L. Macfie and D. D. Raphael, eds., *The Theory of Moral Sentiments*, in the Glasgow Edition of the Works and Correspondence of Adam Smith, bk. 2, sec. 2, chap. 2, 82–85: "Of the sense of Justice, of Remorse, and of the consciousness of Merit." For the indispensability of the sense of justice to society, see chap. 3, "Of the utility of this constitution of Nature," 86.

22. On moral sentiments, see Macfie and Raphael, eds., *The Theory of Moral Sentiments*, pt. 1, "Of the Propriety of Action," sec. 1, "Of the Sense of Propriety," chap. 1, "Of Sympathy," 9–13.

23. See Ronald L. Meek, *Social Science and the Ignoble Savage* (Cambridge: Cambridge University Press, 1976).

24. See Wightman, *Essays on Philosophical Subjects*, 31–105.

25. See R. L. Meek, D. D. Raphael, and P. G. Stein, eds., *Lectures on Jurisprudence*, in the Glasgow Edition of the Works and Correspondence of Adam Smith, Report of 1762–63, 14. The four stages are not as clearly enunciated in Hume's essay "Of Commerce" (*E* 253–67), but the sharp periodic distinction between commercial and precommercial societies is symptomatic of the shared conceptual approach of Hume and Smith.

26. See J. C. A. Gaskin, ed., *David Hume: Principal Writings on Religion including "Dialogues Concerning Natural Religion" and "The Natural History of Religion"* (Oxford: Oxford University Press, 1993), 134–96.

27. See R. H. Campbell, A. S. Skinner, and W. B. Todd, eds., *An Inquiry into the Nature and Causes of the Wealth of Nations*, 2 vols., Glasgow Edition of the Works and Correspondence, e.g., 1:376–427.

28. Among indications of the influence of this construct in Hume's work, Alfred (*H* 1:81) and Athelstan (*H* 1:88) are both singled out for "remarkable" (*H* 1:88) legislative initiatives, which helped advance the development of "commerce" in their realms.

29. C. B. Macpherson, ed., *Hobbes: Leviathan*, pt. 1, chap. 13.

30. Ibid., chap. 18, p. 233.

31. See *H* 6:153: Hume praised Harrington's *Oceana*, with its plan for an "imaginary republic," as a work "justly admired" for its "genius and invention." He was cool to Harrington's style but much more sympathetic to the "matter" of his work than he was to Hobbes's systematic thought. And this despite his judgment that "the idea . . . of a perfect and immortal commonwealth will always be found as chimerical as that of a perfect and immortal man." Cf. Hume's essay "Idea of a Perfect Commonwealth" (*E* 512–29), esp. at 514.

32. Montaigne, "Of Experience," in *The Complete Essays of Montaigne*, trans. D. M. Frame (Stanford: Stanford University Press, 1958), 821–22.

33. Recall the bewildered Hume at the end of the section on skeptical philosophy at *T* 1.4.7/269. Quoted below at n. 42.

34. Montaigne, *Essays*,"Of Experience," 836.

35. Montaigne, *Essays*, "Of Vanity," 730. He adds, "These great, lengthy altercations about the best form of society and the rules most suitable to bind us, are altercations fit only for the exercise of our minds; as in the liberal arts there are several subjects whose essence is controversy and dispute, and which have no life apart from that."

36. "Mutual complaisance": Cf. Hobbes's treatment of "compleasance" as the foundation of "sociability": "A fifth law of nature is COMPLEASANCE; that is to say, *That every man strive to accommodate himself to the rest.* . . . The observers of this Law, may be called SOCIABLE, (the Latines called them Commodi)" (Macpherson, ed., *Hobbes: Leviathan*, pt. 1, chap. 15, p. 210). Adam Smith was to dramatize the effects of "surprise" and "wonder" on the human imagination at greater length in his essay "The Principles which Lead and Direct Philosophical Inquiries; Illustrated by the History of Astronomy" (Wightman, *Essays on Philosophical Subjects*, 34–39).

37. See the discussion of Carneades's lectures in *Sextus Empiricus: Selections from the Major Writings on Scepticism, Man, and God*, ed. P. P. Hallie, trans. S. G. Etheridge (Indianapolis: Hackett, 1985): "on the first day he 'proved' that justice was metaphysically founded in universal, natural law; on the second day he 'proved' that justice was nothing but *ad hoc* expediency" (20). See 39–40 for an explanation of "The Criterion of Scepticism."

38. Ibid., 64.

39. Donald W. Livingston, *Hume's Philosophy of Common Life* (Chicago: University of Chicago Press, 1984), chap. 5, "Time and the Moral World"; see esp. 116.

40. The age of progress was to make much of the idea of a natural flow of the imagination into the future. Another strategic "ascent" into the past, however, would be necessary to chart retrospectively that progressive flow. Such was to be the methodology of Adam Smith's conjectural history, a methodology only embryonically present—if that—in Hume's *History*.

41. See R. G. Collingwood, *The Idea of History* (Oxford: Clarendon Press, 1946), especially the section entitled "History as Re-enactment of Past Experience." There, Collingwood writes that "the historian must re-enact the past in his own mind" (282).

42. "Where am I, or what? From what causes do I derive my existence, and to what condition shall I return? Whose favour shall I court, and whose anger must I dread? What beings surround me? and on whom have I any influence, and who have any influence on me? I am confounded with all these questions, and begin to fancy myself in the most deplorable condition imaginable, inviron'd with the deepest darkness, and utterly depriv'd of the use of every member and faculty" (*T* 1.4.7.8/269).

43. We do well to recall that the full title is, of course, *A Treatise of Human Nature: Being An Attempt to introduce the experimental Method of Reasoning into Moral Subjects*.

44. George Grant, *Time as History*, ed. William Christian (Toronto: University of Toronto Press, 1995), 3–15.

45. Ibid., 13. The same point is made in a different context by James Tully in his introduction to Pufendorf's *On the Duty of Man and Citizen* (Cambridge: Cambridge University Press, 1991), xvii, where he observes that in place of "the Aristotelian and Thomistic concept of nature as a

purposeful realm ordered by intrinsic teleological dispositions," "the philosophers of the new natural sciences advanced a concept of nature as a non-purposive realm of atoms [exhibiting] ... motion and an extrinsic order of efficient causes or regularities."

46. Grant, *Time as History*, 52.

47. See *The Prince* in *The Portable Machiavelli*, ed. and trans. P. Bondanella and M. Musa (Harmondsworth: Penguin, 1979), 131.

48. This general principle would seem to belie the extensiveness, vividness, and conclusiveness of the many compelling character sketches that punctuate the text of the *History*—unless the purpose of the *History* is instruction and entertainment rather than the discovery of ultimate truth. Parables are not invalidated by being in some degree caricatures.

49. "Of the Populousness of Ancient Nations" (*E* 377–464), "Of the Original Contract" (*E* 465–87), and "Idea of a Perfect Commonwealth" (*E* 512–29) provide only a sampling of Hume's delight in "debunking," or dethroning, the most dogmatically held and deeply embedded of historical general "truths."

THE "MOST CURIOUS & IMPORTANT OF ALL QUESTIONS
OF ERUDITION": HUME'S ASSESSMENT OF THE
POPULOUSNESS OF ANCIENT NATIONS

M. A. Box and Michael Silverthorne

1. Overview

One hundred and eight of the 304 pages in the second edition of David Hume's *Political Discourses* belonged to "Of the Populousness of Antient Nations," 101 pages of 270 in the third edition. The version of that discourse in the 1772 *Essays and Treatises on Several Subjects* included over 260 footnotes, many lengthy and impressively erudite. Plainly, Hume deemed that discourse a major work warranting far more space and documentation of sources than any other of his essays.[1] It is remarkable then that the annual bibliographies in *Hume Studies* list not one article on that essay. Roland Hall's enumerative bibliography for the years from 1925 to 1976 lists only the three following discussions: a few pages in James Bonar's 1929 lectures on theories of population, slightly more than two pages of Eugene Rotwein's introduction to his collection of Hume's essays, and a 1949 article by Ernest Campbell Mossner on the Ancient-Modern controversy.[2] Secondary literature that is valuable for gaining perspective on the essay might not focus on the essay or deal with it at all and hence evades the notice of the indexes.[3]

The reason for Hume's heavy investment in that essay is straightforwardly proclaimed: it dealt with "the most curious and important of all questions of erudition," as Hume says in his footnote saluting Robert Wallace's work on the topic.[4] It is important because of its profound implications: "the comparative populousness of ages or kingdoms . . . commonly determines concerning the preference of their whole police, manners, and constitution of government" (159 = ¶ 4). Hume condenses Wallace's version of the same point. The question,

Wallace says, "is closely connected with the deepest policy and with the most intimate constitution of human society," namely the circumstances, favorable or not, for procreation and family life: "The question concerning the number of mankind in antient and modern times, under antient or modern governments, is . . . of the greatest importance; since it must be a strong presumption in favour of the customs or policy of any government, if, *cæteris paribus*, it is able to raise up and maintain a greater number of people."[5] Hume builds his case on the same premise:

> For a like reason, every wise, just, and mild government, by rendering the condition of its subjects easy and secure, will always abound most in people, as well as in commodities and riches. A country, indeed, whose climate and soil are fitted for vines, will naturally be more populous than one, which produces only corn, and that more populous than one, which is only fitted for pasturage. But if every thing else be equal, it seems natural to expect, that wherever there are most happiness and virtue, and the wisest institutions, there will also be most people. (160 = ¶ 4)

Putting aside the effects of "*Physical* causes" not under human control like disease, population levels provide a measure of the quality of the "police," manners, and constitution of civilizations.[6] For population to have declined—as Montesquieu, Vossius, and Wallace claimed—would be an indictment crying out for reform taking its example from the ancients.

The question is both important, in its implications, and "curious," that is, exact, subtle, requiring nice diligence and accuracy.[7] Curiousness and importance are not incompatible, but, in his peculiar ambidextrous way of doing more than one thing at a time, Hume made the two point in different directions. In its curious aspect, the essay is a virtuoso examination of a historical question about comparative populations; in its implications, it is a polemic about police, manners, and constitutions. The thesis of the curious examination is expressly skeptical, prescribing suspension of judgment. That of the polemic is an endorsement of modernism and a condemnation of the ancients' ways exerting a dangerous attraction on intellectuals like Fénélon, Montesquieu, Fletcher of Saltoun, Adam Ferguson, and Smollett. These two theses might be inconsistent and render the essay incoherent. They might be consistent logically but in tension rhetorically, for suspension of judgment is a notably weak way to make a polemical case against emulating the ancients. Perhaps Hume makes one a foil for the other and offers suspension of judgment as a formality behind which a firm conviction is discernible that the ancient world was, beyond a reasonable doubt, less populous because of circumstances largely of the ancients' own creation. Perhaps the skeptical thesis is all he deliberately intended to argue and the polemical one is an accidental effect. The question is not strictly capable of proof, though it is arguable. Our contention is that Hume offers two essays in one, with the polemical one enhanced in its pungency by its delivery in the form of a curious enquiry into a question of history.

The polemic is not delivered through a transparently weak or preposterous ostensible essay that Hume undercuts with irony. This essay is not Swiftean satire, but a work of history. Hume argues the curious question with formidable if sometimes peccable scholarship and a detail shaped and probably assisted—it should be acknowledged—by his conning of Wallace's dissertation.[8] For that reason the argument is best examined in relation to Wallace rather than to Montesquieu, Vossius, or other famous luminaries.

Wallace's thesis was that by comparing the conditions where history affords evidence, particularly in those countries near the Mediterranean Sea, we find "that in most of those countries whose antient and present state is best known, there have been fewer inhabitants in later ages, there are fewer at present, than were in more antient times, and that these countries were better peopled before the *Roman* empire was established, than they have ever been at any succeeding period." These countries "must have been best peopled . . . about the time of *Alexander the Great*, and before the *Roman* empire had enslaved the world" (*Dissertation*, 32, 147). Hume's stated thesis was skeptical. All he "aspires" to show is that, confining "ourselves to the scene of antient history, *Europe* and the nations about the *Mediterranean*," the "conclusion is not so certain as is pretended, in favour of antiquity" (158–59 = ¶ 3). Such a milk-and-water thesis from someone as provocative as Hume was often pleased to be seems a bit mincing, but he reiterated it several times (as in ¶¶ 110, 134, 136). In the letter to Clephane of 18 April 1750, Hume described the essay as "a very learned, elaborate discourse, concerning the populousness of antiquity; not altogether in opposition to *Vossius* and *Montesquieu*, who exaggerate that affair infinitely; but, starting some doubts, and scruples, and difficulties, sufficient to make us suspend our judgment on that head." When in the third edition of the *Political Discourses* he changed the footnote to acknowledge the recent publication of the *Dissertation*, he wrote, "So learn'd a refutation would have made the author suspect, that his reasonings were entirely overthrown, had he not us'd the precaution, from the beginning, to keep himself on the sceptical side; and having taken this advantage of the ground, he was enabled, tho' with much inferior forces, to preserve himself from a total defeat. That Reverend gentleman will always find, where his antagonist is so entrench'd, that it will be very difficult to force him. *Varro*, in such a situation, could defend himself against *Hanniabal*, *Pharnaces* against *Caesar*."[9]

2. Hume's Skeptical Argument

As a matter of logic Hume could not prove that populations were larger in his day by demolishing the arguments of Vossius, Montesquieu, and Wallace. Refuting their arguments establishes no conclusion about comparative populousness, only the failure of their particular arguments. Formally, and officially, the essay ends with no more than a negative result about others' arguments. Readers might not feel so agnostic, however, upon reaching the end, where Hume implicitly upbraids Montesquieu through a criticism of Plutarch: "The humour of blaming the present, and admiring the past, is strongly rooted in human nature, and has an influence, even on persons, endu'd with the profoundest judgment and most extensive learning" (262 = ¶ 186). The compliment to Montesquieu's judgment and learning only adds to the debunking effect of the sentence, and Hume ends on an assertive note when he might have ended by asking, "Que sais-je?"[10]

Nevertheless, the skeptical argument that we are reduced to agnosticism by a lack of reliable information cannot be impugned. Its systematic construction means that it submits itself fairly well to outlining.[11]

I. Physical causes, i.e., unaffected by human behavior (¶¶ 1–2)
   A. General: eternalism dismissed, its alternative moot (¶ 1)
   B. Particular (¶ 2)
      1. Diseases sufficient as *explanation* for but not *proof* of modern depopulation
II. "Moral" causes, i.e., human nature as cause (¶¶ 3–186). *Procedural steps:* (*a*) reasoned surmise & (*b*) assessment of available facts (¶ 3). Moral causes pertain to the first step.
   A. Reasoning on probable causes (¶¶ 4–93)
      1. *Premise:* Given the opportunity, men and women will have children, so, other things being equal, population growth attends happiness & virtue, the precondition for which are good "police," manners, & constitutions of nations (¶ 4; cf. n. 13).
      2. *Procedural steps:* probable reasonings divided into (*a*) domestic & (*b*) political (¶ 5)
         a. Domestic economy, ancient vs. modern (¶¶ 6–43)
            i. Ancient slavery vs. modern service: "All I pretend to infer from these reasonings is, that slavery is in general disadvantageous both to the happiness and populousness of mankind, and that its place is much better supplied by the practice of hired servants" (¶¶ 6–38 at 34).

ii. Ancient infanticide vs. modern monasticism (¶¶ 39–43)
   (a) *Concession:* Paradoxically infanticide might encourage marriages, & modern "hospitals" might subvert them (¶¶ 42–43).
b. Political economy, ancient vs. modern (¶¶ 44–94)
   i. Advantages of ancients: Small polities foster civil liberty & comparative equality of fortune (¶¶ 45–52).
   ii. Disadvantages of ancients (¶¶ 53–93)
      (a) Bloody and severe maxims of war (¶¶ 54–62)
      (b) Inhumane, immoderate maxims of peace: "factions and revolutions" (¶¶ 63–82)
      (c) Industry & commerce (¶¶ 83–92)
      (d) Summary of disadvantages (¶ 93)
III. Matters of fact: what available facts indicate, if anything (¶¶ 94–186)
A. Facts are "uncertain," i.e., unascertainable (¶ 94).
   1. Presumption against any numbers implausible prima facie
      a. Textual corruption (¶ 95)
      b. Scantiness of statistics (¶ 96)
      c. Unknown variable of slave population (¶ 97)
      d. Fabulous exaggeration & carelessness in history (¶¶ 98–109)
         i. Ancient cities and environs (¶¶ 110–33)
            (a) Greece (¶¶ 111–33)
               1) Athens (10 points, ¶¶ 111–21)
               2) Note that population figures refer to the whole territory of a city-state and not just the city, at Athens and elsewhere (¶¶ 122–23).
               3) Rhodes, Thebes, Mantinea, Sparta (¶¶ 124–27)
               4) Ætolia, Achaia, Thessaly, Epirus (¶¶ 128–32)
               5) Greece as a whole (¶ 133)
            (b) Rome & Roman Italy (¶¶ 134–51)
               1) The population of the city of Rome (¶¶ 135–47)
                  a) From the physical size of the city (¶ 135)
                  b) From the numbers receiving the corn dole (¶¶ 136–40)
                  c) Slave numbers at Rome (¶ 141)
                  d) Numbers of deaths (¶ 142)
                  e) Effect of corn dole on the rest of Italy (¶ 143)
                  f) Comparison of Rome with Antioch and Alexandria (¶¶ 144–45)
                  g) Size of Nero's palace (¶¶ 146–47)

            2) The emptiness of the rest of Italy (¶¶ 148–51)
    2. Maximum size of cities "in the nature of things" (¶¶ 152–54)
        a. Aristotle's unaccountable mistake (¶ 152)
        b. Actual logistical restraints (¶ 153)
            i. Empire
            ii. Commerce
            iii. London's synthesis allows the maximum (¶ 154).
            iv. Exceeding the maximum prompts expansion of prosperity out to provinces, making regions the better measure of populousness, as exemplified in the region around the Channel and North Sea.
    3. The warming of Europe is a possibility suggesting deforestation and increased cultivation as its cause (¶¶ 155–64).
    4. Comparing ancient and present "situations" of nations (¶¶ 165–76)
        a. Turkey in Africa (Egypt) & Turkey in Europe (¶ 165)
        b. Eastern Europe: Poland/Sarmatia, Muscovite Europe/Scythia, Scandinavia (¶ 166)
        c. Germany, Britain, France/Gauls, Switzerland/Helvetia, Netherlands/Batavia, ancient & modern Spain (¶¶ 167–74)
        d. Ancient & modern Italy (¶¶ 175–76)
    5. Disconfirmation of Montesquieu's thesis that large empires subvert themselves and their population (¶¶ 177–85)
        a. Roman Empire, including Roman Greece
            i. The effect of Roman dominion on Grecian population
            ii. Montesquieu's citation of incredible testimony by Plutarch
            iii. *Conclusion:* Testimony is always fallible, one reason being the natural inclination to blame the present found in Plutarch, Diodorus, & (implicitly) Montesquieu (¶ 186).

The structure of the argument, strikingly similar to Wallace's expository procedure, is designed to assess the question systematically, as completely as its nature allows.[12] Hume examines both physical and moral causes, concluding that, everything considered, the case for depopulation is unsuccessful. He then reinforces this conclusion in the second half of the essay by examining what the available facts indicate, thus dividing the essay into two units of 92 or 93 paragraphs, the first devoted to reasoned surmise, the second to assessment of "facts."

Hume uses physical causes as his introduction, giving "*general Physical* causes" and "*particular physical* causes" one paragraph each. For the former he rebuts the vague notion that because the world is corruptible, mankind would have been more populous in times closer to its inception than in the Georgian age of lead. The corruptibility of the world cannot explain, much less prove, a decline because "history and tradition" do not afford the perspective for us to locate mankind's stage of development. The species is as likely to be thriving as decaying. After this introductory flourish, Hume considers particular physical factors likely to affect populousness, specifically modern diseases. Hume's unexplained conclusion is that modern diseases like smallpox and the Great Pox could explain an established fact of depopulation but not prove an unestablished claim. Modern diseases must be factored in among other causes, most of which will emerge in the course of 93 paragraphs as favoring increasing populousness (156–57 = ¶¶ 1–2).

The distinction between physical and moral causation is familiar from "Of National Characters" (see e.g. ¶¶ 2–4), not to mention the *Treatise* (2.3.1.15/404–5). Wallace states it succinctly: some causes "may be called physical, as they depend entirely on the course of nature, and are independent of mankind. Others of them are moral, and depend on the affections, passions and institutions of men" (*Dissertation*, 12). The latter pertain to the causation of volition and yield probabilities inasmuch as human nature shapes behavior predictably. Thus human nature enables Hume (and Wallace) to treat as a premise "the general rule, that the happiness of any society and its populousness are necessary attendants" (166–67 n. = ¶ 13).[13] Men and women are such that, unhindered, they probably will procreate (¶ 4). (Exceptions merely prove the rule, even perhaps today after birth control has disconnected sexuality from procreation.) Some hindrances are manmade, variable over the ages, and, in principle, remediable.

Infelicitously, Hume informs us that he "shall, *first*, consider, whether it be probable, from what we know of the situation of society in both periods, that antiquity must have been more populous. *Secondly*, Whether in reality it was so" (159 = ¶ 3). By "in reality" he means whether "facts" such as statistics have survived that can overrule or confirm the probable reasonings he offers in the first 93 paragraphs. In a couple of paragraphs he will speak of assessing probabilities by "moral causes." Probable moral causes affecting procreation and longevity he divides into domestic and political aspects (161 = ¶ 5).

Those immersed in Hume's epistemology might be more tempted than others into confusion about these terms. Students of the *Treatise* might be prone to think of probability as opposed to demonstration, but, approaching the topic from that angle, we would find that even facts are probable in their degrees. Matters of fact are not capable of demonstration and hence resolve into probable causes, some so convincing however that in commonsense language we speak of "proof."[14] From one standpoint, familiar from book 1 of the *Treatise*, knowledge of even mathematics and physical causes is conditioned by the laws of human nature. In "Populousness," however, Hume is using ordinary language opposing "probable" to factual, and if facts are doubtful in this context it is not due to epistemological skepticism. The facts are data, or evidence, and the moral considerations are happiness or unhappiness created by good or bad police, manners, and constitutions.[15] The data are a kind of testimony and, like that in the four gospels, must be assessed in light of other facts. Such facts include the human proclivities to exaggerate, be credulous or delusional, make mistakes, be biased, lie. That testimony is false can never be incredible, and the content of testimony often is dubious. Hume's approach is very moderate, mitigated skepticism, not epistemology at its extremity. Hume is just being a critical historian. He tells us to suspend judgment not because knowledge is impossible, but because our information is inadequate.

The domestic economy of the ancients is compared to that of the moderns through the likely effects on populousness of slavery and modern service, respectively. "All I pretend to infer from these reasonings," Hume says, "is, that slavery is in general disadvantageous both to the happiness and populousness of mankind, and that its place is much better supply'd by the practice of hir'd servants" (177 = ¶ 34). (Whether the discussion of slavery does no more than Hume says is a question to which we will turn in section 4 below.) Following this discussion is one setting the practice of infanticide among the ancients against modern monasticism. It is possible, Hume concedes, that against expectations, the availability of infanticide might actually remove a disincentive to marriage and that the availability of foundling hospitals (like Captain Coram's, opened in London in 1741) might subvert the nuclear family. Hume need not explicitly adduce the high infant mortality in the hospitals, for the fact was notorious. Nevertheless, it would be difficult to suppose that monasticism and foundling hospitals harm population as much as slavery and infanticide. Wallace had in fact argued that celibacy had hindered population growth in papist countries and that slavery had promoted it in the ancient world by keeping productive those who otherwise could not "maintain families" (*Dissertation*, 86–89).

Comparing the political economy of the ancients and moderns allows for another concession: the small size of polities and the "equality of fortune among the citizens" before "the full establishment" of Roman hegemony would have been "favourable to industry and agriculture; to marriage and propagation!" (This concession will need examination below to see whether Hume's exclamation point indicates an emphatic tone suffused with irony.) Offsetting any advantage of "the great equality of fortune" (183–84 = ¶¶ 45–46) are the disadvantages under which the ancients suffered. Hume summarizes 39 paragraphs on the disadvantages thus: their "wars were more bloody and destructive; their governments more factious and unsettl'd; commerce and manufactures more feeble and languishing; and the general police more loose and irregular" (210–11 = ¶ 93). The advantages had needed all of 8 paragraphs.

From surmise about the effect on population of the ancient way of life Hume proceeds to "matter of fact," to what available facts indicate, such as they are. The answer will be that the "facts" are "uncertain" (211 = ¶ 94); that is, the evidence is scanty and unreliable. For several reasons statistics in extant writings are dubious, not least because of carelessness and love of fabulous exaggeration. In the most substantial part of the essay for classical historians, Hume scrutinizes the numbers recorded in literature from varying standpoints, such as the numbers receiving the corn dole in Rome. Implicitly the argument accords with that concerning testimony: there are too many reasons why reports of numbers could be wrong to overrule any prima facie implausibility in any number.[16]

Next comes a discussion of how logistical restraints would keep a city from growing beyond 700,000, whether the city's vibrancy arises from empire or commerce. Modern London, combining "extensive commerce and middling empire" (243 = ¶ 154), shows the maximum population a city can reach before its economy is distorted by prodigality and idleness in its ruling classes or checked by inflation, the inherent drawback of success. This check Hume had explained in "Of Money" (¶ 3).

Moving on from numbers to other "facts," Hume takes a hint from the Abbé Dubos about the salubrious warming of the globe due to deforestation in the modern age.[17] Such an improved environment could help explain, if not prove, a growth in populousness.[18] Following is a sequence of contrasts between regions in their modern and ancient "situations": Ottoman Africa and Ottoman Europe versus their ancient counterparts in Egypt and Greece, eastern Europe versus ancient Sarmatia and Scythia, and so on. Spain probably had not decayed since Roman times (however much it had decayed in modern times from the effects of its imperialism), and the acknowledged decay of Italy should not be exaggerated. The argument concludes with a rebuttal of Montesquieu's thesis, defended by Wallace in his appendix, that "extensive dominion" and absolute rule are "destructive to population" and contain their own "poison" (256–57 = ¶ 177). Hume cites *L'Esprit des lois* 23.19 and attacks its use of Plutarch's "On the Obsolescence of the Oracles" (*Moralia* 413f414a) as evidence. Hume's target is the thesis that the Roman Empire was an initiating cause of a decline in population continuing into the heyday of the First British Empire.[19]

3. Hume's Scholarship

The skeptical argument is only as good as Hume's scholarship.[20] Hume makes use of all the well-known classical historians and a great number of other writers. The historians whom he cites most frequently in the essay are Diodorus (21 times); Thucydides, and Xenophon, and Polybius (15, 14, and 13 times, respectively); then Tacitus, Livy, and Suetonius (10 times each). Other historians include Caesar and Appian (9 citations each), Suetonius (7), Herodotus (5), Sallust (2), and Arrian (1). Nonhistorical works frequently cited are the *Geography* of Strabo (19), and Pliny the Elder's *Natural History* (12), as well as the speeches of Lysias (16 times), Demosthenes (13), and Cicero (7). Most cited is Plutarch, whose *Lives* and *Moralia* are cited 12 times each. Hume offers brief judgments of most of these authors' credibility.[21]

It might seem surprising that Hume makes so much use of Diodorus, who does not have a high reputation today. But Diodorus's comprehensive compilation of Assyrian, Egyptian, Greek, and Roman history was the only connected narrative of large stretches of ancient history to have survived from antiquity, and he was indispensable to writers on ancient history. Charles Rollin made extensive use of Diodorus in his account of the Egyptians and Assyrians.[22] Diodorus was also extensively employed, though with reservations, in Temple Stanyan's *Grecian History*, the first independent narrative of Greek history to be written in English. Stanyan offers this assessment of him: "Diodorus Siculus *is to be valu'd for his laborious Collections; and tho' he takes in too many of the Fables of his Predecessors, and adheres too much to the Traditions of the* Aegyptian *Priests, he serves very well to supply, and compare with others.*"[23] Hume was very aware of his failings: "*Diodorus Siculus* is a good writer; but 'tis with pain I see his narration contradict, in so many particulars, the two most authentic pieces of all *Greek* history, *viz. Xenophon*'s expedition, and *Demosthenes*'s orations" (213 n. = ¶ 98).

Polybius is one of Hume's favored sources. He is not reluctant to express his prejudices, but on the major charge that he wrote to please the Romans, as a Greek who had been taken into the highest levels of Roman society during the Roman conquest of Greece, Hume insists that though Polybius sometimes displays "caution," he never indulges in "flattery" (258 n. = ¶ 180). More positively, in a letter to Montesquieu, Hume says that, on the question whether the Spartans derived their famous way of life from Crete, he prefers the testimony of Polybius to that of Plato and Aristotle, which Montesquieu had accepted: "le profond sens de cet historien," says Hume, "rend son autorité très considérable" (10 April 1749, *L* 1:134).

Thucydides and Xenophon are trusted sources. Of Thucydides, Hume says, "The first page of *Thucydides* is, in my opinion, the commencement of real history. All preceding narrations are so intermixt with fable, that philosophers ought to abandon them, in a great measure, to the embellishment of poets and orators" (212 = ¶ 98). Hume is seconding Thucydides's own sharp distinction of himself from earlier writers such as, by implication, Herodotus, by the care he took to draw his conclusions only from the evidence available, unlike the poets and "storytellers" (*logographoi*) who preceded him (*History* 1.21.1). This favorable judgment of Thucydides has become the widely accepted view, though it is challenged from time to time.

Xenophon's reliability as a historian rests for Hume on his being a contemporary of the events he narrates. Hume calls the *Anabasis*, Xenophon's account of the unsuccessful attempt to help Cyrus usurp the throne of Persia and the desperate return journey that Xenophon himself led, one of "the two most authentic pieces of all *Greek* history" (213 = ¶ 98), the other being the speeches of Demosthenes. Hume makes use of Xenophon chiefly for details of Athenian economic and social conditions, citing such works as the *Ways and Means* and the *Oeconomicus*, as well as the *Memorabilia*, but not the *Hellenica*, Xenophon's history of his own times, which is not now highly regarded.

Hume makes some distinctions in his estimate of Plutarch. He praises Plutarch's "plain sense" (thinking chiefly of Plutarch's "philosophical compositions" in the *Moralia*) and attempts to excuse the religious essays (such as "On the Obsolescence of the Oracles" or "On the Delays of the Divine Vengeance") as dialogues that might not straightforwardly express the views of Plutarch himself. But in the same footnote Hume says that Plutarch as a historian is "as superstitious as *Herodotus* or *Livy*" (260 n. = ¶ 186), presumably because all three pay attention to oracles and omens and tend to see the hand of the gods in historical events. Plutarch's *Lives* are used with caution by the modern scholar as Plutarch employed sources of varying quality and shaped his *Lives* to portray good and bad character traits.

Herodotus and Livy had been said to be "these two *Princes* of *Greek* and *Roman History*," but for Hume it was not so.[24] Indeed Hume's judgment of Livy seems excessively negative. The "superstitious" Livy, he says, with regard to the early history of Rome, is "an historian, who had so little morals or judgment, as to indulge himself in fiction and romance," and adds that "he is at last shock'd himself with the incredibility of his narration."[25] In his manuscript "Memoranda," Hume criticizes him as "thoughtless" because he is ignorant of the value of a balance of power.[26] However, Hume finds pertinent social and political material in Livy and at least once accepts a story—about the resentment of the Papirian tribe at Rome against the Pollian—that modern scholars find puzzling.[27]

Hume includes Herodotus, the third of the "superstitious" historians, among the fabling predecessors of Thucydides. Though it became commonplace by

Cicero's time to credit Herodotus as "the father of history," Hume seems deliberately to reject this judgment, as we have seen, by describing the "first page of Thucydides" as "the commencement of real history" and "all preceding narrations," which must include the *History* of Herodotus, as fit only for poets and orators to embellish (212–13 = ¶ 98).[28] In reference to the size of the army alleged by Herodotus to have been brought by Xerxes for the invasion of Greece, Hume asks, "will any rational man cite *Herodotus*'s wonderful narrations as an authority?" (215 = ¶ 103). Hume displays no understanding of the range and originality of Herodotus's "inquiry" (*historie*) into the Persian Wars and the diverse customs and histories of the cities and peoples on both sides who fought in them.

Tacitus, who claimed to write history "without anger or favour" (*Annals* 1.1.3), is in a different category. Hume cites him for evidence 10 times in the essay without any adverse or skeptical comment, and the same implicit and perhaps exaggerated trust appears in the other essays. Hume also occasionally turns to Tacitus for a political maxim ("Of Public Credit," ¶ 31; "Parties of Great Britain," n. to ¶ 4), a use of Tacitus that had a long tradition by Hume's time.[29]

Interestingly, Sallust receives only two mentions. He is one of those "*Latin* classics, whom we peruse in our infancy," as Hume puts it.[30] A good reason might be that Hume rejected the thesis for which Sallust was the best-known authority, that the Roman republic suffered a serious moral decline because of the increase of its wealth and power as it gained its empire. This animus against luxury had its place in the ideology against which "Populousness" sets itself in its polemical aspect.

Hume makes two general comments about the ancient historians. First, they had "more candour and sincerity" than the moderns because less swayed by partisanship and religious prejudice, but they also showed "less exactness and care." Second, many of them failed to make use of contemporary documents when they were available. For instance Plutarch and Appian "seem scarce ever to have read *Cicero*'s epistles," though they were writing about the period covered by Cicero (213 n. = ¶ 98).

Hume put some stress on the use of contemporary testimonials. In a letter to Wallace he says, "As to the Argument, I shall only observe to you . . . that when I dispute the positive Testimony of antient Authors, it is only or commonly their Testimony of Facts so much beyond their own Time, that there may remain some Suspicion of Mistake" (1753, *NL* 32–33). In line with this quest for contemporary evidence, Hume, we have seen, put some trust in Thucydides and Xenophon, who write about their own times. He also makes use of contemporary evidence from the speeches of Cicero, making seven citations from the speeches and the epistles. But the two witnesses whom Hume makes most use of in the essay are Demosthenes and Lysias. Their legal and political speeches, cautiously interpreted, are a rich source of contemporary evidence about the social and political conditions of Athens in the fourth century. Hume uses them to build up his portrait of slavery and of the virulence of ancient Greek political conflict.

Strabo and Pliny the Elder are in a separate category. Strabo is the author of a comprehensive *Geography* not only describing the physical state of the various parts of the Greek and Roman world in the time of Augustus, but also offering insight into social and political conditions and including short historical narratives. It is a mine of information. Hume took particular trouble to obtain an edition of Strabo for this project.[31] With a total of 19 citations, Strabo is the most quoted author in the essay apart from Plutarch and Diodorus.

Another encyclopedic writer mined by Hume for this project is Pliny the Elder (12 citations), whose *Natural History* is an immensely informative if not altogether reliable source on a vast variety of topics. Hume uses Pliny throughout the essays, in "Populousness" chiefly as an informant on agricultural slavery and the size of the city of Rome. The Roman agricultural writers Columella (9 citations), Varro (8), and Cato the Elder (2) are also brought in as contemporary witnesses to Roman agricultural practice, particularly to the way in which slaves were treated.

In a letter to Gilbert Elliot of Minto, Hume reveals something about his reading of these and other materials in preparation for writing this essay: "I have amus'd myself lately with an Essay or Dissertation on the Populousness of Antiquity, which led me into many Disquisitions concerning both the public & domestic Life of the Antients. Having read over almost all the Classics both Greek and Latin, since I form'd that Plan, I have extracted what serv'd most to my Purpose" (*L* 1:152–53). Hume does indeed cite a very wide range of authors. In addition to the historians and other frequently quoted writers whom we have mentioned above, he cites poets; letter writers; orators; writers of miscellanies, particularly Athenaeus; philosophers; and an occasional playwright.[32] All are cited in support of some fact. Thus Aristotle is cited for the size of the slave population of Aegina (n. for ¶ 122) and Sextus Empiricus for a law of Solon (n. for ¶ 40). Some texts that scholars have been able to use as sources of information about Greek society he virtually ignores, such as the very rich evidence of Greek comedy. Tragedy and epic, both Greek and Latin, he ignores completely. This omission is surely deliberate. The use Wallace and others made of Homer's figures for the Greek forces at Troy and his lines about Egyptian Thebes as the city with a "hundred gates" may suggest a reason for Hume's caution.[33]

The letter to Elliot indicated that Hume had "extracted what serv'd most to [his] Purpose." This phrase suggests that in preparation for writing the essay

Hume copied out or made extracts of the passages that he thought he might want to use in the essay. Some of the notes that go under the name of Hume's "Memoranda" seem likely to be among the passages and citations that Hume extracted. It is certainly the case that a good number of the memoranda are carried over into the essays. For example, a footnote for paragraph 47 contains material on the pay of soldiers that corresponds with memorandum 223. One for paragraph 84 on an aspect of interest rates at Athens draws on memorandum 233, and memorandum 249 rehearses several of the arguments in a long passage about the population of Athens (¶¶ 111–21).[34] There are many others.

Hume seems to have made do with whatever editions of these texts were available to him. The limitations under which he worked are made clear in the letter to Elliot. Hume says, "But I have not a Strabo, & know not where to get one in this Neighbourhood. He is an Author I never read. I know your Library (I mean the Advocates') is scrupulous of lending Classics; but perhaps that Difficulty may be got over. I shou'd be much oblig'd to you, if you coud procure me the Loan of a Copy, either in the original Language or even in a good Translation."[35] In this request for a Strabo, Hume does not mention any particular editions, not even the great edition of Isaac Casaubon. He is glad to get what is available.

The case is similar for his edition of Demosthenes, who is cited often as a reliable contemporary witness. Hume cites him from an Aldine edition of 1504, though several more recent editions had appeared with commentary, and perhaps the reason is that there was a copy of this edition in his own library.[36] For the ubiquitous Diodorus, Hume cites an edition of 1604 that contains the Greek text, a Latin translation, and some notes.[37] For Xenophon he used one of a number of identically paginated editions by A. Portus with the Latin translation of J. Leunclavius (Frankfurt in 1594 and 1596, and Paris 1625).[38] For Thucydides, we infer from the page numbers he gives us in memoranda 249 and 236 that he used the edition of Thucydides published at Frankfurt in 1594 and edited by H. Stephanus with the translation of L. Valla and notes.[39] This material is carried over to paragraph 121 and the footnote for paragraph 85, respectively. Finally, in a footnote Hume refers to "the *Greek* translation" of Caesar's Gallic War (252 n. = ¶ 171). This translation, which is not genuinely ancient, appears to have been printed in no edition of Caesar except that of John Davies published at Cambridge in 1706.[40] Apart from Demosthenes, none of these identifiable editions is in the *Hume Library*. However, the *Hume Library* does contain editions of Polybius,[41] Livy,[42] Cicero,[43] and Lysias,[44] which might have been available for Hume's use in writing "Populousness," though there is no conclusive proof that these are the editions he used.

But though Hume seems almost casual about his choice of editions, he was, at least in the composition of "Populousness," presenting himself as more than a gentlemanly amateur of the classics in the manner of Sir William Temple.[45] He gives the impression, and he clearly wishes to give the impression, of careful investigation, extensive reading, and scrupulous citation, together with profound thought about his subject. It is an original reading of the texts that he offers, an independent and direct confrontation with them, neither dilettantish nor mediated through layers of prior scholarship.

The presentation is governed by his aim to "start some doubts" about the claim to the greater populousness of antiquity. The skeptical aspect of his endeavor comes out very notably in the magnificently concentrated passage in which he scrutinizes the figures given by Athenaeus for the population of Athens, and particularly for the slave population (¶¶ 111–21). Athenaeus gives the figures of 21,000 citizens, 10,000 "strangers,"[46] and no less than 400,000 slaves. Wallace accepts the figure of 400,000 for the slaves (*Dissertation*, 55). Hume systematically scrutinizes the figure and "starts some doubts" about it. These "doubts" have since been considered a notable contribution to the study of the slave population of ancient Athens, and William Linn Westermann says, "Since Hume's day all attempts to re-establish confidence in these figures [of Athenaeus] have been in vain."[47]

Hume's method is to apply "probable reasoning" to the figure in 10 numbered arguments. (1) The first argument shows up the implausibility of such a large number. Since it is clear that the figure for the citizens is the figure for the adult males only, we must (by Halley's rule) multiply it by four to get the full number of citizens, including women and children.[48] We may plausibly do the same in the case of the "strangers," but if we do this for the slaves, we will reach a total population for ancient Athens of 1,720,000, "larger than London and Paris united"—a result, Hume implies, that is self-evidently absurd.

Hume's assumption that this figure is absurd might seem simply to imply a premise that the ancient world was inferior to the modern world in respect of population, presuming the point at issue. To the proponents of the ancient ways, numbers of this magnitude were not absurd. Wallace accepts Athenaeus's figures not only for Athens, but also for the slave population of Arcadia at 300,000, of Corinth at 460,000, and of the comparatively small island of Aegina at no less than 470,000 and concludes, "where there was such a great number of slaves, we must conclude, that there was proportionally a great number of free citizens; and, upon the whole, that *Greece* was extremely populous" (*Dissertation*, 57–58). However, in order to show how implausible Athenaeus's figure is for the slave population of Athens, Hume sets it against nine other pieces of evidence (denominated "*Secondly*" to "*Tenthly*" in Hume's text). These are collected from contemporary sources and therefore would, by Hume's principle of reliability, have greater authority than the evidence of a late author like Athenaeus.[49]

(2) According to a contemporary, Xenophon, there were only 10,000 houses in Athens. (3) Though Thucydides, an admired contemporary, reports the circuit of the walls of Athens to be 18 miles and more, another contemporary, Xenophon, tells us that there was "much waste ground" (222 = ¶ 114) within the walls. (4) Surely so large a number of slaves would have attempted frequent insurrections, but we hear of only one. (5) Contemporary witnesses (Xenophon, Demosthenes, and Menander) tell us that the Athenians' treatment of their slaves was "gentle and indulgent," but this could not have been the case if there were 20 times as many slaves as free citizens.[50] (6) The number of slaves possessed by people described by contemporaries as rich are quite small, ranging from 10 to 60. (7) Thucydides, ever a reliable witness and a genuine historian, reports that when at a difficult point in the Decelean War more than 20,000 Athenian slaves deserted to the Spartans, it caused great distress in Athens; but it would not have been so distressing "had they been only the twentieth part."[51] (8) Furthermore, some 70 years later Xenophon proposed in his *Ways and Means* that the Athenian state should maintain 10,000 slaves, arguing that this would be thought a sustainable number to anyone who considers how many slaves Athens maintained during the Decelean War. This supposition, in Hume's view, implies a total slave population at that time much lower than the 400,000 of Athenaeus. (9) The total value of private property in Athens, reported by Demosthenes, a contemporary, implies a very low number of slaves, on the basis of the value of slaves given by our sources. (10) Sparta is implied by Thucydides to have more slaves than any other Greek city, but it would be impossible to maintain more than 400,000 slaves in "a narrow, barren country, such as *Laconia*, which had no trade" (225 = ¶ 121).

Following these 10 numbered arguments, Hume deploys some lesser considerations and reports that the figures we hear for the populations of other cities are much lower than those of Athens. It must be said that not all the figures for other cities that Hume uses in these latter paragraphs are from contemporary writers. And he uses a passage from Justin that is generally considered to be unreliable in order to arrive at a total for the population of Greece at the time of its conquest by Philip II. Hume is on good ground when he criticizes the passage about the population of Athens in Athenaeus since he adduces other, more reliable, more contemporary witnesses, but in the case of other cities he himself accepts numbers from other authors that he should have approached with equal caution.[52]

A major topic for admirers of antiquity was the size, populousness, and grandeur of the city of Rome. A common opinion is expressed by Addison: "We may reckon, by a very moderate Computation, more Inhabitants in the *Campania* of old *Rome*, than are now in all *Italy*."⁵³ Hume rightly insists that there is great difficulty in fixing the size of the population of Rome and Italy from the scattered evidence but concludes that there is "no reason to support those exaggerated calculations, so much insisted on by modern writers" (230 = ¶¶ 134). For the size of the population Hume uses some of the materials still familiar to students of ancient population, such as the few statistics we have of the death rate, the number of Romans eligible for the free corn distribution, and so on (¶¶ 134–51).

Hume's long footnote on the physical size of the city of Rome is itself perhaps the most striking instance of his skeptical approach to traditional, grandiose interpretations of the sources. He bases his argument on the interpretation of a very difficult passage in the elder Pliny (*Natural History* 3.5.66–67). First he insists on a correct version of the text: after quoting the passage in Latin, Hume says, "ALL the best manuscripts of *Pliny* read the passage as here cited, and fix the compass of the walls of *Rome* to be 13 miles" (232 = ¶ 135). This is directed against a different reading of the text, accepted by Isaac Vossius, which would put the circumference of the walls at 30 miles. Hume insists that this reading is found only in a "manuscript, of no authority" (233 n. = ¶ 135), and indeed it is ignored by recent editors. Hume then gives his interpretation of the passage. As he sees it, Rome was semicircular in shape "of 13 miles circumference" (232 n. = ¶ 135). It had 37 gates, but only 12 of the streets leading from these gates went all the way in to the central Golden Milestone ("Milliarium Aureum"). These 12 streets, taken together, make up 30,775 paces, or about 30 miles. Hence each of the 12 streets that go from the Milestone to the 12 gates was 2½ miles in length. The radius of the semicircle is therefore 2½ miles, yielding a circumference for the semicircle of about 8 miles for the curved portion and about 5 miles for its base, which lay along the Tiber River. This makes up the 13 miles which Pliny gives as the length of the walls of Rome. Such is Hume's interpretation of the passage.

He then criticizes two other interpretations: Jean Hardouin's on the one hand and Vossius's on the other. Hardouin's approach, as reported by Hume, is similar to Hume's.⁵⁴ It too consists of making sense of the 30,775-pace length of all the roads taken together and of deflating estimates of the size of Rome. But Hardouin proposed to divide it, not by 12, as Hume proposes, but by 37 since he assumes that a road ran back from every one of the 37 gates to the Golden Milestone. However, Hume points out that, apart from other objections, each of the roads from the Milestone to the 37 gates would, on this hypothesis, be only 800 paces long; and a semicircle with such a short radius would not yield a total circumference of nearly 13 miles, the figure Pliny gives us.

On the other hand, Vossius goes wildly in the other direction.[55] Not only does he follow a reading of a manuscript that in Hume's view was "of no authority," giving the length of the walls of Rome as 30 miles (not 13); he then also supposes that this applies only to the semicircular portion, and therefore he adds the supposed length of the straight diameter or base of the semicircle. This makes for an enormous area for the city. Hume counters this with a close interpretation of the text of Pliny designed to show that Pliny cannot have intended what Vossius read in him. Hume adds four other arguments: first, a statement in the *Historia Augusta* (which he does not regard with sufficient suspicion, in view of the critical work that had been done on it by his time) that the emperor Aurelian extended the walls to 50 miles. Secondly, there are no remains of ancient buildings that come near Vossius's envisaged scope and range. Vossius supposes that they are buried 60 feet under the present city, which Hume says "seems absurd."[56] Third, two historians, admittedly very late ones, say that Rome had only between forty and fifty thousand houses. Finally the "extravagance of the consequences drawn by this critic ... destroys the foundation on which they are grounded" (234 n. = ¶ 135). Hume here refers to Vossius's figure of 14 million inhabitants for the city. Lipsius is included in the reproach. His figure was 2 million citizens plus 3 or 4 million slaves.[57]

It might seem that Hume's argument about the size of Rome has not the sharpness and careful use of contemporary evidence that is apparent in his discussion of the number of slaves at Athens. It has not found approval in the way that the Athenian passage has. A recent authoritative text says that the problem of Pliny's passage is intractable: "Pliny's description ... of the size of the city in his day is a bewildering set of statistics from which it is impossible to wrest more than a general meaning."[58]

Time and again, on a smaller scale, Hume finds pertinent details in a wide variety of ancient authors, many of whom were intent on making another point than the one Hume seizes on. He considers that remarks made by writers "by the bye" as "oblique propositions" might be more authentic than deliberate statements (258 n. = ¶ 180). Hume is reading "against the grain," extracting what he needs.[59] These isolated facts he relates and accumulates in large numbers.

Hume prefaces his argument about ancient slavery with an exploration of its inhumanity. The discussion is vivid and convincing by its wealth of detail. He notes Cato the Elder's recommendation to sell old slaves rather than to keep them going at great expense. He notes the practices of housing slaves in underground *ergastula*, of keeping a chained slave porter as a doorkeeper, of permitting slaves to give evidence in court only under torture. He finds significance in the fact that Seneca regards flogging slaves for discipline at night as a sign of disorder in the household rather than cruelty. In an orderly household,

Seneca had argued, it would be done during the day (¶¶ 7–12). Hume's thesis about ancient slavery is that it was inimical to populousness. He draws arguments from many disparate sources to question the widespread assumption that the ancients practiced slave breeding on a large scale. Why then were the Romans constantly importing slaves, as shown by not only direct evidence, but also the fact that slaves' names indicate that most slaves were foreigners? Moreover, enumerations of slaves and their tasks rarely mention female slaves. Xenophon recommends keeping the sexes apart, slave rooms were too small for families, several legal texts imply that breeding was not a habitual practice, and, when Cato lists the number and kind of slaves needed to run a vineyard, he mentions a wife only for the overseer (¶¶ 15–36). In all Hume cites over 50 passages in the course of this argument.

He extracts a similar mass of instances to illustrate his contention that the savagery of ancient warfare (¶¶ 54–62) and internal faction (¶¶ 63–82) were also inimical to the growth of population. The depth of the battle lines in ancient warfare almost ensured that battles were bloody (¶ 56). According to Hume's interpretation of a passage in Tacitus's *Histories*, never was quarter given in battle, except to save enemies to sell into slavery (¶ 57 and n.). That is why civil wars were especially bloody: as in civil wars prisoners were not sold, no prisoners were taken. Hume's point may be confirmed by Plutarch, who visited this same battlefield (at Bedriacum in A.D. 69) and reflected, "It is natural that in civil wars, when a rout takes place, more men should be killed, because no quarter is given, there being no use for prisoners" (*Life of Otho* 14.1–2). Hume gives several cases from Livy, Polybius, and Appian in which the men in besieged cities killed their wives and children and then fought to the death rather than surrender to the brutality of the besieger (¶ 59). There are almost no instances of "cartels," or exchanges of prisoners (¶ 62).

The evidence for the brutality of internal faction is taken from a wide range of authors. Hume does not miss Thucydides's famous reflective passage in book 3[60] about the brutal progress of revolution (¶ 66), but the burden of the argument is again carried by an accumulation of instances. He adduces from several texts the large numbers of citizens killed by both sides in the *stasis*, or civil strife, of the Greek cities in the later fifth and the fourth centuries (¶ 67) and appends a comprehensive footnote on the massacres and other brutalities recorded by Diodorus from the same period, which was "the most shining age of *Greece*" (196 n. = ¶ 67). The numbers involved in these disorders, which he takes at face value, he regards as astonishing for so small a country, as when Alexander ordered the return of political exiles and their number was found to be 20,000 (¶ 68). Also adduced are the massacres committed by tyrants (see Hume's note on Agathocles at ¶ 67 and cf. ¶ 73).

On the insecurity of property in the ancient world, Hume's inferences seem strained, for example when he recounts the complaint attributed to the wealthy Charmides that he had been impoverished by the Athenian people, or takes a remark from Lysias to indicate that Lysias regarded it as "a maxim of the *Athenian* people, that, whenever they wanted money, they put to death some of the rich citizens as well as strangers, for the sake of the forfeiture" (198 = ¶ 71). Apart from the fact that this seems to exaggerate what Lysias says, Hume ignores the rhetorical situation of the rich speaker before a popular law court. The same may perhaps be said of Hume's take on Lysias's account of the proportion of a rich man's fortune spent on public festivals, including drama and religious choruses, which Hume contemptuously calls "rareeshows and figur'd dances" (198 and n. = ¶ 72).

But there are also times when he refuses a piece of evidence in his own favor when it seems preposterous. He refuses to use a judgment of Aristotle which he interprets as meaning that "a city cannot subsist, if it either have so few inhabitants as ten, or so many as a hundred thousand" (241 = ¶ 152). Aristotle says "citizens" here, that is, adult males with political rights, rather than the whole population, and he was concerned with the conditions for creating a self-governing *polis* rather than for simply populating a city. Wallace better divines Aristotle's intent when he says in his rejoinder to Hume that Aristotle "is speaking of the numbers, which a well-ordered and regulated city ought to contain" (app., *Dissertation* 325–26).

In his appendix, Wallace was able to reply to many of Hume's points. Anyone who accumulates as much evidence as Hume has will find that much of it can be contested and that some is vulnerable. It remains true that Hume accumulated from his having "read over almost all the Classics both Greek and Latin" an astonishing amount of evidence, much of which scholars of population in antiquity still use today, and that he deployed it relentlessly to question, and in many cases, to invalidate definitively, the overconfident generalizations of those admirers of antiquity who had uncritically exaggerated its populousness.

4. Ancient Virtue versus Modern Luxury

Aside from the critical scrutiny of testimony, much of the content of the argument is that populousness could not have been greater before "the encrease of the *Roman* power, or rather, till its full establishment" (183= ¶ 45), because the police, manners, and constitutions were worse. The premise is that "if every thing else be equal, it seems natural to expect, that wherever there are most happiness and virtue, and the wisest institutions, there will also be most people" (160 = ¶ 4). A conclusion follows from Hume's establishment that the ancients were less happy and virtuous and did not enjoy wise institutions. Hume's argument mirrors Wallace's, reversing the assessments of the happiness, virtue, constitutional wisdom, and populousness. Less happy, the ancients were therefore less populous. To construe this argument so as to yield suspension of judgment instead of an outright verdict, we can refer to the qualifier, "if every thing else be equal." The conclusion holds only *cæteris paribus*, for we have been eliminating variables so as to reduce the question to a size allowing examination. Though we can disprove arguments, the unknown variables mean that we cannot prove anything concerning populousness.

Readers of the essay need to remind themselves of the unknown variables, for without our keeping them in mind, the argument points us forcefully toward the moral certainty that the ancient world was less populous because unhappy. How unhappy is expounded in relentless and horrifying detail unnecessary to a purely skeptical result about population levels. Hume's motive is not likely to be antagonism toward the ancients, much less triumphalism for the modern age that invented religious bigotry, feudalism, and the national debt, but rather apprehension of the effects of a false nostalgia for police, manners, and constitutions aimed at inculcating ancient virtue. This virtue, defined for "Patriots" by neo-Machiavellian ideology, set itself against the humdrum virtues of a polite and commercial people. When not defined in opposition to luxury, virtue involves frugality as part of industry rather than as part of an ideal of "simplicity." Along with industry this virtue involves a humanity that will recoil from slavery. It involves a notion of honor different from that which had been tied to class hierarchy. An ascetic virtue, pagan or Christian, should not be inculcated at the expense of a virtue that educates children, supports friends, and relieves the poor.[61] In short, Hume favors the virtue developed as people pursue their sundry happinesses and learn to accommodate others' pursuits.

The polemical aspect of the essay is located mostly in the portion devoted to moral causation and the effects of the ancient police, economy, maxims of peace and war, manners, and so on (¶¶ 6–93). Thereafter comes the skeptical survey of what purport to be facts. It is curious that Hume reverses Wallace's procedure. Both Wallace and Hume see moral rather than physical causes as the important factors, and both divide discussion largely into two steps: moral causes and data from testimony. Wallace starts with testimony in the form of statistics to establish the likelihood that population had declined and then enumerates moral causes to provide an explanation.[62] In contrast, and without explanation, Hume begins with moral causes and then proceeds to skepticism about testimony. The result is to put the denunciation of ancient ways in the first step and skepticism concerning the "facts" in the second. Purely as an order of reasoning, this choice seems backward since discrediting the testimony is a precondition of showing that the issue is alive and must be approached through surmise concerning salubrious or insalubrious ways of life. Hume's order of investigation makes more obvious sense as rhetoric than logic, but even viewing it as rhetoric there are two ways of looking at the result. One is that Hume is enabled to finish the essay with a skeptical survey and his goal of suspension of judgment. Another is that this order brings to the fore and confronts readers from the start with ancient slavery, infanticide, and other horrors.

Comparing chattel slavery with hired service or infanticide with foundling hospitals can take a place in an argument about what is conducive to populousness, but the shocking comparisons seem better chosen for an argument that the modern way of life was not inferior to the ancient. Which aspect is more salient to the reader, the concession that foundling hospitals might damage the nuclear family or the tacit fact that moderns respond with charitable foundations to a problem met by the ancients with infanticide? Here as in other places readers must remind themselves of the point about population but have no trouble seeing a point about whether banning infanticide or slavery is progress.

Insofar as Hume is arguing against a claim that slavery conduced to populousness, he is arguing against Wallace, who expatiates on the topic. Insofar as he is rejecting the notion of chattelism as a remedial response to widespread poverty, he is arguing instead against Bishop Berkeley and Andrew Fletcher of Saltoun. Insofar as he highlights the discrepancy between zealotry for civil liberty and the advocacy of reinstituting chattel slavery, the exemplar of what he attacks would have been recognized as the patriot Fletcher: "Some passionate admirers of the antients, and zealous partizans of civil liberty (for these sentiments, as they are both of them, in the main, extremely just, are also found to be almost inseparable) cannot forbear regreting the loss of this institution; and whilst they brand all submission to the government of a single person with the harsh denomination of slavery, they wou'd gladly subject the greatest part of mankind to real slavery and subjection" (161 = ¶ 6).[63] One senses that we are now in an argument less about population than conflicting visions for the future of Europe and its colonies.

For another six paragraphs Hume continues to embarrass patriot foes of corruption with the corrupting effect on masters of keeping slaves. These paragraphs, which have little to do with population but much with cruelty and tyranny, are brought to a close with the admission that Hume had lost sight of the formal topic: "BUT our present business is only to consider the influence of slavery on the populousness of a state" (165 = ¶ 13). Of course if Hume had really lost control of himself he would have edited out the digression. He incorporates it deliberately and uses a trope to draw attention to it.[64] Its function in "Populousness" is to acknowledge what readers sense, that Hume has been talking about slavery as an abomination rather than as a factor affecting populousness. The climax occurs in a footnote: "Who can read the accounts of the amphitheatrical entertainments without horror? Or who is surpris'd, that the emperors shou'd treat that people in the same way the people treated their inferiors? One's humanity, on that occasion, is apt to renew the barbarous wish of *Caligula*, that the people had but one neck. A man cou'd almost be pleas'd, by a single blow, to put an end to such a race of monsters" (165 n. = ¶ 12). The polemic does not stop with the topic of slavery, however, as Hume highlights the bloodiness of the "almost . . . perpetual war" (188 = ¶ 54) between the ancient polities, followed by 20 paragraphs on the horrors of the "factions and revolutions" (201 = ¶ 76) made furious by ancient maxims of peacetime: "[S]uch inveterate rage betwixt the factions, and such bloody maxims, are found, in modern times amongst religious parties alone" (192 = ¶ 63).

In his appendix Wallace usefully summarizes Hume's concessions. The key ones are the first: "that nothing could be more favourable to the propagation of mankind, than the establishment of small governments and an equality of fortune among the citizens; that agriculture is that species of industry which is chiefly requisite to the subsistence of multitudes of people, and that it flourished greatly in some countries in antient times."[65] Here is a complex of factors with a compelling appeal that Hume understands but could not endorse as a model for policymakers: small polities with "the center of government always very near its frontiers," unthreatened by any hegemonistic universal monarchies, capitals that do not swell to morbidity, equality of riches due to the lack of "opportunities of great encrease" and, in commonwealths, to the sharing of "power and authority" (183–84 = ¶¶ 45–46). Here there was much that was attractive and much that was impractical or problematic. That its anti-Mandevillean animus against luxury puts it in direct conflict with Hume's views is apparent when "Populousness" is read in the context of the book in which it appeared.[66] In "Of Commerce," Hume concluded:

> 'Tis natural on this occasion to ask, whether sovereigns may not return to the maxims of antient policy, and consult their own interest, in this respect, more than the happiness of their subjects? I answer, that it appears to me almost impossible; and that because antient policy was violent, and contrary to the more natural and usual course of things. 'Tis well known with what peculiar laws *Sparta* was govern'd, and what a prodigy

that republic is justly esteem'd by every one, who has consider'd human nature, as it has display'd itself in other nations and other ages. Were the testimony of history less positive and circumstantial, such a government wou'd appear a mere philosophical whim or fiction, and impossible ever to be reduc'd to practice. And tho' the *Roman* and other antient republics were supported on principles somewhat more natural, yet was there an extraordinary concurrence of circumstances to make them submit to such grievous burthens. They were free states; they were small ones; and the age being martial, all the neighbouring states were continually in arms. Freedom naturally begets public spirit, especially in small states; and this public spirit, this *amor patriae*, must increase, when the public is almost in continual alarm, and men are oblig'd, every moment, to expose themselves to the greatest dangers for its defence. A continual succession of wars makes every citizen a soldier: He takes the field in his turn; and during his service he is chiefly maintain'd by himself. And, notwithstanding that this service is equivalent to a very severe tax 'tis less felt by a people addicted to arms, who fight for honour and revenge more than pay, and are unacquainted with gain and industry as well as pleasure. Not to mention the great equality of fortunes amongst the inhabitants of the antient republics, where every field, belonging to a different proprietor, was able to maintain a family, and render'd the numbers of citizens very considerable, even without trade and manufactures. (8–10 = ¶ 8)

The ancient virtue is sustainable only under the stimulus of constant threat of war while modern virtue is stimulated by the complex of effort and achievement described in "Of Luxury" (¶ 3) and "Of Interest" (¶ 11). Equality of fortune is unsustainable without agrarian legislation that Hume judged "impracticable."[67] "WERE the question propos'd, Which of these methods of living in the people, the simple or refin'd, is the most advantageous to the state or public," Hume says in "Of Money," his answer is, "without much scruple," refinement (57 = ¶ 18). And he will tolerate some vicious luxury as the cost of benefiting from innocent luxury ("Of Luxury," ¶ 21).

5. Conclusion: "Thus remote times are always most envy'd and admir'd"

There are different ways to regard Hume's essay on populousness. One can see political arithmetic as paramount, in which case Hume's work might even appear to be "the strawman" for Wallace's dissertation.[68] One can see the issue of population as tacitly subordinate to the polemical one.[69] In this case the academic question on a point of history is merely a vehicle for an ideological debate. One need not go so far. Can one say rather that Hume's essay operates on two levels with two theses that, running parallel, do not converge?

Famously, Bertrand Russell wavered over whether he was accurately called an atheist or an agnostic. The levels of certitude required by practical life run against the skepticism required by investigative rigor. For speculative purposes he was an agnostic, for practical ones an atheist. Likewise Hume could say that the point of his essay is *both* that we cannot know whether population declined after the fall of the Roman Empire *and* that the ancient world was too unhappy a place to be emulated for most practical purposes, including population growth. The unhappiness of the ancients is a premise for the first thesis, but from another standpoint it is more salient than the skeptical conclusion, and we strain to suppose that Hume does not firmly believe in the superior populousness of the modern world and wish us to draw appropriate lessons. Though we cannot prove that population was lower among the ancients, it would be enthusiasm to attempt to fashion society on the supposition that it was higher.

NOTES

1. We need not scruple to denominate as essays what Hume termed political discourses since in his 1758 *Essays and Treatises on Several Subjects* he located the discourses in part 2 of what he titled the Essays, Moral, Political, and Literary and provided an advertisement announcing the change. On the other hand, it does not follow that the terms "essay" and "discourse" were meaningless or synonymous.

2. Roland Hall, *Fifty Years of Hume Scholarship: A Bibliographical Guide* (Edinburgh: Edinburgh University Press, 1978), s.v. "Population"; James Bonar, *Theories of Population from Raleigh to Arthur Young* . . . (London: Allen, 1931); Eugene Rotwein, Introduction, *David Hume: Writings on Economics* (1955; reprint, Madison: University of Wisconsin Press, 1970), lxxxviii–xc; E. C. Mossner, "Hume and the Ancient-Modern Controversy, 1725–1752: A Study in Creative Scepticism," *University of Texas Studies in English* 28 (1949): 139–53. The annual bibliographies in *Hume Studies* have been the diligent work of Roland Hall for 1977–85, William Edward Morris for 1986–2003, and James Fieser since. We (quite fallibly) surmise the contents of the works listed in the bibliographies by conning their titles. The bibliography for 1998, "The Hume Literature, 1997," does list Dean James Peterson's helpful 1994 dissertation on Robert Wallace. Peterson quotes from MS correspondence, unpublished essays, and Wallace's commonplace book, from which Peterson infers that Wallace employed Newton's chronology ("Political Economy in Transition: From Classical Humanism to Commercial Society—Robert Wallace of Edinburgh," [PhD diss., University of Illinois at Urbana-Champaign, 1994], 187). Disentangling "the Hume-Wallace debate" from the anachronism of a teleology leading to Malthus, Peterson recognizes that Wallace is better understood as an exponent of a radical, communitarian Whig ideology emphasizing agriculture over trade and agrarian laws to equalize property.

3. For background see Richard B. Sher, "From Troglodytes to Americans: Montesquieu and the Scottish Enlightenment on Liberty, Virtue, and Commerce," in *Republicanism, Liberty, and*

Commercial Society, 1649–1776, ed. David Wootton (Stanford: Stanford University Press, 1994), 368–402, 477–81, and Frederick G. Whelan, "Populations and Ideology in the Enlightenment," *History of Political Thought* 12 (1991): 35–72. Also see Albert O. Hirschman, *The Passions and the Interests: Political Arguments for Capitalism Before Its Triumph* (Princeton: Princeton University Press, 1977); J. G. A. Pocock, "Neo-Machiavellian Political Economy: The Augustan Debate over Land, Trade, and Credit," chap. 13 of *The Machiavellian Moment: Florentine Political Thought and the Atlantic Republican Tradition* (Princeton: Princeton University Press, 1975); and John Sekora, *Luxury: The Concept in Western Thought, Eden to Smollett* (Baltimore: Johns Hopkins University Press, 1977). Sekora knew of Robert Wallace's anonymously published *A Dissertation on the Numbers of Mankind in Antient and Modern Times* only through its review in *Monthly Review* 9 (March 1753): 191–99. Hence he knew neither that Wallace wrote it nor that it preceded Hume's essay (122–23 and n. 16). Sylvana Tomaselli's article situates Hume's essay within the Enlightenment, and accordingly Montesquieu looms large at the expense of Wallace, the lesser light. From this lofty perspective agreements in principle between Hume and Montesquieu are more salient than their disagreements ("Moral Philosophy and Population Questions in Eighteenth-Century Europe," *Population and Development Review* 14, supp. [1988]: 10, 19–20).

4. *Political Discourses*, 2nd ed. (Edinburgh, 1752), 155n. The content of this footnote changed for the 3rd edition, and the footnote disappeared altogether for the 1770 *Essays and Treatises on Several Subjects*. Normally citations to and quotations from the essay will be from the pages of the 2nd edition of 1752, augmented for readers' convenience by paragraph numbers from the 1772 edition of the *Essays and Treatises on Several Subjects*, the copy text for the forthcoming Clarendon edition of the *Essays, Moral, Political, and Literary*. Hume's footnotes will be cited by the numbers of pages and of the paragraphs with which they are associated. Hereinafter citations to the 1752 edition will appear parenthetically in the text, and those references to other editions will appear in the notes.

5. *A Dissertation on the Numbers of Mankind in Antient and Modern Times* . . . (Edinburgh, 1753), 14 and n. Normally citations to this edition will be parenthetical within the text. Though crossing swords with Montesquieu provided the spectacle for the essay, Hume visibly engages in tacit but direct argument with Wallace's dissertation, which Hume had read in some permutation subsequent to its presentation before the Philosophical Society of Edinburgh. After the appearance of Hume's essay, Wallace published the dissertation "*in its original Form*," as he said misleadingly, with "*only some inconsiderable Additions*" (iii). But Yasuo Amoh reports that the book significantly augments the paper ("Ancient-Modern Controversy in the Scottish Enlightenment," in *The Rise of Political Economy in the Scottish Enlightenment*, ed. Tatsuya Sakamoto and Hideo Tanaka [London: Routledge, 2003], 69–85). Whether Hume read the original paper or the augmented version, he will not have seen when he wrote his essay Wallace's very considerable rejoinder appended to the published *Dissertation*.

6. Sir William Blackstone: "By the public police and oeconomy, I mean the due regulation and domestic order of the kingdom" (*Commentaries on the Laws of England*, 4 vols. [London, 1765–69; facsimile reprint, Chicago: University of Chicago Press, 1979], 4:162). "Manners," the subject of Voltaire's *Essai sur les moeurs*, was defined by John Kersey as "*good, or ill conditions, institutions, rules of life, behaviour*, & c." (*A New English Dictionary* [London, 1702; facsimile reprint, Menston: Scolar, 1969]). It supports Hume's argument for the direction of developments and the superiority of modernity that we now expect governments to exert some control over diseases. It would not seem reasonable in Hume's day to hold governments accountable for depopulation due to AIDS or influenza.

7. Samuel Johnson, *A Dictionary of the English Language*, 4th ed., 2 vols. (London, 1773), s.v. "Curious."

8. Wallace delivered his paper before the Philosophical Society not later than 1745 (*NL* 28–29 at 29 n. 2). Hume's memoranda suggest an interest in the topic before Hume would have seen Wallace's MS. See M. A. Stewart, "The Dating of Hume's Manuscripts," in *The Scottish Enlightenment: Essays in Reinterpretation*, ed. Paul Wood (Rochester: University of Rochester Press,

2000), 287–88. A letter to John Clephane of 18 April 1750 describes what must be a substantial draft. Other letters suggest that Hume was still working on the essay around 18 March 1751 (*L* 1:140, 152–53, 157, 159).

9. *L* 1:140; *Political Discourses*, 3rd ed. (Edinburgh, 1754), 135 n. The refutation of which Hume speaks would be Wallace's appendix rebutting Hume's essay point by point. The "Hanniabal" of the text is undoubtedly a corruption of "Hannibal." A letter to Montesquieu of 26 June 1753 reiterates the skeptical purport of the essay (*L* 1:177).

10. Cf. Adam Smith's comparatively innocuous formulation of a similar point in *Wealth of Nations* 2.3, ¶ 33: "The annual produce of the land and labour of England, for example, is certainly much greater than it was, a little more than a century ago, at the restoration of Charles II. Though at present, few people, I believe, doubt of this, yet during this period, five years have seldom passed away in which some book or pamphlet has not been published, written too with such abilities as to gain some authority with the publick, and pretending to demonstrate that the wealth of the nation was fast declining, that the country was depopulated, agriculture neglected, manufactures decaying, and trade undone." *An Inquiry into the Nature and Causes of the Wealth of Nations*, ed. R. H. Campbell, A. S. Skinner, and W. B. Todd, 2 vols., corr. reprint (Oxford: Clarendon, 1979; Indianapolis: Liberty Classics, 1981), 1:344.

11. Once again, the paragraph numbers are from the 1772 copy text so as to match with those in the Clarendon edition. We admit that our outline runs into trouble beginning at ¶ 152 and devoutly wish that others will be able to improve on our effort. This outline was worked out at the behest of and with the participation of our colleague David Harvey, and this is a good point at which to acknowledge that his expert labors in annotating the essay for the Clarendon edition are the foundation of our understanding of it. We have benefited greatly from comments on a draft of this article from Harvey as well as from Tom Beauchamp. We have relied on Beauchamp's collations of the editions.

12. It is a question whether Hume wrote his essay having read the MS of the original paper or an augmented dissertation like the book that Hume saw through the press for Wallace (Amoh, "Ancient-Modern Controversy," 69–70 and nn. 2–3). If when composing his essay Hume read a version of Wallace's dissertation close in content to the published book minus the appendix, many of the parallels between the essay and the book would seem to be reactions to Wallace. If on the other hand Hume was reacting only to Wallace's paper, then some of the parallels could easily reflect Wallace's reactions to Hume's published essay. Our expedient in view of this unanswered question is to speak neutrally about the parallels so as not to indicate who reacted to whom.

13. For an excellent explanation see Ephraim Chambers's *Cyclopaedia: Or, An Universal Dictionary of Arts and Sciences . . .* , 2 vols. (London, 1728), s.v. "Moral." Lexicons of Hume's day, including Samuel Johnson's s.v. "Happy" and "Unhappy," did not make a sharp distinction between "happiness" as felicity and as a psychic state of sustained joy or contentment. Kersey defines "happy" as "*blessed, lucky*, or *fortunate*," as when in "Of the Rise and Progress of the Arts and Sciences" Hume speaks of "a happy climate" (*E* 120 = ¶ 20). This is the meaning that applies to Hume and Wallace's reasoning, though they might not deny that melancholics are hindered in procreating. Hume appears to equivocate between the two meanings when he says, "A master, from humour or interest, may make his slaves very unhappy, and yet be careful, from interest, to encrease their number" (166–67 n. = ¶ 13). Though both Hume and Wallace tend to focus discussion on procreation, longevity obviously is important in itself and as a precondition of procreation.

14. Hume follows what he calls "the common signification of words" when he says, "By knowledge, I mean the assurance arising from the comparison of ideas. By proofs, those arguments, which are deriv'd from the relation of cause and effect, and which are entirely free from doubt and uncertainty. By probability, that evidence, which is still attended with uncertainty" (*T* 1.3.11.2/124).

15. Hume and Wallace can use "fact" in an unusual but not unprecedented sense, illustrated in Wallace's *Various Prospects of Mankind, Nature, and Providence* (London, 1761), 57: "supposing

the fact to be true" (3.2). Such a "fact" purports to be true but might collapse under examination. In one footnote Hume speaks of "facts, which are indeed entirely absurd and impossible" (a phrase added in *Essays and Treatises on Several Subjects*, 2 vols. [London, 1764], 1:462 n. = ¶ 122). A "fact" is something that might be adduced and discounted as evidence.

16. As an illustration, see the footnote in which Hume says with exaggerated deference that it is "difficult, tho' not altogether absurd, to suppose, that such a man as *Columella* might be mistaken" (157 n. = ¶ 1).

17. Hume cites pt. 2, § 16, of Dubos's *Reflexions critiques sur la poësie et sur la peinture*. The copy listed in the *Hume Library* is the "Nouvelle" ed., 3 vols. (Utrecht, 1732–36). Whether the globe is warming is a question affected by points of comparison and frames of reference, spatial and temporal. Neither Dubos nor Hume could have guessed that, by generally accepted standards today, they lived at the end of the "Little Ice Age." See H. H. Lamb, *Climate, History, and the Modern World*, 2nd ed. (London: Routledge, 1995), chaps. 12–13. The beginning of the modern age is similarly dated according to frames of reference. In another context, Hume, Bacon, Harrington, and others would date it from Henry VII's reign and the passing of the Middle Ages. In the context of the *querelle des anciens et des modernes*, the setting for Hume's debate with Wallace, the modern age begins after the fall of the Roman Empire.

18. Does the discussion of global warming belong among the matters of fact rather than among the probable causes? It appears to be intruded into the end of the essay, and indeed outlining the essay in the vicinity of that discussion is vexed. One suspects an unintegrated interpolation on Hume's part.

19. To be sure, Hume was no more in favor of extensive empires or absolutism than Wallace was of slavery. See "Of Refinement in the Arts," ¶ 13; "Idea of a Perfect Commonwealth," ¶ 70.

20. The essay has been regarded as "epoch-making" by authorities on the subject. See P. A. Brunt, *Italian Manpower, 225 B.C.–A.D. 14*, corr. reprint (Oxford: Clarendon, 1987), 11; J. Beloch, *Die Bevölkerung der Griechisch-Römischen Welt* (Leipzig, 1886), 34–35.

21. For current judgments of these and all other classical authors mentioned, see *The Oxford Classical Dictionary*, ed. S. Hornblower and A. Spawforth, 3rd ed. (Oxford: Clarendon, 1994).

22. Charles Rollin, *The Ancient History of the Egyptians, Carthaginians, Assyrians, Babylonians, Medes and Persians, Macedonians, and Grecians* [*Histoire ancienne*, 1730–38], trans. anon., 2nd ed., 10 vols. (London, 1738–40).

23. Temple Stanyan, *The Grecian History*, 2 vols. (London, 1707–39), 1:a5^r.

24. Anthony Blackwall, *An Introduction to the Classics . . . with an Essay, on the Nature and Use of Those Emphatical and Beautiful Figures . . .* , 3rd ed. (London, 1725), 25.

25. "Of the Balance of Power," *Political Discourses*, 105–6 n. This passage was deleted for the 3rd edition of *Political Discourses* (1754).

26. E. C. Mossner, "Hume's Early Memoranda, 1729–1740: The Complete Text," *Journal of the History of Ideas* 9 (1948): 512.

27. M. P. Oakley, *A Commentary on Livy, Books VI–X*, 4 vols. (Oxford: Clarendon, 1998), 2:755.

28. On Herodotus as "the father of history," see Cicero, *De legibus* 1.1.5. Cf. Blackwall, *An Introduction to the Classics*, 36.

29. The best-known example is perhaps Justus Lipsius's *Politicorum sive civilis doctrinæ libri sex* (Leiden, 1589).

30. "Of Luxury," *Political Discourses*, 33 = ¶ 12. The title of this essay changed to "Of Refinement in the Arts" for the 1760 *Essays and Treatises on Several Subjects*.

31. See the letter of 18 February 1751 to Gilbert Elliot of Minto, *L* 1:152.

32. Here is a list of the rest of the authors or works Hume cites: Aeschines, Lucius Afranius, Ammianus Marcellinus, Aelius Aristides, Aristophanes, Aristotle, Asconius's commentary on Cicero's speeches, Athenaeus, Aurelius Victor, Catullus, Quintus Curtius Rufus, Diogenes Laertius, Donatus's commentary on Terence, Florus, Herodian, Hesiod, Horace, Isocrates, Josephus, Julian, Justin, Justinian's *Digest* and *Institutes*, Juvenal, Lucan, Lucian, Martial, Nepos, Olympiodorus, Ovid, Pausanias, Petronius, Plato, Plautus, Pliny the Younger,

"Publius Victor," the *Scriptores Historiae Augustae*, Seneca the Elder, Seneca the Younger, Sextus Empiricus, "Suidas," Terence, Tertullian, Theocritus, Valerius Maximus, Velleius Paterculus, Virgil, Vitruvius.

33. *Dissertation*, 37–38 (on Homer, *Iliad* 2.484–785, the "catalogue of the ships") and 43 (referring to *Iliad* 9.381–84). Similarly Hume ignores what the Old Testament says about Israel while Wallace does not.

34. Mossner, "Hume's Early Memoranda, 1729–1740: The Complete Text," 514–17. On the dating of the memoranda see Stewart, "The Dating of Hume's Manuscripts," 276–88.

35. *L* 1:153. Hume did not become the keeper of the Advocates Library, which gave him sources for his *History of England*, until 1752.

36. *Demosthenis orationes duae & sexaginta*, ed. Aldus Pius Manutius, 2 pts. (Venice, 1504). For Hume's library see D. F. Norton and M. J. Norton, *The David Hume Library* (Edinburgh: Edinburgh Bibliographical Society, 1996).

37. *Diod. Siculi Bibliothecae historicae libri XV*, ed. Laurentius Rhodomanus, 2 vols. in 1 (Hanover, 1604).

38. *Xenophontis quae exstant opera*, 2 vols. in 1, ed. Aemilius Portus, trans. Ioannes Leunclavius (Francofurti, 1594, 1596), and *Xenophontis . . . quae extant opera*, ed. J. Leunclavius, 2 vols. in 1 (Paris, 1625). The practice of setting type for one edition in imitation of an earlier one results in identical pagination in different editions, denying us a deduction of which edition Hume used on the basis of his page references.

39. *Thucydidis . . . de bello Peloponnesiaco libri octo*, ed. H. Stephanus (Frankfurt, 1594). See Mossner, "Hume's Early Memoranda, 1729–1740: The Complete Text," 515–17.

40. *C. Julii Caesaris quae exstant omnia*, ed. John Davies (Cambridge, 1706).

41. *Polybii historiarum libri qui supersunt*, ed. Jacobus Gronovius, trans. Isaac Casaubon, 3 vols. (Amsterdam, 1670). The *Hume Library* indicates only two volumes, suggesting that the commentaries and index comprising volume 3 were detached from the set.

42. *T. Livii Patavini historiarum ab urbe condita libri qui supersunt omnes*, ed. A[rnoldus] Drakenborch, 7 vols. (Amsterdam, 1738–46).

43. *M. Tullii Ciceronis opera*, ed. Pierre-Joseph Thoulier Olivet, 9 vols. (Paris, 1740–42);*Lettres de Ciceron à Atticus*, ed. and trans. l'abbé [Nicolas Hubert] Mongault, Latin text by J. G. Grævius, 6 vols. (Amsterdam, 1741). The presence of Hume's bookplate in the copy of Olivet's edition in the *Hume Library* and Hume's citation of "*Nicolaus Hortensius de re frumentaria Roman.*" (235 = n. for ¶ 138) make it highly likely that Hume used this edition, which appended Hortensius's short dissertation to volume 4.

44. *Lysiæ orationes*, ed. Iodocus Vander-Heidius (Hanover, 1615).

45. See Temple, "Upon Ancient and Modern Learning"(1690) and Richard Bentley, "A Dissertation on the Epistles of Phalaris, Themistocles, Socrates, Euripides and the Fables of Aesop," appended to William Wotton, *Reflections upon Ancient and Modern Learning . . .* , 2nd ed. (London, 1697).

46. "Strangers" were resident aliens, normally now called "metics" after the Greek *metoikoi*.

47. W. L. Westermann, *The Slave Systems of Greek and Roman Antiquity* (Philadelphia: American Philosophical Society, 1955), 7.

48. The source of this ratio is Edmund Halley's rule that the number of "*Fencible Men*" (i.e., "those between 18 and 56") will normally be "somewhat more than a *Quarter*" of the population. See "The Value of Annuities upon Lives, Drawn from the Bills of Mortality at Breslaw," in *The Philosophical Transactions and Collections to the End of the Year 1700. Abridg'd and Dispos'd under General Heads*, ed. John Lowthorp, 3 vols. (London, 1705), 3:669. Hume would have encountered the ratio in Wallace's attempt to corroborate it, if not elsewhere (*Dissertation*, 40–42). (See n. 12 above.) Hume applies it in "Populousness," ¶ 100, by multiplying the number of adult males by four to reach the total population of Agrigentum.

49. Athenaeus, from Naucratis in Egypt, lived about A.D. 200. He tells us (*Deipnosophists* 6.272c) that he takes the figures he gives from the *Chronicles* of Ktesikles. Nothing is known about Ktesikles.

50. Menander: Hume cites Plautus's *Stichus*, but though *Stichus* is a Roman play of 200 B.C., it is based on a Greek play by Menander of a century earlier.

51. The Decelean War is the final part of the Peloponnesian War between Athens and Sparta, which ran in its entirety from 431 to 404 B.C. The desertion of the slaves took place in 413.

52. Wallace counters Hume's population figures for some of these other cities (app., *Dissertation*, 295–302).

53. Joseph Addison, *Remarks on several Parts of Italy . . . in the Years 1701, 1702, 1703* (London, 1705), 180, quoted by Wallace in the 2nd edition of the *Dissertation* (Edinburgh, 1809), 60.

54. Hardouin published an edition of Pliny's *Natural History* in 1685 with annotations, but he does not give a full interpretation of this passage in that edition. We have been unable to trace the work of Hardouin that Hume criticizes here.

55. Vossius, *Variarum observationum liber* (London, 1685), 1–14. The passage of Pliny is quoted on page 3. A map on page 13 illustrates the semicircular reconstruction.

56. Cf. Addison, *Remarks*, 300–301 ("Fourteen or Fifteen Feet").

57. I. Vossius, *Variarum observationum liber*, 32; J. Lipsius, *Admiranda sive De magnitudine romana libri quatuor* in *Roma Illustrata, sive Antiquitatum Romanarum breviarium* (Amsterdam, 1657), 282–84.

58. L. Richardson, *A New Topographical Dictionary of Ancient Rome* (Baltimore: Johns Hopkins University Press, 1992), 331 (s.v. "Regiones Quattuordecim").

59. See Moritz Baumstark's excellent "Hume's Reading of the Classics at Ninewells, 1749–51," *Journal of Scottish Philosophy* 8, no. 1 (2010): 63–77 at 71.

60. Thucydides, *History* 3.81–83.

61. The examples of virtuous behavior come from "Of Luxury" (or "Of Refinement in the Arts"), ¶ 20. Doubtless Wallace would see the choice between different virtues as a false dilemma. For a judicious analysis that surveys the recent secondary literature, see Ryu Susato, "Hume's Nuanced Defense of Luxury," *Hume Studies* 32 (2006): 167–86.

62. See Amoh, "Ancient-Modern Controversy," 72–76. Wallace explains his two-step procedure with more lucidity than Hume does his. See *Dissertation*, 33, 79–80.

63. See George Berkeley, *The Querist*, in *The Works of George Berkeley, Bishop of Cloyne*, ed. A. A. Luce and T. E. Jessop, 9 vols. (Edinburgh: Nelson, 1948–57), 6: 136–37 (nos. 379–88), and the second of Fletcher's *Two Discourses concerning the Affairs of Scotland, Written in the Year 1698* (Edinburgh, 1698). A more recent patriot defense of slavery than Fletcher's was "The African Slave Trade Defended: And Corruption the Worst of Slaveries," *Common Sense*, no. 191 (4 October 1740), reprinted in *London Magazine* 9 (1740): 493–94.

64. "Correction," according to Blackwall, "is a Figure whereby a Man earnestly retracts and recalls what he had said or resolv'd" (*An Introduction to the Classics* 2.4.3). This trope had formed a sort of crescendo in the treatment of Pyrrhonian skepticism in the *Treatise* (T 1.4.7.8–1.4.7.10/268–70), and appears in the second *Enquiry* (*EPM* 2.5/177): "But I forget, that it is not my present business to recommend generosity and benevolence, or to paint, in their true colours, all the genuine charms of the social virtues." Hume pretends to have slipped into a panegyric on virtue, an admission that the panegyric is there and that he had not edited it out.

65. *Dissertation*, 164–64. Wallace paraphrases from Hume's ¶¶ 45–46, 88.

66. Robert Luehrs, "Population and Utopia in the Thought of Robert Wallace," *Eighteenth-Century Studies* 20 (1987): 326–27.

67. "Idea of a Perfect Commonwealth," *Political Discourses*, 283 = ¶ 5. The complex of effort and achievement is applied to the love of truth in *T* 2.3.10.1–2.3.10.10/448–52.

68. John M. Hartwick, "Robert Wallace and Malthus and the Ratios," *History of Political Economy* 20 (1988): 373. This article seeks to situate Wallace in the development of political economy and in relation to Malthus.

69. "The fundamental issue in the Wallace-Hume debate," says Luehrs, "was really the relative merits of an agrarian versus a commercial society in best fulfilling the needs and desires of its citizens" ("Population and Utopia," 320). Luehrs's summary of Wallace's argument (321–25) complements Amoh's summary.

Selected Bibliography

An Account of the Liverpool Mechanics and Apprentices' Library. . . . Liverpool, 1824.
Adams, John. *Diary and Autobiography of John Adams.* Edited by L. H. Butterfield. 4 vols. Cambridge: Harvard University Press, 1961.
———. *Papers of John Adams.* Edited by Robert J. Taylor. 16 vols. Cambridge: Harvard University Press, 1977–.
Addison, Joseph. *The Freeholder.* Edited by James Leheny. Oxford: Clarendon Press, 1979.
Allan, David. *Making British Culture: English Readers and the Scottish Enlightenment, 1740–1830.* Abingdon: Routledge, 2008.
———. *A Nation of Readers: The Lending Library in Georgian England.* London: British Library, 2008.
———. "Some Methods and Problems in the History of Reading: Georgian England and the Scottish Enlightenment." *Journal of the Historical Society* 3, no. 1 (2003): 91–124.
———. *Virtue, Learning, and the Scottish Enlightenment: Ideas of Scholarship in Early Modern History.* Edinburgh: Edinburgh University Press, 1993.
Amoh, Yasuo. "Ancient-Modern Controversy in the Scottish Enlightenment," in *The Rise of Political Economy in the Scottish Enlightenment,* ed. Tatsuya Sakamoto and Hideo Tanaka. London: Routledge, 2003.
Anscombe, G. E. M. "Hume and Julius Caesar." *Analysis* 34, no. 1 (1973): 1–7.
Armitage, David. Introduction to *Political Writings,* by Lord Bolingbroke. Cambridge: Cambridge University Press, 1997.
Austen, Jane. *Mansfield Park.* Edited by Kathryn Sutherland. Harmondsworth: Penguin, 2003.
Authentic Account of the Proceedings of the Congress Held at New York. . . . London, 1767.
Baier, Annette C. *A Progress of Sentiments: Reflections on Hume's "Treatise."* Cambridge: Harvard University Press, 1991.
Baumstark, Moritz. "Hume's Reading of the Classics at Ninewells, 1749–51," *Journal of Scottish Philosophy* 8, no. 1 (2010): 63–77.
Bailyn, Bernard. *The Ideological Origins of the American Revolution.* Cambridge: Harvard University Press, 1967, 2nd enl. ed., 1992.
Beal, P. "Notions in Garrison: The Seventeenth-Century Commonplace Book." In *New Ways of Looking at Old Texts,* edited by W. Speed Hill, 131–47. Binghamton, NY: Medieval and Renaissance Texts and Studies, 1993.
Bell's Common Place Book, Form'd generally upon the Principles Recommended and Practiced by Mr. Locke. London: John Bell, 1770.
Blair, Ann. "Humanist Methods in Natural Philosophy: The Commonplace Book." *Journal of the History of Ideas* 53, no. 4 (1992): 541–51.
Bolingbroke, Henry St. John, Viscount. *The Works of the Late Right Honorable Henry St. John, Lord Viscount Bolingbroke.* 5 vols. London, 1754.
Bondanella, P. and M. Musa, trans. *The Portable Machiavelli.* Harmondsworth: Penguin, 1979.
Bongie, Laurence L. *David Hume: Prophet of the Counter-Revolution,* 2nd. ed. Indianapolis: Liberty Fund, 2000.
Box, M. A. *The Suasive Art of David Hume.* Princeton: Princeton University Press, 1990.
Boyle, Emily C., ed. *The Orrery Papers.* 2 vols. London: Duckworth, 1903.
Braudy, Leo. *Narrative Form in History and Fiction.* Princeton: Princeton University Press, 1970.

Breisach, Ernst. *Historiography: Ancient, Medieval, Modern.* Chicago: University of Chicago Press, 2006.
Brewer, John. *Party Ideology and Popular Politics at the Accession of George III.* Cambridge: Cambridge University Press, 1976.
[Brown, John]. *An Estimate of the Manners and Principles of the Times.* 2 vols. London, 1757–58.
Brown, Stewart J., ed. *William Robertson and the Expansion of Empire.* Cambridge: Cambridge University Press, 1997.
Browning, Anthony. "History." In *Fortuna Domus*, edited by J. B. Neilson. Glasgow: University of Glasgow Press, 1952.
Brumfitt, J. H. *La philosophie de l'histoire.* 2nd rev. ed. Vol. 59 of *Les oeuvres complètes de Voltaire.* Geneva: Institut et Musée Voltaire; Toronto: University of Toronto Press, 1969.
Buckle, Stephen. "Philosophy, Historiography, and the Enlightenment: A Response to Green." In *Hume and the Enlightenment*, edited by Craig Taylor and Stephen Buckle, 53–64. London: Pickering and Chatto, 2011.
[Burgh, James]. *Political Disquisitions; or An Enquiry into Public Errors, Defects, and Abuses.* 3 vols. London, 1774–75.
———. *Thoughts on Education: Tending Chiefly to Recommend to the Attention of the Public, Some Particulars Relating to that Subject; which are not Generally Considered with the Regard their Importance Deserves.* Boston, 1749.
Burke, Edmund. *Reflections on the Revolution in France.* Edited by J. G. A. Pocock. Indianapolis: Hackett, 1987.
Burke, Peter. *The Renaissance Sense of the Past.* London: Arnold, 1969.
Burton, J. E. Hill, ed. *Letters of Eminent Persons Addressed to David Hume.* Bristol: Thoemmes Press, 1995. First published in Edinburgh in 1849.
Butterfield, L. H., et al., eds. *Adams Family Correspondence.* Cambridge: Harvard University Press, 1963.
Cameron, William. *Poetical Dialogues on Religion, in the Scots Dialect, between Two Gentlemen and Two Ploughmen.* Edinburgh: Peter Hill, 1788.
Campbell, R.H., A.S. Skinner, and W.B. Todd, eds. *An Inquiry into the Nature and Causes of the Wealth of Nations*, 2 vols. in the Glasgow Edition of the Works and Correspondence of Adam Smith. Indianapolis: Liberty Classics, 1976.
Capaldi, Nicholas. "The Preservation of Liberty." In *Liberty in Hume's History of England*, edited by Nicholas Capaldi and Donald W. Livingston, 195–224. Dordrecht, Netherlands: Kluwer Academic Publishers, 1990.
Capaldi, Nicholas and Donald W. Livingston, eds. *Liberty in Hume's History of England.* Dordrecht, Netherlands: Kluer Academic Publishers, 1990.
Carr, David. *Time, Narrative and History.* Bloomington: Indiana University Press, 1986.
Carte, Thomas. *A General History of England.* 4 vols. London, 1747–55.
Chalmers, George. *The life of Thomas Ruddiman.* Edinburgh: John Stockdale; London: William Laing, 1794.
Chapman, Alister, John Coffey, and Brad S. Gregory, eds. *Seeing Things Their Way: Intellectual History and the Return of Religion.* Notre Dame: University of Notre Dame Press, 2009.
Chapone, Hester. *Improvement of the Mind.* London, 1773.
Clark, J. C. D. *The Language of Liberty, 1660–1832: Political Discourse and Social Dynamics in the Anglo-American World.* Cambridge: Cambridge University Press, 1994.
———. "Providence, Predestination, and Progress: Or, Did the Enlightenment Fail?" *Albion* 35, no. 4 (2004): 559–89.
Cobbett's Parliamentary History of England from the Norman Conquest, in 1066, to the Year, 1803. 36 vols. London: R. Bagshaw, 1806–20.
Cohen, Alix. "In Defence of Hume's Historical Method." *British Journal for the History of Philosophy* 13, no. 3 (2005): 489–502.
Cohen, Lester H. *The Revolutionary Histories: Contemporary Narratives of the American Revolution.* Ithaca: Cornell University Press, 1980.

Colbourn, Trevor. *The Lamp of Experience: Whig History and the Intellectual Origins of the American Revolution.* Indianapolis: Liberty Fund, 1998.
Colclough, Stephen. "Recovering the Reader: Commonplace Books and Diaries as Sources of Reading Experiences." *Publishing History* 44 (1998): 5–37.
Collingwood, R. G. *The Idea of History.* Oxford: Clarendon Press, 1946.
Cohen, Ralph. "The Rationale of Hume's Literary Inquiries," in *David Hume: Many-Sided Genius,* ed. Kenneth R. Merrill and Robert W. Shahan. Norman: University of Oklahoma Press, 1976.
Conniff, James. "Hume on Political Parties: The Case for Hume as a Whig." *Eighteenth-Century Studies* 12, no. 2 (1978/79): 150–73.
Costelloe, Timothy M. *Aesthetics and Morals in the Philosophy of David Hume.* London: Routledge, 2007.
Cottret, Bernard. *Bolingbroke's Political Writings: The Conservative Enlightenment.* New York: St. Martin's, 1997.
Coutts, James. *A History of the University of Glasgow.* Glasgow: Maclehose and Sons, 1909.
[Cradock, J.] *Village Memoirs.* . . . London, 1765.
Dacome, Lucia. "Noting the Mind: Commonplace Books and the Pursuit of the Self in Eighteenth-Century Britain." *Journal of the History of Ideas* 65, no. 4 (2004): 603–26.
Damrosch, Leo. *Fictions of Reality in the Age of Hume and Johnson.* Madison: University of Wisconsin Press, 1989.
Darnton, Robert. "Extraordinary Commonplaces." *New York Review of Books,* 21 December 2000, 82–87.
———. "First Steps Toward a History of Reading." *Australian Journal of French Studies* 23, no. 1 (1986): 5–30.
———. "In Search of the Enlightenment: Recent Attempts to Create a Social History of Ideas." *Journal of Modern History* 43, no. 1 (1971): 113–32.
Davidson, Donald. "On the Very Idea of a Conceptual Scheme." *Proceedings of the American Philosophical Association* 47 (1973/74): 5–20.
DeMaria, Jr., Robert. *Samuel Johnson and the Life of Reading.* Baltimore: Johns Hopkins University Press, 1997.
Dibdin, Thomas Frognall. *Bibliomania.* London, 1809.
Dickinson, H. T. *Bolingbroke.* London: Constable, 1970.
Donoghue, Frank. *The Fame Machine: Book Reviewing and Eighteenth-Century Literary Careers.* Stanford: Stanford University Press, 1996.
d'Orleans, Pierre Joseph. *The History of the Revolutions in England under the Family of Stuarts.* London, 1711 [1693–94].
Dunstan, Vivienne S. "Glimpses into a Town's Reading Habits in Enlightenment Scotland: Analysing the Borrowings of Gray Library, Haddington, 1732–1816." *Journal of Scottish Historical Studies* 26, no. 1/2 (2006): 42–59.
Echard, Laurence. *The History of England, From the First Entrance of Julius Caesar.* . . . 3 vols. London, 1707–18.
Elliott, J. H. *Spain and Its World, 1500–1700.* New Haven: Yale University Press, 1989.
Emerson, Roger L. *Academic Patronage in the Scottish Enlightenment: Glasgow, Edinburgh, and St. Andrews Universities.* Edinburgh: Edinburgh University Press, 2008.
———. *Essays on David Hume, Medical Men, and the Scottish Enlightenment: "Industry, Knowledge, and Humanity."* Farnham, UK: Ashgate, 2009.
———. "Hume and the Bellman, Zerobabel MacGilchrist," *Hume Studies* 23 (1997): 9–28.
Encyclopédie, ou Dictionnaire raisonné des sciences, des arts et des métiers Metiérs. . . . Paris: Brisson, David, Le Breton, and Durand, 1751. Reprinted in 5 vols., New York: Readex Microprint Corporation, 1969.
Evnine, Simon. "Hume, Conjectural History, and the Uniformity of Human Nature." *Journal of the History of Philosophy* 31 (1993): 589–606.
Fackenheim, Emil L. *Metaphysics and Historicity.* Milwaukee: Marquette University Press, 1961.

Fain, Haskell. *Between Philosophy and History*. Princeton: Princeton University Press, 1970.
Farr, James. "Hume, Hermeneutics, and History: A 'Sympathetic' Account." *History and Theory* 17, no. 3 (1978): 285–310.
Fieser, James, ed. *Early Responses to Hume*. 10 vols. 2nd rev. ed. Bristol: Thoemmes Continuum, 2005.
———. "The Eighteenth-Century British Reviews of Hume's Writings." *Journal of the History of Ideas* 57, no. 4 (1996): 645–58.
Fletcher, Andrew. *Two Discourses concerning the Affairs of Scotland, Written in the Year 1698*. Edinburgh, 1698.
Forbes, Duncan. *Hume's Philosophical Politics*. Cambridge: Cambridge University Press, 1975.
———. Introduction to *The History of Great Britain: The Reigns of James I and Charles I*, by David Hume. London: Penguin, 1970.
Force, James E. "Hume and Johnson on Prophecy and Miracles: Historical Context." *Journal of the History of Ideas* 43 (1982): 463–75.
Frame, D.M., trans. *The Complete Essays of Montaigne*. Stanford: Standford University Press, 1958.
Francesconi, Daniele. "The Languages of Historical Causation in David Hume's *History of England*." *Cromohs* 6 (2001): 1–11. http://www.cromohs.unifi.it/6_2001/francesconi.html.
Frazer, Catherine S. "Pattern and Predictability in Hume's *History*." *Enlightenment Essays* 1 (1970): 27–32.
Fukuyama, Francis. *The End of History and the Last Man*. New York: Free Press, 1992.
Garrett, Don. *Cognition and Commitment in Hume's Philosophy*. Oxford: Oxford University Press, 1997.
Gerrard, Christine. *The Patriot Opposition to Walpole: Politics, Poetry, and National Myth, 1725-1742*. Oxford: Oxford University Press, 1994.
Gibson-Wood, Carol. "George Turnbull and Art History at Scottish Universities in the Eighteenth Century." *Revue d'art canadienne / Canadian Art Review* 28 (2001–3): 7–18.
Ginzburg, Carlo. *The Cheese and the Worms: The Cosmos of a Sixteenth-Century Miller*. Translated by John and Anne Tedeschi. Baltimore: Johns Hopkins University Press, 1980.
Glover, Katharine. "The Female Mind: Scottish Enlightenment Femininity and the World of Letters; A Case Study of the Women of the Fletcher of Saltoun Family in the Mid-Eighteenth Century." *Journal of Scottish Historical Studies* 25, no. 1 (2005): 1–20.
Goldie, Mark. "The English System of Liberty." In *The Cambridge History of Eighteenth-Century Political Thought*, edited by Mark Goldie and Robert Wokler, 40–78. Cambridge: Cambridge University Press, 2006.
Goldsmith, Oliver. *An History of England, in a Series of Letters from a Nobleman to his Son*. 2 vols. London, 1764.
Gouget, Antoine. *The Origin of laws, sciences and their progress among the most ancient nations*. Paris, 1758.
Gould, Eliga H. *The Persistence of Empire: British Political Culture in the Age of the American Revolution*. Chapel Hill: University of North Carolina Press, 2000.
Grafton, Anthony. "Is the History of Reading a Marginal Enterprise? Guillaume Bude and His Books." *Papers of the Bibliographical Society of America* 91, no. 2 (1997): 139–57.
Graham, Roderick. *The Great Infidel: The Life of David Hume*. Edinburgh: John Donald, 2005.
Grant, George. *Time as History*, ed. William Christian. Toronto: University of Toronto Press, 1995.
Green, Karen. "Will the Real Enlightenment Historian Please Stand Up? Catharine Macaulay versus David Hume." In *Hume and the Enlightenment*, edited by Craig Taylor and Stephen Buckle, 39–51. London: Pickering and Chatto, 2011.
Gregory, Brad S. "The Other Confessional History: On Secular Bias in the Study of Religion." *History and Theory* 45, no. 4 (2006): 132–49.
Grene, Marjorie. "Hume: Sceptic and Tory?" *Journal of the History of Ideas* 4 (1943): 333–48.

Grimm, Friedrich Melchior. *Correspondance littéraire, philosophique et critique par Grimm, Diderot, Raynal, Meister, etc.* Edited by Maurice Tourneux. Vol. 7. Paris: Garnier Frères, 1879.

Guthrie, William. *A General History of England from the Invasion of the Romans . . . to the late Revolution.* 4 vols. London, 1744–51.

Hall, Roland. *Fifty Years of Hume Scholarship: A Bibliographical Guide.* Edinburgh: Edinburgh University Press, 1978.

Hamilton, Elizabeth. *Memoirs of Modern Philosophers.* Bath, 1800.

Harrington, James. *The Political Works of James Harrington.* Edited by J. G. A. Pocock. Cambridge: Cambridge University Press, 1977.

Hartwick, John M. "Robert Wallace and Malthus and the Ratios." *History of Political Economy* 20 (1988): 357–79.

Havens, Earle. *Commonplace Books: A History of Manuscripts and Printed Books from Antiquity to the Twentieth Century.* New Haven: Yale University Press, 2001.

Hay, Carla H. "Catharine Macaulay and the American Revolution." *Historian* 56, no. 2 (1994): 301–16.

Hegel, Wilhelm Friedrich. *Lectures on the Philosophy of World History. Introduction: Reason in History.* trans. H.B. Nisbet. Cambridge: Cambridge University Press, 1975.

Herder, Johann Gottfried. *Another Philosophy of History and Selected Political Writings.* trans. Ioannis D. Evrigenis and Daniel Pellerin. Indianapolis: Hackett, 2004.

Herdt, Jennifer A. *Religion and Faction in Hume's Moral Philosophy.* Cambridge: Cambridge University Press, 1997.

Herodotus. *The Histories.* Translated by Aubrey de Sélincourt. Revised by A. R. Burn. Harmondsworth: Penguin, 1972.

Hicks, Philip. "Catharine Macaulay's Civil War: Gender, History, and Republicanism in Georgian Britain." *Journal of British Studies* 41, no. 2 (2002): 170–98.

———. *Neoclassical History and English Culture: From Clarendon to Hume.* New York: St. Martin's, 1996.

———. "The Roman Matron in Britain: Female Political Influence and Republican Response, ca. 1750–1800." *Journal of Modern History* 77, no. 1 (2005): 35–69.

Hill, Bridget. *The Republican Virago: The Life and Times of Catharine Macaulay, Historian.* Oxford: Oxford University Press, 1992.

Hirschmann, A.O. *The Passions and the Interests: Political Arguments for Capitalism Before Its Triumph.* Princeton: Princeton University Press, 1977.

Historical Manuscripts Commission: *Report on the Manuscripts of the Marquess of Downshire.* Vol. 1, pt. 2. London: His Majesty's Stationery Office, 1924.

The History of Melinda Harley. London, 1779.

Hurd, Richard. *Works.* 8 vols. London, 1811.

Hyde, Edward, first Earl of Clarendon. *The History of the Rebellion and Civil Wars in England* [1702–4]. Edited by W. Dunn Macray. 6 vols. Oxford, 1888.

Jackson, Ian. "Approaches to the History of Readers and Reading in 18th-Century Britain." *Historical Journal* 47, no. 4 (2004): 1041–54.

Jones, Peter. "On Reading Hume's *History of Liberty.*" In *Liberty in Hume's History of England,* edited by Nicholas Capaldi and Donald W. Livingston, 1–23. Dordrecht, Netherlands: Kluwer Academic Publishers, 1990.

Jordan, Will R. "Religion in the Public Square: A Reconsideration of Dave Hume and Religious Establishment," *Review of Politics* 64, no. 4 (2002): 687–713.

Jung, Sandro. *David Mallet, Anglo-Scot: Poetry, Patronage, and Politics in the Age of Union.* Newark: University of Delaware Press, 2008.

Kaufman, Paul. *Borrowings from the Bristol Library, 1773–1784: A Unique Record of Reading Vogues.* Charlottesville: Bibliographical Society of the University of Virginia, 1960.

[Kennett, White]. *A Complete History of England; With the Lives of All the Kings and Queens....* 3 vols. London, 1706.

Kidd, Colin. "Religious Realignment Between the Restoration and Union." In *A Union for Empire: Political Thought and the Union of 1707*, edited by John Robertson, 145–68. Cambridge: Cambridge University Press, 1995.

———. *Subverting Scotland's Past: Scottish Whig Historians and the Creation of an Anglo-British Identity, 1689–c. 1830.* Cambridge: Cambridge University Press, 1993.

Klancher, Jon P. *The Making of English Reading Audiences, 1790–1832*. Madison: University of Wisconsin Press, 1987.

Kramnick, Isaac. Introduction to *Historical Writings*, by Lord Bolingbroke. Chicago: University of Chicago Press, 1972.

Laird, John. *Hume's Philosophy of Human Nature*. New York: Dutton, 1932.

Lamb, H.H. *Clilmate, History, and the Modern World*. 2nd. ed. London: Routledge, 1995.

Lee, Charles. *The Lee Papers, 1754–1811*, 4 vols. *Collections of the New York Historical Society for the Years 1871–1874* (New York, Printed for the Society, 1872–75).

The Library; or Moral and Critical Magazine, for the year 1761, by a Society of Gentlemen. London, 1762.

Livingston, Donald W. "Hume on the Problem of Historical and Scientific Explanation." *New Scholasticism* 47, no. 1 (1973): 38–67.

———. "Hume's Historical Conception of Liberty." In *Liberty in Hume's History of England*, edited by Nicholas Capaldi and Donald W. Livingston, 105–53. Dordrecht, Netherlands: Kluwer Academic Publishers, 1990.

———. *Hume's Philosophy of Common Life*. Chicago: University of Chicago Press, 1984.

———. *Philosophical Melancholy and Delirium: Hume's Pathology of Philosophy*. Chicago: University of Chicago Press, 1998.

Long, Douglas. "Hume's 'Imagination' Revisited," in *Lumen: Selected Proceedings from the Canadian Society for Eighteenth-Century Studies* 17 (1998), ed. C. Gibson-Wood and G.D. Fulton.

Lottenbach, Hans. "Monkish Virtues, Artificial Lives: On Hume's Genealogy of Morals." *Canadian Journal of Philosophy* 26, no. 3 (1996): 367–89.

Ludlow, Edmund. *Memoirs of Edmund Ludlow....* [1698–99]. 2nd ed. 3 vols. London, 1720–22.

Luehrs, Robert. "Population and Utopia in the Thought of Robert Wallace." *Eighteenth-Century Studies* 20 (1987): 313–335.

Macaulay, Catharine. *The History of England from the Accession of James I to that of the Brunswick Line*. 8 vols. London, 1763–83.

Macfie, A.L. and D.D. Raphael, eds. *The Theory of Moral Sentiments*, in the Glasgow Edition of the Works and Correspondence of Adam Smith. Indianapolis: Liberty Classics, 1976.

MacIntyre, Alasdair. *Whose Justice? Which Rationality?* Notre Dame: University of Notre Dame Press, 1988.

Macpherson, C.B. ed. *Hobbes: Leviathan*. Harmondsworth: Penguin, 1968.

Marsden, George. *Jonathan Edwards: A Life*. New Haven: Yale University Press, 2003.

Matthew, H. C. G., and Brian Harrison, eds. *Oxford Dictionary of National Biography*. 60 vols. Oxford: Oxford University Press, 2004.

McArthur, Neil. *David Hume's Political Theory: Law, Commerce, and the Constitution of Government*. Toronto: University of Toronto Press, 2007.

McGinn, Colin. *Mindsight: Image, Dream, Meaning*. Cambridge: Harvard University Press, 2004.

McKendrick, Neil, ed. *Historical Perspectives: Studies in English Thought and Society*. London: Europa Publications, 1974.

Meek, Ronald. *Social Science and the Ignoble Savage*. Cambridge: Cambridge University Press, 1976.

McIntyre, Lee C. "Reduction, Supervenience, and the Autonomy of Social Scientific Laws." *Theory and Decision* 48, no. 2 (2000): 101–22.

Melaney, William D. "Hume's Secular Paradigm: Skepticism and Historical Knowledge." *History of Philosophy Quarterly* 25, no. 3 (2008): 243–57.

Merlan, Philip. "From Hume to Hamann." *Personalist* 32 (1951): 11–18.

Mijers, Esther. "_News from the Republic of Letters": Scottish Students, Charles Mackie, and the United Provinces, 1650–1750_. Leiden: Brill, 2012.

Miller, David. *Philosophy and Ideology in Hume's Political Thought*. Oxford: Clarendon Press, 1981.

Miller, Eugene F. "Hume on Liberty in the Successive English Constitutions." In *Liberty in Hume's History of England*, edited by Nicholas Capaldi and Donald W. Livingston, 53–103. Dordrecht, Netherlands: Kluwer Academic Publishers, 1990.

———. "Hume on the Development of English Liberty," *Political Science Reviewer* 16 (Fall 1986): 127–83.

Montesquieu. *Considerations on the Causes of the Romans' Greatness and Decline*. Dublin: Hafner Press, 1734.

———. *The Spirit of the Laws*. Translated by Thomas Nugent. Edited by Franz Neumann. New York: Hafner, 1949.

More, Hannah. *Hints Towards Forming the Character of a Young Princess*. London, 1805.

Moss, Ann. *Printed Commonplace-Books and the Structuring of Renaissance Thought*. Oxford: Clarendon Press, 1996.

Mossner, Ernest Campbell. "An Apology for David Hume, Historian." *Modern Language Association Publications* 16, no. 3 (1941): 657–90.

———. "Hume and the Ancient-Modern Controversy, 1725–1752: A Study in Creative Scepticism," *University of Texas Studies in English* 28 (1949): 139–53.

———. "Hume's Early Memoranda, 1729–1740: The Complete Text," Journal of the History of Ideas 9 (1948): 492–518.

———. *The Life of David Hume*. Edinburgh: Thomas Nelson and Sons, 1954. 2nd rev. ed., Oxford: Clarendon Press, 1980.

———. "Was Hume a Tory Historian? Facts and Reconsiderations." *Journal of the History of Ideas* 2, no. 2 (1941): 225–36.

Mossner, E.C. and I.S. Ross, eds. *Correspondence of Adam Smith*, in the Glasgow Edition of the Works and Correspondence of Adam Smith. Indianapolis: Liberty Classics, 1987.

Myers, Deborah C., Michael S. Moss, and Miles K. Oglethorpe, eds. *Visions of Scotland's Past: Looking to the Future; Essays in Honour of John R. Hume*. East Linton: Tuckwell, 2000.

Myers, Robin, and Michael Harris, eds. *Property of a Gentleman: The Formation, Organisation, and Dispersal of the Private Library, 1620–1920*. Winchester: St. Paul's Bibliographies, 1991.

Nagel, Ernest. *The Structure of Science*. New York: Harcourt, Brace, and World, 1961.

Noggle, James. "Literary Taste as Counter-Enlightenment in Hume's *History of England*." *Studies in English Literature 1500–1900* 44, no. 3 (2004): 617–38.

Norton, David Fate. "History and Philosophy in Hume's Thought." In *David Hume: Philosophical Historian*, edited by David Fate Norton and Richard Popkin, xxxii–l. Indianapolis: Bobbs-Merrill, 1965.

Norton, David Fate, and Mary J. Norton. *The David Hume Library*. Edinburgh: Edinburgh Bibliographical Society, 1996.

Norton, David Fate, and Richard H. Popkin, eds. *David Hume: Philosophical Historian*. New York: Bobbs-Merrill, 1965.

O'Brien, Karen. "Catharine Macaulay's Histories of England: A Female Perspective on the History of Liberty." In *Women, Gender, and Enlightenment*, edited by Sarah Knott and Barbara Taylor, 523–37. Basingstoke, Hampshire: Palgrave Macmillan, 2005.

———. *Narratives of Enlightenment: Cosmopolitan History from Voltaire to Gibbon*. Cambridge: Cambridge University Press, 1997.

Okie, Laird. "Ideology and Partiality in David Hume's *History of England.*" *Hume Studies* 11, no. 1 (1985): 1–32.

Oldmixon, John. *A Review of Dr. Zachary Grey's Defence of our Ancient and Modern Historians.* London, 1725.

Oxford English Dictionary. 2nd ed. Oxford: Oxford University Press, 1989.

Paul, James Balfour, ed. *Diary of George Ridpath, Minister of Stitchel, 1755–1761.* 3rd ser. Vol. 2. Edinburgh: Scottish Record Society, 1922.

Pearson, Jacqueline. *Women's Reading in Britain, 1750–1835: A Dangerous Recreation.* Cambridge: Cambridge University Press, 1999.

Pennington, Lady Sarah. *Advice to Daughters.* 4th ed. London, 1767.

Perinetti, Dario. "Philosophical Reflection on History." In *The Cambridge History of Eighteenth-Century Philosophy*, edited by K. Haakonssen, 2:1107–40. 2 vols. New York: Cambridge University Press, 2006.

Phillips, Mark Salber. "'If Mrs Mure Be Not Sorry for Poor King Charles': History, the Novel, and the Sentimental Reader." *History Workshop Journal* 43 (1997): 111–31.

———. *Society and Sentiment: Genres of Historical Writing in Britain, 1740–1820.* Princeton: Princeton University Press, 2000.

Phillips, Mark Salber, and Dale R. Smith. "Canonization and Critique: Hume's Reputation as a Historian." In *The Reception of David Hume in Europe*, edited by Peter Jones, 299–313. London: Thoemmes Continuum, 2005.

Phillipson, Nicholas. *Hume.* London: Weidenfeld and Nicolson, 1989. 2nd rev. ed. published as *David Hume: The Philosopher as Historian.* London: Penguin, 2011.

Pocock, J. G. A. *Barbarism and Religion.* 5 vols. Cambridge: Cambridge University Press, 1999–.

———. "Catharine Macaulay: Patriot Historian." In *Women Writers and the Early Modern British Political Tradition*, edited by Hilda L. Smith. Cambridge: Cambridge University Press, 1998.

———. *The Machiavellian Moment: Florentine Political Thought and the Atlantic Republican Tradition.* Princeton: Princeton University Press, 1975.

———. *Politics, Language, and Time: Essays on Political Thought and History.* New York: Atheneum, 1971.

———. *The Ancient Constitution and the Feudal Law: A Study of English Historical Thought in the Seventeenth Century.* Cambridge: Cambridge University Press, 1957.

Pompa, Leon. *Human Nature and Historical Knowledge: Hume, Hegel, and Vico.* Cambridge: Cambridge University Press, 1990.

Popkin, Richard H. "David Hume: Philosophical versus Prophetic Historian," in *David Hume: Many-Sided Genius*, ed. Kenneth R. Merrill and Robert W. Shahan. Norman: University of Oklahoma Press, 1976.

Popkin, Richard. "Skepticism and the Study of History." In *David Hume: Philosophical Historian*, edited by David Fate Norton and Richard Popkin. Indianapolis: Bobbs-Merrill, 1965.

Potkay, Adam. "Hume's 'Supplement to Gulliver': The Medieval Volumes of *The History of England.*" *Eighteenth-Century Life* 25, no. 2 (2001): 32–46.

Pownall, Thomas. *Principles of Polity, being the Grounds and Reasons of Civic Empire.* London, 1752.

Purviance, Robert, ed. *Narrative of Events Which Occurred in Baltimore Town During the Revolutionary War.* Baltimore: Jos. Robinson, 1849.

Ralph, James. *The History of England during the Reigns of K. William, Q. Anne and K. George I. . . .* 2 vols. London, 1744–46.

Raphael, D.D. "'The True Old Humean Philosophy' and Its Influence on Adam Smith," in *David Hume: Bicentenary Papers*, ed. G.P. Morice. Austin: University of Texas Press, 1977.

Rapin de Thoyras, Paul. *The History of England. . . .* Translated by Nicholas Tindal. 15 vols. London, 1725–31.

Raven, James. *The Business of Books: Booksellers and the English Book Trade.* New Haven: Yale University Press, 2007.

———. "New Reading Histories, Print Culture, and the Identification of Change: The Case of Eighteenth-Century England." *Social History* 23 (1998): 268–87.

Raven, James, Helen Small, and Naomi Tadmor, eds. *The Practice and Representation of Reading in England.* Cambridge: Cambridge University Press, 1996.

Raynor, David R. "Hume and Robertson's *History of Scotland*." *British Journal for Eighteenth-Century Studies* 10 (1987): 59–63.

Richards, Jeffrey H., and Sharon M. Harris, eds. *Mercy Otis Warren: Selected Letters.* Athens: University of Georgia Press, 2009.

Richter, Melvin. *The Political Theory of Montesquieu.* Cambridge: Cambridge University Press, 1977.

Ridpath, George. *Diary of George Ridpath, Minister of Stitchel 1755–61.* Edited by Sir J. Balfour Paul. Edinburgh: Scottish History Society, 1922.

Ring, Benjamin A. "David Hume: Historian or Tory Hack?" *North Dakota Quarterly* (1968): 50–59.

Robbins, Caroline. *The Eighteenth-Century Commonwealthman: Studies in the Transmission, Development and Circumstance of English Liberal Thought from the Restoration of Charles II until the War with the Thirteen Colonies.* New York: Atheneum, 1968.

Robertson, William. *The History of America.* London, 1777.

———. *The History of the Reign of the Emperor Charles V.* 3 vols. London, 1769.

Rogers, Nicholas. *Crowds, Culture, and Politics in Georgian Britain.* Oxford: Oxford University Press, 1998.

Rose, Jonathan. "Rereading the English Common Reader: A Preface to a History of Audiences." *Journal of the History of Ideas* 53 (1992): 47–70.

Rotwein, Eutene, "Introduction" in *David Hume: Writings on Economics.* Madison: University of Wisconsin Press, 1970.

Sabine, George H. "Hume's Contribution to the Historical Method." *Philosophical Review* 15 (1906): 17–38.

Sabl, Andrew. *Hume's Politics: Coordination and Crisis in the "History of England"* Princeton and Oxford: Princeton University Press, 2012.

Schama, Simon. *Citizens: A Chronicle of the French Revolution.* London: Penguin, 1989.

Schelling, F.W.J. *System of Transcendental Idealism.* trans. Peter Heath. Charlottesville: University of Virginia Press, 2001.

Schmidt, Claudia M. *David Hume: Reason in History.* University Park: Pennsylvania State University Press, 2003.

Seed, John. "The Spectre of Puritanism: Forgetting the Seventeenth Century in David Hume's *History of England*." *Social History* 30 (2005): 444–62.

Shackleton, Robert. *Montesquieu: A Critical Biography.* Oxford: Oxford University Press, 1961.

Sher, Richard B. *The Enlightenment and the Book: Scottish Authors and Their Publishers in Eighteenth-Century Britain, Ireland, and America.* Chicago: University of Chicago Press, 2006.

———. "From Troglodytes to Americans: Montesquieu and the Scottish Enlightenment on Liberty, Virtue, and Commerce," in *Republicanism, Liberty, and Commercial Society, 1649–1776,* ed. David Wootton. Stanford: Stanford University Press, 1994.

Sheridan, Thomas. *A Plan of Education for the Young Nobility and Gentry of Great Britain.* London, 1769.

Siebert, Donald T. *The Moral Animus of David Hume.* Newark: University of Delaware Press, 1990.

Siebert, Donald T. "The Sentimental Sublime in Hume's *History of England*." *Review of English Studies* 40 (1989): 352–72.

Skinner, Quentin. *The Foundations of Modern Political Thought*. 2 vols. Cambridge: Cambridge University Press, 1978.

———. "The Principles and Practice of Opposition: The Case of Bolingbroke versus Walpole." In *Historical Perspectives: Studies in English Thought and Society in Honor of J. H. Plumb*, edited by Neil McKendrick, 93–128. London: Europa Publications, 1974.

Sloan, Kim. *Enlightenment: Discovering the World in the Eighteenth Century*. London: British Museum Press, 2003.

Smith, Nigel. "Popular Republicanism in the 1650s: John Streater's 'Heroick Mechanicks.'" In *Milton and Republicanism*, edited by David Armitage, Armand Himy, and Quentin Skinner. Cambridge: Cambridge University Press, 1995.

Somerville, Martha. *Personal Recollections, From Early Life to Old Age of Mary Somerville*. London, 1873.

Spadafora, David. *The Idea of Progress in Eighteenth-Century Britain*. New Haven: Yale University Press, 1990.

Spencer, Mark G. *David Hume and Eighteenth-Century America*. Rochester: University of Rochester Press, 2005. 2nd rev. ed., 2010.

———. "Hume and Madison on Faction." *William and Mary Quarterly*, ser. 3, vol. 59 (2002): 869–96.

———. *Hume's Reception in Early America*. 2 vols. Bristol, UK: Thoemmes Press, 2002.

———. "Hume's Reception in Eighteenth-Century Philadelphia." In *New Essays on David Hume*, edited by Emilio Mazza and Emanuele Ronchetti, 287–308. Milan, Italy: FrancoAngeli, 2007.

St. Clair, William. *The Reading Nation in the Romantic Period*. Cambridge: Cambridge University Press, 2004.

Stanhope, Philip Dormer, fourth Earl of Chesterfield. *Letters to His Son*. 2 vols. Washington: Universal Classics Library, Oliver H. G. Leigh, 1901.

Stevenson, David R. "David Hume, Historicist." *Historian* 52 (1990): 209–18.

Stewart, John B. *The Moral and Political Philosophy of David Hume*. New York: Columbia University Press, 1963.

———. *Opinion and Reform in Hume's Political Philosophy*. Princeton: Princeton University Press, 1992.

Stewart, M.A. "The Dating of Hume's Manuscripts," in *The Scottish Enlightenment: Essays in Reinterpretation*, ed. Paul Wood. Rochester: University of Rochester Press, 2000.

Stockton, Constant Noble. "Hume—Historian of the English Constitution." *Eighteenth-Century Studies* 4 (1970/71): 277–93.

Stuart, Gilbert. *A View of Society in Europe, in its Progress from Rudeness to Refinement*. Edinburgh, 1778.

Tacitus. *The Complete Works of Tacitus*. Translated by A. J. Church and W. J. Brodribb. New York: Modern Library, 1942.

Thompson, C. Bradley. *John Adams and the Spirit of Liberty*. Lawrence: University Press of Kansas, 1998.

Thomson, James. *Liberty, The Castle of Indolence, and Other Poems*. Edited by James Sambrook. Oxford: Oxford University Press, 1986.

Towsey, Mark. "'All the Partners May Be Enlightened and Improved by Reading Them': The Distribution of Enlightenment Books in Scottish Subscription Library Catalogues, 1750–c. 1820." *Journal of Scottish Historical Studies* 28 (2008): 20–43.

———. "'An Infant Son to Truth Engage': Virtue, Responsibility, and Self-Improvement in the Reading of Elizabeth Rose of Kilravock, 1745–1815." *Journal of the Edinburgh Bibliographical Society* 2 (2007): 69–92.

———. "First Steps in Associational Reading: Book Use and Sociability at the Wigtown Subscription Library, 1795–1799." *Papers of the Bibliographical Society of America* 103, no. 4 (2009): 455–95.

———. "Imprisoned Reading: Napoleonic Prisoners of War at the Selkirk Subscription Library, 1809–1815." In *Civilians and War in Europe, 1640–1815*, edited by E. Charters, E. Rosenhaft, and H. Smith, 241–61. Liverpool: Liverpool University Press, 2012.

———. "'Observe Her Heedfully': Elizabeth Rose on Women Writers." *Women's Writing* 18, no. 1 (2011): 15–33.

———. "'Patron of Infidelity': Scottish Readers Respond to David Hume, c. 1750–c. 1820." *Book History* 11 (2008): 89–123.

———. "'Philosophically Playing the Devil': Recovering Readers' Responses to David Hume and the Scottish Enlightenment." *Historical Research* 83, no. 220 (2010): 301–20.

———. *Reading the Scottish Enlightenment: Books and Their Readers in Provincial Scotland, 1750–1820*. Leiden: Brill, 2010.

Trevor-Roper, H. R. "David Hume, Historian." In *History and the Enlightenment*, edited by John Robertson, 120–28. New Haven: Yale University Press, 2010.

———. "Three Historians: II: David Hume." *Listener* (7 October 1965): 521–24.

van Holthoon, Frederic. "Hume and the 1763 Edition of His *History of England*." *Hume Studies* 23, no. 1 (1997): 133–52.

———. *Een Dialoog over David Hume*. Amsterdam: Boom, 2007.

Vickery, Amanda. *The Gentleman's Daughter: Women's Lives in Georgian England*. New Haven: Yale University Press, 1998.

Vincent, David, ed. *Testaments of Radicalism: Memoirs of Working-Class Politicians 1790–1885*. London: Europa, 1977.

Wallace, Robert. *A Dissertation on the Numbers of Mankind in Antient and Modern Times*. Edinburgh, 1753.

———. *Various Prospects of Mankind, Nature, and Providence*. London, 1761.

Warren-Adams Letters: Being Chiefly a Correspondence Among John Adams, Samuel Adams, and James Warren. 2 vols. Boston: Massachusetts Historical Society, 1917–25.

Wertz, S. K. *Between Hume's Philosophy and History: Historical Theory and Practice*. Lanham: University Press of America, 2000.

———. "Hume, History, and Human Nature." *Journal of the History of Ideas* 36 (1975): 481–96.

———. "When Did Hume Plan a History?" *Southwest Philosophical Studies* 3 (1978): 30–33.

Wexler, Victor G. *David Hume and the History of England*. Philadelphia: American Philosophical Society, 1979.

Wightman, W.P.D. ed. *Essays on Philosophical Subjects*, in the Glasgow Edition of the Works and Correspondence of Adam Smith. Indianapolis: Liberty Fund, 1980.

Whelan, Frederick G. "Church Establishments, Liberty, and Competition in Religion," *Polity* 23, no. 2 (1990): 155–85.

———. "Populations and Ideology in the Enlightenment," *History of Political Thought* 12 (1991): 35–72.

Wodrow, Robert. *Analecta or Some Remarkable Providences. . . .* 4 vols. Edited by Mathew Leishman. Glasgow: Maitland Club, 1842–43.

Wood, Gordon S. "Conspiracy and the Paranoid Style: Causality and Deceit in the Eighteenth Century." *William and Mary Quarterly*, 3rd ser., vol. 39 (1982): 401–41.

———. *The Creation of the American Republic 1776–1787*. Chapel Hill: University of North Carolina Press, 1969. Reprint, 1998.

Wootton, David. "David Hume: 'The Historian.'" In *The Cambridge Companion to Hume*, edited by David Fate Norton and Jacqueline Taylor, 447–79. 2nd rev. ed. New York: Cambridge University Press, 2009.

———, ed. *Republicanism, Liberty, and Commercial Society, 1649–1776*. Stanford: Stanford University Press, 1994.

Worden, Blair, ed. *Edmund Ludlow: A Voyce from the Watch Tower*. London: Royal Historical Society, 1978.

———. "Providence and Politics in Cromwellian England." *Past and Present* 109 (November 1985): 55–99.
Works of Thomas Jefferson. Edited by Paul L. Ford. 12 vols. New York: G. P. Putnam's Sons, 1904–15.
Wrangham, Francis. *The British Plutarch*. 6 vols. London, 1816.
Yeo, Richard. "Ephraim Chambers' *Cyclopaedia* (1728) and the Tradition of the Commonplaces." *Journal of the History of Ideas* 57 (1996): 157–75.

David Allan is Reader in the School of History at the University of St. Andrews. He has held visiting fellowships at Harvard, Yale, and Brown and is the author of *Commonplace Books and Reading in Georgian England* (2010); *Making British Culture: English Readers and the Scottish Enlightenment 1740–1830* (2008); *A Nation of Readers: The Lending Library in Georgian England* (2007); *Adam Ferguson* (2006); *Scotland in the Eighteenth Century: Union and Enlightenment* (2001); *Philosophy and Politics in Later Stuart Scotland* (2000); and *Virtue, Learning, and Scottish Enlightenment: Ideas of Scholarship in Early Modern History* (1993).

M. A. Box is Emeritus Professor of English at the University of Alaska Fairbanks. He is the author of *The Suasive Art of David Hume* (1990). With David Harvey and Michael Silverthorne, he has edited Hume's pamphlet *A True Account of the Behaviour and Conduct of Archibald Stewart* (*Hume Studies* 2003). He is a co-editor, with Tom Beauchamp, of the forthcoming *Essays, Moral, Political, and Literary*, volumes 6 and 7 in the Clarendon edition of the works of David Hume.

Timothy M. Costelloe is Associate Professor of Philosophy at the College of William and Mary. He is the author of *Aesthetics and Morals in the Philosophy of David Hume* (2007) and *The British Aesthetic Tradition: From Shaftesbury to Wittgenstein* (2013), and the editor of *The Sublime: From Antiquity to the Present* (2012). His work has also appeared in a variety of collections and journals, including *Hume Studies*, *Journal of the History of Philosophy*, and *History of Philosophy Quarterly*.

Roger L. Emerson is an emeritus professor who spent most of his career teaching European and British social and intellectual history at the University of Western Ontario. He has published many articles on Scottish thought and institutions. In addition to having edited several volumes, he is the author of *Professors, Patronage, and Politics: The Aberdeen Universities in the Eighteenth Century* (1992); *Academic Patronage in the Scottish Enlightenment: Glasgow, Edinburgh, and St. Andrews Universities* (2008); *Essays on David Hume, Medical Men, and the Scottish Enlightenment* (2009); and *An Enlightened Duke: The Life of Archibald Campbell (1682–1761), Earl of Ilay, 3rd Duke of Argyll* (2013).

Jennifer A. Herdt is Gilbert L. Stark Professor of Christian Ethics at Yale University. She is the author of *Religion and Faction in Hume's Moral Philosophy* (1997 and 2008) and *Putting On Virtue: The Legacy of the Splendid Vices* (2008 and 2012). She served as editor for a special issue of the *Journal of Religious Ethics*, entitled "Eighteenth-Century Ethics" (2000), and for a special issue of the *Journal of Medieval and Early Modern Studies*, entitled "Virtue, Identity, and Agency: Ethical Formation from Medieval to Early Modern" (2012). She is an associate editor for the *Journal of Religious Ethics*.

Philip Hicks is Professor of Humanistic Studies at St. Mary's College, Notre Dame, Indiana. He is the author of *Neoclassical History and English Culture: From Clarendon to Hume* (1996), as well as essays on Catharine Macaulay, Abigail Adams, Lord Bolingbroke, and aspects of feminist argument and classical antiquity in eighteenth-century British historical writing, most recently, "The Ancient Historians in Britain," in *The Oxford History of Classical Reception in English Literature*, volume 3, 1660–1790, edited by David Hopkins and Charles Martindale (2012).

Douglas Long is Associate Professor in the Department of Political Science at the University of Western Ontario, Canada, and honorary senior research associate at the Bentham research project, University College London. He is a member of the editorial board of *Utilitas* and of the executive committee of the International Society for Utilitarian Studies. He is the author of *Bentham on Liberty* (1977) and is editing *Preparatory Principles of Jurisprudence*, a forthcoming volume in the *Collected Works of Jeremy Bentham*. His other publications include articles on Hume's idea of the imagination, Hume's understanding of "utility," and Hume's role in the secularization of modern political thought.

Claudia M. Schmidt (1961–2011) was Associate Professor in the Department of Philosophy at Marquette University. Her research interests included the development of different approaches to human nature and history in modern philosophy since the eighteenth century, and the issues of psychologism and cognitive theory that are raised by considering the works of various philosophers, especially Hume and Kant, in this context. Her publications include *David Hume: Reason in History* (2003) and articles on Hume, Kant, and the philosophy of history.

Michael Silverthorne taught classics at McGill University. He has translated a number of Neo-Latin texts, including Bacon's *Novum Organum* and Spinoza's *Tractatus Theologico-Politicus* and works of Gershom Carmichael and Francis Hutcheson. He is associate editor of the Clarendon edition of Hume's *Essays*. He is currently translating Sir Isaac Newton's theological notebooks for the Newton Project.

Mark G. Spencer is Associate Professor of History and Chair of the Department of History at Brock University, Ontario. His monograph *David Hume and Eighteenth-Century America* (2005) was reissued in a paperback edition in 2010. His edited and co-edited books include *Ulster Presbyterians in the Atlantic World: Religion, Politics, and Identity* (2006); *Utilitarians and Their Critics in America, 1789–1914* (2005); and *Hume's Reception in Early America* (2002). He is a past president of the Eighteenth-Century Scottish Studies Society and is a member of the editorial board of *Hume Studies*.

Jeffrey M. Suderman teaches a wide range of courses on early modern Europe and Britain and the history of science at the University of Calgary and at Mount Royal University in Calgary, Alberta. He is the author of *Orthodoxy and Enlightenment: George Campbell in the Eighteenth Century* (2001). His current research is on the relationship between philosophy and religion in eighteenth-century Scotland.

Mark Towsey is Lecturer in Modern History at the University of Liverpool, having previously held fellowships at the University of London, Yale and Harvard Universities, and the Huntington Library. His first monograph, *Reading the Scottish Enlightenment: Books and Their Readers in Provincial Scotland, 1750–1820*, was published in 2010. He has published extensively on book history, the history of reading, and the cultural history of libraries in the eighteenth and nineteenth centuries. He is editor-in-chief of *Library and Information History* and vice president of the Eighteenth-Century Scottish Studies Society.

CONTRIBUTORS

F. L. van **Holthoon** is Professor Emeritus at the University of Groningen, Netherlands. His publications include *The Road to Utopia: A Study of J. S. Mill's Social Thought* (1971); *Mensen in Europa* (1985); *De Nederlandse Samenleving sinds 1815* (Dutch society since 1815) (1985); *Common Sense: The Foundation for Social Science* (with D. Olson) (1987); a variorum edition of Hume's *History of England* (2000); *State and Civil Society: Theories, Illusions, Realities; A Survey of Political Theories in the 19th Century Western World* (2003); and *A Dialogue on David Hume: On His Revision of "A Treatise of Human Nature"* (2009). His translations into Dutch include *David Hume: Traktaat over de Menselijke Natuur* (A treatise of human nature) and *David Hume: Mens en Werk* (The man and his work) (2009).

Index

absolutism, 114, 137, 140 n. 3, 152, 156–57
   Elizabeth I and, 150–51
   freedom and, 8, 140
   of Tudor kings, 1, 149–50
Adams, Abigail, 5, 73
Adams, John, 5, 72–73, 78 n. 42
Addison, Joseph, 91, 240–41
Aegina, 237, 239
Aelius, 252 n. 32
Aeschines, 252 n. 32
Aeneas, the Roman founder, 26
Aeneas Sylvius, 33
Afranius, Lucius, 252 n. 32
aesthetics, 9, 169, 172
Alexander the Great, 189, 227, 243
Alfred the Great, 27, 131–32, 139,
   death of, 130, 140 n. 6
   Hume admiration for, 7, 123–24, 135, 206, 221–22 n. 10, 222 n. 28
   as warrior and scholar, 123–24, 139
Allan, David, 6–7, 28, 103–20, 265
Allen, John, 109
Alphonsus Ligouri, Saint, 30
American Revolution, 5, 72–73
Ammianus Marcellinus, 252 n. 32
"Amusements in Solitude," 86–87, 97
analytic philosophy of history, 9, 169–71, 173–75
Anderson, William, 22
Anglicism. *See* Church of England
Annual Register, 89
Appian, 234, 236, 243
Arcadia, 239
Aristides, 252 n. 32
Aristophanes, 252 n. 32
Aristotle, 163, 230, 234, 237, 244, 252 n. 32
Arrian, 234
artificial lives, 3–4, 37, 53–54, 56
   sympathetic understanding and, 42–47
Asconius, 252 n. 32
Ashbourne, 105
Astruc, Jean, *Conjectures sur les mémoires originaux*, 29
Athenaeus, 11, 237, 239–40, 252 n. 32, 253 n. 49

Athens, 11, 41, 229, 237–40, 242, 254 n. 51
Atholl, Duchess of, 5, 84
Atholl, Duke of, 95–96
Augustine, Saint, 20, 28, 163
Aurelius Victor, 252 n. 32
Austen, Jane, *Mansfield Park,* 109
authority, 146, 153
   History of England as study of, 8, 149–54
   liberty and, 71, 148, 150, 151, 152
   See also kingship

Bacon, Francis, 66, 174, 252 n. 17
Baier, Annette, 58 n. 41
barons, 136–37, 143 n. 19, 150, 152–53
   feudalism and, 152
   tyranny of, 135, 142 n. 18, 149
   See also nobility
Bath, 108–9
Baxter, John, *A New and Impartial History of England,* 116
Bayle, Pierre, 14, 25, 29
Beaton, Cardinal David, 15
Beattie, James, 81
   Essay on Truth, 85, 94
Becket, Thomas à, 48, 131–32, 146, 193, 206, 222 n. 11
Berkeley, Bishop, 246
bias, 26, 86, 92, 157, 160, 205, 232
Bible, 23, 29–30
   and history, 13, 21, 28, 188
Binford, Thomas, 106
Birch, Dr., 149, 161 n. 15
Blackstone, Sir William, 250 n. 6
Blackwell, Thomas, 30
blasphemy, 18, 34 n. 15
Blount, Charles, 23
Bolingbroke, Viscount (Henry St. John), 75 n. 9, 76 n. 18, 162 n. 32
   Hume treatment of, 71, 139, 141 n. 10
   "spirit of liberty" and, 4, 61–64, 67–68, 73, 76 n. 16
   Walpole and, 4, 63–64, 74
   works: *A Dissertation upon Parties*, 76 n. 15; *Remarks on the History of England,* 63, 65

INDEX

Bonar, James, 225
Bongie, Laurence, 188
Bossuet, Bishop Jacques-Bénigne, 18
Box, M. A., 11–12, 225–54, 265
Boyle, David, 5, 82, 91–93, 96–7, 98 n. 3, 101 n. 48
Brady, Robert, 82, 98 n. 4, 152
Braudy, Leo, 149
Bristol, eighth Earl of, 104
British Library, 1
Brooke, Zachary, 105
Brown, John, 5, 73
    An Estimate of the Manners and Principles of the Times, 70–71
Buchanan, George, *History of Scotland*, 25
Buckle, H. T., 167
Buffon, Comte de, *Natural History*, 107
Burgh, James, 70
Burke, Edmund, 146, 158, 162 n. 32
Burns, Robert, 104
Butts, Robert, 174

Caesar, Julius, 72, 227, 234, 238–9
Caligula, 247
Calmet, Dom, 20
Calvinism, 17, 22–23, 30, 57 n. 14, 58 n. 31
Cambridge, 92, 238
Camden, William, 197
Cameron, William, 5, 84–85
Campbell, George, 29, 81
Campbell, Hugh, 108
Campbell, John, 95
Campbell, Matthew, 89
Canterbury, 110
capitalism, 150, 159–60
Carneades, 212, 223 n. 37
Carr, David, 9, 165
Carre, Robert (Viscount Rochester), 195
Carte, Thomas, 65
Catholicism, 3, 18, 20–21, 23, 28, 30
    Hume on, 17, 33, 113
    papacy in, 24, 33
Cato the Elder, 237, 242, 243
Catullus, 252 n. 32
causation, 170, 219–20
    cause and effect, 173–74, 196
    physical and moral, 231, 245
celibacy, 44, 232
Chapman, Richard, 105
Chapone, Hester, 93
Charlemagne, 27
Charles I, 8, 71, 93, 193
    character analysis, 48, 65–66, 142 n. 23, 149, 153
    duplicitous reputation, 149, 161 n. 15
    spirit of liberty and, 66–67, 68

Charles II, 68, 206, 222 n.12
Charmides, 244
Chesterfield, fifth Earl of, 104
Chesterfield, Lord (Phillip Stanhope), 15–16
Chisholm, Duncan, 5, 88
chivalry, 129, 130
Christianity, 14, 17, 19–20, 32, 42, 55. *See also* Calvinism; Catholicism
chronology, 26, 137, 142 n. 21, 196
Church of England, 19–20, 28, 110
Church of Scotland, 18, 21, 28, 30
Cicero, 62, 234, 236, 238
civility
    as Hume's theme, 7, 122, 137, 140 n. 2
    kings and, 122, 123, 133, 136, 138–39
civilization, 146, 173, 178 n. 24
Clanricarde, fourteenth Earl of, 104
Clarendon, first Earl of, 65, 76 n. 19, 198
Clarke, Thomas, 105
Clephane, John, 77 n. 31, 84, 99 n. 12, 149, 227, 251 n. 8
clergy, 19, 84, 107, 154
    History of England read by, 105–6
    kings and, 130, 131, 136, 222 n. 11
Clerk, John, 24
cognitive momentum, 204, 207
Coke, Sir Edward, 152
Collingwood, R. G., 163
    on historical narrative, 216, 223 n. 41
    on Hume, 2, 40, 49
    Idea of History, 175
Columella, 237, 252 n. 16
commerce, 141 n. 10, 159. *See also* "Of Commerce"
common life, 39, 40, 42, 49, 54–55, 125, 215
commonplace books, 90, 101 nn. 42–43
    "Amusements in Solitude," 85, 86–87, 97
    History of England in, 6, 90–92, 113–17
Commons, 137, 153, 156
    House of, 72, 127, 135, 143 n. 19
"complaisance," 212, 216, 223 n. 36
Comte, Auguste, 9, 163, 166–67, 172–73, 178 n. 24
Condorcet, Marquis de, 172
consensus, 148
Constable, William, 6, 113
constitution, English, 63–64, 66–67, 150
    Euthanasia of, 157–58
    freedom and, 68, 70
context, 41, 171, 175, 201, 220
Cooke, John and Charles, *Hume's History*, 88
Corinth, 239
corruption, 138, 154, 246
Costelloe, Timothy M., 9–10, 181–99, 265

Country opposition, 62–63, 70–71
Cowper, third Earl, 104
The Craftsman, 63
Crawford, Matthew, 22
critical philosophy of history, 9, 164
Critical Review, 5, 87, 90
Crofts, Thomas, 105
Cromwell, Oliver, 62, 71
Crusades, 16
cultural history, 144, 176, 179 n. 36
Cuming, Patrick, 3, 22–24, 29, 35 n. 30
curiousness, 226

d'Alembert, Jean le Rond, 16–17, 32, 34 nn. 10–11
Dalrymple, David, 35 n. 36
Dalrymple, Sir John, *Memoirs of Great Britain and Ireland,* 106
Darnton, Robert, 81
de Brosses, Charles, 29
debt, public, 159–60
Decelean War, 240, 254 n. 51
de Henault, Jean-François, 29
deism, 14, 16–18, 23, 28–29, 33 n. 3
deity, 44–45, 51–52, 55, 64, 176, 210. See also theism
democracy, 156, 158, 160
    ancient, 151–52
Demosthenes, 234–35, 237–38, 240
Descartes, René, 163
descriptivism, 40, 56
Dibdin, Thomas Frognall, 105
Dilthey, Wilhelm, 163, 165, 175
Diodorus Siculus, 230, 234, 238, 243
Diogenes of Sinope, 42
Diogenes Laertius, 252 n. 32
distance, historical, 161
Dodwell, Henry, Sr., 24
Donatus, 252 n. 32
Drummond, Jean, 95, 96
Dubos, Abbé, 233, 252 n. 17
Duclos, Charles, 29
Dunlop, William, 21–22, 24
Durham, 110
Durkheim, Émile, 55

ecclesiastical history, 2–3, 13, 16, 20–21
    biblical criticism and, 29–30
    Cumings on, 22–24
    Hume and, 13–14, 16–17, 20, 29–30, 32–33
    Mackie on, 24–26
    Rouet on, 26–28
    Voltaire on, 31–32
Echard, Laurence, 65

Edinburgh, 2–25, 35 n. 32, 37, 84, 111, 174
    Philosophical Society of, 25, 35 n. 28, 250 n. 5
    Review, 89
    University of, 21–25, 35 n. 34
Edward I, 7, 132–35, 137, 138, 141 nn. 12–13
Edward II, 7, 126, 127
Edward III, 63, 121, 128–30, 141 n. 10, 189–90
Edwards, Jonathan, 17
    History of the Work of Redemption, 35 n. 30
Edwards, Nathaniel, 106
Edward VI, 84
Elizabeth I, 8, 66, 77 n. 24, 92, 101 n. 53, 110, 137, 197
    absolutism of, 150–51
    liberty and, 68, 144
Elliot, Gilbert, 35 n. 38, 208, 237–38
Emerson, Roger L., 2–3, 13–36, 265
Encyclopédie ou dictionnaire raisonné des sciences, des arts et des métiers, 31, 34 n. 10, 36 n. 48
English civil war, 4, 33 n. 1, 61–66, 71–72
enthusiasm, 17, 85, 171
    liberty and, 4–5, 68–69, 71
Episcopalians, 28
eternity, 213, 217–18
Eusebius of Caesarea, 20, 29
exchequer courts, 133
executive governance, 7, 122, 138
existentialism, 175
existential philosophy of history, 9, 165–66, 171–72, 175–76
experience, 183–84, 191
Exeter, nineteenth Earl of, 107

fact, 154, 229, 246
    fiction and, 181
    history and, 9–10, 87, 91, 146, 171, 181–88, 190, 192, 194
faction, 22, 48, 63, 65, 68–69, 82, 127, 157, 160, 188, 219, 229, 243, 247
Falkenheim, Emil, 9, 165
fanaticism, 16, 73, 202
    religious, 68–69, 71, 74, 86, 116, 202
Farmington, Conn., 106
Farr, James, 57 n. 9, 205, 207, 221 n. 6
female readers, 83, 93–94, 101 n. 49, 106–7
Fénélon, François, 226
Ferguson, Adam, 226
    History of the Roman Republic, 107
feudalism, 71, 131–32, 137, 152, 245
fiction, 9, 94, 109, 169, 181, 183, 185, 190, 192, 194, 199 n. 5, 216, 235
Five Knights' case, 66

INDEX

Fletcher of Saltoun, Andrew, 226, 246, 254 n. 63
Flexman, Roger, 5, 86–87
Florus, 252 n. 32
Fontenelle, Bernard de, 14, 26
Forbes, Duncan, *Hume's Philosophical Politics*, 98 n. 6, 145–46
Forbes, James, 82–83, 96
forgeries, 26, 35 n. 37
France, 16–17, 28, 30, 34 n. 13, 76 n. 18, 104, 129, 142 n. 26, 156, 230
    England and, 129, 141 n. 10, 152, 159
    French Revolution, 61, 74 n. 3, 82, 110
    Hume's reception in, 97, 129, 188
    monarchy in, 48, 52, 161 n. 17
freedom, 30, 33, 66, 112, 116–17, 123, 127, 136, 142 n. 19, 153, 248
    absolutism and, 8, 140
    English constitution and, 68, 70, 83
    See also liberty
Fukuyama, Francis, 155
future, 21, 45, 48, 125, 155, 177, 179 n. 37, 192, 207, 214, 246
    past and, 158, 167, 171, 215–16, 223 n. 40
    present and, 51–53, 148

Gambier, James, 6–7, 115–16
George II, 146
George III, 111, 139, 158
George IV, 108
Giarizzo, Giuseppe, 157–58, 162 n. 33
Gibbon, Edward, 160, 188
    Decline and Fall of the Roman Empire, 107
Gibbons, Thomas, 109
Glasgow, 22, 177 n. 4
    Literary Society, 36 n. 44
    University of, 21–22, 26, 35–36 n. 39, 82, 98 n. 3
global warming, 233, 252 nn. 17–18
God. *See* deity
Godwin, Charles, 109
Golden Tooth legend, 14, 26
Goldsmith, Oliver, *An History of England*, 71
Grant, George, *Time as History*, 218
Gray Library, 5, 89
Greece, ancient, 41, 155, 168, 195, 229–30, 233–34, 236, 239–40, 243
Gregory, Pope, 19
Gregory of Tours, 25–26
Grimm, Friedrich Melchior, 16, 34 n. 9
Grotius, Hugo, 27, 210
Guicciardin, 195
Guthrie, William, 65

Haddington, 5, 89, 100 n. 35
Hall, Roland, 225
Hall-Stevenson, John, 114
Hamann, J. G., 179 n. 37
    Golgotha and Sheblimini!, 176
Hamilton, Elizabeth, *Memoirs of Modern Philosophers*, 94
happiness, 76 n. 17, 137, 159, 217, 232
    populousness and, 226, 228, 231–32, 244–45, 247, 249, 251 n. 13
Hardouin, Jean, 241, 254 n. 54
Harrington, James, 62, 252 n. 17
    Oceana, 158, 210, 223 n. 31
Hartington, 108
Harris, H. S., 173
Hazard, Samuel, 109
Hearne, Thomas, 28, 140 n. 6
Hegel, G. W. F., 9, 147, 163–66, 173
Heidegger, Martin, 163, 165
Helvetius, Claude Adrien, 16
Hempel, Carl, 9, 163, 166
    "The Function of General Laws in History," 174, 179 n. 30
Henry, Robert, 35 n. 31
    History of Great Britain, 49, 107
Henry I, 130–31, 141 n. 11
Henry II, 131–32, 146, 153
    and Becket, 131, 206, 222 n. 11
Henry III, 133, 136–37, 192, 196
Henry III (of France), 48
Henry VI, 93
Henry VII, 125, 149–50, 252 n. 17
Henry VIII, 32, 90
Herder, Johann Gottfried, 9, 163–64, 175–76
Herdt, Jennifer A., 3–4, 37–59, 265
hereditary monarchy. *See* kingship
Hereford, 109
Herodian, 252 n. 32
Herodotus, 11, 189, 234–36
    The Histories, 75 n. 7
Herschel, John, 9, 174
Herschel, William, 174
Hesiod, 252 n. 32
Hickes, George, 28
Hicks, Philip, 4–5, 61–79, 143, 145, 265–66
Hirschmann, Alfred, *The Passions and the Interests*, 159
Historia Augusta, 242
history and historiography, 9–10, 138, 145, 236
    Bible as, 13, 21, 188
    causality and contingency in, 219–20
    chronology in, 26, 137, 142 n. 21, 196
    context and, 41, 171, 175
    criticism and, 194–98
    cultural, 144, 176, 179 n. 36

ecclesiastical, 2–3, 13–33
end of, 155–56
as entertainment, 116, 193
error and, 189–90
evidence and proof in, 187, 191–92, 194, 231–32, 251 n. 14
fact and, 187–88, 190, 192, 194
four stages theory of, 154–55, 209, 222 n. 25
good-bad division of, 63
Hegel on, 163, 164, 165–66, 173
historian's craft, 190–94
human actions and, 174–75
Hume's contribution to, 37–38, 93
imagination and, 187, 191, 192, 194, 195, 198, 201–2, 203–7
imitation of nature and, 196–97
as literary art form, 192, 202
medieval chroniclers, 188
memory and, 187–90, 191–92, 198
methodology of, 38, 209
narrative character of, 161 n. 4, 169, 191, 194, 195, 202, 206
past and, 148, 192, 193, 196
plan and design in, 195–96
poetry and, 181–82, 186–87, 192, 194, 195, 196, 198
progress and, 172–73
providential, 14, 33 n. 2, 48–54, 69–70, 188
readers of, 5–7, 103, 193–94, 221
reason in, 8, 143, 146–47, 166, 216–17
as rhetoric, 54–56
secular, 23–24, 44, 188, 213–14
social history, 144, 154
style in, 169, 203
sympathetic understanding and, 40–41, 193, 207
temporality and, 193, 196, 197, 215, 218
tradition in, 58–59 n. 42, 63, 137
See also philosophy of history
History of Melinda Harley, 94
Hobbes, Thomas, 10, 29, 163, 201–2, 209–11, 223 n. 36
Hume and, 210, 220–21, 223 n. 31
Leviathan, 209–10, 212
Holden, John, 105
Homer, 23, 29, 237
honor, 41, 132, 134, 142 n. 20, 172, 245
Hopper, George, 103–4
Horace, 62, 252 n. 32
House of Commons, 66, 72, 112, 127, 135, 142 n. 19
Hudson, Charles, 106
Huguenots, 30, 140 n. 4

human nature, 9, 71, 85, 138, 165, 220, 228, 231
Hume on, 41, 52–53, 168, 211, 232, 248
sympathy and, 205, 219
Hume, David
atheism alleged in, 81, 85, 91, 249
common life philosophy of, 39–40, 49, 54–55, 125
conservatism of, 157–60, 162 n. 33
descriptive method of, 4, 40
in France, 28–29
"historian" label for, 1, 9–10, 160–61
history-philosophy connection in, 1–2, 21, 38–39, 218, 221
influence on philosophical historians, 27, 167, 172–77
irony by, 31, 70, 232
irreligion of, 14, 18, 81, 84, 85, 86, 95, 97
on moderation, 6, 33, 61, 148, 157, 177, 202–3
naturalist ontology of, 49, 212
as neoclassicist, 8, 143–45
optimism of, 3, 41, 42, 177
as philosopher of history, 10, 70, 121, 167–72, 209
as political thinker, 64, 97, 122, 145–46
scholarship and sources of, 11, 14, 227, 234–44
skepticism of, 12, 38–39, 94, 112, 210–12, 217, 220, 227, 232, 245–46
as student, 21–22
Tory reputation of, 8, 92, 112, 114, 153
and Whigs, 117, 122, 140 n. 4, 146–47
writing style of, 95–96, 116, 143, 203, 221 n. 10
Hume, David, works
The Dialogues concerning Natural Religion, 13–14, 17, 176
An Enquiry concerning Human Understanding, 2, 4, 38, 50–52, 145, 167, 169–71, 182–84, 186, 189–90, 195–97; "Of Miracles," 39, 170; "Of the Association of Ideas," 169
An Enquiry concerning the Principles of Morals, 2–4, 41–43, 205, 218; "A Dialogue" appendix, 3, 41–45, 50, 141 n. 9, 155, 167, 170, 184–86, 189, 193–95, 197, 199 nn. 5, 10, 205, 254 n. 64
Essays, Moral, Political, and Literary (Hume), 2–4, 8, 11, 14, 17, 38, 64–65, 68, 122, 135, 138–39, 140 n. 5, 141 nn. 10, 16, 154, 156, 159–60, 167–69, 172, 178 n. 23, 217, 219, 225, 238, 250 n. 4

Hume, David, works (cont.)
    Essays, Moral, Political, and Literary, Part I:
        "Of Eloquence," 169; "Of National
        Characters," 17, 34 n. 12, 231; "Of
        Simplicity and Refinement in Writing,"
        169, 184; "Of Superstition and
        Enthusiasm," 17, 68–69; "Of the
        Independency of Parliament," 219;
        "Of the Origin of Government," 156,
        162 n. 31, 219; "Of the Parties of Great
        Britain," 64, 157, 236; "Of the Rise and
        Progress of the Arts and Sciences,"
        178 n. 23, 219–20, 251 n. 13; "Of the
        Standard of Taste," 185; "Of Tragedy,"
        169; "That Politics may be reduced to a
        Science," 142 nn. 24, 26, 156
    Essays, Moral, Political, and Literary, Part II
        [Political Discourses], 29, 141 n. 16, 156,
        159, 178 n. 23, 225, 227, 249 n. 1; "Idea
        of a Perfect Commonwealth," 158,
        223 n. 31, 224 n. 49, 252 n. 19, 254 n. 67;
        "Of Commerce," 141 n. 16, 154, 159, 209,
        222 n. 25, 247–48; "Of Interest," 248;
        "Of Luxury" (see "Of Refinement in the
        Arts"); "Of Money," 233, 248; "Of
        Refinement in the Arts," 141 n. 16, 248,
        252 n. 19, 252 n. 30, 254 n. 61; "Of Some
        Remarkable Customs," 170, 220; "Of the
        Balance of Trade," 141 n. 10; "Of the
        Coalition of Parties," 71; "Of the
        Jealousy of Trade," 141 n. 10, 159; "Of
        the Populousness of Ancient Nations,"
        11–12, 221 n. 9, 225–49, 245–46, 248–49,
        251–52 n. 15
    essays withdrawn: "A Character of Sir
        Robert Walpole," 142 n. 26; "Of the
        Middle Station of Life," 140 n. 5; "Of the
        Study of History," 11, 103, 107, 167, 169,
        211, 221
    Essays and Treatises on Several
        Subjects, 81, 85, 225, 249 n. 1, 250 n. 4,
        252 n. 15
    The History of England, from the Invasion of
        Julius Caeser to the Revolution in 1688:
        abridgments, 91–93; "The Anglo-Saxon
        Government and Manners" appendix
        to, 151; appendices and endnotes in,
        8, 28, 69, 70, 144, 150, 153, 155; on
        Catholicism, 33, 113; character analysis
        in, 122–35, 149, 202; chronological
        construction, 137, 196; commonplace
        books on, 6, 90–92, 113–17; ecclesiastical
        history in, 3, 14, 17, 32–33; editions and
        translations, 88; ending, 155–56, 162 n.
        29; on English civil war, 61, 65–67;
        71–72; as entertainment, 116, 193; on
        events of 1688, 8, 72, 146–47, 151, 153, 155,
        158; as evidence-based, 187; excising of,
        144–45, 161 n. 6; on imagination, 10,
        215–16, 217; as influential work, 6, 73,
        96–97, 173; on liberty, 64–65, 67–69, 74,
        139, 147–48; in libraries, 87–89, 97,
        107–10; "My Own Life" in, 47–48, 81, 97,
        203, 221 n. 4; as narrative, 144, 149, 215;
        as neoclassical history, 8, 143–45; as
        philosophical history, 10, 209; as
        political history, 112, 121–40, 145–46, 173;
        in private collections, 104–7,
        117–18; providential character of, 49,
        69–70, 188; published reviews of, 5–6,
        86–88, 90; readers' annotations in, 6–7,
        110–13; readership and popularity, 1,
        5–6, 74, 82, 88, 106, 115; reading abroad
        of, 103–4; reading aloud of, 94–95; on
        reason in history, 8, 143, 146–47; on
        religion, 14–15, 48; Romantic critique of,
        58–59 n. 42; on Scottish-English union,
        96–97, 134; seen as subversive and
        dangerous, 111–12, 115, 116;
        sentimentality in, 48, 93; "spirit" use in,
        61, 64–65, 67; as study of authority, 8,
        149–54; sympathetic understanding in,
        47–48; title, 161 n. 2; and Whigs, 8, 117,
        122, 140 n. 4, 143, 146–47
    "Memoranda," 235, 238, 250 n. 8,
        253 n. 34
    "My Own Life," 47–48, 81, 97, 102 n. 71, 203,
        221 n. 4
    The Natural History of Religion, 2, 17, 31,
        44, 209
    "On Chilvary and Modern Honour," 172
    Political Discourses. See Essays Moral,
        Political, and Literary: Part II
    A Treatise of Human Nature, 1–3, 38, 40, 141
        n. 14, 147, 155, 167, 174, 176, 203, 219, 223
        n. 43, 231–32; historical features of, 2,
        142 n. 21, 145, 169–70; on imagination,
        9, 10, 219; on self, soul, and substance,
        205–6, 215; on sympathy, 205, 219; on
        time and space, 212–15, 218–19
Hume, Hanna, 5, 83, 85, 87
Hume Library, 238
Hume Studies, 225, 249 n. 2
Hunter, Robert, 118
Hurd, Richard, 115
Husserl, Edmund, 165
Hyde, Edward. See Clarendon, first Earl of

idealism, 175
Ilay, Earl of, 22

imagination, 204, 216–17, 219
  history and, 187, 191–92, 194–95, 198, 201–2, 203–7
  in Hume's writing, 9, 10–11, 201, 214
  ideas and, 182–83
  memory and, 181–83, 190–91, 202
  poets and, 183–84, 186
  Smith on, 207–8, 222 n. 16
  sympathetic and constructive, 201, 205–8, 219–20
  time/space and, 214–15
infanticide, 41, 232, 246
Innes, Thomas, 35 n. 36
Inverness, 5, 88
Ipswich, 108, 110
Isocrates, 252 n. 32

Jackson, Noel, 53
Jacobites, 83, 112
James I, 63, 91–92, 110–11, 153, 160
  and liberty, 65–68
James II, 111, 125, 141 n. 8
James V, 195
Jameson, William, 21
Jansenists, 30–31, 42
Jefferson, Thomas, 116
Jerningham, Edward, 106
Jesuits, 16, 30, 34 n. 10, 36 n. 51
Jews, 18, 20, 29, 32, 34 n. 22
Joan, Pope, 26
Joan of Arc, 171, 203
John I, 7, 124–25, 137, 153, 189
Jones, John, 109
Josephus, 252 n. 32
Julian, 252 n. 32
justice, 67, 131–34, 215, 219
Justin, 133, 240, 252 n. 32
Juvenal, 252 n. 32

Kames, Lord [Henry Home], *Sketches of the History of Man*, 106
Kant, Immanuel, 163, 175–76
Kelso, 87
Kendal, 107
Kennett, White, 65
Kent, 19, 109
Kersey, John, 250 n. 6, 251 n. 13
Kidd, Colin, 28
kingship, 7–8, 91–92, 121–40, 152
  absolute power and, 137, 140 n. 3, 150–51, 156–57
  arbitrariness and, 72, 126, 128–29, 131, 133, 135
  feudalism and, 152
  governance and, 138, 146

hereditary, 139, 142 n. 27
military prowess and, 124, 128–29
Parliament and, 137, 156, 158
rule of law and, 127, 130, 132, 135–36, 138–39, 140 n. 3, 142 n. 24
stability and, 8, 128, 153–54, 156
See also authority
Kirk. *See* Church of Scotland
Knox, John, 14, 22

La Peyrère, Isaac de, 23
Lawson, George, 89
Le Blanc, Abbé, 29
Lee, Charles, 6, 114–15, 117
Leo X, Pope, 33
Lessing, G. E., 29
Leunclavius, J., 238, 253 n. 38
liberty, 7, 127, 132, 153, 154
  authority and, 71, 148, 150–52
  Bolingbroke on, 4, 61, 62–64, 67–68
  Elizabeth I and, 68, 144
  enthusiasm and, 4–5, 68–69, 71
  history and, 146–48
  Hume view of, 61–62, 64–65, 67, 71, 74, 117, 139
  James I and, 65–66
  kingship and, 122–23, 136, 139
  language of, 72, 76
  Magna Carta and, 137
  rule of law and, 67, 122, 140 n. 3
  See also spirit of liberty
libraries
  History of England in, 87–89, 97, 107–10
  Hume use of, 238, 253 n. 35
  types of, 89–90, 107–10
Library; or Moral and Critical Magazine, 87–88
Lichfield, 108
Lipsius, 242, 252 n. 29
literature, 185–86, 192
  plan and design in, 186
Livingston, Donald, 3, 39, 48–49, 54, 57 nn. 7, 9, 12, 18, 142 n. 21, 214
  on philosophical theism, 58 nn. 21, 35
  on providential history, 38, 49–53
Livy, 21, 32, 63, 123, 189, 235
  as Hume source, 11, 234, 238, 243
Logan, John, *Elements of the Philosophy of History*, 164, 177 n. 5
London, 1, 16, 92, 101 n. 48, 104, 106, 109, 137, 232
  population of, 230, 233, 239
Long, Douglas, 10–11, 201–24, 266
longevity, 231, 251 n. 13
Lottenbach, Hans, 58 n. 41
Louis XIV, 30, 160, 219

Lowth, Bishop Robert, 29–30
Lucan, 252 n. 32
Lucian, 252 n. 32
Ludlow, Edmund, 62, 64
Lyotard, Jean-François, 178 n. 17
Lysias, 234, 23–38, 244

Mabillon, Jean, 24
Macaulay, Catharine, 5, 70
   The History of England from the Accession of James I to that of the Brunswick Line, 71–72, 74
   on Hume, 159, 162 n. 38
   political radicalism of, 71–72
Machiavelli, Niccolò, 4, 62, 74, 163
   Discourses on Livy, 63
   The Prince, 219
MacIntyre, Alasdair, 40
Mackie, Charles, 3, 24–26, 35 n. 34
Magna Carta, 63, 72, 133, 137, 149–50, 153
Mallet, David, 15–17
Malton, James, 104
Manchester, 106, 112
manners, 144, 155, 202, 226, 250 n. 6
Marks, Joseph, 105
Martial, 252 n. 32
Marvell, Andrew, 62
Marx, Karl, 163, 166–67
Mary I (of England), 84, 93, 112
Mary I (of Scotland), 83, 115
Mather, Cotton, 24
McKeand, Robert, 89
Meinecke, Friedrich, 143
Melvil, James, 14–15
memory, 9
   history and, 187–92, 198
   imagination and, 181–83, 190–91, 202
mercantilism, 159
metaphysics, 38, 175, 212, 217
   naturalism and, 55
Methodists, 18, 30
Michaelis, Johann David, 29
Middleton, Conyers, 14, 33 n. 3
Mill, J. S., 9, 174
Millar, Andrew, 15, 140 n. 1
Millar, John, 141 n. 13
Milton, John, 62
miracles, 13–14, 17, 28, 31, 171, 188–89
moderation, 97, 142 n. 18, 148, 222 n. 11
   of Hume, 6, 33, 61, 148, 157, 177, 202–3
modernism, 11, 226
monarchy. *See* kingship
monasticism, 19, 24, 229, 232
monkishness, 4, 44, 46–47, 56, 188, 202, 213, 221 n. 3

Monro, John, 106
Montaigne, Michel de, 10, 201, 211–12, 223 n. 35
Montesquieu, 27, 31, 76 n. 18, 154, 226
   on antiquity, 152, 227
   Hume and, 11, 228, 230, 233, 250 n. 3
   on intermediate powers, 137, 142 n. 20
   works: *Considerations on the Causes of the Romans' Greatness and Decline*, 65, 76 n. 17; *The Spirit of the Laws*, 61, 64–65
Monthly Review, 5, 86
morals and morality, 209
   as causative factor, 228, 245
   Hume and, 42, 48–49, 85, 155, 221 n. 1
   imagination and, 201–2
More, Hannah, 93
More, Sir Thomas, 48, 140–41 nn. 7–8
Moses, 23, 32
Mossner, Ernest Campbell, 225
Mountfort, Simon de, 153, 162 n. 21
Munro, William, 5, 88
Murdoch, Patrick, 106
Murray, George, 88, 96
Murray, John, 95
Murray, Lady Charlotte, 95

Nagel, Ernest, 47
national animosities, 129, 188
naturalism, 49, 212
   methodological, 38, 55
nature, 208, 211
   art and, 186
   history and imitation of, 196–97
Nedham, Marchamont, 62
Nepos, 252 n. 32
Neville, Henry, 62
Newark, 108
Newton, Thomas, 105
Nietzsche, Friedrich, 163, 210
nobility, 126, 136–37, 142 n. 18. *See also* barons
Norman Conquest, 132, 152, 188–89
Northumberland, Earl of, 144
Norton, David Fate, 3
   David Hume: Philosophical Historian, 38–39
Norwich, 7, 108, 117
Nouvelles Ecclesiastiques, 31
Nottingham, 107

Olympiodorus, 252 n. 32
Onslow, Arthur, 112, 117
Orwell, Harriet, 94
Ovid, 252 n. 32
Oxford, 92, 110

INDEX

Palamedes, 41, 42
Palmer, George Joseph, 111
papacy, 24, 33
Parliament, 126–27, 152–53
    king and, 137, 156, 158
parties, political, 48, 92, 157, 162 n. 32
Pascal, Blaise, 42, 45–46
passion, 203
    reason and, 147, 216–17
past
    future and, 215–16, 223 n. 40
    history and, 148, 192–93, 196
    present and, 51, 53
Pausanias, 252 n. 32
Pennington, Lady Sarah, 93
Penrith, 109
Pentateuch, 29
Percy, Thomas, 144
Petronius, 252 n. 32
Phillips, Mark Salber, 161
Philosophical Transactions of the Royal Society of London, 25
philosophy, 39, 208
    of common life, 39–40, 42, 49, 54–55
philosophy of history, 163, 164–67
    analytic, 9, 169–71, 173–75
    critical, 9, 64
    existential, 165–66, 171–72, 175–76
    hermeneutic, 3, 37–38
    Hume and, 10, 56, 70, 121, 143–44, 167–72, 186–87
    imagination and, 186–87, 209
    influence of Hume in, 172–77
    speculative, 167–69, 172–73
Pied Piper of Hamelin, 26
Pitt, William, 139, 142 n. 26
Plato, 218, 234, 252 n. 32
Plautus, 252 n. 32
Pliny the Elder, 11, 234, 237, 241, 242
Pliny the Younger, 252 n. 52
Plutarch, 11, 122, 233, 234, 243
    Hume on, 228, 235, 236
Pocock, J. G. A., 95
poetry
    art of, 183–85
    history and, 181–82, 186–87, 192, 194–96, 198
    imagination and, 183–84, 186
    nature and, 197
politics, 25, 28, 30
    general maxims in, 156, 220
    History of England as history of, 112, 121–40, 145–46, 173
    imagination and, 219
    partisan, 61, 72
    religion and, 16, 19, 28

Polybius, 11, 234, 238, 243
polytheism, 44
Popkin, Richard, 3, 50, 188, 238
    David Hume: Philosophical Historian, 38–39
Portus, Aemilius, 238, 253 n. 38
positivism, 137, 166, 175
    Hume and, 37, 174
Pownall, Thomas, 70
pragmatism, 39
Presbyterians, 23, 28
Prideaux, Humphrey, 24
Priestley, Joseph, 52
printing, 187
procreation, 231, 251 n. 13
progress
    history and, 172–73
    Hume on, 146, 154, 168
    Spadafora definition of, 154, 162 n. 25
proof, 231–32, 251 n. 14
property, 219, 244
prophetic tradition, 188
providential history, 14, 33 n. 2, 48–53, 69–70, 188
    Hume rejection of, 38, 50–54
    on past, present, and future, 51, 52
Puritans, 5, 55, 68–70, 160

Quincy, Josiah, Jr., 5, 73
Quintus Curtius, 189, 252 n. 32

Raleigh, Sir Walter, 197
Ralph, James, 65
Rankenian Club, 25, 35 n. 32
Raphael, David, 207
Rapin de Thoyras, Paul, 65, 140 nn. 4, 6
Raynal, Abbé Guillaume, 29
reading
    in family circles, 94–95
    by women, 93–94, 106–7
realism, 28, 204
reason
    history and, 8, 143, 146–47, 166
    passion and, 147, 216–17
Reformation, 24, 27, 33, 92
regimen mixtum, 154, 155–58, 160
Reid, Thomas, 81
Reimarius, Samuel, 29
religion, 3–4, 14–15, 17, 23, 42, 188
    enthusiasm and, 68, 69
    fanaticism and extremism in, 68–69, 71, 74, 85–86
    Hume's irreligion, 14, 18, 81, 84–86, 95, 97
    popular, 50
    religious beliefs, 13, 18, 48, 56, 93
    superstition and, 19–20, 23, 85–86

republic, 142 n. 27, 156, 158, 160
rhetoric, 48, 221 n. 10, 246
　history as, 53–56
　political, 61, 64, 70–72
Rhodes, Ebenezer, 106
Richard, Duke of York, 125
Richard I, 128
Richard II, 126–27, 141 n. 8
Richard III, 7, 125–26, 140–41 n. 7
Ridpath, George, 22, 87
Roberts, Clayton, *The Logic of Historical Explanation*, 174
Robertson, William, 5, 14, 33 n. 2, 83, 101 n. 49
　The History of America, 85, 106
　The History of Scotland, 106, 141 n. 12
　The History of the Reign of the Emperor Charles V, 29, 71, 106, 141 n. 10, 160
Robert the Bruce, 189
Rollin, Charles, 20, 234
　Ancient History, 25, 27
Romantic ideal, 58–59 n. 42
Rome, ancient, 227, 233, 240–42, 248
Rose, Elizabeth, 84, 92–94, 96
Ross, Charles, 140–41 n. 7
Rotwein, Eugene, 225
Rouet, William, 3, 26–28, 36 n. 39
　"Lectures on Ancient Painting," 28, 36 n. 44
rule of law, 67, 137, 139
　kings and, 127, 130, 132, 135–36, 138–39, 140 n. 3, 142 n. 24
　liberty and, 67, 122, 140 n. 3
Russell, Bertrand, 249
Rymer, Thomas, *Foedera*, 25

Sade, Marquis de, 104
Saladin, 128
Sallust, 234, 236
Sandys, Edwin, 66
Saracens, 128
Sarpi, Fra Palo, 14
Schelling, Friedrich, 164
Schlegel, Friedrich von, 164
Schmidt, Claudia M., 8–9, 10, 146–47, 163–79, 266
Schumpeter, Joseph, 159
Scotland, 2, 21–22, 82, 189
　Church of, 18, 21, 28, 30
　Edward I and, 134, 141 n. 13
　England union with, 30, 95–97, 134
　Hume reception in, 81–82, 88–89
secularization, 23–24, 44, 188, 213–14
self, soul, and substance, 201, 205–6, 214, 216, 220

self-consciousness, 166, 177
Selsey, Dowager Lady, 106
Seneca the Elder, 253 n. 32
Seneca the Younger, 242–43, 253 n. 32
sentimentality, 48, 93
Seven Years' War, 129
Sextus Empiricus, 237, 253 n. 32
Shaftesbury, Lord, 220
Sheffield, 106, 109
Sher, Richard, 88
Sheridan, Thomas, 91, 92
Shrewsbury, 108
Sibbald, Sir Robert, 35 n. 37
Sidney, Algernon, 62
Silverthorne, Michael, 11–12, 225–54, 266
simplicity, 44, 186, 197, 245
Simson, Andrew, 89
Simson, John, 22
skepticism, 39, 220
　of Hume, 12, 38–39, 94, 112, 210–12, 217, 220, 227, 232, 245–46
slavery, 11, 136, 150, 228, 232, 246–47
　in Greece, 239–40
　in Rome, 242–43
Smith, Adam, 10, 159, 201, 209, 217
　on history, 161 n. 4, 163, 208, 223 n. 40
　Hume and, 97, 159, 208–9, 222 n. 25
　on sympathy and imagination, 207–8, 209, 221 n. 8, 222 n. 16, 223 n. 36
　Theory of Moral Sentiments, 209
　The Wealth of Nations, 209, 251 n. 10
Smith, James, 7, 117
Smollett, Tobias, 5, 87, 226
　History of the World, 104
social history, 144, 154
Somerville, Mary, 95
Soulby, Anthony, 109
space, 218–19
　time and, 16, 191, 195–96, 212–15, 217–18, 220
Spadafora, David, 154, 162 n. 25
Spanheim, Friedrich, 24
Sparta, 234, 240, 247–48
speculative philosophy of history, 167–69, 172–73
Spelman, Sir John, 140 n. 6, 152
Spencer, Mark G., 1–12, 34 n. 14, 266
Spengler, Oswald, 167
Spinoza, Baruch, 23, 29
spirit of liberty
　American Revolution and, 72–73
　British civil war and, 66–67
　history of phrase, 4, 62
　Hume on, 61–62, 64–65, 67–69, 71
　Macaulay on, 71–72

Montesquieu on, 65, 76 n. 17
republican tradition and, 70
See also liberty
Sprange, Jasper, 109
Stafford, 108
Stamford, 107
Stanley, Thomas, *History of Philosophy*, 25
Stanyan, Temple, *Grecian History*, 234
St. Clair, William, 88
Stephanus, 238
Steuart, Sir James, 5, 35 n. 38, 83–84
Stewart, John B., 158, 221 n. 1
Stewart-Mackenzie, James Alexander, 88, 96
St. John, Henry. *See* Bolingbroke, Viscount
St. John, thirteenth Baron, 104–5
Strabo, 11, 234, 237–38
Strahan, William, 1, 149, 157
Stuart dynasty, 8, 65, 82–83, 91–92, 146, 149
demise of, 67, 153
Suderman, Jeffrey M., 7–8, 121–42, 266
Suetonius, 234
suffering, 45–46
superstition, 17, 85, 171
Hume critique of, 14, 86, 202, 221 n. 3
Surtees, John, 5, 88
sympathy and sympathetic understanding, 48–49, 56
artificial lives and, 42–47
communication and, 205, 206–8, 221 n. 6
Enquiry concerning the Principles of Morals on, 41–43
history and, 40–41
in *History of England*, 47–48
human nature and, 205
imagination and, 201, 205–8, 219–20
Smith-Hume differences on, 10, 208

Tacitus, 34 n. 22, 62, 151, 189, 197, 243
Hume and, 11, 21, 145, 234, 236
Temple, Sir William, 239
Terance, 253 n. 32
Tertullian, 253 n. 32
testimony, 191
Hume on, 170–71, 236–37, 245–46
theism, 44–45
Hume on, 37–38, 44–45, 57 n. 14
Livingston on Hume and, 58 nn. 21, 35
Theocritus, 253 n. 32
Thomson, Christopher, 109
Thomson, James, 4, 64, 74
Thucydides, 21, 195, 240
as Hume source, 11, 234–36, 238, 243
Timæus, 189

time and temporality, 217–19
eternity and, 218
history and, 193, 196–97, 215, 218
space and, 16, 191, 195–96, 212–15, 217–18, 220
Todd, William B., 219
Toland, John, 29–30, 62
Towsey, Mark, 5–6, 81–102, 266
Toynbee, Arnold J., 167
Trevelyan, Mrs. George, 106
Tudor dynasty, 87–88, 127–28, 149, 153–54
absolutism of, 1, 137, 149–50
Tully, James, 223 n. 45
Turgot, Anne-Robert-Jacques, 20, 172
Turretin, J. A., *Compendium Historiae Ecclesiasticae*, 22
tyranny
of barons and nobility, 135, 142 n. 18, 149
Hume use of term, 7, 127
of kings, 124–25, 127, 136–37
Tyssen, Samuel, 105
Tytler, Alexander, *Elements of General History*, 107

Valerius Maximus, 253 n. 32
van Holthoon, F. L., 8, 143–62, 267
Varro, Marcus Terentius, 20, 26, 227, 237
Vellus Paterculus, 253 n. 32
Vernet, Jacob, 20
Verstehen, 49, 175
Vico, Giambattista, 163
Virgil, 253 n. 32
Vitellius, 197
Vitruvius, 253 n. 32
Voltaire, 3, 27, 32, 76 n. 18, 172, 250 n. 6
Church and blasphemy laws attacked by, 16, 34 n. 10
on ecclesiastical history, 16, 18–19, 31–32, 34 n. 6
on history, 31, 160, 164, 177 n. 2, 179 n. 36
Hume and, 19, 29, 34 n. 18
works: *An Essay on the Manners and Spirit of Nations*, 18–19, 65; *Une historie des Croisades*, 16, 34 n. 6; *La Philosophie de l'histoire*, 164, 177 n. 2
Vossius, Isaac, 11, 227–28, 241–42

Wales, 133–34
Wallace, Robert, 231, 239, 250 n. 3
appendix rebuttal to Hume, 244, 247, 251 n. 9
dissertation by, 227, 248, 250 n. 5, 250–51 nn. 8–9, 251 n. 12
Hume on, 11, 225–28, 237, 250 n. 4
Walpole, Horace, 141 n. 8

Walpole, Robert, 4, 63–64, 74
Warburton, Bishop William, 29
Ward, William, 109
Warenne, John de, 112
warfare, 210, 243, 248
War of the Roses, 63, 154
Warren, Mercy Otis, 5, 72
Waszek, Norbert, 173
Watson, Robert, *History of Philip the Second of Spain*, 106
Weber, Max, 175
Westermann, William Linn, 239
Whigs, 62–63, 136–37, 141 n. 8, 142 n. 18, 157
    History of England and, 8, 117, 143, 146–47
    Hume and, 122, 140 n. 4, 146–47, 213
    origin of term, 111
Whitchurch, 110
Whitehaven, 108
Whitmore, George, 104
Wigtown, 89, 200 n. 33
Wilkes, John, 72, 157–58
William and Mary, 112–13
William III, 142 n. 22
William the Conqueror, 63, 128, 152–53
Winchester, 108
Windham, Joseph, 105
Wittenagot, 151
Wodrow, Robert, 22, 24
    History of the Church of Scotland, 21
Wolverhampton, 107
Worcester, 108, 115
Wrangham, Francis, 115, 120 n. 47
Wray, Sir William, 105

Xeno, 212–13
Xenophon, 240, 243
    as Hume source, 11, 234–36, 238
    Ways and Means, 235, 240
Xerxes, 236

www.ingramcontent.com/pod-product-compliance
Lightning Source LLC
Chambersburg PA
CBHW021356290426
44108CB00010B/271